The Contribution of Cambridge Ecclesiologists
to the Revival of Anglican Choral Worship 1839–62

For my parents,
Layen and Shirley Adelmann

The Contribution of Cambridge Ecclesiologists to the Revival of Anglican Choral Worship 1839–62

DALE ADELMANN

LONDON AND NEW YORK

First published 1997 by Ashgate Publishing

Reissued 2018 by Routledge
2 Park Square, Milton Park, Abingdon, Oxon, OX14 4RN
711 Third Avenue, New York, NY 10017, USA

Routledge is an imprint of the Taylor & Francis Group, an informa business

Copyright © Dale Adelmann, 1997

The author has asserted his moral right under the Copyright, Designs and Patents Act, 1988, to be identified as the author of this work.

All rights reserved. No part of this book may be reprinted or reproduced or utilised in any form or by any electronic, mechanical, or other means, now known or hereafter invented, including photocopying and recording, or in any information storage or retrieval system, without permission in writing from the publishers.

Notice:
Product or corporate names may be trademarks or registered trademarks, and are used only for identification and explanation without intent to infringe.

Publisher's Note
The publisher has gone to great lengths to ensure the quality of this reprint but points out that some imperfections in the original copies may be apparent.

Disclaimer
The publisher has made every effort to trace copyright holders and welcomes correspondence from those they have been unable to contact.

A Library of Congress record exists under LC control number: 97039983

ISBN 13: 978-1-138-34034-3 (hbk)
ISBN 13: 978-1-138-34035-0 (pbk)
ISBN 13: 978-0-429-44070-0 (ebk)

Contents

Editor's Foreword		vii
Acknowledgements		viii
Preface		ix
Abbreviations		xiv
1	Introduction and context	1
2	Cambridge ecclesiologists 1839–49: the formative years	19
3	The Ecclesiological late Cambridge Camden Society 1850–55: champions of choral service	63
4	Contributions of individual ecclesiologists to the revival of church music	92
	The Venerable Thomas Thorp	92
	The Revd Professor William Hodge Mill	102
	The Revd Benjamin Webb	108
	Alexander James Beresford (Beresford) Hope, M.P.	115
	The Revd John Mason Neale	123
	The Revd Thomas Helmore	125
	The Revd Henry Lascelles Jenner	129
	The Revd Samuel Stephenson Greatheed	132
	The Revd John Lake Crompton	136
	Francis Henry Dickinson, Esq.	137
	John David Chambers, Esq.	139
	William Dyce, Esq.	140
5	The ecclesiological apologetic for church music	143
6	The Ecclesiological Society 1856–62 and the diffusion of the Anglican choral revival	175

*Appendix – Music performed by the Ecclesiological Motett Choir
1853–62* 218

Bibliography – Manuscripts 222

Bibliography – General 226

Index 238

Editor's Foreword

So much of our 'common' knowledge of music in nineteenth-century Britain is bound up with received attitudes. The modern musicologist working in this field contends not only with the hermeneutical contextualization of contemporary writings but also with undoing the often undiscriminating evaluatory processes of later and more modern generations of scholars. In some instances the historiographical calculus is so soritical that groundwork revision becomes a primary necessity. In other cases, despite a facade of impartiality, one detects some trace apologetic, be it aesthetic, theological, political, or otherwise. Given either situation, however, there exists the fundamental need to reassess the work of the period, as well as the work about the period, and in addition to explore areas of the topic which have hitherto remained unknown. The current series of Music in Nineteenth-Century Britain, of which Dale Adelmann's is the first to be published, is designed to fill these lacunae.

In respect of such needs, Dr Adelmann's book comes as a welcome addition to this expanding corpus of research. Especially at a time when manifold changes are being made to the nature of Anglican choral worship it is right that the process of reassessment include examination of its more recent nineteenth-century origins. Such a study, as is here presented, provides not only a formative reevaluation of the place of Anglican choral worship in the middle part of the century but also places the role of the Cambridge ecclesiologists in its rightful context as a primary force behind the revival. Clarification of ecclesiological influence is provided through a rich matrix of contemporary documentation, including amongst other things substantive personal diaries, correspondences, occasional papers and pamphlets, as well as newspapers and more formative critical writings of the time. Views of more modern writers are reconsidered, chiefly in light of the reputed influence of the Oxford Movement, Tractarianism, the episcopal hierarchy, and the cathedral institutions. Adelmann's work, therefore, adopts a mainly revisionist posture towards prevailing mythologies of the revival, particularly where modern misconceptions have become muddled up with the generally uninformed historiographical attitudes of the past. In this research Dr Adelmann delineates fact from fiction and introduces key figures with clarity and concentrated attention. Indeed, the role and influence of individual ecclesiologists and their circle of ecclesiology is here, for the first time, presented without a hidden apologetical agenda, and readers can assess, for themselves, the extent to which such men directed theological and aesthetic values of the times.

Bennett Zon, Hull

Acknowledgements

I wish to express my profoundly felt thanks to all of my colleagues and friends who have encouraged me throughout the process of researching, writing, and revising this book.

In the first instance I would like to express my gratitude to my supervisors at the University of Cambridge, Dr Roger Bowers and the Revd Dr Nicholas Thistlethwaite, for their support during the writing of the Ph.D. dissertation which comprises the body of this work. The staff of the University Library at Cambridge was unfailingly helpful, as were the staffs of the Wren Library at Trinity College, Cambridge; the Bodleian Library, Oxford; and the Royal Institute of British Architects in London. Specifically I would like to thank Mr Malcolm Underwood, archivist of St John's College, Cambridge; Mrs Margaret Cranmer, Rowe Music librarian at King's College, Cambridge; the Rt Revd Peter Mann, Dunedin, New Zealand; Ms Diane Scoggin, Diocese of Pietermaritzburg, South Africa; Stephen Kogut; and the archivists of Christ's, Corpus Christi, Jesus, Peterhouse, and Queens' Colleges, Cambridge; all of whom graciously assisted me in locating manuscripts and other sources that were critical to the completion of my work.

Without the financial support of the Fulbright Commission, the American Friends of Cambridge University, and the Master and Fellows of St John's College, Cambridge, it would have been impossible for me to undertake this research. To them I am forever grateful. I would also like to thank the Very Revd Allen Farabee and the Vestry of St Paul's Cathedral, Buffalo, New York, for granting me the sabbatical leave which was necessary to revise the manuscript and prepare it for publication.

Without the encouragement and support of Dr Bennett Zon this work might never have been published. It was he who brought it to the attention of Ashgate Publishing, and my gratitude to him is immense. I wish to thank my editors, Rachel Lynch and Caroline Cornish, for their good-humoured assistance and care to ensure that the typescript conforms to current conventions of British spelling and punctuation; and Vera Kozak, for her helpful suggestions.

My brothers, their families, and dear friends too numerous to name have been a constant and incalculable source of encouragement, and I am ever mindful of the great fortune that is mine to be surrounded and cared for by such good people. Finally, I would like to thank my parents, for having loved and supported me in everything I have ever set out to do.

Dale Adelmann, Cambridge

Preface

It was both an academic and a performance interest in the Anglican choral tradition that originally compelled me to undertake this research. How, I wondered, had the performance standards of modern English choirs come to be so remarkably high? A glance at the history of choirs during the first decades of the nineteenth century within the Church of England revealed that, at that time, musical excellence was the exception rather than the rule. When did the improvement begin, and what happened to turn the tide? Most importantly, how was an ecclesiastical climate created in which Anglican choral worship could flourish?

The pursuit of answers to this pivotal, final question led me back to the 1840s and 50s, but not to the discovery of sweeping encouragement by the leaders of the Oxford Movement, and not to the bishops or cathedrals of the Church of England. Neither did it lead me to the careers of heroic musicians (though there were some of them), nor to the examples set by the colleges of Cambridge and Oxford whose choirs bring them such honour today. To my surprise it led to a group of Cambridge undergraduates. With the formation of the Cambridge Camden Society in 1839, they dedicated themselves to the revival of Anglican worship, determined to recapture the deep aura of spirituality which they perceived to be exemplified in medieval art and architecture, in all of its aesthetic and symbolic richness. It is largely to their efforts that the mid nineteenth-century Ecclesiological Movement may be attributed.

The primary importance of this book will lie in its revelation and clarification of the role of Cambridge ecclesiologists (theoretically, practically, and as individuals) in the post-Tractarian revival of choral worship within the Church of England. That their participation in the revival of Anglican choral worship 1839-62 was immensely more significant than has hitherto been recognized will become obvious as the history unfolds. It is a side of the Ecclesiological Movement that has been largely concealed, one which will perhaps garner more regard for the work of ecclesiologists than they have often received.

Much has been written about the immense ferment within the Anglican Church during the nineteenth century, and it cannot be the purpose here to encapsulate and rewrite the immense contextual considerations that are examined in a dozen other books. To do so would be needlessly repetitious for scholars and would quickly obscure the work at hand, which is of sufficient interdisciplinary interest in its own right. Given the great interest which the clergy and laity of the Anglican Communion possess for this period of history, however, salient aspects of the broader context will be drawn out as necessary to understand the present narrative.

For readers interested in the period and subject matter dealt with by the present book, two classic works have stood pre-eminent: Bernarr Rainbow's *The Choral Revival in the Anglican Church 1839–1872* (1970)[1] and James F. White's *The Cambridge Movement: the Ecclesiologists and the Gothic Revival* (1962). Neither of them, however, makes more than superficial reference to the involvement of ecclesiologists in the Anglican choral revival, and consequently the critical role which the Ecclesiological Movement played in it has hardly been suspected. Rainbow identifies a few strands of the ecclesiologists' story in his interesting book, and White also moves beyond the traditional myth that the ecclesiologists' primary interest in church music centred on the dilemma of where to locate an organ within a church building. Placement of the organ was indeed the point of departure for *The Ecclesiologist's* first general article on church music (1843), but over the long term organs were a comparatively minor musical concern of the leaders of the Ecclesiological Movement. In the four pages White devotes to music late in his book, he gives a summary of their views which overlooks both the principles behind them and the later developments which those principles engendered.[2]

Unlike these two standard works, the research presented in this book is a general history neither of the Anglican choral revival nor of ecclesiology. It does, however, reveal that ecclesiologists were a critical source of influence in the revival of choral worship, and it exposes a side of ecclesiology which is remarkable as much for its breadth and importance as for the fact that it has largely lain concealed to scholars until now. Students of nineteenth-century ecclesiology will also recognize that several traditional views of the movement are fundamentally challenged and reinterpreted here.

About the text

Numbers in the text which follow a colon and are enclosed by parentheses are cross references, and refer to page numbers elsewhere in the present book.

A certain amount of confusion exists over the various names of the Ecclesiological Society. It was founded in 1839 as the Cambridge Camden Society. For ten years after its disassociation from the University of Cambridge (May 1846–April 1856) its official name was the 'Ecclesiological late

---

[1] It is anticipated that the forthcoming publication of Bennett Zon, *The English Plainchant Revival* (Oxford University Press) will considerably augment this work.
[2] White (1962) 98, 211, 216–219. Indeed, the first two hundred pages of his book cite views stemming primarily from the childhood of the Cambridge Camden Society, especially when his purpose is to criticize; in the remaining twenty-five pages of his text our headstrong Cambridge undergraduates are never quite allowed to grow up.

Cambridge Camden Society.' The name was formally shortened to the 'Ecclesiological Society' at the 17th Anniversary Meeting of the Society on 23 April 1856.[3] In reference to specific periods of the Society's existence, its official title for each respective period will be used. The designation, 'Ecclesiological (late Cambridge Camden) Society', i.e. with parentheses enclosing the 'late Cambridge Camden' portion of the name, will be used for the sake of convenience here to designate references made to principles, convictions, or acts of the Society which are not limited to a period designated by any of the more specific permutations of its name.

Much confusion also exists over the name of one of the main figures in the present history. Born A.J.B. (Alexander James Beresford) Hope, Mr Hope added a second 'Beresford' upon the death in 1854 of his stepfather, Lord Beresford, whose fortune he mainly inherited.[4] This he used as a double-barrelled surname, although he did not hyphenate it. He will be referred to in the text as 'Hope' in references up to 1854, and as 'Beresford Hope' thereafter.

It is clear that the influence of the Ecclesiological Movement extended throughout the British Isles, the worldwide Anglican Communion, and even transcended denominational boundaries. The leaders of the movement were, nonetheless, English, and it was in England that they worked and had the most influence as individuals within their own lifetimes. Prevailing attitudes referred to in this text as 'English' certainly existed elsewhere, but it will be our purpose only to address the immediate cultural and ecclesiastical sphere in which leaders of the movement lived and worked. Realizing that there are 'Anglicans' throughout the world, it is hoped that use of that term here in the narrower sense of English Anglicanism (unless the Anglican Communion is specified) will be understood by readers in other parts of the world merely to be a matter of literary convenience.

Deciding how to designate the churchmanship of key figures in the Ecclesiological Movement, as well as the degree to which their views were formed by the various theological currents of the day, is problematic to say the least. The jump from 'exposure' to 'influence' is often dubious in its own right, and far more so the leap from there to 'adherent' or 'disciple.' One might observe that reading the Tracts did not necessarily make one a Tractarian (i.e. a disciple of the Oxford Movement) any more than reading the Bible necessarily makes one a Christian. It is sensible that some ecclesiologists may have been attracted to the aesthetic aspect of the Victorian Church revival because it seemed to be a logical adjunct to the principles of Tractarians, but it is a diffi-

---

[3] *The Ecclesiologist* 17/CXIV (June 1856) 219. White (1962) 198, incorrectly states that the name was shortened in 1852; Davies 4 (1962) 120, mistakenly writes that this name change took place in 1846.
[4] Law (1925) 274.

cult thing to prove. Many ecclesiologists came from traditional High Church backgrounds. Others were High Churchmen who read the Oxford Tracts before they were attracted to Cambridge ecclesiology, yet considered themselves to be High Churchmen throughout their lives. Several leading ecclesiologists came from Evangelical backgrounds, and it could as reasonably be argued that this was at least as formative of their mature religious character as the fact that they had read some or even all of the Tracts. It is often beside the point of the present work to quibble about variations in churchmanship. Ecclesiology united many in a common cause, and there is seldom much to be gained by seeking to divide them.

Nonetheless it does need to be pointed out that the term 'Tractarian' has been used far too indiscriminately to describe ecclesiological and ritualistic developments in worship throughout the remainder of the nineteenth century.[5] Regarding our present subject matter in particular, the Oxford Movement has far too sweepingly been identified as the impetus for the revival of choral worship which began to take shape in the 1840s.[6] An impetus it certainly was, but in light of the present research, it is arguably far more accurate to attribute the formative groundwork for the revival of choral worship to the Ecclesiological Movement. The authors of the Tracts made no significant pronouncements on church music whatsoever.

It is a misrepresentation of ecclesiologists in general to call them 'Tractarians' and to ascribe credit for their work to the Oxford Movement.[7] The Ecclesiological Movement did not emanate from Oxford, though it

---

[5] An observation supported by Yates (1984) 36. Gerald Parsons writes of the tendency to credit the Oxford Movement with every reform or pastoral and theological advance in the Victorian Church of England: 'This, as Yates himself adds, is absolute nonsense. But it is nonsense with an extraodinarily tenacious and persistent influence.' Unfortunately he later perpetuates the myth that ecclesiologists were Tractarians, a party designation their leaders never applied to themselves. Parsons (1988) 17, 33. It is also critical to note that ecclesiology and the movement during the second half of the nineteenth century known as Ritualism are not synonymous either, although individuals may certainly be identified who were proponents of both.

[6] To cite but a few examples from the most thorough treatment of the Anglican choral revival, see Rainbow (1970) 4, 6, 12, 86, 109 and appendix 4.

[7] Davies 3 (1962) 245, 271, and 4 (1962) 120 calls ecclesiologists 'second generation' Tractarians, which also implies a more thoroughly formative lineage than is certifiable. Chandler's recent biography of John Mason Neale too readily perpetuates the largely unsubstantiated implication of the original, highly romanticized biography of John Mason Neale by Eleanor Towle, namely that the Tracts so deeply formed Neale that he may be called a Tractarian. In reality the Tracts were but one of many formative influences upon him, and they were not one that he absorbed uncritically. To give just one example, in 1844 Neale wrote to Webb, 'I hope and trust you are not going to Oxonianize. It is clear to me, that the Tract writers missed one great principle, namely the influence of Aestheticks, and it is unworthy of them to blind themselves to it.' Lawson (1910) 70.

certainly found supporters there. Ecclesiology was largely the work of the next generation after the Tract writers, and 'Tractarian' is a party designation that the leaders of the Ecclesiological (late Cambridge Camden) Society never applied to themselves. To give the Oxford Movement credit for the work of ecclesiologists is only slightly more sensible than it might be for musicologists to give Charles Villiers Stanford credit for the works of Benjamin Britten. The designation 'Tractarian', therefore, will be used here only when clearly identified Tractarian ideas or persons are involved.

Abbreviations

CCCA	Corpus Christ College Archives, Cambridge
CCS	Cambridge Camden Society
CUL	Cambridge University Library
ECCS	Ecclesiological late Cambridge Camden Society
ed.	edited by
edn	edition
f., ff.	folio, folios
KCRML	King's College, Rowe Music Library, Cambridge
Lambeth	Lambeth Palace Library
LJRO	Lichfield Joint Records Office
MS, MSS	manuscript, manuscripts
OBL	Oxford, Bodleian Library
ref.	refer to
RIBA	Royal Institute of British Architects, Library of
SJC	St John's College, Cambridge
SJCA	Archives of St John's College, Cambridge
TCWL	Trinity College, Wren Library, Cambridge
vol., vols.	volume, volumes

CHAPTER ONE

Introduction and context

It would be quite logical for one to wonder how and why the Ecclesiological Movement of the mid-nineteenth century ever broadened to include the consideration of church music, since ecclesiologists are primarily remembered for their work in the field of church architecture. Ecclesiastical buildings were indeed their first consideration, but it shall be seen that their efforts to revive Gothic church architecture quickly widened to include an integral aspect of the worship which they envisioned should take place within those sacred spaces, specifically the revival of 'choral service.'[1] The *raison d'être* of this book shall be to expose the Ecclesiological Movement's significant role in the creation of a climate within the Church of England in which choral worship could flourish.

Critical analysis of the Ecclesiological Movement has normally taken place at one of two poles, on the one hand as if it were some disembodied juncture of theological and aesthetic thought, devoid of real individuals who lived in a unique cultural context,[2] and on the other hand as if the worth of the movement could be understood merely by considering the churches and church restorations which were influenced by its ideas.[3] Such fault-finding approaches have failed to consider both the breadth of the movement and the contemporary logic behind it.[4] Moreover the lives and individual efforts of

---

[1] Ecclesiologists typically spoke of 'choral service' rather than 'choral services.' They considered it a duty to render such service unto God. In their understanding of the term, 'choral' could be either fully congregational or choir-led, and referred more to the fact that the service was sung than to the presence of a choir. (: 155)
[2] The standard history of ecclesiology, J.F. White's *The Cambridge Movement* (1962), contains very little biographical information about any of the key men responsible for the development of ecclesiological thought, and provides virtually no documentation of ecclesiology's effectiveness in actual parishes.
[3] In *The Gothic Revival, an Essay in the History of Taste*, Kenneth Clark admits his personal bias against Gothic Revival architecture and goes on to lay waste to ecclesiologists with little regard for the issues of spirituality which motivated them or the cultural logic that gave rise to their views. His work is remembered primarily for his oft-quoted characterization of ecclesiologists as 'ruthless and infallible tyrants' and the stigma he attached to them by musing, 'It would be interesting to know if the Camden Society destroyed as much mediaeval architecture as Cromwell. If not it was lack of funds.' Clark (1928) 162, 173.
[4] White (1962) ix–xi, for instance, sets out with the peripheral agenda of challenging the validity of the Ecclesiological Movement's theological presuppositions and

almost all of its key leaders have remained unexamined.[5] By avoiding the reconciliation of its apparent views with the individuals who actually led the Cambridge Camden Society and its subsequent, London-based incarnations, the broader worth and significance of the Ecclesiological Movement has been obscured, even trivialized. The clearest and most accurate understanding of ecclesiology may be seen only in an aggregate reflection of the individuals who led it, men of broad learning, exceptional intellectual acuity and immense spiritual depth, whose sincerity and fervour to revive the Anglican Church in their own day merits regard by comparison to the efforts of any age.

The history which is about to be recounted will expand the traditional understanding of the Ecclesiological Movement by revealing a sphere in which the depth of its influence has been virtually unknown, that of the revival of music in Anglican worship. The architectural views of ecclesiologists will be the subject matter here only insofar as they relate to their views on the music of the Church, and indeed it will become apparent that their contribution to the revival of choral worship was effected in much the same manner as they championed the Gothic Revival. Considerable attention will be given to pertinent biographical information about the men who founded the movement, and who were largely responsible for its prosperity throughout the period framed, 1839–62. Indeed, what follows is primarily a story about a collection of remarkable individuals, friends who allied themselves in a common cause, who were not merely products of the times in which they lived, but men who worked with vigour to change and improve them. It will be seen that they laboured to identify and uphold ancient, Catholic aspects of worship which they believed were the rightful inheritance of the Church of England, and used every fibre of their creativity and intellectual acumen to work for the spiritual revival of the Anglican Church.

Their first work was in the field of church architecture, but having chosen a style of Christian architecture to emulate, specifically the period of Gothic which they called Middle Pointed or Decorated (1260–1360 A.D.),[6] it was logical that they would soon move on to consider how to worship in the liturgical spaces they were creating and restoring. The vast majority of ecclesiologists were, it is critical to remember, clergymen. As their work evolved,

---

liturgical models for modern times, rather than evaluating them strictly within the context of its own era.

[5] John Mason Neale is the only leader of the Ecclesiological (late Cambridge Camden) Society who has ever received significant scholarly attention. The mistaken notion that Neale can uncritically be regarded as the archetypal ecclesiologist has been responsible to a large degree for many of the widespread misunderstandings of the Ecclesiological Movement as a whole. (: 16–18)

[6] Cambridge Camden Society, *A few words to Church builders*, 3rd edn (1844) 5–6; see also *The Ecclesiologist*, 2/14 (October 1842) 5–6; and the introduction by J.M. Neale and Benjamin Webb to Durandus, *The Symbolism of Churches* (1843) xxiv.

INTRODUCTION AND CONTEXT 3

they came to define ecclesiology ever more broadly, and eventually all of the ecclesiastical arts were claimed to lie within their purview. By 1847 they declared ecclesiology to be 'the science of Christian Æsthetics' and 'the systematic study of the requirements of Divine Worship.'[7] This included not merely architecture but sculpture, stained glass, wood carving, brass work, polychrome, embroidery and, much more significantly than has hitherto been thought, church music. Thus widening the scope of their labours, ecclesiologists sought a unity of principle among the arts which had been a trend in English aesthetic thought since the late eighteenth-century writings of Sir Joshua Reynolds. (: 40) It has been well documented that, 'during the years of the Gothic Revival the majority of artists, critics, and aestheticians regarded the interchangeability of principles between art forms as a matter of course and quite consciously drew parallels and sought correspondences between poetry, painting, sculpture, music, and architecture.'[8]

An overview

The dates that form the boundaries of the present study (1839–62) have been chosen because the Cambridge Camden Society was formed in 1839,[9] and the Ecclesiological Society disbanded its musical committee in 1862.

Chapters two, three, and six deal specifically with the three phases of ecclesiological involvement in the revival of choral worship. The first phase encompasses the 1840s. During this time ecclesiologists worked out in theoretical and practical terms how the Church principles propounded by old-style High Churchmen and Tractarians should be applied to the aesthetic aspects of worship, i.e. architecture and the ecclesiastical arts, including music. The revival of choral worship was intimately linked, both theoretically and practically, with other aspects of ecclesiology.

During the second period, 1850 to early 1856, ecclesiologists recruited to their ranks the leading advocates of choral worship who did not already number among them, and became the foremost champions of choral service within the Established Church. It will become apparent that it was during the first decade and a half of the revival of choral worship (1841–56) that the vital thought and dissemination of concepts took place which were decisive for the revival's subsequent general prosperity. Ecclesiologists amassed an impressive and convincing apologium for choral worship during this period, and continually brought it before the public. These efforts were targeted primarily

---

[7] *The Ecclesiologist*, 7/57 (March 1847) 85; 7/60 (June 1847) 234.
[8] Bright (1984) 76.
[9] Coincidentally, Frederick Oakeley also introduced choral services at Margaret Chapel in 1839. Rainbow (1970) 4, 15.

at the clergy, who were deemed to be the group most able either to encourage or to thwart such worship. The apologium for choral worship thus established (detailed in chapter five) was perhaps the Ecclesiological Movement's single greatest contribution to the success of the Anglican choral revival.

The third period began in 1856. By this time the theoretical battle for choral worship had essentially been won, and *The Ecclesiologist's* articles on musical subjects during the next six years turned to more practical subjects. These included debates on such topics as how to point and sing psalms, and ecclesiologists who had previously agreed in theory began to diverge from one another in practice. During the late 1850s the movement to revive choral service quickly reached a size and breadth impossible for any single party of the Church to control. As the movement attracted the widespread interest of churchmen from many shades of Anglican parishes, popular musical opinion began to exert a telling influence upon the course of the revival.

Because of its importance as a cradle of the Ecclesiological Movement, the University of Cambridge will receive specific consideration, and the music of the Cambridge college chapels throughout the period will be detailed. Ecclesiologists were highly critical of the choral foundations of Cambridge and repeatedly lamented the dearth of opportunities for University students who intended to take holy orders either to learn about the history of church music or to participate in the practice of it. There were encouraging signs of improvement in the late 1840s and early 1850s, but it will be seen that the University trailed well behind parish churches in the revival of choral service. Having noted the growth of interest in choral worship at Cambridge, Bernarr Rainbow states:

> To estimate the effect of those developments upon the undergraduate community of the day at large would be a formidable task. Nevertheless, there can be little doubt that regular attendance at the choral services held in their own college chapels exerted telling influence upon those undergraduates who were earnestly preparing for ordination.[10]

The influence of ecclesiologists upon the clergy, especially young clergy and undergraduates preparing for ordained ministry, will be a recurrent theme throughout the present work. At the risk of stating the obvious, it is a general presupposition of this book that for theological, liturgical, or musical innovations to become sufficiently widespread to be considered a 'movement' within the Church, the prevailing support of a considerable proportion of the clergy had to be won. Leaders of the Ecclesiological Movement believed this, and they intentionally aimed their persuasive efforts at the clergy, because it was the clergy who were in a position to implement most quickly and efficiently the changes ecclesiologists advocated.

---

[10] Rainbow (1970) 218.

Several misconceptions about the theory and work of the ecclesiologists will also be discussed. Just how radical were they? Were they really antiquarians and ultra-conservatives? Much of the confusion over this point arises because the long-term role of John Mason Neale as a leader of the Ecclesiological Movement has been significantly overestimated. Extensive reference to the diaries of the Cambridge Camden Society's co-founder, Benjamin Webb, will prove that Webb's role in the earliest days of the Society's existence was at least equivalent to Neale's, and that Webb had much the greater role both in the running of the Society and in the development of its policies throughout its mature period. Very little has ever been written about Webb, and his role has been further obscured by the fact that most of his voluminous writings were published anonymously. Neale, on the other hand, who was undoubtedly one of the great minds in the history of Anglicanism, has taken on such heroic stature posthumously that he has, often by default, received more credit for the movement than is his due.[11] The following work will begin to redress the imbalance by illuminating the role played by Benjamin Webb.

The context for ecclesiology

Any widespread revival is inevitably the result of a confluence of ideas and trends and events of the time in which it occurs; the Ecclesiological Movement and the revival of Anglican choral worship during the reign of Queen Victoria are no exception. Several other identifiable movements contributed to the creation of the climate in which the 'science' of ecclesiology was born and flourished.

Within the sphere of the Church, the most well documented antecedent to ecclesiology is the Oxford Movement. The beginning of the Oxford Movement is traditionally dated from the delivery of John Keble's 'Assize Sermon' at Oxford on 14 July 1833, when he called the British government to account for national apostasy by its suppression of ten Irish bishoprics through the Irish Church Temporalities Bill.[12] Publication of the *Tracts for the Times* began the following autumn. Tractarians, as writers and supporters of the Tracts came to be known, defended the national Church against the perceived threat of political interference, and swiftly moved on to demonstrate that the Anglican Communion formed a true branch of the Catholic and Apostolic Church, a *via media,* as John Henry Newman called it, between the errors of Roman

---

[11] Conversely Neale's excesses, particularly in the earliest years of the Ecclesiological Movement, have caused harsher judgements to be made of ecclesiologists in general than are fair.
[12] Chadwick 1(1971) 56–60, 70; Green (1964) 263–4; Parsons (1988) 29–30; White (1962) 18–19.

Catholicism and Protestantism on either extreme.[13] The two fundamental principles that Anglicanism needed to recover were, 'first, the Church's apostolic descent as the real ground of its authority, and secondly, the dependent principle that the sacraments, not preaching, are the covenanted sources of divine grace.'[14]

At least by any subsequent standard for judgement, it has never been convincingly argued that the general state of the Established Church in England could be described as extraordinarily healthy during the early decades of the nineteenth century. A major cause of this was widespread clergy pluralism, a practice whereby senior or socially well-connected clergymen received income from several parishes that were not necessarily even in the same part of the country, thus ensuring that the spiritual needs of many went unmet. Not uncommonly these incumbents underpaid curates to actually do the work of caring for the spiritual needs of multiple and remote parishes, while the incumbent himself lived in absenteeism.[15] The situation was so bad that Parliament finally stepped in and passed the Pluralities Act in 1838, limiting the number of benefices a clergyman could hold to two.[16] The Evangelical Movement of the late eighteenth and early nineteenth centuries affected the universities of both Cambridge and Oxford, and had gone some way to correct the 'spiritual torpor' which characterized much of Anglicanism at the time, but its effects were by no means all-pervasive.[17] Frequent admonishments to observe the rubrics of the *Book of Common Prayer* were made by Tractarians after 1833 and ecclesiologists in the 1840s and 50s, suggesting that compliance with them was certainly not universal. Outside of cathedrals the daily offices were seldom offered publicly, except on Sundays, and they were almost never sung. It was rare for the sacrament of Holy Communion to be celebrated more than once a quarter, if that often.[18] In the eyes of many,

---

[13] Davies 3 (1962) 259–60, 262; Rainbow (1970) 6; Reardon (1980) 94–6; Green (1964) 265–70.

[14] Reardon (1980) 97.

[15] Parsons (1988) 18–19; Rainbow (1970) 8; White (1962) 16–17. University divines could be no less guilty of pluralism. When Richard Watson was appointed Bishop of Llandaff in 1782, he retained the Regius Professorship of Divinity at Oxford, complaining that otherwise he would have an income of only £1,200 per annum. Many curates in his remote diocese subsisted on only £50 per year. Green (1964) 225–7.

[16] These had to be within ten miles of one another and could not be worth a joint annual income of more than £1000. Neither benefice could have a population of more than 3000 people, limiting to a more reasonable number the souls entrusted to a clergyman's care. Furthermore bishops were given the authority to require two Sunday services, each with sermon, and their power to enforce residence within the parish was strengthened. Chadwick 1 (1971) 136–7.

[17] Green (1964) 224, 241–51.

[18] Chadwick 1 (2nd edn, 1970) 514; Yates (1991) 134–6. Wakeling (1895) 27–8, 60, states that the reestablishment of daily services and weekly Communion by those

worship had become too Protestant. The movement to revive Anglicanism, therefore, was in part a reaction against the Calvinistic tendencies of worship since the Restoration of the Monarchy (1660),[19] which of course followed what ecclesiologists commonly called 'the Rebellion', referring to the eleven destructive years of Cromwell's iconoclastic brand of Puritanism during the Commonwealth (1649–60). Reports of irreverences such as altar tables being used as repositories for gentlemen's hats were common.[20] Cathedral choirs were often in a miserable state of inefficiency,[21] and such musical ensembles as existed in the west galleries of parishes were often said to be more remarkable for their personal displays than their musical ability to transport the assembled congregation into the courts of heaven by the beauty or devotion of their offerings. Many clergy tried to reform these latter ensembles out of existence.[22] The historical predisposition of High Churchmen was to be somewhat wary of hymn singing, which was a characteristic of Evangelical and Nonconformist worship; they tended instead to favour metrical psalms.[23] In any case the repertoire was limited to a few well-known tunes, and most often the psalms and canticles were merely read.[24]

The development in the musical world that most enabled the widespread revival of Anglican choral worship was the singing movement. Although it began during the late 1830s, it grew with astonishing speed following the decision by the National Society for Promoting the Education of the Poor to sponsor evening classes to teach sight singing to schoolmasters. The instruction method of Louis Bocquillon Wilhem, then popular in France, was adapted for use in England by John Hullah, whose classes began on 1 February 1841 in Exeter Hall. One hundred men were enrolled, and so great was the demand for admission that by 24 March 1841 there were four separate classes of one hundred members each (three of men, one of women). By spring Hullah had been so besieged by applications for entry from persons who were not

---

affiliated with what he calls the 'Church Movement' was an immensely positive influence on the life of the Church.
[19] Rainbow (1970) 4–5; Gatens (1986) 20–26.
[20] Wakeling (1895) 60–3, 73. See also Rainbow (1970) 7–8 for an entertaining summary of impieties common in early nineteenth-century parish churches.
[21] Chadwick 1 (1971) 140: 'No one knew what cathedrals were for. By the beauty of their music and singing they set forth the glory of God; and yet it was confessed that if the choirs of Durham and Canterbury were models of decorum and art, the choirs of some cathedrals, including, St. Paul's and Westminster abbey [sic], were renowned for slipshod irreverence.'
[22] Rainbow (1970) 11–12; Temperley (1979) 151–62, 239–42.
[23] Temperley (1979) 262. Nonconformists are those who do not conform to the Established Church.
[24] Congregations primarily in urban Evangelical parishes and choirs in High Church parishes were occasionally encouraged to chant the psalms and canticles during the early decades of the nineteenth century. Temperley (1979) 219–25.

involved in teaching that additional classes were opened for the general public. By autumn of the same year, it was felt necessary to provide some opportunity for those who had completed the elementary training to advance their skills further, and on 1 December 1841 two hundred and fifty people joined the first Upper Singing Class. The first public demonstration of the participants' new-found skill took place in April 1842, when 1500 persons performed, 'the majority adults, who, a year before, had possessed no knowledge of music; many, indeed, in our classes having made their first attempts to utter musical sounds.'[25] From the beginning pupils were taught with the expectation that they would thereby acquire the skills necessary to become teachers of the Hullah method. It is nonetheless astonishing that, during a speech before the House of Lords on 13 July 1842 in support of a bill to fund national musical education, Lord Wharncliffe stated that a total of 50,000 people had already enrolled in Hullah's classes.[26]

The timely coincidence that singing became popular in the 1840s did not, however, mean that the revival of choral worship was an inevitability. (: 70–3, 78–9) The fact that ecclesiologists so strongly advocated choral service (singing of the responses, psalms, canticles, and eventually hymns) as the Catholic and rightful inheritance of the Anglican Church was certainly one of the significant developments which assured that an essentially secular movement would benefit the sacred sphere. Leading ecclesiologists effectively turned their own parishes into models for imitation, became potent apologists for choral service, and effectively propounded their case in various organs of the national press. These efforts were key components in paving the way for the fruit of the secular singing movement to be appropriated to the benefit of the Church.[27]

The movement which pervaded all others, arguably the one whose influence is at once most certain and yet most nebulous, was Romanticism,[28] sometimes referred to as 'romantic medievalism', the driving force behind the Medieval Revival. In a very thorough treatment of the aesthetic motive behind this revivalism, Bright explains that early Victorians considered the Renaissance to be the start of their own era:

> Believing that with the Renaissance things had begun to go wrong and that the predicament of modern times was largely due to the false steps taken at that period, the Revivalists sought in the Middle Ages, the wise and true grandparent, answers to their questions, solutions to their problems, values for their void of them, order for their chaos. Young Englanders sought political solutions in the feudal rapport of lord and serf, Tractarians sought religious

---

[25] J. Hullah (1846), 23–4.
[26] F. Hullah (1886) 35. See also Rainbow (1970) 43–8.
[27] Ecclesiologists' example as creators of model parishes is documented in chapter four, their labour as apologists for church music is detailed in chapter five.
[28] Yates (1991) 129–30.

solutions in an unreformed church, Pre-Raphaelites sought artistic solutions in the unconventionalized naturalism of early Christian painting, and Gothic Revivalists sought architectural solutions in a Christian, national, and uncorrupted style.[29]

Unlike Classical architecture, Gothic architecture had arisen in an era of Christian faith and in perceived response to its needs. Although the Gothic style had originated in France, it had arrived in England during the style's infancy and had a long history of development on native soil. It was deemed by ecclesiologists, therefore, to be an honest expression of English Christianity,[30] and was particularly attractive for its rich symbolism.[31]

According to many contemporary and subsequent critical analyses, several of which are cited below, it was the field of literature that played the greatest role in the popularization of things medieval. Foremost among the authors responsible for this development was Sir Walter Scott. In the creation of a new respect for and fascination with what were clearly not Dark Ages, the influence of his novels was acknowledged by ecclesiologists on several occasions. (: 183–4) As early as 1846 they wrote:

> like many other signs of hope in the present day, we are disposed to trace the progress which has of late been made in a considerable degree to the writings of Sir Walter Scott: and whatever be his place among the chiefs of English Literature, he will we believe earn from posterity a higher praise than is ever the lot of any mere literary man, from the purity of his writings, and the lessons which his readers could not fail to draw from the truthful and attractive pictures he has given of those times which the grossness of a later age had treated with unmixed contempt.[32]

---

[29] Bright (1984) 30–31. He cites W. Jackson Bate, *The burden of the past and the English poet*, page 22, that in this revival of certain medieval traits they partook in 'the "leapfrog" use of the past for authority or psychological comfort: the leap over the parental—the principal immediate predecessors—to what Northrop Frye calls the "modal grandfather".'

[30] In this ecclesiologists found strong support from A.W.N. Pugin (1836) 2–3, but the view was not universally accepted. Ruskin, for instance, preferred Italian architecture and protested that the French had both originated and perfected Gothic. Bright (1984) 94–6.

[31] See also Durandus. Davies 3 (1962) 277–8; White (1962) 73–9.

[32] In 'The French Académie and Gothic Architecture', *The Ecclesiologist* 6/51 (September 1846) 83. A footnote in the article mentions 'as deserving of our gratitude for what they wrote or did in the cause of mediæval art' the work of Thomas Warburton (a contributor to *Essays on Gothic Architecture* 1800, and author of various late eighteenth-century histories of English poetry), Bishop John Milner (author of accounts of the history and antiquities of Winchester 1798, and its cathedral 1801), and John Carter (early nineteenth-century author of many beautifully illustrated books on medieval architecture). Architect G.E. Street also acknowledged Sir Walter Scott's influence in *The Ecclesiologist* 19/127, (August 1858) 233. See also Davies, 4 (1962) 44 and 3 (1962) 243.

In the field of painting, the Pre-Raphaelites were indeed more evidence of romantic medievalism.[33] One of the founders of this school of artists, William Morris, stated his belief that 'the revival of the art of architecture in Great Britain may be said to have been a natural consequence of the rise of the romantic school in literature.'[34]

The Gothic Revival in architecture was the most visible expression of the growing cultural fascination with medieval times.[35] Although the movement began as early as the 1750s with the construction of Horace Walpole's villa Strawberry Hill, and was fostered in the ecclesiastical arena when 174 of the 214 churches resulting from the Church Building Act of 1818 were in neo-Gothic style,[36] it was largely through the efforts of ecclesiologists that the case was made and won for Gothic as the architecture of Christianity.[37] Ecclesiologists did not start the Gothic Revival any more than they originated the revival of choral worship. Theirs was the work of seeking Christian truth in what they considered to be the spiritual purity of medieval, Catholic forms of artistic expression, studying them, reviving them, and forming an apologetic to encourage others to follow their lead. Others had begun the research and practice. The ultimate concern of ecclesiologists was the encouragement of Christian devotion and the pursuit of truth. A vast proportion of ecclesiologists were priests. As devout churchmen there can be no doubt that they revived medieval forms and practices first and foremost for pastoral reasons, based on the presupposition that the reappropriation of ancient Catholic *forms* would foster, as it were, a deeper spiritual *content*.[38] This, as shall become obvious below, is constantly manifest in their writings.

It cannot be denied that ecclesiologists' labours to revive Gothic church architecture, plainsong, and the polyphonic church music of the sixteenth and seventeenth centuries, though driven by spiritual goals, were linked to nineteenth-century England's fascination and increasingly spiritual identification with the Middle Ages. Considered at this cultural level, it may be observed that they employed the pragmatic pastoral technique of appropriating popular architectural and artistic forms to the benefit of the Church. The

---

[33] *The Ecclesiologist*, 21/139 (August 1860) 245–7; Rainbow (1970) 4.
[34] William Morris in *The Revival of Architecture*, cited in Michael Bright (1984) 85.
[35] Bright (1984) 4. Bright also argues that it is the most important expression of nineteenth-century medievalism.
[36] Bright (1984) 6; White (1962) 8.
[37] The advancement of ecclesiology found significant support in the work and writings of A.W.N. Pugin, although ecclesiologists always believed that his actual influence was seriously limited by the fact that he 'found among Roman Catholics less sympathy and encouragement than he deserved.' *The Ecclesiologist*, 13/92 (October 1852) 352–3. The vociferousness of his Roman Catholicism certainly decreased his contemporary influence among Anglicans. White (1962) 9–10, 14.
[38] Chandler (1995) 46, notes that J.M. Neale wrote as 'a man with pastoral concern for the community served by a church, and not exclusively as an antiquarian.'

critical difference between their use of this technique and that of the Church in more modern times, however, is that ecclesiologists decided which styles of Christian art and architecture were worthy and ought to be popular, and worked to make them so. They were absolutely convinced that art which emanated from a medieval sense of piety would captivate and enhance the religious sensibilities of their own age.

The co-founders: Benjamin Webb and John Mason Neale

Benjamin Webb was born on 28 November 1819 at Doctors Commons in the City of London. His father, a London businessman, had been raised a Quaker and was not baptized until a few months prior to his son's ordination in 1842. Benjamin Webb's mother, however, was a member of the Church of England and saw to it that her children were brought up in the Church. Benjamin attended St Paul's School, and showed early signs of being 'religiously disposed', including not merely frequent attendance at church (three times each Sunday) but forays out to attend occasional meetings of the Protestant Association and to hear the popular Evangelical preacher Henry Melvill.[39]

That Benjamin Webb was more than superficially interested in theology and church music well before he came up to Trinity College, Cambridge in the Michaelmas term 1838 is plainly evident from his diaries. In March and April 1837 (age 17) he attended lectures in London on 'Ecclesiastical Music' given by Dr Gauntlett, and references to outings to hear performances of oratorios in Exeter Hall appear with some regularity. He spent his eighteenth birthday reading *Ivanhoe* and confirming his 'resolution to take Holy Orders',[40] having recently 'Read *Oxford Tracts* for first time, and liked them much, though doubting – at first – about Baptismal Regeneration in Tract 3.'[41] Webb's diaries show that he devoured two more novels by Sir Walter Scott, *The Monastery* and *The Abbot*, in December 1837. Webb was an avid reader and no doubt enjoyed the attractive picture Scott painted of the Middle Ages.

Benjamin Webb's attraction to the High Churchmanship for which he was known in later life seems to have been gradual, fed by a curiosity which led him to seek out all manner of religious experiences in the late 1830s. His son records that Webb did 'not at once break off from the interest of the Evangelical forms of religious activity which had previously attracted him', but in his

---

[39] Clement C.J. Webb, 'Benjamin Webb,' *Church Quarterly Review*, LXXV (October 1912 – January 1913) 331–2.
[40] Webb diaries, 28 November 1837.
[41] Webb diaries, 16 November 1837. He also mentions reading the Tracts on 19 April 1839, and a sermon preached against them by Scholefield at the University Church, Great St Mary's, on 1 November 1840. On 21 March 1841 he noted that he had 'read Tract 90 with approbation,' and four days later that Harvey Goodwin spoke against it.

later school years began attending choral services and going to hear High Church preachers such as Bishop Phillpotts (Exeter) and Dr Hook (Leeds Parish Church). He read voluminously on religious subjects, and his diaries show that he admired the work of the Oxford Tractarians.

John Mason Neale was born on 24 January 1818 in London, grandson of James Neale, a prosperous china manufacturer and strict Evangelical, and son of Cornelius Neale, who had reformed from his earlier 'dangerous inclinations and dispositions' to take Holy Orders in 1822.[42] One year following his ordination, Cornelius Neale died leaving the five-year-old John Mason Neale and his sisters to be raised by their severe and strictly Evangelical mother, née Susannah Mason Good.[43] Soon after her husband's death, she moved her young family to Shepperton, where at age six John Mason Neale was entrusted to the daily care of the parish rector, the Revd W. Russell, who became a beloved mentor. In 1829 Neale was sent away to school at Blackheath, thence to school at Sherborne 1833–35, followed by a brief time at Farnham. He possessed an extraordinarily serious temperament, and was by nature something of a loner. There is little to suggest that he had much of a boyish childhood, for he would seem to have read without ceasing, and typically books on church history, theology, poetry, or languages. In 1836 Neale was sent to live with Dr Challis, Professor of Astronomy at Cambridge and rector of Papworth St Everard, under whom he prepared for the University entrance exams. He matriculated at Trinity College, Cambridge, having won a scholarship, in the Michaelmas term 1836.

John Mason Neale's spiritual pilgrimage was formed by a far stricter and more potent dose of Evangelicalism than Benjamin Webb's. Having been raised in that milieu, Neale's character was deeply formed by it, whereas Webb's voluntary exposure to Evangelicalism was merely one facet of his personal quest. Like Webb's, though, Neale's transformation to High Churchmanship was gradual and independent, and the Oxford Tracts were among the many things he read on religious topics. Yet his Evangelical upbringing wrought in him a seriousness, zeal, and certitude about his religious convictions that was a permanent and unshakeable aspect of his very character. 'He retained with faithful tenacity his hold upon evangelical truth, whilst

---

[42] Early biographical details are taken from Eleanor Towle, *John Mason Neale D.D.: a Memoir* (1906). Cornelius Neale's tendency toward waywardness apparently evidenced itself in that he 'became an inordinate reader of fiction, a constant frequenter of London theatres.' Towle (1906) 4.

[43] Her Sunday rota was to take her young children to hear the sermons at the long morning and evening services at the local Chapel, and in between she would spend a portion of the afternoon reading them one of Dr Doddridge's published sermons. Towle (1906) 12. During a visit to the Neales, Benjamin Webb recorded in his diary, 'The Neales very Evangelical and stiff,' and the next day, 'None of the Neales to church... Neales go to Vaughan's chapel.' 9 and 10 January 1841.

slowly and surely gaining clearer views of the doctrines of the Catholic Church as taught in her creeds and formularies. And he fought his battle single-handed,' writes his first biographer, Eleanor Towle.[44] During his first months in Cambridge he is known to have come under the influence of the great Cambridge evangelical leader, Charles Simeon, and was deeply touched by the account of Simeon's death later the same year.[45]

In October 1840, Neale mysteriously 'migrated' to Downing College,[46] allowing him to stay briefly on in Cambridge and to continue working for the Cambridge Camden Society. According to Towle, he was appointed assistant tutor and chaplain, but the latter must have taken place the following year, for he was not ordained deacon until Trinity Sunday, 6 June 1841. In October 1841, 'Neale announced he must resign his post at Downing,'[47] presumably to undertake parochial work in the parish of St Nicholas, Guildford. This was not to be, however, for Bishop Sumner of Winchester was suspicious of the Cambridge Camden Society and refused to license him. Disappointed, Neale returned briefly to Cambridge.[48] On Trinity Sunday, 22 May 1842, Neale was ordained priest, and the next day he accepted the parish living of Crawley in Sussex. Again his hope to proceed in parochial work was short-lived, for in early July he was forced to resign due to chronic lung problems.[49] Approximately half of the next three years was spent in Madeira for health reasons. The extent to which he was able to remain abreast of the daily workings of the Cambridge Camden Society during that time was largely due to frequent correspondence with Benjamin Webb.

The establishment of friendship

The formation of a short-lived High Church club called the Ecclesialogical Society in March 1839 occasioned Webb's introduction to Harvey Goodwin,[50] (: 19–21) and Goodwin in turn introduced Webb to John Mason Neale.[51] Common interests and intellectual prowess resulted in the rapid formation of a deep friendship between Webb and Neale. Towle describes Webb as:

---

[44] Towle (1906) 30.
[45] Chandler (1995) 7.
[46] Webb diaries, 24 October 1840.
[47] Webb diaries, 11 October 1841. The entry for that date continues, 'Bought Vol. 1 of Tracts for the Times.' It is interesting to note that the Cambridge Camden Society was more than two years old at this point; until this time Webb had only read a few of the Tracts.
[48] Towle (1906) 53–6.
[49] Towle (1906) 59, 66.
[50] Webb diaries, 9 March 1839.
[51] Webb diaries, 11 March 1839. Goodwin and Neale had met in 1836 as fellow pupils preparing for entrance to the University under Dr Challis, Professor of Astronomy and rector of Papworth St Everard. Towle (1906) 22.

a man of great critical ability, an iron will, and, together with a comprehensive grasp of great subjects, surprising patience in working out details. In many ways the friends were fitted to supplement each other. Neale's impetuosity was restrained by Webb's calmer judgment, and his rash conclusions corrected by the relentless force of logic.[52]

A walking tour in June solidified their friendship[53] and by midsummer of 1839, less than four months after their first acquaintance, they agreed to keep the canonical hours together using Bishop Cosin's *Devotions*.[54] During the summer of 1840 Webb attended Margaret Chapel for the first time,[55] something he often did on visits to London in the early years after he left Cambridge,[56] and Neale and Webb made a trip through the north of England, where they met Dr Hook at Leeds.[57]

Church music formed a part of their discussions at least by October 1839, when Webb noted a long conversation on Latin hymns, and by the summer of 1840 Neale's views on ecclesiastical music were sufficiently codified to enable him to deliver a paper on the subject.[58] Webb and Neale evidently met regularly to participate in the making of sacred music, since the latter's published letters include one to Webb in 1841 instructing him to have the piano tuned which lay at their disposal: 'I hope to return on S Mark's Eve; and on S Mark's [April 25] we will, all well, open our Sacred Concerts with Jackson's *Te Deum*, which I have been diligently studying.'[59] Life in Cambridge was not without its musical diversions, whether an evening of singing at Burton's[60] assisted by several King's College choristers and the deputy organist, [John] Robson; the novelty of hearing Harvey Goodwin play the cornopeon; a Septett Club chamber concert at Downing, where a young lady sang excerpts from Hummel's *First Mass*;[61] or merely reading up on music history.[62] Visits home

---

[52] Towle (1906) 33. However romanticized this characterization sounds, it would appear to be quite accurate.
[53] Webb diaries, June 1839.
[54] Webb diaries, 8 July 1839.
[55] Webb diaries, 21 June 1840.
[56] Webb diaries, 29 March 1842; 21, 26, and 28 January 1844; 7 April 1844 (Easter evening); 9 and 23 June 1844; 20 October 1844; December 1844; and many more.
[57] Webb diaries, 7 July 1840: 'By 6 a.m. we left York for Leeds. Dr Hook had invited his architect & committee to meet us yesterday.' Leeds Parish Church was completed a year later.
[58] Webb diaries, 29 October 1839 and 20 July 1840.
[59] Lawson (1910) 24. This would suggest that Neale's minimal musical ability did not always subdue his zeal. See (: 34 footnote 76, : 125)
[60] Thomas Jones Burton, matriculated at Peterhouse in Michaelmas 1836, B.A. 1841. He served 1843–4 as curate to J.F. Russell (a member of the inner circle of ecclesiologists and editor of *Hierurgia Anglicana*) at St James, Enfield, Middlesex. Venn, *Alumni Cantabrigienses* and *Clergy List*.
[61] Webb diaries, 27 February 1840, 31 February 1841, 9 March 1841.
[62] Webb diaries: Burney's history on 7 March 1841, Hogarth's on 17 September 1841.

during University recesses found Webb attending choral services in St Paul's Cathedral,[63] playing the flute accompanied by his sister on the piano,[64] or listening to the great works of Handel in Exeter Hall.[65] In 1841 Neale and Webb both subscribed to the recently formed Musical Antiquarian Society (1840–7),[66] and Webb, at least, consulted with Burns, the publisher, about joining the Motett Society.[67] As we shall see, these last two associations gained in significance with the passage of time.

Benjamin Webb took his BA degree on 22 January 1842,[68] but remained in Cambridge for some time to continue his work for the Cambridge Camden Society. During an extended vacation in London, however, Webb records the establishment of a 'Hullah singing-class' under Mr Jay on 12 March 1842. It seems probable that he participated in the classes until his return to Cambridge on 9 April, since less than a week later he notes, 'Lent my Hullah to Mrs Mill.'[69] Webb's interest in Hullah's work was ongoing. In the spring of 1843 he attended one of Hullah's singing classes in the Merchant Taylors School, and in early February 1844 they met one another in Cambridge to discuss the formation of a singing class locally. Although Hullah had visited Cambridge already in the first year of the singing classes (1841–2) and is known to have begun a lifelong friendship with William Whewell at that time,[70] the 1844 discussion which included Webb would seem to have occasioned the first local Hullah singing classes. They were started on 27 February 1844 under the direction of one Banister. Twenty men attended the first meeting; forty attended the second one the next evening. The classes would seem to have met frequently. On 2 May 1844 Webb left the singing class for unspecified reasons, and later that month he notes that he 'met Hullah and had a talk.'[71] Thus, Webb was one of the very early beneficiaries of Hullah's singing method, and would have attended not only because of his own love of music, but for the purpose of obtaining sufficient skill to be able to set a good example and give proper instruction in his future parishes.

---

[63] Webb diaries, April 1839, December 1840, and 20 August 1841.
[64] Webb diaries, 20 August 1841.
[65] Webb diaries, 12 March 1841
[66] Webb diaries, 18 March 1841.
[67] Webb diaries, 28 June 1841.
[68] Webb diaries, 22 January 1842. He notes with satisfaction, 'When I took my degree, the CCS was cheered.'
[69] Webb diaries, 12 March and 15 April 1842. Mrs Mill was married to the Revd W.H. Mill (beloved and influential ECCS advisor, Regius Professor of Hebrew at Cambridge 1848–d.1853). Mrs Mill became Webb's mother-in-law on 21 April 1847.
[70] F. Hullah (1886) 29, 88–9, 92.
[71] Webb diaries, 29 April 1843; 23 February 1844; 26 May 1844.

The archetypal ecclesiologist: John Mason Neale or Benjamin Webb?

It has always been clear that Benjamin Webb's role in the formation and running of the Ecclesiological (late Cambridge Camden) Society was central throughout the earliest and greatest period of its existence; however, the absence of any biography of him has obscured his importance. Nearly all of his voluminous writings were published anonymously in various periodicals of the day, and therefore his thinking and real influence have been difficult to trace. Exhaustive biography of John Mason Neale and the genius of his signed publications have tended to cast shadows over the work of Benjamin Webb and other leading ecclesiologists.

Close examination of the letters which passed between the two men shows that, once Neale left Cambridge, Webb took primary responsibility for editing *The Ecclesiologist*. When the deterioration of Neale's health led to the necessity that he spend the winters of 1843, 1844, and 1845 in Madeira,[72] the difficulty of keeping abreast of Cambridge Camden Society developments was complicated by his residence abroad. Despite the fact that this could have provided him with total leisure to research and write articles, James Stewart Forbes (later Bishop of Brechin) wrote to Neale in 1845, 'We look forward to *The Ecclesiologist* to support the cause of Catholic art; *but you do not write for it enough.*'[73]

In 1851 Neale began to write three 'leaders' a week, at A.J.B. Hope's request, for the *Morning Chronicle*. He later admitted that he was forced to write primarily for the *Morning Chronicle* and the *Christian Remembrancer* because, unlike *The Ecclesiologist*, they paid him to do so.[74] Neale's earliest biographer tells us that by the time of Neale's death (1866) his contributions to *The Ecclesiologist*, which had concerned mainly ritual and liturgical subjects, had long since ceased, and that he no longer took any part in the management of the Society.[75] These facts are corroborated in a letter written by Benjamin Webb in 1865, in which Webb asked Neale why he no longer kept in contact

---

[72] He was ordered to Madeira by his doctor in January 1843, and the first journey lasted 2 February–1 June 1843. Towle (1906) 76, 85. The second trip lasted from October 1843 to May 1844. Chandler (1995) 22. By the end of the third winter abroad, 1844–45, it was thought that he was cured, and that autumn he moved with his family to Reigate, where he stayed until his appointment as warden of Sackville College, East Grinstead, in May 1846. Towle (1906) 96, 121, 132, 140.
[73] Towle (1906) 120.
[74] In the same letter to Benjamin Webb (11 November 1859) in which Neale admitted this financial necessity, Neale refers several times to Webb's management of *The Ecclesiologist*. Towle (1906) 191; Lawson (1910) 309. The value of the Sackville College wardenship was only £24 plus accommodation in the College. Towle (1906) 139; Lawson (1910) 95.
[75] Towle (1906) 136.

with his ecclesiological friends, and never communicated the results of any of his research to the pages of *The Ecclesiologist*.[76]

When the Revd Professor W.H. Mill died in late 1853, *The Ecclesiologist* recorded that Mill had been 'united in the closest ties of affinity' with the 'one to whom *The Ecclesiologist* is more indebted than to any of its contributors, as its responsible conductor from the first.'[77] This can only refer to Webb, who was married to Mill's only daughter. In each of the years 1855 and 1857, Neale attended only two of the Society's seven Committee meetings, while Webb and A.J.B. Beresford Hope had perfect attendance records, followed closely by such men as the Revds W. Scott, S.S. Greatheed, H.L. Jenner, Thomas Helmore; and Messrs Chambers, France, and F.H. Dickinson.[78] In 1885 the *Saturday Review* offered its assessment: 'Neale with all his genius was not judicious, and how much the worship movement owes to Webb's wise, tolerant judgment cannot be overstated.'[79] It is, in fact, evident that history has substantially understated Webb's role.

The steady decline of J.M. Neale's participation in the affairs of the Ecclesiological (late Cambridge Camden) Society and his influence upon its policies is but one indication that the development of the Society's policies and principles lay increasingly elsewhere. From the known writings of Benjamin Webb on the revival of Christian art, it would seem that, after the earliest years of the Cambridge Camden Society, he was the driving force in the ongoing codification and development of the Ecclesiological (late Cambridge Camden) Society's principles in that area. In 1860 Neale himself admitted to Webb, 'As to ritual Ecclesiology, I believe that I am your equal; but as to aesthetic, no one ever was nor ever could be.'[80] Later in the same year he restated his conviction thus: 'I know how infinitely inferior I am to you in all ritual matters connected with Art.'[81] Neale was not the sort of person to feign humility if he was actually expert in something.

So closely do Benjamin Webb's diaries anticipate the evolution of the musical views of the Ecclesiological (late Cambridge Camden) Society, that it would seem clear that he was primarily responsible for its direction in that regard throughout the 1840s. The diaries also reveal that he remained intimately involved in the musical interests of the Society through the early 1860s. Moreover, as the editor who held principal responsibility for *The Ecclesiologist*, the organ by which the views of the Ecclesiological (late

---

[76] Letter from Webb to Neale, 9 June 1865. Lambeth Palace Library, Letters and Papers of W.H. Mill, MS 1491, f.183–4.
[77] *The Ecclesiologist*, 15/100 (February 1854) 4.
[78] Attendance statistics derived from the Minute Book of the Ecclesiological Society, 1854–66. RIBA: ES/1.
[79] Obituary of Benjamin Webb, *Saturday Review*, 12 December 1885.
[80] Letter to Benjamin Webb, 28 March 1860. Cited in Lawson (1910) 312.
[81] Lawson (1910) 329.

Cambridge Camden) Society were primarily made known over the long term and, therefore, the chief means by which its ongoing influence was wielded, it may more convincingly be argued that Benjamin Webb should bear the mantle of 'archetypal ecclesiologist' rather than John Mason Neale. To realize the full import of this assertion would require a complete reconsideration of the Ecclesiological Movement, for the mature Benjamin Webb was a moderate man who typically saw a much broader picture than the more dogmatic Neale. Such a re-examination would go considerably beyond the scope of this book, nonetheless a significant beginning will be made as the Ecclesiological Movement's role in the revival of Anglican choral worship is considered.

The overestimation of Neale's role as a leader in the Ecclesiological (late Cambridge Camden) Society has allowed unfair judgements to be formed of the whole movement. It is largely because Neale has so often been treated as the archetypal ecclesiologist, and his views accepted as synonymous with those of ecclesiology that, for instance, William Gatens can label ecclesiologists 'ultra-conservatives' and equate their views with pure antiquarianism.[82] No doubt some, like Neale, were ultra-conservatives, and some, unlike Neale, were motivated by antiquarian, in addition to or rather than religious, considerations. But an examination of the principles which motivated the Society and the personal lives and practices of leading ecclesiologists will allow general charges of neither ultra-conservatism nor antiquarianism to be sustained.

---

[82] Gatens (1986) 65, 66, 70. Thomas Helmore is partly to blame for this interpretation, but it will be demonstrated that even he was more moderate than some of his statements may seem to indicate. (: 128–9)

CHAPTER TWO

Cambridge ecclesiologists 1839–49: the formative years

The primary source of details regarding the formation of the Cambridge Camden Society (1839) has traditionally been the memorial written in 1888 by the Revd E.J. Boyce (Trinity College), one of the founding members. Presumably written in preparation for the fiftieth anniversary of the establishment of the Society, it has been treated by scholars as authoritative. The comparison of it with the diaries of Benjamin Webb,[1] however, reveals errors in detail which one might expect after the lapse of a half century. These could be passed over in silence did they not tend to obscure the early relationship between the study of church architecture and High Churchmanship.

Boyce states that he, John Mason Neale (Trinity College), Harvey Goodwin (Caius College), and 'two or three more' informally associated themselves to study church architecture during the academic year 1837–8, 'but it was upon the coming up to the University of such men as [James Gavin] Young, [Benjamin] Webb, [Edmund] Venables, and others, that a small society of men interested in this study began to be formed under definite laws and with definite objects.' No explanation is given for the rather confusing succession of names attributed by Boyce to the new society, which he states were supposed to have included the 'Ecclesiological Society', the 'Camden Society', and finally, in May 1839, the 'Cambridge Camden Society.'[2]

Benjamin Webb came up to Trinity College, Cambridge, at Michaelmas 1838. On Sunday, 3 March 1839, he notes, '[H.L.] Jenner of Trinity Hall called on me. We this day talked of founding a High Church Club.' Less than two weeks passed before Webb recorded:

[March] 15th. First meeting of our Society: Codd, Colson, Goodwin, Neale, Poynder, and I: Hough coming in afterwards. Goodwin, President; Colson, Secretary and Treasurer, to meet every Wednesday from 5 to 7. Name of Ecclesialogical chosen, borrowed from the British Critic.[3]

Following the Easter vacation, the Ecclesialogical Society lost no time in pursuing its studies. Webb's first paper for the Society, 'Apostolical Fathers', was 'very kindly received', and he was assigned the 'Similitudes of Hermas'

---

[1] Benjamin Webb kept an almost daily diary from 1837 until the end of his life.
[2] Boyce (1888) 8.
[3] Webb diaries, 15 March 1839.

for his next topic. John Mason Neale spoke on 'The merit of works', Harvey Goodwin on 'The necessity of Creeds', and Keble's views on tradition were read aloud by the meeting.[4]

On 6 May 1839 Benjamin Webb, by then a neighbour of John Mason Neale in Bishop's Hostel, noted: 'Neale admired my models of fonts; and announced himself as fond of Church Architecture.' The following day Neale introduced him to E.J. Boyce, and Neale and Webb 'made plans for an Architectural Society.' Characteristically, no time was lost in bringing the new scheme to fruition. Potential members were approached, and the new organization came into being on 9 May 1839, only three days after Webb and Neale's first discussion of church architecture:

> Neale gave a wine party to Thomas, Lewthwaite, Lingham, Boyce, Colson, and me. All joined the new Society: Neale made President & I Sec[retary] & Treasurer. Chose the name of Cambridge Camden Society. We drafted a Church Scheme and sent it out to be printed.[5]

Less than two weeks elapsed before the infant Society experienced its first crisis:

> Halliwell of Jesus preferred starting a Rival Society, to be called the Fullerian: whereupon Neale, Boyce & I took the Brass of Wm de Fulbourne to Archdn Thorp, and asked him to become our President. He assented joyfully.[6]

With sanction from Thorp, a senior member of the University and tutor of Trinity College, the Cambridge Camden Society's purpose and mission immediately took on a seriousness and public respectability which gained it the support of university men of all ranks. Professor G.E. Corrie (later Master of Jesus College) and William Whewell (elected Master of Trinity College in 1841) became members, as did Harvey Goodwin (later Dean of Ely, then Bishop of Carlisle). The Cambridge Camden Society was poised to move forward with authority. Published membership statistics for 1843 show that after just four years the Society included, as patrons or honorary members: two archbishops, sixteen bishops, thirty-one peers and members of parliament, seven deans and chancellors of dioceses, twenty-one archdeacons and rural deans; plus more than seven hundred ordinary members.[7]

Thus the Ecclesialogical Society and the Cambridge Camden Society were actually formed within two months of one another as distinct societies, and

---

[4] Webb diaries, 18 April 1839. The views on tradition referred to were a published sermon, *Primitive Tradition Recognised in Holy Scripture*, preached by John Keble at Winchester in 1836, which elicited published responses by four other Anglican clergymen in 1837.
[5] Webb diaries, 6–9 May 1839. The Society's name derives from William Camden (1551–1623), one of England's great, early antiquarians. White (1962) 31.
[6] Webb diaries, 20 May 1839.
[7] Boyce (1888) 10.

what were to become three highly influential clerics of the Victorian era, Neale, Webb, and Goodwin, were active in both organizations. The two societies coexisted, each active in its separate sphere, through the Long Vacation term of 1839. In August Webb was fined by Goodwin for having missed a meeting of the Ecclesialogical Society, which was reported to have been reading *Ancient Christianity*.[8] By late autumn some sort of rift had developed, Webb was 'disgusted with Goodwin's Radicalism'[9] (although this did not adversely affect their long-term friendship), and in December 1839 an amicable agreement was reached to dissolve the Ecclesialogical Society. Webb and Neale hoped to form another, more select and practically oriented association.[10] This, however, never came to pass. The obvious reason was that, as the Cambridge Camden Society grew, the job of organizing the architectural information they solicited and answering the requests for advice which came in from around the country (and eventually from around the world) came to occupy an ever-increasing amount of their time. No doubt this more than fulfilled any desire they felt to work out High Church principles in a practical way.

Within a few years the ostensibly inauspicious architectural inquiries of a few Cambridge undergraduates and fellows had attracted interest which crossed international boundaries, a fact which amazed no one more than the founders themselves. By February 1841 the amount of work related to the Cambridge Camden Society had grown to be so voluminous that Webb had to be persuaded not to resign as secretary. In spite of the appointment of an assistant, the work remained 'incessant' and, added to the normal demands made upon a conscientious undergraduate, Benjamin Webb frequently felt 'overwhelmed' by it.[11] By January 1846 the leaders of the Cambridge Camden Society were prepared to claim full credit for the movement to revive church architecture, consenting to share centre stage only with the Oxford Architectural Society. Pugin, they admitted, had published similar ideas earlier than they, but they claimed that he had no followers, even in his own Communion, and therefore the movement could not be attributed to him. Yet they were quick to add, 'It was the Lord's doing; and it was marvelous in our eyes. Those who were then engaged in the work can never forget their astonishment at the spread of their principles.'[12]

---

[8] Webb diaries, 15 August 1839.
[9] Webb diaries, 1 and 5 November 1839.
[10] Webb diaries, 3 December 1839.
[11] Webb diaries, 2 February, 5 May, September 6, 22 December 1841.
[12] *The Ecclesiologist*, 5/– (January 1846) 4.

The Ecclesiologist

On 23 October 1841 the Committee of the Cambridge Camden Society, with Dr W.H. Mill in the chair, resolved to begin publication of a periodical to be entitled *The Ecclesiologist*. With typical speed, the first issue appeared on 4 November 1841.[13] It was published bi-monthly throughout most of its existence, except during 1842 when eleven monthly issues appeared, and 1846 when it appeared every month. The choice of this name for the periodical is indicative of the close association of its goals with the aims of the short-lived High Church 'Ecclesialogical Society' of 1839. In spite of the objectivity and freedom from party polemics which *The Ecclesiologist* liked to assert for itself in the early days, it was clear from the beginning that the periodical was more than just an architectural magazine. Boyce claims credit for the idea that it would be useful to have some means of maintaining contact with members who had left the University, but recognized that within its first three years, the periodical became 'scarcely so much a mere report of the doings of the C.C.S., as a general organ of Ecclesiology; that peculiar branch of science to which this very magazine gave first its *being* and its *name*.'[14]

From the beginning Neale and Webb saw *The Ecclesiologist* as a means of extending the influence of the Society, not only through its widespread circulation, but also in terms of subject matter. In the prefatory article to the first number, F.A. Paley proclaimed that, in addition to ecclesiastical architecture, it would consider 'Church Musick and all the Decorative Arts which can be made subservient to Religion' to fall within its scope.[15]

Contributors to *The Ecclesiologist* spared no means of persuasion in their articles and reviews. Through careful study of ancient models, they sought to identify the principles that had motivated medieval architects and divines, those who had lived in what ecclesiologists came to believe was the greatest age of faith. They arrived at the conviction that the purest and best expressions of Christian art had flourished during the centuries of fervent belief which preceded the Commonwealth, and attempted to redress the decay which had occurred since then by aiming 'to derive all our notions of what is orthodox or beautiful from the *best* period of the art.'[16] In doing so they developed a concept of 'correctness' of principles, which they proceeded to profess dogmatically for the unabashed purpose of influencing the course of the wider revival of the Church. As headstrong young champions of good, beauty, and orthodoxy, they felt justified in intimidating any who wittingly or unwittingly dissented from their views. This they did in scathing reviews of architectural

---

[13] Webb diaries.
[14] Boyce (1888) 11.
[15] Boyce, 11.
[16] *The Ecclesiologist*, 5/– (June 1846) 252.

works and publications of any sort that did not meet their standards, as well as by unprovoked attacks on whatever or whoever they felt merited them.[17] Giving the impression that they had already won the larger aesthetic and intellectual battle was a powerful tool to convince the public that to disagree would be backward, and the less well informed were sometimes brought into line simply through the fear of being held up to public scorn for ignorance. These methods of persuasion extended to their other publications as well. A classic example that employs all of these tactics is found in the lead article for November 1845, in which the Cambridge Camden Society upbraided its own alma mater for the miserable liturgical arrangements of the University Church:

> It is a significant circumstance, as illustrating the apathy into which great and prosperous corporate bodies are ever prone to fall, – that while the movement in favour of Church restoration has extended over the length and breadth of the land, that church which is at once the most indecently and puritanically arranged in the whole kingdom, and in some sort the mother church of a vast body of our clergy, should have remained to this day unaltered. To say that Great S. Mary's could not have been, or might not now be, made in every respect fit for the service of the Church, and worthy of the University, in whose occupancy it has long been, [is] absurd.[18]

Looking back from the vantage of its one hundredth number (February 1854), *The Ecclesiologist* admitted that they had begun by doing 'a rough work in rough fashion':

> Clearing the back-woods is a work not to be achieved in drawing-room costume... We had to affront a good many persons, and not a few assumptions, as well as sundry convictions. It was a weary work, and we counted the cost. That cost was personal popularity; but the end was general success.[19]

The self review continues:

> as our principles won their way, the water became more smooth around us. Relieved from the necessity of mere guerilla warfare, we had time to elaborate principles. Church architecture is no longer tentative. It approaches to something of the completeness of an exact science. It is admitted to be a subject not so much of taste as of facts. It has rules, principles, laws.[20]

The brashness of the early writings of the Cambridge Camden Society, then, was seen as bitter but necessary medicine to deliver the Church from an illness characterized by complacent acceptance of the status quo and ignorance of its own history and Catholic heritage.

Given these methods of operation, it is hardly surprising that controversies were sparked which led to trouble within the ranks. Beginning with the very

---

[17] This will be obvious to any reader of *The Ecclesiologist*, and has been noted by White (1962) 36.
[18] *The Ecclesiologist*, 4/– (November 1845) 253.
[19] *The Ecclesiologist*, 15 (February 1854) 2.
[20] *The Ecclesiologist*, 15 (February 1854) 3.

first number of *The Ecclesiologist* some members of the Society were offended by its general tone. A petition against it was circulated and the Bishop of London withdrew his membership, but Webb reported that he and the Committee 'agreed to hold our ground.'[21] In December 1841 the evangelical Low Church publication, the *Record*, attacked the Cambridge Camden Society, and Webb was accused of being a Roman Catholic in disguise.[22] There were setbacks, such as the resignation of William Whewell and Professor Willis following a quarrel in April 1842,[23] and encouragements, including a letter which expressed 'Mr Keble's great delight in *The Ecclesiologist*.'[24] Indeed through the influence of *The Ecclesiologist* and several key publications discussed below, the work of the Cambridge Camden Society continued to expand at such a rate that, in 1842–3 alone, its Committee received no fewer than ninety-eight applications for advice on church restorations, new buildings, internal arrangements, ornaments, and church plate.[25]

There can be no doubt that, over the next two decades, it was primarily through the medium of *The Ecclesiologist* that its editors so widely and effectively spread the views and influence of the Cambridge Camden Society. With the cessation of the Tracts for the Times in 1841, it was precisely this centralized, fully identifiable and intentional means of proselytizing which the Oxford Movement lacked. Although there were national journals that carried on standards of churchmanship which were arguably the logical continuation of Tractarianism, and there were individual parishes whose Tractarian rectors created early and inspiring models of worship for any who wished to observe them, after 1841 there was little identifiable Tractarian unity in devising new goals and next steps for the revival of the Anglican Church. With John Henry Newman's withdrawal from public life and eventual secession to Rome in 1845, what remained of the Oxford Movement's identity, i.e. the group of individuals who had comprised its focal point, was lost. Beginning in the early 1840s the Ecclesiological Movement largely filled the void,[26] and the identification, refinement (where it was thought necessary), and spreading of the principles for which the Cambridge Camden Society became known took place primarily within the pages of *The Ecclesiologist*. It was therefore the core group of leaders who saw to its publication, under the constant care of

---

[21] Webb diaries, 27, 29, and 30 November 1841.
[22] Webb diaries, 18 December 1841.
[23] Webb diaries, 18 April 1842.
[24] Webb diaries, 8 June 1842, conveyed in a letter from P. Young to Webb.
[25] Boyce (1888) 22.
[26] Even the early Tractarian centre, Margaret Chapel, was taken on as a special project with the intention of making it a model of ecclesiological perfection. (: 118–21)

Benjamin Webb as its 'responsible conductor from the first,'[27] who wielded the influence of the Society as a whole.

With the real power of the Cambridge Camden Society so firmly centralized in the hands of its committee, it is hardly surprising to find that the management of *The Ecclesiologist* was not always a wholly peaceful affair.[28] An incident in 1846 reveals the real crux of the tension. Benjamin Webb proposed that Alexander James Beresford Hope be added to the number of proprietors. This occasioned a characteristically blunt reply from J.M. Neale:

> Every day I see more and more clearly... how thoroughly opposed he [Hope] is to that dogmatic spirit which I consider to be the life and soul of *The Ecclesiologist* and of the C.C.S. I am sure he believes himself to be actuated by principle only. But I feel it to be impossible for a man, unless he lives a truly ascetic life, to move in the rank in which he moves, and to mix with high life, without being infected with the miserable compromising spirit of the day... Now, I cannot consent to have an element of compromise introduced into *The Ecclesiologist. Pace tua*, you are not wholly free from fault in that way.[29]

Interestingly, this 1846 letter is early evidence that Webb, however bluntly he may have expressed himself in private letters to Neale, was more inclined to act in moderation, and that he was apt to perceive a broader picture than his longtime friend and confidant. It was a part of Neale's core nature, on the other hand, to express his convictions with absolute certainty. Once Neale's powers of reason had arrived at what he considered to be the principle of a matter, it was settled. A later editorial dispute occasioned the following statement by Neale to Webb: 'I don't like Tentative papers. I would never write anything till I was sure of the principle: and being sure of it, why should I, or you, pretend to be doubtful?'[30]

For men like Webb and Neale, consistency in the development of ecclesiological principles was an intellectual necessity; but then the vehemence with which they sometimes expressed them also demanded it, for challenges to their principles were an inevitability. It is not surprising, therefore, that the school of thought which ecclesiologists developed to guide the revival of Gothic church architecture carried over, as we shall see, to their views on sacred music.

---

[27] *The Ecclesiologist*, 15/100 (February 1854) 4.
[28] An editorial dispute in 1842 is noted in Webb's diaries: Phillip Freeman resigned from the CCS Committee on 22 October and rejoined it two days later. On 5 November, 'after much disputing, Venables carried his point, & took the Ecclesiologist from me to P Freeman alone.' On 11 November Webb records, 'a stiff visit from Freeman' and the next day, 'Freeman resigned, & I was re-instated. Venables and JJ Smith very angry.' Webb's diaries give no indication of any further challenges to his management of *The Ecclesiologist*.
[29] Lawson (1910) 93. Letter dated 1st Sunday in Lent, 1846.
[30] Lawson, (1910) 155. Letter dated S. Matthew (21 September), 1850.

Early publications

There is no doubt that the remarkable expansion of the Cambridge Camden Society's influence was aided substantially through the wide readership reached by its series of publications beginning *A Few Words to...* Two versions of *A Few Words to Churchwardens on Churches and Church Ornaments* appeared: *No.I. Suited to country parishes*, and *No. II. Suited to town and manufacturing parishes*. Both of these invited inquiries to be directed either to the Cambridge Camden Society or to the Oxford Architectural Society. Published in 1841 and highly commended to the public by the *Times* in a leading article, authorship is traditionally attributed to John Mason Neale, but Webb's diaries appear to claim for himself sole credit for at least one of them.[31] So practical and popular were these pamphlets that in just five years *No. I* reached a fourteenth edition, and the Society noted with pleasure that the wish it had expressed when the pamphlet was first published, that every parish in the country might be provided with a copy, had been, as far as the number sold was concerned, more than fulfilled.[32] These publications were followed closely by *A Few Words to Church Builders* in 1841 (second edition, 1842); and *A Few Words to Parish Clerks and Sextons of Country Parishes* in 1843, which recommended a proverb that was the practical theme of all the pamphlets, 'If a thing is worth doing at all, it is worth doing well.'[33]

So rapidly did the views of the Cambridge Camden Society develop during its first five years of existence, and so popular was *A Few Words to Church Builders*, that it reached a third, greatly expanded and revised edition in 1844. The question of architectural style had still been open to debate in the second edition of 1842,[34] but by 1844 the question was utterly settled.[35] The rationale for the decision set forth at that point is so fundamental to understanding the manner in which ecclesiologists reasoned and proceeded thenceforward, that it merits careful consideration:

---

[31] Webb diaries, 15 April and 4 September 1841. Regarding the *Times* notice, Webb refers to them as 'our' *Few Words*, which could refer either to a joint authorship or the collective nature of the publication, which was sanctioned by and published under the name of the Cambridge Camden Society. On a visit to the Neales in September 1841, however, Webb records, 'Neale read my "Churchwardens" aloud to his mother and sisters.'

[32] *The Ecclesiologist*, 7/60 (June 1847) 233.

[33] Cambridge Camden Society, *A Few Words to Parish Clerks*, 3.

[34] 'It will, generally speaking, be better to adopt that which prevails in the district in which the church is to be built. The number of worshippers will much affect the style.' It was thought that Early English was best for small chapels. Cambridge Camden Society, *A Few Words to Church Builders* (2nd edn, 1842) 4.

[35] The adoption of Middle Pointed Gothic as the preferred style was put forth in *The Ecclesiologist*, 2/14 (October 1842) 5–6, and in the introduction by Neale and Webb to Durandus, (1843) xxiv.

> We are not now called on to prove that Gothick is the only Christian Architecture. We believe that, after a well-fought battle, this point has been conceded: and that, though second-rate architects may, for a few years yet, employ Romanesque or revived Pagan, those who are at the head of their profession will be guilty of such serious errours no longer. The subject is amply discussed in the *Ecclesiologist*, Vol. II p.5.
>
> 12. We wish however to restrict the choice of style still further than this. No one can, sensibly, employ Norman, and perhaps not judiciously even Perpendicular, when free to choose another style. Early English, though it must perhaps be allowed occasionally, should be used very sparingly. The Decorated or Edwardian style, that employed, we mean, between the years 1260 and 1360, is that to which only, except from some very peculiar circumstances, we ought to return. The reason for this is plain. During the so-called Norman era, the Catholick Church was forming her architectural language: in the Tudor period, she was unlearning it. What should we say of him, who wishing to acquire the elegances of a polished and expressive tongue, should select his models from a period, either before that tongue had emerged from barbarism, or after the process of over-refinement had reduced it to frivolous debility?[36]

The justification continued:

> Once more, it is agreed on all hands that the greatest glory which Christian Architecture has yet attained was reached in the early part of the Decorated Style: the Art had followed the true clue till that period, or at least not long after that she began to lose it. Now, if we really indulge the hope that there is yet a higher pitch of glory to be attained, and which future architects may hope to reach, we may well go back to that point where decay and debasement began, if so be, that we may thence strike out a more real and more faithful course; more real, because Perpendicular employed meretricious enrichments, and *made* ornament for its own sake; more faithful, because the Tudor architects forgot their high vocation of setting forth truth by beauty and symbolised worldly pomp instead of the Catholick Faith; instead of the teachings of the Church, the promptings of Erastianism. And let it not be said that the time we have marked out, as that of which the art alone was to be imitated, would leave the architect too little scope for his ability and imagination. None can make this assertion who is, in the slightest degree, acquainted with the marvelous variety and flexibility of the Decorated style.[37]

The methods of reasoning used here, as well as the principles derived from them for future application (in reference to music as well) are critical:

1. Gothic was chosen because it was an essentially Christian style. Note that the pre-Christian origins of Classical architecture earned it the designation 'Pagan.'
2. Artistic forms have a beginning, or infancy; a middle, or maturity; and an end, or degeneracy. Clearly the mature manifestations should be held in highest honour. This view of artistic achievement related closely to

---

[36] Cambridge Camden Society, *A Few Words to Church Builders* (3rd edn, 1844) 5–6.
[37] Cambridge Camden Society, *A Few Words to Church Builders*, (3rd edn, 1844) 6.

William Crotch's thoughts on the history of English music and, as we shall see, was applied by ecclesiologists to music during this same period of time. (: 40–2, 134–5)
3. The Renaissance was a fundamentally secular influence on the Church and society which precipitated the decline of art. The means of its rescue should be to return to the point prior to that at which art had peaked, and to proceed from there.
4. Artists have a vocation to set forth truth by beauty.
5. Modern artistic invention would find wide scope once the spirit of medieval art in its prime was regained and, if revived on that basis, there was hope of 'yet a higher pitch of glory to be attained.'[38]

The Symbolism of Churches and Church Ornaments: a Translation of the First Book of the Rationale Divinorum Officiorum, written by William Durandus has been called the Cambridge Camden Society's most important publication (1843), since it 'marked the real adoption of symbolism as a significant feature of ecclesiology.'[39] The publication was actually issued under the names of the editors, John Mason Neale and Benjamin Webb, who collaborated on the eleven chapters of introduction as well as on the translation itself. The purpose of issuing it was to bring to contemporary attention the 'sacramental character of Catholick art.' This they understood to mean that 'by the outward and visible form, is signified something inward and spiritual: that the material fabrick symbolizes, embodies, figures, represents, expresses, answers to, some abstract meaning.'[40] Various methods were employed by the editors to demonstrate this, one of which included the insistence that, by analogy, Christian architecture must be symbolic because the other religious arts were symbolic. Among them, Neale and Webb wrote, 'Musick... has the strongest claims to our notice. We know, for example, that each instrument symbolizes some particular colour. So, according to Haydn, the trombone is deep red, – the trumpet, scarlet, – the clarionet, orange' and they went on to explain how Haydn had used these colours to cause the sun to rise at the beginning of *The Creation*. This served as 'a specimen of the manner in which the expressions of one art may be translated into that of another, because they each and all

---

[38] This commonly accepted line of reasoning was acknowledged by T.G. Jackson in one of the earliest histories of the Gothic Revival: 'Nothing is more certain than the impossibility of our inventing a new style directly, and the necessity of our choosing some appropriate style out of which the new style, if it ever comes, will naturally and insensibly develope [*sic*] itself. If we make a right choice, and if we succeed in making our adopted art *live again* in any degree... if we raise it from the condition of a dead language to that of a living vernacular, then a new style will inevitably be developed out of it... we can attain this result in no other way.' Jackson (1873) 13.
[39] White (1962) 68–9.
[40] Durandus (1843) xiii, xxvi.

symbolize the same abstraction',[41] and marks an important step in the solidification of the ecclesiologists' theory that underlying principles of Christian art applied to all of its branches.

Durandus met with mixed reaction. High Churchmen and Tractarians generally loved it: on a visit to Hursley in 1844, Webb recorded that 'Keble talked of Neale and expressed his great delight with our Durandus', and by 1847 it had been translated into French.[42] But such a symbolical understanding of Christian art naturally aroused suspicion among those who were inclined to fear 'popery.' On account of *Durandus* Archbishop Sumner threatened to refuse to license Webb to a curacy in his archdiocese in 1848; and there is no doubt that *Durandus* contributed to fuel the controversies of 1844 and 1845 discussed below.

Formation of the Ecclesiological late Cambridge Camden Society

Whatever the objective practical usefulness of the Cambridge Camden Society's work, popular and often negative identification of Cambridge ecclesiology with Tractarianism continued to gain in strength until prejudicial tensions reached a breaking point in late 1844. In the midst of a long court battle over the erection of a stone altar during restoration work on the Round Church (St Sepulchre's), Cambridge, the Revd Francis Close published his infamous sermon for Guy Fawkes' Day 1844, *The Restoration of Churches is the Restoration of Popery*.[43] Mr Close's stated purpose was:

> to show that as Romanism is taught *Analytically* at Oxford, it is taught *Artistically* at Cambridge – that it is inculcated theoretically, in tracts, at one University, and it is *sculptured*, painted, and *graven* at the other... in a word, that the *'Ecclesiologist'* of Cambridge is identical in doctrine with the Oxford *Tracts for the Times*.[44]

In an effort to distance the Cambridge Camden Society from controversy, *The Ecclesiologist* was officially disassociated from it in January 1845 but continued publication under Webb's general editorship. Public pressure was too great, however, and Close's sermon coupled with the resignation of several influential members contributed to lead the Committee to recommend the dissolution of the Cambridge Camden Society in February 1845.[45] Neale wrote from Madeira to say that he was averse to dissolution, but that he 'should like

---

[41] Durandus (1843) xlvii.
[42] Webb diaries, 14 April 1844; Webb received a copy of the French translation on 12 September 1847.
[43] Chadwick, 3rd edn, I (1971) 221.
[44] Quoted in White (1962) 142.
[45] Webb diaries: committee decision taken 7 February, announced at a public meeting 13 February 1845.

[the Society] to be freed from an University yoke, and then set going again.'⁴⁶ When it became apparent that dissolution could not be effected legally without the unanimous consent of the membership, the Committee was requested to reorganize the Society, and Neale's wish became reality. London became the new headquarters for the 'Ecclesiological late Cambridge Camden Society' (hereafter the ECCS).⁴⁷ The general feeling of relief among the Committee members at this release from constraints is testified to by F.A. Paley, who wrote, 'I trust now the makeweight of the Society is providentially removed, we shall go *with full sail and colours up.*'⁴⁸ Having weathered the storm, *The Ecclesiologist* was formally reassociated with the ECCS on 12 May 1846, since it had to be admitted that the purposes of the two were 'absolutely identical.'⁴⁹

The new freedom felt by the leaders of the Society quickly revealed itself in the pages of *The Ecclesiologist*. If any uncertainty existed as to the boundaries of the province which ecclesiologists considered to fall under their jurisdiction, articles in the January and March 1847 issues of *The Ecclesiologist* claimed a whole empire. J.M. Neale declared:

> Ecclesiology is the science of Christian Æsthestics; and if æsthetics be of such infinite importance in the service of GOD, of infinite importance must they also be in fitting children for that service: which is education.⁵⁰

A.J.B. Hope proceeded to define ecclesiology as the 'science' devoted to the 'systematic study of the requirements of Divine Worship',⁵¹ and *The Ecclesiologist* stated bluntly that this included Ritualism.⁵² A warning was sounded, however, that attention to aesthetics did not necessarily yield true religion. *The Ecclesiologist* hoped to point out the 'pole-wide difference between the cultivation of Ecclesiology and that fatal error of substituting the type in place of the reality which it symbolises.'⁵³

---

⁴⁶ Lawson (1910) 84. Letter to Benjamin Webb dated Easter Monday 1845.
⁴⁷ The name 'Camden Society' was already in use by an antiquarian society in London.
⁴⁸ Letter to the Revd John Charles Chambers, 3 June 1845, original underlined rather than italicized. Lambeth, MS 2677, f. 27.
⁴⁹ *The Ecclesiologist*, preface to volume five, vi.
⁵⁰ 'Schools.' *The Ecclesiologist*, 7/55 (January 1847) 2. Attribution of authorship derived from Lawson (1910) 100.
⁵¹ *The Ecclesiologist*, 7/57 (March 1847) 85
⁵² *The Ecclesiologist*, 7/60 (June 1847) 234. What mainstream ecclesiologists would have regarded as ritualism in 1847, however, was considerably tamer than the Ritualism which became a party designation by the late 1850s. It must also be remembered that J.M. Neale's views on ritualism by the 1850s were considerably less moderate than Webb's or A.J.B. Hope's.
⁵³ 'Æsthetics and Religion.' *The Ecclesiologist*, 7/57 (March 1847) 126. The author of this article was A.J.B. Hope, according to a letter from G.W. (probably the Revd Gordon Williams, King's College, Cambridge) in the *Guardian*, 696 (6 April 1859) 303.

External influences on the musical views of the ECCS

As mentioned earlier, both Benjamin Webb and John Mason Neale subscribed to the Musical Antiquarian Society (1840–7) in March 1841.[54] It had been formed 'for the publication of scarce and valuable works by the early English composers', supplied to members for an annual subscription of one pound. By the end of its first year the Society boasted nearly one thousand members. William Chappell, music publisher, was the 'projector' of the Society and acted as treasurer and manager of publications for five years before being succeeded by his younger brother, Thomas.[55] Among the other founders of the Society was E.F. Rimbault, who held the office of Secretary and served as a primary editor of its publications.[56]

The Motett Society 'evolved' out of the Musical Antiquarian Society[57] in 1841, due to the need felt by William Dyce (:32–3, 140–2) and others for a society dedicated not only to the publication but to the practice and public performance of the ancient church music of all Catholic countries. Three key members were Dyce (the chief promoter and Secretary), Dr Edward Rimbault, and the publisher, James Burns (Dyce's cousin[58]). They collaborated to issue three volumes of sacred music, including works by Palestrina, Victoria, Lassus, Marenzio, Tallis, Farrant, Byrd, Gibbons, Blow, and Purcell. Rimbault edited the music, and Dyce translated the texts into English and fitted them to the vocal parts. A typical array of music sung at one of the early meetings of the Motett Society included two 'hymns' and three 'anthems' by Palestrina (adapted to English texts), Tye *The Lord descended*, Gibbons *Almighty and everlasting God*, Byrd *Bow thine ear*, and the Credo from Palestrina's *Missa Eterna Christi munera*. In noticing this event the editor of the *English Churchman* added his opinion, 'Those who wish to know what ecclesiastical music really is, and to enjoy the compositions of the great masters, should not neglect this opportunity.'[59] Ecclesiologists admitted later in the same year that two significant influences on their musical views were the Motett Society of London and the model services of St Mark's Training College, Chelsea. In the same article *The Ecclesiologist* voiced its unqualified support and gratitude to

---

[54] Webb diaries, 18 March 1841.
[55] 'Musical Antiquarian Society,' *Grove's Dictionary* (3rd edition) and *New Grove Dictionary* (6th edition).
[56] 'Rimbault, Edward Francis,' Brown and Stratton, *British Musical Biography*.
[57] Pointon (1979) 74–5. The Motett Society was not formed in 1844, as Pointon asserts; see *The Ecclesiologist*, 14/97 (August 1853) 274–5; 23/142 (October 1862) 299.
[58] Pointon (1979) 53.
[59] *English Churchman*, 1/17 (27 April 1843) 271.

William Dyce for his exquisite edition of *The Order of Daily Service... with Plain Tune*.[60]

In 1842 the Revd Thomas Helmore was appointed to train the students of the recently founded (1841) National Training College in Chelsea to sing daily services, first in its 'Model' School and later, after its opening on 7 May 1843, in the College Chapel, St Mark's. The task of teaching the students to sing at sight had already been entrusted to John Hullah and his assistant, Edward May. Helmore became closely involved with the Motett Society, first through the liturgical use of its publications at St Mark's.[61] When the meetings of the Motett Choir ceased 'principally from want of funds' in 1845, Helmore soon revived them privately at the request of a group of amateur volunteers. This was the basis of the Motett Choir to which he would act as Precentor well into the 1860s.[62]

Benjamin Webb seems to have been the primary ecclesiological link to the Motett Society. Whether or not his inquiry into membership on 28 June 1841 resulted in a formal affiliation with the Society remains unrecorded, but it does prove that he was one of the Motett Society's earliest supporters. His diaries confirm that he received its publications with pleasure[63] and attended its meetings when he was in London.[64] Beginning in October 1843 Webb added the services at St Mark's College, Chelsea, to those he attended on his occasional visits to London, which was an additional, if indirect, exposure to the music and ideals promoted by the Motett Society.[65] Even the temporary break in the Motett Choir's official activities in 1845 did not halt its key members from making music. Private 'madrigal parties' were thrown with regularity. The first of these recorded by Webb took place on 13 January 1845, and was attended by the Revds Thomas Helmore, William Scott[66], T.M. Fallow[67], Gordon, G.F. Forbes, J.F. Russell,[68] and C.W. Page;[69] and William

---

[60] 'Organs,' *The Ecclesiologist*, 3/25 (September 1843) 2.
[61] Although founded in 1841, the College was not christened St Mark's until the opening of the Chapel. Rainbow (1970) 64–7; *The Ecclesiologist*, 23/142 (October 1862) 299–300.
[62] *The Ecclesiologist*, 25/160 (February 1864) 47; 14/97 (August 1853) 274–5, public meetings ceased again during the years 1849, 1850, and 1851.
[63] Webb diaries, 15 June 1842.
[64] Webb diaries, 1 May 1843; 5 and 19 June 1843; 22 April 1844.
[65] Webb diaries, 15 and 22 October 1843; 20 June 1845. Webb would have been curious to attend the services here after reading the high praise given them in the *English Churchman*, 1/21 (25 May 1843) 333–4.
[66] William Scott, BA 1835, Queen's College, Oxford, served as perpetual curate of Christ Church, Hoxton 1839–63; and vicar of St Olave's, Jewry 1863–d.1872. Foster, *Alumni Oxonienses...1715–1886*. He became a stalwart member of the ECCS Committee.
[67] T.M. Fallow was vicar of St Andrew's, Wells Street, and a founding member of both the Motett Society and the Society for Promoting Church Music. His obituary in the *Parish Choir*, 1/21 (September 1847) 179, stated: 'We believe that there are few

Dyce, Esq. This was Webb's first personal introduction to Dyce, with whom he recorded 'an interesting talk about the proposed church at Hong Kong, and then about Beauty and the Secret of Gothic, as to which he has a numerical theory; which he proceeded partly to unfold. He is a most clever man.'[70] Webb loved this kind of social evening, and he attended and hosted them regularly throughout the rest of his life. During the next thirteen months further madrigal and motet parties were held in the homes of the Revd J.F. Russell and James Burns, and Webb reciprocated their hospitality by sponsoring two of his own.[71] It is probable that these meetings led James Burns and T.M. Fallow to join the ECCS as ordinary members during the course of 1846, while William Dyce was made an honorary member.[72] Among the other distinguished guests on these occasions were the Revds J.M. Neale and J. Haskoll, Dr Robert Brett,[73] Mr and Mrs Jay,[74] as well as the architects, Butterfield and Carpenter.

Development of a church music policy

In spite of the fact that the prefatory article to the first volume of *The Ecclesiologist* (1841) claimed church music as one of the publication's concerns, the first significant treatment of the subject did not appear until September 1843.[75] The problems presented to church builders in regard to the physical location of organs proved a convenient springboard from which to discuss organs and church music in general.

---

persons who have done more than he did towards diffusing a knowledge of and taste for the true Church style.'
[68] John Fuller Russell, Peterhouse, Cambridge, SCL 1837, LLB 1838; served as curate of St Peter, Walworth 1838–40, and perpetual curate of St James, Enfield, Middlesex 1841–54. He was a member of the inner circle of ecclesiologists, editor of *Hierurgia Anglicana*, published by the Cambridge Camden Society, and co-editor of several works with Dr Hook and Dr Irons. *Crockford's* 1876, 1894.
[69] Cyril William Page, BA 1823, Christ Church, Oxford, served as perpetual curate of Christ Church, Westminster 1843–d.1873.
[70] Webb diaries, 13 January 1845.
[71] Webb diaries, 13 (location unknown) and 22 January 1845 (hosted by Webb); 4 February 1845 (Russell); 27 November, 9 and 23 December 1845 (Burns); 5 January 1846 (Russell); and 18 February 1846 (Webb).
[72] *The Ecclesiologist*, 6/49 (July 1846) 26; 6/54 (December 1846) 227.
[73] Brett was a surgeon, who later was a central figure in the building of the Tractarian church, St Matthias, Stoke Newington.
[74] Jay taught the Hullah singing class that Webb attended in the spring of 1842. Webb diaries, 12 March 1842.
[75] *The Ecclesiologist*, 3/24 (September 1843) 1–5.

The anonymous article would appear to have issued from the pen of Benjamin Webb.[76] The author suggests that one reason for *The Ecclesiologist's* virtual neglect of church music to that point was 'the disgraceful neglect of this church-art in our University.'

> A few miserable and effete singers running about from choir to choir,[77] and performing, to a crashing and bellowing of organs, the most meagre and washy musick; how could Church men learn anything, under such a system, of the depth and majesty and sternness and devotion of true church musick?[78]

The most prominent contemporary influences for the good of church music were identified as follows:

> the exertions of the Motett Society of London, the example of S Mark's Training College at Chelsea, and the high principles respecting this art maintained by our contemporary the *English Churchman*, have already done wonders in showing what are the nature, rules, and requirements of *old* church musick. It is now beginning to be recognized that church musick is almost exclusively *vocal*: at any rate the Gregorian chants, the canto-fermo, and the responses, according to the original musical notation of our Prayer-book (beautifully edited by W. Dyce, Esq. and published by Mr Burns), clearly are better without any instrumental accompaniment whatever.[79]

The opinion expressed about the physical placement of an organ (on the ground at the west end either in the nave or a side aisle) is the article's most original contribution to the contemporary discussion of church music. The more general thoughts expressed mirror and expand upon those of the *English Churchman* so closely, both in theory and the manner in which they are

---

[76] This article's recommendations for the placement of the organ agree with those of *A Few Words to Churchwardens...No. II*, which Webb probably wrote (: 26 footnote 31); and on at least one other occasion Neale is known to have suggested that Webb treat the subject of organs. Towle (1906) 136. Furthermore, a footnote within the article (page 2) refers to the courtesy with which strangers were admitted to meetings of the Motett Society, a fact which is stated to be the personal observation of the author. Webb's diaries confirm that he attended numerous meetings of the Motett Society during this period of time; whereas Neale did not even learn to intone until 1849. Lawson (1910) 128. One of the reasons Neale offered for refusing the deanery of the new cathedral in Perth, Scotland, was the fact that he possessed zeal but little skill in music. Towle (1906) 184–5. Another footnote refers to the haunting effect of the organ when heard at a distance in the Cathedral of Amiens; Webb and Neale had made an ecclesiological tour of France in 1841. Towle (1906) 54. The article refers to St Mark's, Chelsea; although Webb's diary gives the impression that 15 October 1843 was the first time he attended services there, he would certainly have known of its influence from others and from reading about it in the *English Churchman* earlier that year.

[77] Until 1856 a single set of lay clerks sang at King's, Trinity, and St John's Colleges, and the latter two also shared a set of choristers. The choristers of King's did double duty for the University Sermon at Great St Mary's, the University Church. (: 47, 56)

[78] *The Ecclesiologist*, 3/25 (September 1843) 2.

[79] *The Ecclesiologist*, 3/25 (September 1843) 2.

expressed, that the *English Churchman* saw fit to reprint the article in its entirety the following month, followed closely by an expression of congratulation and thanks for the 'powerful aid' which *The Ecclesiologist* had afforded it.[80]

The Ecclesiologist pointed out that music had become an integral part of Christian worship long before organs were perfected, stated that organs were therefore unnecessary to contemporary worship,[81] that they hid the real beauty of music which was intended to be sung unaccompanied, and that too often they tempted an organist to inappropriate technical display. It objected to the theory that organs were a musical 'improvement' in worship, insisting that they destroyed the effect of antiphonal singing by constantly emitting sound from the same location. By too often drowning the efforts of the choir through sheer volume, *The Ecclesiologist* went on to suggest that, 'We owe to [the organ] in great measure the disgraceful appearance of most of our choirs at the Divine office: we have seen in cathedrals *two* vicars-choral on *one* side, and perhaps three boys on the other,' a state of degeneracy which would have been impossible in the absence of instrumental accompaniment.[82] It complained that cathedral music had come to be 'done by deputy.'[83] Furthermore, organs caused problems in church arrangement by blocking west windows or chancel arches, or by obscuring the baptismal font under an organ gallery.[84] The parallel was drawn: 'Like the improvements in architecture itself, and other church-arts, the effect has been entirely to supersede the old ways, to bring in a showy but hollow secularity without a particle of solemnity or devotion.'[85] Although the organ was deemed unnecessary, *The Ecclesiologist* attested to its grandeur and propriety in large churches and cathedrals; but it felt that the 'entrancing effect' of hearing an organ from a distance was lost in smaller churches, that parishes would do better to spend money on architectural

---

[80] *English Churchman*, 1/40 (5 October 1843) 636–7; and 1/43 (26 October 1843) 684.
[81] The success of the full choral service instituted by the Revd E. Shuttleworth at St Mary's, Penzance, was cited as proof of this. The opening of this church and the 'grand simplicity and depth of devotional feeling' of its choral service were lauded in *The English Churchman*, 1/18 (4 May 1843) 278.
[82] These views were echoed two years later in Druitt's *A Popular Tract on Church Music* (1845) 52–4. As founder of the Society for the Promotion of Church Music and editor of the *Parish Choir* (1846–51), Druitt would prove a powerful ally to ecclesiologists on matters musical.
[83] Many of these ideas were expounded upon earlier the same year in an article about St Mark's College, Chelsea in *The English Churchman*, 1/21 (25 May 1843) 333–4.
[84] Jebb also complains about problems of organ placement, (1843) 202–3.
[85] *The Ecclesiologist*, 3/25 (September 1843) 3.

improvements than on an organ, and that it would be advantageous to divert the stipend of the organist to employ an additional curate.[86]

This earliest pronouncement on church music revealed the basic assumptions from which the musical views of the Society would develop:

1. Church music had been on a continual decline since the Rebellion, and therefore true church music at the present could most surely be found in old church music.
2. Anglican worship is inherently choral (i.e. sung) in nature.
3. Gregorian chant is conducive to congregational participation.
4. True church music, once introduced, would become popular, 'since it is simpler and easier, as well as being so exactly suited to the wants and feelings of every Catholic mind.'[87]

In addition, the unacceptable state of ecclesiastical music in the universities was identified as a primary cause of its degraded state throughout the Church at large.

In February 1844 the receipt of a 'valuable and courteous letter' from the Revd John Jebb was acknowledged, in addition to other correspondence on the subject of church music and organs, but the editors of *The Ecclesiologist* felt compelled to defer further consideration of the matter:

> Suffice it for the present to say, that we see no reason to recede from the positions laid down in our former paper; which indeed, as a whole, and in all important aspects, are allowed by the correspondents now alluded to, and have met with acceptance and support from other quarters. In the mean while we must add our own testimony to the want expressed elsewhere of some choral school[88] for the instruction both of our clergy and others. There is absolutely no provision made anywhere for education in this important requirement for the proper performance of the Divine Offices. We are not in a condition to suggest any scheme for supplying this want, nor would it be our immediate province to do so. But it is much to be deplored that no means are taken to remedy a defect which is daily becoming more universally felt and lamented.[89]

---

[86] *The Ecclesiologist*, 3/25 (September 1843) 4–5. The *English Churchman* replied that the organist's stipend should be spent on a choirmaster rather than on an additional curate. *English Churchman*, 1/43 (26 October 1843) 684.

[87] *The Ecclesiologist*, 3/25 (September 1843) 4.

[88] Possibly a reference to *The English Churchman's* calls for the clergy to be trained in music. The idea of a choral school for potential choir members was later championed by the Society for Promoting Church Music, *Parish Choir*, 3/44 (August 1849) 13–15.

[89] *The Ecclesiologist*, 3/29-30 (February 1844) 83–4. Rainbow construes Jebb's letter to have been an unfriendly attack, and implies that it proves an early drawing of lines between enemy camps: 'And we cannot fail to remark that the doctrine thus propounded in the *Ecclesiologist* quickly drew a critical letter from John Jebb – a letter which was acknowledged in a later issue of the journal without formal reply.' Rainbow (1970), 89. Jebb and ecclesiologists had much in common, and there is no evidence to suggest that this letter was anything but amicable. Many years later Jebb became a

Thus *The Ecclesiologist's* first two important statements on church music both expressed great concern over the lack of opportunities in the universities for the future clergy to be educated in the music of the Church.

In May 1846 *The Ecclesiologist* returned to the same attack in a review of several collections of traditional Anglican cathedral chants in four-part harmony, including one by the Professor of Music at Cambridge, Thomas Attwood Walmisley. 'Mr Walmisley's work is one that must be very much regretted, if only as showing that there can be no general chanting of the Psalms by priests or laymen in the University of Cambridge.'[90]

More than that, the review provided a forum to ask, given a *Book of Common Prayer* which instructed that psalms be sung in every liturgy, why did no one sing them? And whose duty was it? The reviewer's analysis was:

> The Psalms are not sung, because singing has come to be considered the duty of a trained quire; but if Psalm singing were meant to be confined to such a quire, the direction would have been, "In quires and places where they sing" here followeth the singing of the Psalms. But there is nothing of the sort. The antiphonal chanting of the Psalms is meant to be congregational: whether the congregation be a large body of ecclesiasticks alone, or a mixed one. It is altogether an abuse that the chanting of Psalms has come to be thought a *quire* instead of a *common song*. When singing ceased to be regarded as the duty of all equally, those on whom the task devolved began to feel it irksome, and imitated their superiors in neglecting it. A silent Dean made a silent Chapter: the congregation ceased to sing when the Priest no longer led.[91]

Although they thought it 'altogether an abuse that the chanting of Psalms has come to be thought a *quire* instead of a common song,' they hastened to allow for the work of choirs:

> It is almost needless to say it, but we may add by way of avoiding all misunderstanding, that while we condemn the attempt to introduce elegant harmonized music for the Psalter, we are far from arguing against the use of the very highest specimens of art in the Services of the Church. The Anthem, parts of the Communion Office, &c., for instance, may be sung to the grandest and most artistic compositions, provided that they be in a solemn and devotional style. In this case the people are intended to listen and to be edified, – not as in the Psalms and Hymns, in which they are on the contrary to take a constant and audible part.[92]

---

member of the Committee of the Ecclesiological Society. *The Ecclesiologist,* 21/139 (August 1860) 238.
[90] *The Ecclesiologist,* 5/– (May 1846) 174. Less than a year later an article suggesting the redecoration of Trinity College Chapel repeated the hope that the 'general taste for church-music' which was spreading so quickly would mean that, by the time their suggestions might be implemented, undergraduates would be 'willing and able to bear their part in the solemn celebration of the Divine worship.' *The Ecclesiologist,* 7/57 (March 1847) 85.
[91] *The Ecclesiologist,* 5/– (May 1846) 172.
[92] *The Ecclesiologist,* 5/– (May 1846) 172, 174.

This qualification was due in part to a recent attack by John Hullah on what he misunderstood to be the musical stance of ecclesiologists.[93] On 19 February 1846 Hullah had delivered a lecture in Leeds at the invitation of the parish rector, Dr Walter Farquhar Hook. It was an able defence of the appropriateness of music in worship and the duty of Christians, especially the clergy, to acquire the skill to participate in it. Hullah had been a member of the Cambridge Camden Society since November 1843,[94] but the zealousness of some members for plainsong sung in unison had given him the impression that they wished to exclude all other types of music from worship. He was prepared to admit that such restraint might sometimes be necessary or even prudent, but thought it ludicrous to 'propose the permanent abasement of the choral service to the level of the musical ignorance of the great mass of English people.' Ecclesiologists ignored the fact that harmony was an inherently Christian science, he asserted. Hullah was not one to mince words, and went on to accuse them of being inconsistent,

> who think no amount of pains thrown away on the study of architecture, sculpture, or painting; who derive all their notions of what is orthodox or beautiful from the *best* periods of those arts, but who would settle the question of ecclesiastical *music* alone, by appealing for precedent to the practices of ages when, as an art, it can scarcely be said to have existed at all: – such appeals being generally wound up by some tribute to the 'beauty of simplicity.'
>
> Now it may be observed that whenever people are called upon to perform tasks to which they are incompetent, or unwilling, they generally begin to talk of the 'beauty of simplicity.' It is a nice compact little phrase, conveniently susceptible of an infinite variety of meanings and uses. It is not impossible that the musical incapability of some of our modern Ecclesiologists may have had something to do with the different views they take of music from those they take of architecture, sculpture, or painting. For, be it observed, they are not called upon to build churches, carve finials, or paint frescos; their's [sic] is the easier task of talking about them. But the delegation of Church singing to others is another matter. There has happily grown up a feeling of late, that they should do this duty for themselves; and seeing no ready mode of raising their powers to the standard of what the Church requires, it is not very surprising that they should have striven here and there to lower the standard to their powers.[95]

An accusation of inconsistency was the sort of criticism that the Cambridge Camdenians could not bear to let pass unnoticed. Hullah was wrong in assuming that they wanted to restrict music to 'plainsong, in unison.' This they wished only for the psalms, which they stated had been sung to Gregorian chants up until the Rebellion. 'When we translate the psalms and canticles into fluent newspaper English, it will be time enough to admit such a developement [sic] of Church music as Mr Walmisley's double chant', they wrote.

---

[93] This attack is replied to in the same issue of *The Ecclesiologist*.
[94] *The Ecclesiologist*, 3/28 (November 1843) 44.
[95] J. Hullah (1846) 10–11.

Why, – because we prefer for the Psalter a kind of chant which is ancient, Catholick, and authorized, besides being the only kind that combines solemnity and dignity with the practical objects that are intended to be answered by musical recitation, to the meretricious style which has become common with us since the Restoration; are we stigmatized as insensible to the merits of "that eminently Christian science, harmony"? This is indeed hard upon those whose devotion to Palestrina in music has exposed them to many a smile from the votaries of Balfe or Verdi.

As to Hullah's charge of inconsistency, *The Ecclesiologist* replied:

we may take Palestrina for our highest idea of religious music, and Mr Hullah may, (if he likes), take Rossini. But then the question is quite another one. We are quite ready to defend our 'Middle Pointed' of Palestrina against the beautiful debasements (as we believe) of Pergolesi or Haydn. Then however Mr Hullah's charge of 'inconsistency' vanishes away: for in music also, as he approvingly acknowledges we do in other arts, we profess "to derive all our notions of what is orthodox or beautiful from the *best* period of the art." [96]

The Ecclesiologists' response to Hullah concluded with an expression of regret that he had misrepresented the school of ecclesiologists, and stated, 'Probably he could not write any praise of Christian harmony which it would be too strong for us to join in.'[97] This statement should have dispelled the notion that ecclesiologists were only interested in promoting services in which the congregation did all of the singing. Clearly there was an honoured place for choir music within the liturgies of the Anglican tradition.

This was also the first of several comparisons of church music to ecclesiastical architecture within the pages of *The Ecclesiologist*. It should be noted that the 'Middle Pointed' or mature period of music was identified as that of Palestrina (the sixteenth century), rather than the musical style chronologically concurrent to Middle Pointed Gothic architecture (1260–1360). This is possible because of the ecclesiologists' view that every art form had an infancy, maturity, and degeneracy (: 27–8), and there was, therefore, no intellectual inconsistency in their opinion that music had matured and declined in a different era than the one they identified for architecture.

The correlation of sixteenth- and early seventeenth-century polyphonic motets and anthems to their preferred style of architecture, Middle Pointed or Decorated, was in fact an intellectual necessity. Their view was that the art of composing truly sublime church music had been interrupted at 'the Rebellion' and was never regained after the Restoration of the Monarchy in 1660. The blame for this loss was normally attributed to the rise of opera and Charles II's

---

[96] *The Ecclesiologist*, 5/– (May 1846) 251–2.
[97] *The Ecclesiologist*, 5/– (May 1846) 252.

predilection for the lighter, secular style of music then fashionable on the Continent.[98]

One of the sources for this view was certainly William Crotch, who in 1831 had published the *Substance of Several Courses of Lectures on Music, read in the University of Oxford*, where he was Professor of Music. These lectures were widely read and quoted for several decades after their publication. In April 1846 (fifteen years after the original publication), excerpts from Crotch's views were taken up in an influential contemporary journal, the *Parish Choir*. The first three numbers of the *Parish Choir* were briefly reviewed in *The Ecclesiologist* the next month, and even if the reviewer was previously unaware of Crotch's theories, he would have come across the substantial quotation from them there.[99] Two years later an attempt was made in *The Ecclesiologist* to reinterpret Crotch's three styles in relation to yet other periods of music and architecture.[100]

The second chapter of William Crotch's lectures was entitled 'On the three styles of Music – the Sublime, the Beautiful, and the Ornamental.' He traced the aesthetic lineage for his views to Sir Joshua Reynolds, who had asserted in the seventeenth century:

> "All arts having the same general end, which is to please, and addressing themselves to the same faculties through the medium of the senses, it follows that their rules and principles must have as great an affinity as the different materials, and the different organs or vehicles by which they pass to the mind, will permit them to retain."[101]

Crotch proceeded to adapt Reynolds' styles of painting to the realm of music (admitting that this had been done previously by Samuel Wesley in his *Lectures on Music*). Crotch's purpose was to enable the student's taste to be developed, 'And if, by this mode of considering the subject, we find that the art is on the decline, let us not regret that we have discovered Truth... Her brightness, which enables us to detect our error, will also help us to recover it.' The nineteenth-century belief is clearly apparent here that, in order to rescue art from its contemporary state of degradation, it would be necessary to return to the point immediately prior to its decline. Indeed, Crotch devotes chapter five of his published lectures to this very point. It is also clear that the purpose in reviving old art forms would not merely be antiquarian amusement. Crotch

---

[98] William Dyce had propounded this view very thoroughly in the early 1840s. *Christian Remembrancer*, 1 (February 1841) 105–110. (: 141)

[99] *The Ecclesiologist*, 5/– (May 1846) 171–4. See also the *Parish Choir*, 1/3 (April 1846) 24, 'Dr Crotch on Different Styles of Music', in which his views on the sublime, beautiful, and ornamental styles were quoted.

[100] *Parish Choir*, 1/3 (April 1846) 24; *The Ecclesiologist*, 9/68 (October 1848) 111. (: 134–5)

[101] Quoted in Crotch (1831) 27. Crotch's 'ornamental' style corresponded to Reynolds' picturesque.

asserted, 'Let the higher walks of the art be pointed out, and new productions will soon spring up and adorn them.'[102]

The sublime style was 'founded on principles of vastness and incomprehensibility', it was 'high, lofty, elevated' and never 'small, delicate, light, pretty, playful, or comic.' Indeed, 'infinity, and, what is next to it, immensity, are among the most efficient causes of this quality,' Crotch proclaimed. He believed that 'uniformity is not only compatible with the sublime, but is the cause of it,' and both simplicity and its opposite, intricacy (which yielded incomprehensibility), were sublime. For architecture, then, this could apply to the simple grandeur of a Roman aqueduct or the intricate sublimity of a Gothic cathedral. In music, he qualified, it was important not to mistake grandeur or magnificence for sublimity, and stated that the choruses of Haydn, Mozart, and Beethoven frequently embodied the former, but rarely the latter.[103]

Crotch continued that the beautiful style, 'in all the arts, is the result of softness, smoothness, delicacy, smallness, gentle undulations, symmetry, and the like', whereas the ornamental style was 'the result of roughness, playful intricacy, and abrupt variations',[104] and was the lowest of the three styles. He cited the 'well known rebuke from his master of the young Grecian painter, for having decked his Helen with ornaments, because he had not the skill to make her beautiful.'[105]

Crotch believed that elements of the three styles often coexisted in individual works of art, but his view was clearly that the sublime was the noblest of them all, a belief that later lay at the very foundation of ecclesiological thought. Crotch summarized, in a way which any ecclesiologist could have endorsed,

> Admiration, wonder, awe, and even terror are produced in the mind by the sublime style; beauty pleases, soothes, and enamours; ornament dazzles, delights, amuses, and awakens curiosity... To be amused and delighted is a meaner enjoyment than that of being soothed and charmed; while both are less noble to the mind than feeling itself elevated and expanded.[106]

Ecclesiologists would have parted ways with Crotch at the point of drawing parallels between his three styles and architecture.[107] His thought is important, nonetheless, for the skill with which he championed the concept of a sublime style, because it embodied the aura of medieval spirituality that was so sought

---

[102] Crotch (1831) 32.
[103] Crotch (1831) 32–4.
[104] Crotch (1831) 35.
[105] Crotch (1831) 38–9.
[106] Crotch (1831) 41.
[107] He suggested that Norman English and Doric Greek architecture would constitute the sublime, Early Pointed English and Ionic Greek architecture the beautiful, and Decorated or Perpendicular English and Corinthian Greek architecture the ornamental. Crotch (1831) 42.

after by ecclesiologists. Considering the frequency with which he was quoted and the similarity of subsequent nineteenth-century thought on Anglican church music to his, Crotch's influence was clearly pervasive.[108]

It is also clear that Crotch's lectures had a profound influence on the young Thomas Helmore, who was later recruited to chair the Ecclesiological late Cambridge Camden Society's musical committee and to spearhead their musical activities.[109] In Crotch's lecture entitled 'The Rise, Progress, and Decline of Art,' he stated his belief that ecclesiastical music had been in a state of perfection in the mid-seventeenth century, and that it had been 'gradually, though not imperceptibly, losing its character of sublimity ever since.'[110] He continued,

> The remedy is obvious, let the young composer study the productions of the sixteenth and seventeenth centuries, in order to acquire the true church style, which should always be sublime and scientific, and contain no modern harmonies or melodies. There will still be room for the exercise of genius, without servile plagiarism.[111]

The composers recommended for study were those specifically named and advocated so often by ecclesiologists: Palestrina, Tallis, Byrd, Tye, Lassus, and Gibbons.[112]

Later in 1846, *The Ecclesiologist* welcomed the publication of a collection of precisely that repertoire, *Anthems and Services for Church Choirs*, numbers 1–5 (released by Burns). The review stated with certainty:

> The restitution of a just taste in church music will ever proceed *pari passu* with the revival of true feeling in church architecture: and to the promotion of that object, after the manifold degradations of the present and preceding centuries, a most important step is gained by presenting in this most accessible and cheap form the works of the best masters of ecclesiastical song to the public.[113]

The collection included not only sacred works by Palestrina, Allegri, Gibbons, Farrant, and Tallis, but new works by William Dyce and Dr Gauntlett, 'of which it is no small praise to say that they are not unfit to appear in such

---

[108] It is anticipated that the research of Sibylle Mager will substantially expand the scholarship currently available on the aesthetic and religious debate surrounding ancient and modern church music in Victorian England.

[109] Rainbow (1970) 62, 67. Helmore's role will be discussed at length in chapters three, four, and six.

[110] Crotch (1831) 73.

[111] Crotch (1831) 78.

[112] Crotch (1831) 84, 90.

[113] *The Ecclesiologist*, 6/52 (October 1846) 141–2. It is quite possible that Benjamin Webb was the author of this review. Webb's diary for 11 August 1846 notes, 'Palestrina sung,' during an evening in the Brasted rectory, which is the first time the diaries specifically mention any sixteenth-century composer. The review also mentions the fact that Burney's history of music devotes thirteen quarto pages to Palestrina; Webb appears to have read Burney in one sitting on 7 March 1841.

company.'[114] It is usual to suppose that the ecclesiologists promoted only plainsong and Palestrina, but this shows that, already at this early date (1846), some leading ecclesiologists were prepared to welcome new compositions which they considered to live up to and emanate from the best style of church music.

The *Parish Choir*

Among the significant early manifestations of the will to revive church music was the formation of the Society for Promoting Church Music, announced in February 1846 with the publication of the first number of its journal, the *Parish Choir*. It was the result of camaraderie generated among like-minded High Churchmen and Tractarians following the 1845 publication of Robert Druitt's *Popular Tract on Church Music, with Remarks on its Moral and Political Importance*,[115] about which *The Ecclesiologist* had written, 'We have great pleasure in recommending this pamphlet as an earnest and well written protest in the right direction.'[116] The design of the Society for Promoting Church Music was to develop and to propound an Anglican apologium of church music, while simultaneously providing encouragement, practical hints, and appropriate, inexpensive music to clergymen and schoolmasters who were in a position to support and train parish church choirs. Druitt was the prime mover of the new Society for Promoting Church Music and editor of the *Parish Choir*.

Like *The Ecclesiologist*, the *Parish Choir* suffered from misrepresentation in the popular press during the controversy that raged in late 1846 and early 1847 over the supposed exclusivity of its advocacy of Gregorian chant. Precisely as *The Ecclesiologist* had done, the *Parish Choir* stated unequivocally that it had no desire to banish harmony from the Church:

> We desire... to have the best of music, as of everything else, consecrated to the glory, and employed in the service of God. And, therefore, where there is skill and ability, we could wish the Anthem, for instance, to be as rich in harmony as the Church composer can produce, or the Church choir execute.

---

[114] *The Ecclesiologist*, 6/52 (October 1846) 144. Benjamin Webb's diaries reveal that he attended many musical lectures by Dr Gauntlett, in February and March 1837, and again in April 1846 (accompanied by Thorp, the Mills, A.J.B. Hope, and F.H. Dickinson, among others) and May 1846 (when he encountered William Dyce).
[115] Rainbow (1970) 96. Robert Druitt was an amateur musician and church music enthusiast who made his living as a physician.
[116] *The Ecclesiologist*, 4/– (July 1845) 182.

It was prepared to allow like freedom for the canticles, where there was a highly skilled choir. It was the psalms that it primarily wished to reclaim for the congregation.[117]

An article on 'The Spirit of Divine Worship' in the first number of the *Parish Choir* has been attributed to the Revd W.J.E. Bennett, who is believed to have been one of the founding members of the Society for Promoting Church Music.[118] As vicar of St Paul's, Knightsbridge, he was a leading figure among Tractarian clergy, whose links with ecclesiologists were many and friendly. When the new model church of St Barnabas, Pimlico, was consecrated within Bennett's parish on 11 June 1850, Thomas Helmore directed the music, and Helmore's *Psalter Noted* was adopted for use in the services of that church.[119] J.M. Neale and Dr W.H. Mill preached during the octave of services which followed, and Bennett's great friend and first churchwarden at St Barnabas, Sir John Harington, would shortly thereafter be drafted to join the first musical committee of the ECCS.[120] In 1852 Bennett received the dedication of J.M. Neale's book, *Lectures Principally on the Church Difficulties of the Present Time*.

Another founding member of the Society for Promoting Church Music was the Revd T.M. Fallow, vicar of St Andrew's, Wells Street and an original member of the Motett Society.[121] He had fraternized with Benjamin Webb at the motet parties in 1845 (: 32) and joined the ECCS in 1846. In May of that year *The Ecclesiologist* published a brief review of the first three numbers of the *Parish Choir*, which expressed regret that Anglican chants were countenanced for singing the psalms.[122] To *The Ecclesiologist*, this signaled faulty standards of churchmanship. It contains no further reference to the *Parish Choir* for nearly three years, and by the tone of the *Parish Choir's* reply, one suspects the two societies may have eyed one another somewhat warily in the interim:

> We must take the present state of things as our basis making use of existing elements where possible; always striving after improvement, but never by violent transitions. We have to deal with men as they are, not with men as we wish them to be... To attempt a sudden transition from the modern secularized double chant, and vulgar hymn tunes, to the Gregorian Tones and Elizabethan Anthems would be an absurdity. We have too sincere a respect for the

---

[117] *Parish Choir*, 1/14 (February 1847) 112–113.
[118] F. Bennett, 144.
[119] F. Bennett, 150.
[120] *The Guardian*, 232 (12 June 1850) 428–9; *Parish Choir*, 3/55 (July 1850) 116–119; F. Bennett (1909) 153; and *The Ecclesiologist*, 11/79 (August 1850) 135.
[121] *Parish Choir*, 1/21 (September 1847) 179.
[122] *The Ecclesiologist*, 5/- (May 1846) 171–4.

Gregorian Tones to expose them to the chance of mutilation or factious opposition.[123]

To conclude the *Parish Choir* suggested, 'We fear that some of the objections raised to [Anglican chants] are tainted with not a little of that spirit of Puritanism, which is too apt to be found even amid what is most Catholic in profession.'[124]

One who would later become a key figure in the musical pursuits of the ECCS, the Revd S.S. Greatheed, was certainly a reader of the *Parish Choir* by August 1848, when he wrote a letter to the editor asking about the history of Anglican chant.[125] Yet it was in April 1849 that *The Ecclesiologist* contained a second, considerably more favourable notice:

> We have been remiss in not before congratulating our readers that those principles for which we have so long contended – the necessity of a chancel and the propriety of filling it with the clerici and singers, as well as the officiating clergy – are (so far as our acquaintance, as yet a limited one, with that publication extends) ably and consistently supported by our contemporary the *Parish Choir*. This is the more gratifying as its writers deal with the question in connection with the peculiar object of our own labours, and in a very practical spirit.[126]

Very possibly this notice was elicited by the *Parish Choir's* favourable notice of the publication of J.M. Neale's 'A Song for the Times' in February 1849. Although the editor did not believe that the times were quite as Neale painted them, he wrote, 'we believe that it will contribute to make the times more and more so, to promote the good old music of the Church.'[127]

The *Parish Choir's* rejoinder to *The Ecclesiologist* in May 1849 began with an expression of their great pleasure at receiving such a recognition 'from so estimable a source' as *The Ecclesiologist*. The *Parish Choir* continued by pointing out that, like the human body, the health of the Church depended not merely upon one limb or function, but upon all working together in unity. Ecclesiologists were admonished to keep in mind that their work was a sacred one, and not merely a science or an antiquarian amusement. Accordingly, the work of the two societies would complement one another: if ecclesiologists would restore the House in fulfillment of their motto, *Donec templa refeceris* ('until the Temple has been rebuilt'), then the Society for Promoting Church Music would fill it with the voice of praise and thanksgiving according to theirs, *'Let Thy priests, O Lord, be clothed with righteousness, and let Thy saints sing with joyfulness.'* Clearly the editor of the *Parish Choir* saw the

---

[123] *Parish Choir*, 1/5 (June 1846) 37–8.
[124] *Parish Choir*, 1/5 (June 1846) 38.
[125] *Parish Choir*, 2/32 (August 1848) 88.
[126] *The Ecclesiologist*, 9/76 (April 1849) 336. Clearly this was written by a different reviewer than the June 1846 article on psalms.
[127] *Parish Choir*, 2/38 (February 1849) 143.

work of the two societies to be but different branches of the same mission. With this in mind, one curious statement in the article demands attention:

> We have been induced to make these reflections, in responding to our fellow-labourer's call to union, from our conviction of the necessity that equal attention should be bestowed on all of the accessories of the sanctuary.[128]

The 'call to union', interpreted in the light of the rest of the article and the original statement by *The Ecclesiologist* itself, clearly refers to a theoretical or spiritual rather than literal union. Subsequent developments, however, lead one to surmise that it was more prophetic than the writer may have realized at the time.

This was only the first significant evidence of sympathy between the Society for the Promotion of Church Music and the ECCS. (: 144–6) A friendly connection was further encouraged later that year in Thomas Helmore's article on the church modes, in which he recommended that ecclesiologists obtain further information from 'our excellent contemporary, the *Parish Choir.*'[129] The Motett Society also served as a common ground that brought Helmore, William Dyce, Robert Druitt[130] and ecclesiologists together (: 31–2, 77–81, 145), the significance of which became integral to the Ecclesiological Movement's efforts on behalf of choral worship.

Music in the Cambridge college chapels

Cambridge was the cradle of the Ecclesiological Movement and, as we have already seen, the *Ecclesiologist* was highly critical of the music in its college chapels. It will be informative to look at the music of those chapels not only to find out what was being sung during the undergraduate careers of the original leaders of the Cambridge Camden Society, but to note how the University responded to the general revival of choral worship. We shall also consider the ways in which the Ecclesiological (late Cambridge Camden) Society continued to assert an influence within the University after the inner circle of leadership had graduated and the Society had removed itself to London.

The University of Cambridge of 1839 was comprised of just seventeen colleges, about half the present number, only one of which (Downing) had been founded more recently than the sixteenth century. The colleges were filled with young gentlemen, most of whom came from aristocratic and upper class families or were sons of clergy. The religious character of the University was central to its being. Students had to subscribe to the Thirty-Nine Articles of the Church of England in order to take their degrees, most fellowships

---

[128] *Parish Choir*, 2/41 (May 1849) 168–9.
[129] *The Ecclesiologist*, 10/75 (November 1849) 212.
[130] *The Ecclesiologist*, 14/99 (December 1853) 436–7.

required that their holders be unmarried and in holy orders,[131] Morning and Evening Prayer were said daily in all of the college chapels, and regular chapel attendance was compulsory for all junior members of the University.[132] About 80 per cent of the clergy of the Established Church were graduates of Cambridge or Oxford.[133] In 1841 alone, 270 Cambridge men took holy orders;[134] During the years 1844–53, an estimated 74.4 per cent of Cambridge graduates were subsequently ordained.[135]

The old choral foundations: King's, Trinity, and St John's Colleges

Until the middle of the 1840s, choral services of any note were to be found in only three colleges: King's, Trinity, and St John's. Peterhouse is said to have had something of a 'humble nature' on Sunday evenings,[136] but that 'something' is described elsewhere as the 'slovenly' attempt on the part of a few poorly trained, unsurpliced boys to chant the psalms and canticles from the rear gallery.[137] The daily prayers at the other colleges were said, by a priest-musician writing fifty years later, to have been 'dreary in the extreme.'[138]

If the services which were only read were not such as might incline one to fervent devotion, neither were the choral services all that they might have been. King's, Trinity, and St John's shared one set of six lay clerks. Some of them were elderly, their voices worn out, and the choral services were planned so that they could run from chapel to chapel, singing as many as seven services in the course of a Sunday (if they happened to be called in to sing at the University Church, Great St Mary's). King's College maintained its own set of choristers, as provided for in the original foundation, but Trinity and St John's had shared an organist since 1799[139] and boys since 1819.[140]

The most illuminating record of the general state of the King's College Choir in the 1840s has been left by W.E. Dickson (BA 1846, Corpus Christi; later precentor of Ely), who served as musical assistant to the regular deputy organist at King's, John Robson. Coupled with the memoirs of Thomas Case,

---

[131] Chadwick 1 (2nd edn, 1970) 89–90, 480–1; Green (1964) 229–30, 256, 297.
[132] Green (1964) 230–4. At St John's College, for instance, undergraduates living in college were required to attend nine times and those living in lodgings seven times each week, although attendance twice on Sunday counted as three. SJC Dean's Conclusion Book, 17 December 1838.
[133] Haig (1984) 32.
[134] Chadwick, 1 (3rd edn, 1971, reprint 1987), 522.
[135] Haig (1984) 30–32.
[136] Dickson (1894) 17.
[137] *Parish Choir*, 2/29 (May 1848) 62.
[138] Dickson (1894) 17.
[139] West (1921) 126, 128–9.
[140] SJC Conclusion Book, 10 July 1819.

a chorister at King's 1836–45, a fairly clear picture of the choral services there can be elicited. The unfortunate fact is that the choir at King's was going through particularly hard times. Under the infirm and tyrannical organist, John Pratt, one of whose modes of disciplining a choirboy was to 'take an *ear* in *each hand*, and *shake his head* violently, not always keeping the back of it from the walls,'[141] the efficiency of the choristers had degenerated to a state in which 'not one boy in the choir of sixteen could read his part at sight, or had any acquaintance with rules for the production of voice, or had ever heard of phrasing, or was ever told to attend to marks of Expression.'[142] The thing that seemed shocking to a new generation of undergraduates was that no one seemed to care, if they even noticed.

Choral services were held at King's twice daily during term.[143] During the week, the service settings were by such composers as Farrant, Gibbons, Rogers, Child, and Aldrich.[144] On Sunday afternoon, however, the situation was different. Case stated that these services could hardly be termed 'devotional', and suggested that 'parades' was a rather more accurate description.[145] On such occasions the music was 'usually a noisy service, such as Jackson, Hudson, Nares, &c; the anthem generally an adaptation of Mozart, Hummel, Handel, or Hadyn [sic], with occasionally one from Boyce, or Greene, or Hayes.'[146] These services were evidently the most popular, for seats in the choir not occupied by members of the College were snapped up by outsiders who had gone to the trouble to obtain a written visitor's pass. 'No standing room was allowed *in* the Choir,' we are told, 'but the space under the organ got uncomfortably and unseemly filled by the time the Anthem commenced, and immediately [when] it was over a general stampede was made,' and the space, together with most of the antechapel, would be nearly empty before the final prayers were concluded.[147] 'Public opinion in the University and in the town,' Dickson wrote,

> was altogether laudatory of the music at King's. This is easily explained. The magnificent chapel has a resonance which lends charm to any music performed under its lofty vault, quite independently of the artistic merits or defects of the performance. The voices of the six lay-clerks, half of them worn out; the ill-trained or un-trained voices of the boys; these supported by the majestic tones

---

[141] Case (1899) 33.
[142] Dickson (1894) 19.
[143] *New Guide to the University and Town of Cambridge*, (1831) 89, cited in A.H. Mann's notebook (volume 3), 'Musical events in Cambridge.'
[144] *Parish Choir*, 2/29 (May 1848) 61.
[145] Case (1889) 24; also Dickson (1894) 19–20.
[146] *Parish Choir*, 2/29 (May 1848) 61–2.
[147] Case (1889) 24.

of the organ, produced an *ensemble* in that splendid building which satisfied the ears of uncritical listeners.[148]

Not only was the singing of the boys reprehensible, but Case insists that 'it would be quite impossible to convey to the mind of the modern organist any adequate idea of the vulgarity and tastelessness of poor [Robson's] accompaniment of the service.'[149] Dickson summed up unequivocally, 'The fact remains unshaken that the much-vaunted music at King's in 1842,3 [*sic*] was radically bad.'[150] John Pratt's retention of the post of organist until his death in 1855 effectively prevented any significant improvement being made at King's during the first period of the choral revival.

Under the highly competent leadership of Thomas Attwood Walmisley, the joint choir of Trinity and St John's Colleges fared somewhat better. There are several signs to indicate that Walmisley set out with vigour to improve the standard of the music in the chapels under his care. His predecessor, Samuel Matthews, received £5.2.0 for 'writing music,' i.e. copying anthems into the choir part books, during his last year in office (1832). During 1833 a Mr Piper, one of the lay clerks, was paid £6.9.3 for copying music. Walmisley entered upon his duties roughly halfway through that year. The total bill for new music and copying out parts during 1834 was £33.6.4. The magnitude of that sum becomes clearer when one considers that in the same year it cost Trinity only £21.15.0 to purchase a pianoforte for use in the rehearsals of the choristers.

Walmisley also introduced Cambridge to the keyboard works of Bach, which were then virtually unknown in England,[151] and had the organs rebuilt and greatly enlarged in both college chapels. By 1836 he had succeeded in persuading Trinity to spend £455 for the repair and improvement of the college organ;[152] and during the Michaelmas term 1838, St John's installed a new instrument with three manuals and 'German Pedals' (FF–c), built by William Hill at a cost of £695.[153] The efficiency of the choir was strengthened in late 1843 by pensioning off several of the old lay clerks whose voices had 'decayed',[154] which leads one to suspect that this may have been a direct response to *The Ecclesiologist's* strictures in September of that year against 'a few miserable and effete singers running about from choir to choir' in the University of Cambridge.[155] (: 34) By 1848 Walmisley had obtained the services of three supernumerary lay clerks on weekends and festivals to

---

[148] Dickson (1894) 20.
[149] Case (1889) 21.
[150] Dickson (1894) 23.
[151] Dickson (1894) 26–7.
[152] Trinity College Bursar's Annual Accounts, 1832–6.
[153] Organ contract between SJC and Hill, 1838. SJCA: D33.8.1(2).
[154] See copy of letter, dated 5 January 1844, in reply to the Lay Clerks' protest of this policy in Whewell's Journal, TCWL: O.15.45.
[155] *The Ecclesiologist*, 3/25 (September 1843) 2.

strengthen the ensemble of the Choir. The 'versicles, &c.' were the same harmonized ones as those used at King's, and the litany was sung in harmony. 'The priest's part of the service,' he concluded, 'is now read, but will in the course of a month or two be intoned.'[156]

Choral services were far less frequent at Trinity and St John's than at King's College. The choir sang at Trinity twice on Sundays, and evensong was sung on surplice days.[157] At the beginning of Walmisley's tenure (1833), the services at St John's were choral only on Sunday evenings, twice on Christmas Day, and on the mornings of Easter, Pentecost, and Trinity Sunday;[158] but at some point before 1838 a second choral service was added on Wednesday evenings.[159] So popular did these become that in the following year the Dean of St John's was forced to issue an order that, on evenings of choral service, no visitors could be admitted to seats *in the Chapel* unless they were introduced by the Master or one of the Fellows, or if they produced a written order from the Master, President, or one of the Deans.[160] This may partially be due to the overcrowding which necessitated the building of a larger chapel during the 1860s. On the other hand, the added attraction of choral service alone could well have demanded such a restriction.

Since there were approximately twice as many choral services at Trinity as at St John's, expenses for the joint choir were split in the corresponding ratio of two to one. Consequently it would seem that St John's was always treated as the junior member of the partnership,[161] and most of the impetus for improvement in the choral services of the two colleges, like the infant heartbeat of the Cambridge Camden Society itself, came from within the walls of Trinity College.

William Whewell accepted the mastership of Trinity College in October 1841. Whewell began his lifelong friendship with John Hullah at about this

---

[156] *Parish Choir*, 2/29 (May 1848) 62. The versicles and responses were probably those by Tallis.
[157] 'Surplice days' were those days on which members of college would wear surplices instead of college gowns during chapel services. St John's College retains the custom to this day on Saturday evenings, Sundays, Saints' Days and their Eves.
[158] According to George Garrett, *Eagle* (1891) 227.
[159] SJCA: Dean's Order Book, 20 December 1838. In the *Eagle* (1891) 227, Garrett writes that this second choral service was established 'when the Organ was erected in 1837' and that it was added 'partly as a set-off for the non-observance of Saints' Days.' However, the organ was not erected in 1837, and in fact the sealing of the contract was not approved by the SJC Master and Seniors until 17 December 1838. (SJCA: Conclusion Book) This is just one of several early nineteenth-century details which is incorrect in Garrett's article, hence one must naturally be suspicious about whether the second choral service was actually added in 1837. It is probably safe to assume, however, that it was added sometime after T.A. Walmisley became organist in 1833.
[160] SJCA: Deans Order Book, 23 October 1839.
[161] Garrett, *Eagle* (1891) 228.

time.[162] Under Whewell's leadership, efforts to improve the choral services in chapel found not merely support, but some very specific encouragement. If Walmisley was primarily concerned with the execution of the service settings and anthems, as church musicians are often wont to be, Whewell wanted to hear a marked improvement in the manner of chanting the psalms and to see the services performed with greater devotion. In a letter of 21 October 1844 to the Dean, Whewell made it clear that his wishes had not been satisfactorily met:

> In the execution of the Chants especially the performance of the Singing Men is feeble and interrupted as if for want of continued execution; and in parts which are sung by them, there is a want of agreement in the delivery of the words by different singers, which appears to arise from want of joint practice. I cannot but feel much dissatisfaction that after the efforts we have made to improve our choir it should be in these respects so much inferior as it is to other choirs which I occasionally hear.[163]

The fact that there should have been discrepancies among the men in the chanting of the psalms is hardly surprising, since it is highly unlikely that the Choir ever sang from pointed psalters during Walmisley's tenure as organist. William Glover stated, 'Mr Janes, the organist of Ely Cathedral, published his psalter [1837], pointed for chanting, at a time when singers chose their own divisions from an ordinary Prayer Book. I never saw a "pointed" book in the college chapels', an assertion that is supported by Thomas Case.[164] Hence one could expect there to be disagreement over the pointing of the psalms every time a new lay clerk was hired, until sufficient time had passed for the new man to accustom himself to local practice, to whatever extent that was influenced by Walmisley. Furthermore, the fact that evensong was not sung on a daily basis would have meant that months might pass before any particular psalm would be repeated, and without the daily repetition of the psalms which one would experience in a Cathedral choir, it could easily have taken years for familiarity to breed uniformity. Whewell admitted himself to be quite 'driven' to hear the psalms chanted in the best possible manner. In a letter to the Dean dated 2 February 1846, he encouraged further persistence in the matter:

> I am glad to be able to speak with more satisfaction than on previous occasions of the mode in which the service is performed by the choir. The services have often been performed in a careful and attractive manner and generally better than was the case a little while ago. The chanting of the choristers is good. The

---

[162] F. Hullah, 29, 88–9, 92.
[163] A copy of this letter is found in William Whewell's Journal, TCWL: 0.15.45.
[164] Glover, 1 (1885), p. 195. Case (1889) 27. According to Scholes and Rainbow, Robert Janes' psalter (1837) was the first ever to be published with pointing. Temperley (1979) 220. There is no evidence to suggest that Janes' psalter was ever used in the Cambridge choral foundations.

plan of accentuation and delivery... appears to me very good; they sing for the most part heartily, steadily and carefully.[165]

The anthem repertoire at King's, Trinity, and St John's Colleges, 1844

While the service settings in use at Trinity and St John's under Walmisley were primarily by eighteenth- and nineteenth-century composers such as Kent, Attwood, Greene, Croft, Boyce, and King, the anthems in use were similar in style to those sung at King's. In addition, Walmisley, who was also Professor of Music in the University 1836–56, composed a significant amount of church music which formed a familiar part of the Sunday diet.

The best insight into the choral repertoire sung in the chapels of Trinity and St John's Colleges during the first half of the nineteenth century is provided by two collections of anthem texts, which were printed as devotional aids for the use of the congregations of the two chapels. These are particularly useful because one may reasonably assume that at the time of publication they contained the texts of all the anthems in use in the chapels for which they were printed.[166]

For present consideration the more relevant of the two is *A Collection of Anthems used in the Chapels of King's, Trinity and St John's Colleges*, compiled by Thomas Attwood Walmisley and published in 1844. It is significantly larger than its 1827 forerunner by Samuel Matthews (Walmisley's predecessor), and this is partially explained by the fact that it was designed for use in King's College as well as Trinity and St John's. As such, it reveals the choral repertoire that would have been heard by Cambridge ecclesiologists in the earliest days of their revival of Christian art.

The first edition of Walmisley's collection included 279 titles for 302 anthems, allowing for multiple settings of the same text. Seventy-six composers were represented. Dickson tells us that occasionally some of Samuel Matthew's sacred adaptations of secular works were to be heard at Trinity and St John's, but that 'Walmisley's own leanings were towards the Anglican school of Cathedral music, as represented by Boyce, Croft, Greene, Hayes, and perhaps Kent.'[167] Writing nearly forty years after Walmisley's death, Dickson here demonstrates a remarkably accurate memory. Apart from Handel, who of course does not belong to the Anglican school but whose presence in the music lists was perhaps too obvious to require special mention, and the local composers, John Clarke-Whitfeld (organist of Trinity and St John's 1799–

---

[165] Whewell's Journal, (TCWL: 0 15.45). Benjamin Webb's diaries reveal that he spent most of February and March 1845 in Cambridge, where he frequently attended chapel at Trinity, and continued to be in a position to critique the singing there.
[166] It is possible that a few texts were included which had not yet been introduced, but whose use was anticipated by the respective compilers.
[167] Dickson, (1894) 26.

1822) and Walmisley himself, Dickson recalled virtually the complete list of those composers most highly represented. They are as follows:

Handel	41	Clarke-Whitfeld	10	Mozart	6
Greene	22	Nares	10	Blow	5
Croft	15	Hayes	9	Arnold	4
Purcell	15	Aldrich	7	Battishill	4
Boyce	14	Attwood	7	Gibbons	4
Kent	14	Haydn	7	King	4
Walmisley	11	Child	6	Matthews	4

This is essentially the repertoire concerning which the correspondent to the *Parish Choir* wrote in 1848, 'The style of music prevailing here is very showy, and particularly good of its kind, though it is one which churchmen would be sorry to see generally prevalent.' On Sundays it was not uncommon for chants, service, and anthem all to have been composed by Walmisley. Weekday services were characterized by 'not quite so much display' in their performance.[168]

It is noteworthy that Handel, Haydn, and Mozart are the only foreign composers to be found among the top twenty-one. By 1844 Mendelssohn had made his eighth visit to England, and Coleridge tells us that '[Walmisley's] intimacy with Mendelssohn was a source of great pride to him,'[169] but we must remind ourselves that *Elijah* (1846), which was so popular in service lists later in the century, had not yet been written. One finds that Mendelssohn is generously represented in the appendices added by each of the three colleges after the deaths of Pratt in 1855 and Walmisley in 1856.

Other composers represented include:

three each: Batten, Byrd, Clarke, Corfe, Farrant, Hummel, Mendelssohn, Porter, Rogers, Tallis, Weldon, Wise.
two each: Alcock, Crotch, Goldwin, Graun, Pratt, Pring, Travers, Tye, T.F. Walmisley.
one each: J.S. Bach, Beethoven, Blake, Camidge, Carissimi, Chard, Clari, Creyghton, Henry VIII, Himmel, Jackson, Kelway, Lasso, Lawes, Leo, Loosemore, Luther, Marcello, Mason, Palestrina, Perez, Randall, Reynolds, Richardson, Stroud, Travers, Tucker, Turner, S.S. Wesley, Woodward.

The presence of even one work by J.S. Bach, a translation of his motet *Lobet den Herren*, is noteworthy at this date. At the time Bach's choral works were virtually unknown outside Germany, and the collection predates the first English performance (1854) of the *St Matthew Passion* by ten years. The collection includes several adaptations which borrow from the work of more than one composer. There are twenty-one adaptations of works of continental composers to English sacred texts, not including the eleven by Hugh Bond

---

[168] *Parish Choir*, 2/29 (May 1848) 62.
[169] A.D. Coleridge, 'Walmisley, Thomas Attwood,' *Grove's Dictionary of Music and Musicians 1*, IV (1889) 378–9.

from Handel. Thirteen are by John Pratt, six by Samuel Matthews, and there is one each by Vincent Novello and T.A. Walmisley.

As in its 1827 forerunner, just more than one-quarter of the composers represented in Walmisley's collection are responsible for about three-quarters of the repertoire. From this group, Handel is the only significant non-native influence. The fact that foreign compositions (excluding Handel) represent only 8.5 per cent of the 1827 Collection and 11.6 per cent of that of 1844 reveals the insularity of the early nineteenth-century Anglican choral repertoire, even at one of the nation's great centres of learning, and in spite of the popular adulation of foreign composers for which Victorian England has been well known. To consider that the number of foreign compositions increased by only 3.1 per cent from 1827 to 1844, however, obscures the significance of the rise in the actual numbers of foreign works from eleven (1827) to thirty-five (1844). Walmisley was very interested in the music of the continent, and was an early advocate of Johann Sebastian Bach's supremacy among composers.[170] The fact that the foreign contingent made up exactly one-third of the thirty-three composers whose works were newly introduced into the repertoire in Walmisley's *Collection* is indicative of a trend to appropriate the best sacred music of other Christian traditions for use in the services of the Anglican Communion, however different it was from the foreign church music (e.g. Palestrina) being advocated by ecclesiologists.

Walmisley's anthem collection added thirteen works by five sixteenth- and seventeenth-century English composers who had been entirely neglected in Matthews' *Collection* of 1827: Byrd (three), Gibbons (four), George Loosemore (one), Tallis (three) and Tye (three). This was due to the addition of the King's College Choir's repertoire to the book.[171] They account for only 4.3 per cent of the total collection, yet nevertheless it is not insignificant for the early nineteenth century that they are represented at all. Of these thirteen early English anthems, nine are contained in the Rowe Music Library at King's College in manuscript scores or part books dating from the late eighteenth or early nineteenth century. Of the remaining four, all but one are to be found in A.H. Mann's late nineteenth-century repertoire list for King's College Chapel. Nine of the anthems can also be found in the second volume of Boyce's *Cathedral Music* (1768), and hence may have been introduced at King's under John Randall, organist 1743–99. Trinity College possesses none of its ancient

---

[170] 'In a series of lectures on the "Rise and Progress of the Pianoforte" he spoke incidentally of Bach's Mass in B minor as "the greatest composition in the world," and prophesied that the publication of the cantatas (then in MS.) would show that his assertion of Bach's supremacy was no paradox.' Coleridge, 'Thomas Attwood Walmisley', *Grove 3*, V (1929) 618.

[171] The addition of the King's College repertoire also brought a significant increase in the number of works by Handel and in adaptations of English sacred texts to continental and English secular compositions.

choir part books, and in those found at St John's College, only one of the thirteen, George Loosemore's *Glory be to God on high*, is found. This would suggest that despite Walmisley's broad interest in music, it did not include the introduction of old English music into the repertoire of his choir.

Neither Samuel Matthews' nor Walmisley's anthem collection contains a single Latin text, in spite of the fact that all members of the University were proficient in Latin. No doubt the use of Latin church music would have led to cries of 'popery' at this period. Choral singing in the vernacular was held to be a rule without exception, and foreign works were always sung in English translations.

It is a well-established fact that eighteenth-century England was obsessed with the solo voice. Handel arrived in England (first in 1710, and again to stay in 1712) in an age when the *prima donna* was queen, and public pressure compelled composers of opera to write one show aria after another, drama being quite incidental to the value of the music as a means of entertainment and vocal display. As Christopher Dearnley has pointed out, 'the adulation of the human voice... was bound to leave its mark on music written for the church's services.'[172] Nicholas Temperley writes that, by the Georgian period, cathedral choral singing:

> centred on the glorification of the solo voice, as did the verse and solo anthems that formed the bulk of the repertory. The written line was broken up by ornaments of all kinds; improvised cadenzas were customary at the end of each movement of an anthem; even in the choral sections two or three solo voices would often predominate.[173]

As oratorio became increasingly popular, excerpts began to be admitted in church services in place of the anthem. By that time the soloist had become an established staple of the church music diet. This is evident in the Cambridge anthem collections, for 86 per cent of the entries in Matthews' compilation of 1827 contain solo work, as do nearly 80 per cent of the entries in Walmisley's collection of 1844. It is no wonder that William Glover's review of the 'Trinity' choir's abilities during this time stipulates that it excelled 'especially in quartets and trios.'[174] While the huge increase in the size of the 1844 collection means that a much larger number of anthems is included that contain work for soloists, the small decline in the overall percentage of such works can be attributed to an increase in foreign compositions and the inclusion of early English anthems from the King's College repertoire, which were written for full choir. The 'adulation' of the solo singer persisted in the

---

[172] Dearnley (1970) 130.
[173] Nicholas Temperley, 5 (1981) 182.
[174] Glover, 1 (1885) 148. At this time the 'Trinity' choir also sang at St John's College.

choral foundations of Cambridge into the twentieth century, as long as professional lay clerks of note were retained by the Colleges.[175]

What relatively little music there was in the worship services of Cambridge college chapels in the early 1840s, then, was essentially non-congregational. Only the University Church, Great St Mary's, allowed metrical psalmody to be sung, and it was performed as a prelude to the University sermon by choristers from King's.[176] Thirteen of the colleges, it would appear, held services twice daily without singing of any kind.

Revival of choral service in Cambridge colleges during the late 1840s

Jesus College. The choral revival in Cambridge, as in other cities around the country, began largely as a result of the enthusiasm of a few individuals. The first Cambridge college to be affected in this way was Jesus College, which benefited from the zeal and generosity of a Fellow Commoner, (after 1855, Sir) John Sutton, who had joined the Cambridge Camden Society during his first year in Cambridge (1841).[177]

In December 1846 a meeting of the council requested the master (William French) to convey the 'best thanks' of the College to Sutton,

> for his kind and unwearied exertions in training, and that with so great success, six Boys for the performance of Choral Service; and that he be requested to continue the direction of that part of divine Worship in the College Chapel, so long as may be convenient and agreeable to himself, in the same manner and entirely as if he were appointed to the office of Organist.[178]

Thus it is apparent that Sutton formed a boys' choir at Jesus College not later than Michaelmas 1846, and not, as a correspondent to the *Parish Choir* suggested, in 1847.[179] Not only did Sutton establish the choir, but he personally saw to the schooling of his choristers, even to the extent of staying in residence during vacations to continue teaching them.[180]

---

[175] Mr T.C. Nicholas, who came up to Trinity College, Cambridge as an undergraduate in 1907, remembered particularly that the College Chapel was always extremely full at evensong on Advent Sunday, when townspeople would crowd in to hear the operatic tenor lay clerk, Joss Reed, sing 'Comfort ye' from Handel's *Messiah*. He also recalls that undergraduates commonly referred to another one of the lay clerks, Mr Pink, as 'Thunderguts.' Such a nickname does not suggest that a later twentieth-century ideal of choral blend was likely to have been achieved, but it cannot be surprising that a repertoire which reveals an operatic tendency would have been performed in like manner. Mr Nicholas, interviewed by the author, 29 February 1988.
[176] *Parish Choir*, 2/31 (July 1848) 76.
[177] Davidson (1992) 18–19.
[178] Jesus College Conclusion Book, 18 December 1846.
[179] *Parish Choir*, 2/29 (May 1848) 61, 62.
[180] Morgan (1914) 295; Gray and Brittain (1902, reprinted 1979) 158–9.

According to the pattern that *The Ecclesiologist* predicted in October 1846,[181] the revival of choral worship at Jesus accompanied the restoration of the Chapel. While the works were under way, unaccompanied choral services were begun in the College Hall with the full support of the Dean, John Gibson.[182] In a letter of November 1847 to his good friend and fellow superintendent of the Chapel restoration, the Revd Osmund Fisher, Gibson reported, 'Birkelt now chants the service and very well – our service is now unspeakably delightful.'[183] By May 1848 the correspondent to the *Parish Choir* reported that there were two Fellows who intoned services at Jesus, that the Choir chanted the psalms and canticles antiphonally to chants of 'all kinds, except real Gregorians', that the versicles and litany were sung in a harmonization for two trebles with 'very good effect', and that simple anthems were sung on surplice days. No evidence can be found for the tradition[184] that true Gregorian chants were commonly used in Jesus College Chapel during the 1840s and 1850s. In fact, a letter regarding Sutton's successor, Henry James Brown, states that, many years after the period under consideration here, Brown's affiliation with the College 'was terminated for his absolute refusal to replace the music he loved by Gregorian chant!'[185]

On All Saints' Day 1849 the chapel was reopened with full choral service and Holy Communion. The Professor of Music, Thomas Attwood Walmisley, who was a former student of the college, presided at the organ and composed the anthem *Ponder my words* for the occasion. The chapel organ, by Bishop, was the design and gift of John Sutton, whose biographer identifies the Cambridge Camden Society as a major source of inspiration for Sutton's study of organs.[186]

The following year Sutton printed *A Collection of the Anthems used in Divine Service upon Sundays, Holy-days and their Eves, in Jesus College Chapel, Cambridge* for the devotional use of the College congregation. The eighty-eight anthems included by Sutton were divided into full anthems (forty-three) and verse anthems (forty-five). As compared with those of Matthews and Walmisley, the much higher percentage of full anthems in this collection is probably explained both by the preference for full anthems commonly

---

[181] *The Ecclesiologist*, 6/52 (October 1846) 141.
[182] Morgan (1914) 296.
[183] Letter from Gibson to Fisher, 15 November 1847. Jesus College Archives: Chapel box 2.
[184] Gray and Brittain (1902, reprinted 1979) 158.
[185] Letter from Ethel Christie (granddaughter of H.J. Brown) to the Jesus College archivist, 26 January 1963. Jesus College Archives, Letters of H.J. Brown.
[186] Davidson (1992) 38–41, 47. Benjamin Webb's diary for 22 November 1848 reveals that he visited Jesus Chapel with his wife and mother-in-law, and was 'lionized by Sutton.'

advocated by churchmen of the ecclesiological mould, such as Sutton, and by the fact that the Choir of Jesus College did not employ professional lay clerks.

In 1851 *The Ecclesiologist* lauded the restoration of the chapel, singling out Pugin's organ case for particular praise. 'Whether ritually or architecturally,' it stated, 'few restorations are more complete or correct than that of Jesus College Chapel.'[187] In 1855 it was proposed to ask Sir John Sutton to join the Committee of the Ecclesiological late Cambridge Camden Society (ECCS),[188] but by that time he was primarily resident abroad and, certainly unbeknown to the ECCS committee members, he had embraced the Roman Catholic faith.[189]

Queens' College. Another impressive early move to reintroduce choral worship into the college chapels occurred in the spring of 1848, when 'daily chanting was quite unexpectedly established at Queen's [*sic*] College, conducted and maintained entirely by under-graduates.' The correspondent to the *Parish Choir* believed the improvement to have been a direct result of the interest in worship awakened by restoration work on the Chapel begun in 1846, the expenses of which had been '*entirely* defrayed by the junior members of the college.' He went on to report that a small organ had also been procured, which was played by an undergraduate. As to the singing:

> the chanting of the psalms and canticles is conducted by about a dozen undergraduates. The chants are good, mostly Gregorian, with a few of the best single chants. The choir being composed solely of Tenor and Bass, the chanting has a singular effect, but is notwithstanding very earnest and solemn.[190]

As is the case with many such student-initiated reforms in Cambridge, no records exist in the College archives to indicate any more precisely than this either the nature of these services or how long they continued to be thus performed.

The 'frustration factor'

Writing about the Cambridge of the early 1840s, W.E. Dickson asserts that numerous undergraduates became sympathizers with Tractarian teaching, and, although he himself did not approve of all that was promoted by the Cambridge Camden Society, he admits that it did 'excellent and praiseworthy' work to awaken students to the relation of theology to the ecclesiastical arts. During these years, long before the publication of plainsong manuals and ancient hymns, he wrote,

---

[187] *The Ecclesiologist*, 12/135 (August 1851) 324–5.
[188] RIBA: Ecclesiological Society Minutes, 12 December 1855.
[189] Davidson (1992) 23–4.
[190] *Parish Choir*, 2/31 (July 1848) 77.

already there was a strong leaning towards single chants, and toward a severe and colourless style of church music generally: the maxim, 'That which is new is not good, and that which is good is not new' was received as an axiom: the principle of Self-denial and mortification of the flesh was applied to the music of the Church, and was held to exclude the elements of Grace and Beauty from compositions dedicated to Religion as ministering only to sensuous pleasure. Sad nonsense all of this! but the way was being paved, nevertheless, for an association of Art with Religion to which this country had long been a stranger; and many of our shallow young sciolists were to go down to country curacies with the wish and hope of introducing order and reverence where all had been rude.[191]

This brings us to the 'frustration factor.' This dynamic was very evident in the early writings on church music by ecclesiologists and others. (: 34, 37, 71–3) As an institution, it is clear that one significant way in which the colleges within the University contributed to the revival of choral worship was by engendering frustration among undergraduates, especially among those preparing for the priesthood. In the face of a growing national singing movement and the upheaval caused by post-Tractarian liturgical and musical thought propounded by *The English Churchman*, the *Parish Choir*, and the publications of the ECCS among others, these future ordinands could not understand why the colleges were generally so unwilling to encourage the study and practice of church music in an established capacity, despite having unmatched resources and daily chapel services in which to do so. Endeavours of this sort were left primarily to undergraduates. It is hardly surprising, then, that those who pursued the independent study of church music as undergraduates went down to curacies with the intention of setting their parishes in order. There they functioned as gentle autocrats, and one need only read the 'Ecclesiastical Intelligence' columns in the *Guardian* from the late 1840s and 1850s to see that, before long, the countryside was dotted with parishes where the hearty singing of psalms and canticles could be heard, sung by congregations and choirs that were often trained in the art of singing by the curate himself. To theological students and young curates, the tiny parishes of leading ecclesiologists which held choral services twice daily, such as Kemerton and Sheen,[192] were important models of what could be achieved where vision, enthusiasm and perseverance coincided.

Eclecticism

1847 was an important year in the development of the science of ecclesiology. Not only did the *Ecclesiologist* boldly define it as 'the science of Christian

---

[191] Dickson (1894) 42.
[192] Archdeacon Thorp at Kemerton (:94–6) and Benjamin Webb at Sheen. (: 110–11)

aesthetics' and 'the systematic study of the requirements of Divine Worship', but it helped to codify three theoretical types of architectural restoration. Publication of E.A. Freeman's *Principles of Church Restoration*, its review in *The Ecclesiologist*, and a debate on the subject at the eighth anniversary meeting of the Society on 18 May 1847 combined to yield a general, if rather nebulous, policy. The three methods of restoration were identified as Destructive, Conservative, and Eclectic.[193]

The Destructive method ignored any consideration of the original style, arrangement, and proportion of a building: 'it employs the best style of art, adopts the best conceptions which present themselves, and to these it sacrifices the work of an earlier generation.' This method was 'universally adopted by our ancestors', *The Ecclesiologist* observed. Quoting Freeman it explained, 'Each successive style rose only on the ashes of its predecessor; not only was a ban laid on further working of the old, the very structures that it had already reared must bend to receive the yoke of the new lord of taste and beauty.'[194]

There were several objections to the Destructive method. First, *The Ecclesiologist* stated that contemporary architects did not employ their art as a living one, one which they could manipulate with complete mastery, and therefore there was great risk in destroying old models, for they could not guarantee that they would be able to add new life in their place. As ancient principles were gradually mastered, this argument would become steadily less valid. Second, the feelings aroused through romantic association were new to the Victorian era, and possessed great powers that were unknown to earlier generations. Third, to destroy *anything* ancient was a 'most dangerous experiment.'[195]

The Conservative method had characterized most modern restorations. The goal was not to make any architectural alterations whatever, but rather to preserve a building exactly as it had come down to the time in which the restoration was undertaken: 'Norman, First-Pointed, Middle-Pointed, Tudor work are equally respected; and the church in its new state is a mere facsimile (the decorations of course omitted) of the building unchurchwardenised.' The fact that the Conservative method was the safest of the three was its only recommendation, *The Ecclesiologist* declared, but stated so thankfully, for 'had the destructive or the eclectic spirit prevailed some years back there is no telling what mischief might not have been perpetrated.' The difficulty with the Conservative method was that during the decline of Christian art various travesties *had* been committed in church restorations, and 'it is,' *The*

---

[193] White (1962) 164–70.
[194] *The Ecclesiologist*, 7/49 (May 1847) 162.
[195] *The Ecclesiologist*, 7/49 (May 1847) 164–5; 7/60 (June 1847) 240.

Ecclesiologist reasoned, 'surely too much to be called upon to perpetuate these barbarisms.'[196]

The Eclectic method was a compromise between the other two: 'in certain cases it would simply restore, in others it would re-model.' But no one had yet succeeded in the codification of guidelines, much less principles, to aid in determining which should apply in every given situation.[197] Nevertheless the consensus of the debate at the eighth anniversary meeting of the ECCS was that Eclecticism represented a sort of practical and æsthetic *via media*. The Dean of Chichester, who chaired the meeting, is reported to have summed up:

> Variety, he thought, should pervade art, as it does nature. By adopting the Eclectic theory, we might hope to develop [*sic*] something more beautiful than ever yet known. In the mean time we are not to keep up nor copy deformity, but aim at advancing and developing the ideal of beauty.[198]

Exactly what this meant would be a question confronted anew in each individual case. The discussion does, however, signal a certain flexibility in architectural approach, and gives voice to the hope that modern artists would eventually advance to the point at which their appropriation of carefully selected historical models would mature into an even more beautiful contemporary style.

The ecclesiologists' starting point was to attempt to derive their notions of beauty from the *best* period of art. Thus an agreement that the 'best' of different features might have arisen during different periods, and that these might plausibly be combined to form a new but dignified whole, marks a significant theoretical step forward. We will come to see that ecclesiologists continued to struggle with the question of how to create valid contemporary artistic styles, ones which issued from the best historical precedents.

It is no surprise that a policy which encouraged artists to hearken unto what were perceived as the *best* precedents should have extended to include the insistence that only the best materials should be employed in any artistic undertaking. In 1849 Benjamin Webb wrote a lengthy review for *The Ecclesiologist* of John Ruskin's newly published *Seven Lamps of Architecture*. In it Ruskin had denounced those who aimed to build as much as possible at the least possible expense, since only one's best was worthy of being offered to God. Webb commended this support for a position which Cambridge ecclesiologists had long maintained.[199] 'Let every material employed be real', the Cambridge Camden Society had proclaimed in 1842. 'If we are not ashamed to employ inferior materials, surely we need not be ashamed to

---

[196] *The Ecclesiologist*, 7/49 (May 1847) 162, 166–7.
[197] *The Ecclesiologist*, 7/49 (May 1847) 162–3.
[198] *The Ecclesiologist*, 7/60 (June 1847) 240.
[199] *The Ecclesiologist*, 10/74 (October 1849) 111. Benjamin Webb's authorship of this review is revealed in his diaries, 19 and 20 September 1849.

confess that they are inferior', but it would be well to remember that neither God nor man would be deceived by this.[200] Whatever the branch of art, an offering made to God should be the absolute best offering that it was within the giver's power to make. (: 88, 102, 159–60) John Mason Neale wrote, with his usual simple clarity:

> The first great principle to be remembered is reality... Let everything be real. Never attempt to make beech or deal, if they are used, look like oak. To do so is either a silent confession that such ought to be the materials of which a church is built, or a piece of hypocrisy... This false ornament can arise from only one of two causes: either it has its origin in our own ideas of luxury – ideas which ought to be banished from a church – or from the idea of making our offerings to God appear as great as possible, while the cost to ourselves is as little as may be.[201]

---

[200] Cambridge Camden Society, *A Few Words to Church Builders* (2nd edn, 1842), 4.
[201] Towle (1906) 71.

CHAPTER THREE

The Ecclesiological late Cambridge Camden Society 1850–55: champions of choral service

In November 1849 *The Ecclesiologist* announced that the Revd Thomas Helmore, Priest in Ordinary to the Queen (also Precentor of St Mark's College, Chelsea; Precentor of the Motett Choir; and Master of the Choir at the Chapel Royal, St James), had been elected to membership of the ECCS. In February 1850 it reported that he had been added to the Committee.[1]

Simultaneously the subject of church music began to take on a high profile in the bimonthly issues of *The Ecclesiologist*. The first article was a lengthy communication on 'Ecclesiastical Music' from Thomas Helmore in November 1849. Under the same title, the editors expanded upon the subject in the February 1850 issue, and Helmore returned to the task of education with an article on the 'Cantus collectarum' in April. On 16 May 1850 Helmore continued the discussion and F.R. Wegg Prosser, Esq., M.P., read a paper on modern anthems at the eleventh anniversary meeting of the ECCS, when the annual report stated, 'The greater development which that most important branch of ecclesiological study, Church Music, has lately received in *The Ecclesiologist* will be, the committee are sure, an object of congratulation to the society.'[2] This rapid move to position itself to become a formidable champion of church music revival was completed when, in the summer of 1850, the Ecclesiological late Cambridge Camden Society officially established a musical committee:

> After some discussion, it was agreed to add certain additional members of the society, for the exclusive consideration of musical questions; and the Revd J.L. Crompton, W. Dyce, Esq., R.A., and Sir John Harrington [*sic*], Bart., were so appointed. The Revd T. Helmore accepted the office of honorary secretary of the committee of music.[3]

For the next six years the subject of music was a regular and significant feature among the subjects dealt with by *The Ecclesiologist*, reaching its greatest visibility when it occupied the whole of the first twenty pages of the February 1856 issue. It is clear that Helmore was recruited to guide the ecclesiologists' musical endeavours not only for his knowledge and public status, but because

---

[1] *The Ecclesiologist*, 10/75 (November 1849), 219; 10/76 (February 1850) 349.
[2] *The Ecclesiologist*, 11/78 (June 1850) 28–31, 52, 56.
[3] Report of Committee meetings held on 12 June and 20 July 1850. *The Ecclesiologist*, 11/79 (August 1850) 135. The correct spelling is 'Harington.'

his principles and the example of St Mark's College was in complete sympathy with the direction ecclesiologists felt the church music revival ought to proceed. By undertaking the new duties, Helmore succeeded to the firmly established circle of influence which belonged to the ecclesiologists, and obtained a powerful platform from which to encourage and guide the movement.

In addition to the recruited members of the musical committee listed above, Benjamin Webb was a key participant, as was John Mason Neale during the early 1850s, when the Committee was largely occupied with the publication of the *Hymnal Noted*. By 1853 the musical committee was comprised of the following gentlemen: the Revds Thomas Helmore, Benjamin Webb, John Mason Neale, S.S. Greatheed, H.L. Jenner, and Dr W.H. Mill; plus Messrs A.J.B. Hope, F.H. Dickinson, J.D. Chambers, and W.C. Luard (ECCS treasurer). By that time all but Dr Mill and Mr Luard were instructed 'to prepare for submission to the general committee the translations necessary for Part II of the *Hymnal Noted*.'[4]

The *Hymnal Noted*

The way for publication of the ECCS's first practical contribution to the revival of early church music was prepared by the series of articles beginning in November 1849. Introducing Thomas Helmore's article in that month's issue, *The Ecclesiologist*, while not wishing to commit itself without reservation to the opinions expressed therein, stated that he would be known to all of its readers as 'the most accomplished Church musician of our time', hailed the recent publication of his *Psalter Noted*, and hoped that it would be 'universally adopted as the standard for congregational singing.'

Helmore lost no time in capturing his particular readership's attention. 'There is one branch of Ecclesiology which has scarcely kept pace with the rapid advances made in other departments,' he opened. 'We mean Ecclesiastical Music.'[5] The recent diffusion of the knowledge and practice of music in the secular sphere had been remarkable, but insufficient steps had been taken to reform the music of the sanctuary. 'Why should we provide so magnificently for the eye, and neglect the ear?' he asked. Helmore went on to posit that there were two kinds of church music, choral and congregational, that in the current state of things the latter must demand the most attention, that congregational singing implied singing in unison, and that Gregorian chants were not only best suited to this, but that they were marked by a severity and penitential tone

---

[4] Report of the Committee meeting on 22 February 1853. *The Ecclesiologist*, 14/95 (April 1853) 118. The Revd S.S. Greatheed was appointed a member of the musical committee on 12 June 1851. *The Ecclesiologist*, 12/85 (August 1851) 285.
[5] *The Ecclesiologist*, 10/75 (November 1849) 208.

which had been recognized since antiquity as making them peculiarly appropriate to Christian worship. Music in worship must be subordinate to the sung texts and, unlike Anglican chants, this was an inherent quality of the Gregorian tones. Yet this was frequently difficult to ascertain, because Gregorian chants were so often badly sung, gabbled, or mutilated through false accents in the division of the words at the mediation and termination. In passing, Helmore took issue with a common prejudice among High Churchmen and Tractarians that, because metrical psalms were introduced into English worship by the Puritans, hymns were inadmissible altogether. He appealed to the sanction given to ancient Latin hymns by saints Ambrose and Gregory, and claimed that many of these hymns could be very appropriately sung in contemporary English worship. There was not the same authority for exclusive use of Gregorian hymns as there was for Gregorian psalm tones, but Helmore was prepared to state, 'we think their superiority, as far as we know them, is decided.'[6]

The idea of undertaking a translation of ancient church hymns was not new. The Revd John Jebb had proposed it as early as 1843,[7] and two years later Robert Druitt referred to a recent translation in blank verse by 'that munificent benefactor of the Church' and ecclesiologist, A.J.B. Hope.[8] Hope's translation was evidently intended for meditation and private devotion rather than singing or public worship.

The publication of Part I of the *Hymnal Noted* in 1850 not only represents the first fruit of the ECCS's increased musical labours, but would seem to have been an important catalyst of them. Part I is well known to have been the work of Thomas Helmore and J.M. Neale;[9] it is less well known that the idea for this collaboration originated with the Revd Professor W.H. Mill. Frederick Helmore, Thomas's brother, claims to have been present in Mill's rectory at Brasted, Kent, when the idea was first broached. In consequence, a meeting between Thomas Helmore and J.M. Neale is said to have been arranged at East Grinstead following the annual dedication festivities at Withyham, which Helmore and the Chapel Royal boys had attended.[10] The *Parish Choir*[11] and the Webb diaries confirm that such a meeting took place on 1 August 1849 at Sackville College, the day after festival services at Withyham (the first entry which links the names of Helmore and Neale). The diaries also confirm that Frederick Helmore spent numerous musical evenings at the rectory in Brasted singing Latin hymns with the Mills and the Webbs, though the first mention of these is 20 December 1849. Whether the Webb diaries omit to mention earlier visits *or* Frederick Helmore merely heard of Dr Mill's idea in retrospect is

---

[6] *The Ecclesiologist*, 10/75 (November 1849) 208–217. Quotation, 216.
[7] Jebb (1843) 396–7.
[8] Druitt (1845) 44.
[9] *The Ecclesiologist*, 11/80 (October 1850) 185.
[10] F. Helmore (1891) 65–7.
[11] *Parish Choir*, 3/45 (September 1849) 23–4.

unimportant. What is significant is that the idea for a modern publication of Latin hymns in English translation was first discussed by Thomas Helmore and J.M. Neale on 1 August 1849. Before the end of the year, Helmore's adoption by the ECCS was underway, and a significantly increased attention to sacred music was being manifest in *The Ecclesiologist.*

The ECCS musical committee, formed around midsummer 1850, lost no time in setting to work. By late summer it had obtained sanction to publish the *Hymnal Noted* under the auspices of the Society,[12] which was announced in October 1850.

> Our hymnology is confessedly the weak point of the English Church: heterodoxy in words, and vulgarity in music, will still find their way into churches where, with this exception, the office has ritual propriety and even dignity.

The new hymnal would be based entirely on ancient sources in common Western use prior to the 'so-called Reform of Urban VIII' (Pope, 1623–44), and the English translations would retain the original metres of the Latin poetry so that the original melodies could also be used.[13] Publication by instalments began in January 1851.[14]

During the spring and summer of 1851, Thomas Helmore and Neale read a series of papers before the Society to explain and defend the propriety of re-introducing the ancient hymnody into contemporary worship.[15] Neale explained,

> we could only act on the same principle which we have endeavoured to carry out in all things, that, if we were Catholics in the first place, we were English Catholics in the second. We felt that we could look for our hymns to only one source, the offices... And of the various uses of that Church, the ritual of Sarum had so incomparably the most authority, that its hymns, we felt were to be regarded as our especial inheritance.[16]

The decision to use the music of the ancient Sarum rite was largely due to the influence of William Dyce. In 1850 Thomas Helmore had raised the dilemma with Dyce of which plainsong source to use, making known his preference for the Mechlin version. Dyce replied, 'I quite appreciate the difficulty of deter-

---

[12] Report of committee meetings held on 10 August, 10 and 18 September 1850. *The Ecclesiologist*, 11/80 (October 1850) 185.

[13] *The Ecclesiologist*, 11/80 (October 1850) 175.

[14] *The Ecclesiologist*, 11/81 (December 1850) 251–2, announced the imminent publication of the *Hymnal Noted*, while Lawson (1925) 160, quotes a letter from Neale to Webb dated Epiphany 1851, in which he suggests that it should be published in cheap instalments and lists those hymns which he desired to appear first. *The Ecclesiologist*, 12/82 (February 1851) 11–16, explains why it *has been* published.

[15] *The Ecclesiologist*, 12/85 (August 1851) 241–253.

[16] 'On the history of hymnology.' A paper read before the ECCS on 23 June 1851 by the Revd J.M. Neale. *The Ecclesiologist*, 12/85 (August 1851) 241.

mining nowadays what the music *ought* to be by a comparison of ancient documents', but pointed out that there were fewer differences between the Sarum use and sixteenth-century Roman plainsong than between the latter and the modern Mechlin version. Dyce thought that Helmore would harm the cause if he persisted in being a 'Mecklinite'; but felt that they could not go far wrong if they adopted a source which they knew to have been familiar to, for instance, Tomás Luis de Victoria. Yet Dyce did not consider even that to be the most sensible route:

> why adopt the Roman use when there is an English? Why not follow the steps of Marbeck, who certainly adopted his music from the Sarum books? Why not disarm the objection of many to importation of Roman wares by adopting without enquiry the music of the old English Church such as it existed when the hymns were in use?[17]

With a historical justification for the reintroduction of plainsong hymns firmly in place, Helmore was quick to add that their publication was no narrow, reactionary exercise:

> Without... any disparagement of modern art in its proper place, or opposing ourselves to any genuine improvement, there does appear to me every reason for restoring their use in the offices and liturgy of the Church of England; and this would bring about a change in the musical performance of her services desired by all, and based on the highest religious and artistic principles... retaining all the jewels of our present musical Regalia, but setting them in purer gold chased and embossed in a richer style.[18]

Despite the enthusiasm generated among members of the ECCS for ancient hymnody, the *Hymnal Noted* was by no means universally welcomed. The timing of the publication of Part I left a great deal to be desired, following so closely on the events of October and November 1850: Cardinal Wiseman's announcement of the restoration of the Roman Catholic hierarchy in Britain, the Bishop of London's verbal denunciation of the romanizing tendencies of Tractarians,[19] Lord John Russell's inflammatory letter to the Bishop of Durham,[20] and the widespread rioting which ensued cannot have enhanced the general population's inclination to adopt either pre-Reformation hymn texts or their 'popish' sounding Sarum melodies. When a less-than-enthusiastic review

---

[17] Letter from Dyce to Thomas Helmore, 2 November 1850. Dyce Papers: Tate Gallery Archives, Microfilm TAM 54/22.
[18] 'On the music of the *Hymnal Noted.*' A paper read before the ECCS by the Revd Thomas Helmore on 23 June 1851. *The Ecclesiologist*, 12/85 (August 1851) 253. This paper was also quoted also in the *Guardian*, 291 (2 July 1851) 473.
[19] Chadwick (3rd edn 1971, 1987 reprint) 291–4.
[20] *Morning Chronicle*, 26190 (8 November 1850) 5. Russell warned of 'the danger within the gates from the unworthy sons of the Church of England herself', i.e. romanizing Anglican clergymen who had been 'the most forward in leading their flocks, "step by step, to the very verge of the precipice".'

of the hymnal appeared in the *English Churchman*, which had normally proved itself a firm ally, no fewer than three ecclesiologists wrote letters to the editor in the hymnal's defence. All three were reprinted in the February 1852 issue of *The Ecclesiologist*. J.M. Neale asserted with typical certainty, 'all the present objections against Gregorian music were made against Pointed architecture some twenty years ago. *That* was unreal – *that* gave scandal – *that* would never be received; but Christian architecture triumphed, and so will Gregorianism.' S.S. Greatheed complained that the reviewer had failed to realize that it was nearly impossible to judge impartially between that with which one had been familiar since childhood and that which was completely new to everyone. The ECCS had done a great service in unearthing a neglected treasure, and the result should be given a fair hearing. Thomas Helmore defended his use of the four-line stave and neumes, in the belief that the essence of the music could not be expressed in modern notation, and that to have used it would have invited incorrect associations regarding rhythm. To those who objected on the grounds that they did not think plainsong to be melodious, he stated it was the ancient and, whether they liked it or not, it was the only authorized music of the Church. He suggested that they re-read the preface and appendix to William Dyce's *Book of Common Prayer... with Plain Tune*, which had been so generally welcomed in 1843.[21] No battle lines were drawn, however. The editor of the *English Churchman* (13 November 1851) stated his pleasure in inserting such 'able and temperate' letters, convinced that the objects which all had in mind would eventually be promoted by a discussion so conducted.

More time was taken over the second part of the *Hymnal Noted*, which appeared in 1854 and was very much the result of a committee effort. The Revds Thomas Helmore, J.M. Neale, S.S. Greatheed, and Benjamin Webb were appointed to be the 'responsible editors',[22] although others, including A.J.B. Hope and J.D. Chambers, were involved in the work of translating. Neale referred to these meetings as 'some of the happiest and most instructive hours' of his life:

> It was my business to lay before them the translations I had prepared, and theirs to correct. The study which this required drew out the beauties of the original in a way which nothing else could have done; and the friendly collisions of various minds elicited ideas which a single translator would in all probability have missed.[23]

The corpus of ancient hymn texts and melodies thus revived remains among the ecclesiologists' most significant and enduring gifts to the English-speaking church.[24]

---

[21] *The Ecclesiologist*, 13/88 (February 1852) 21–9.
[22] *The Ecclesiologist*, 14/94 (June 1853) 193.
[23] J.M. Neale, quoted in Towle (1906) 214.
[24] Davies, 3 (1962) 234–6.; Temperley (1979) 263–6; White (1962) 219–20.

The basis of a policy on church music confirmed

Thomas Helmore's article on 'Ecclesiastical Music' in the November 1849 issue of *The Ecclesiologist* hailed the commencement of a new era for the subject among ecclesiologists. In the next issue (February 1850) an editor continued the discussion.[25] The two kinds of church music, congregational and choral, were technically styled the *Canto fermo* and *Canto figurato*, and the article proceeded to discuss congregational singing of the prose psalms. It maintained that the Gregorian tones appointed for them had been passed down inviolate from the Church Fathers; and Merbecke, Cranmer, and Queen Elizabeth's Injunctions all proved that their continued use was intended at the Reformation. (: 152–6) Moving into a discussion of the speed and manner in which the psalms should be chanted, *The Ecclesiologist* cautioned,

> But let it never be forgotten that the Canto fermo is intended, not simply as a convenient vehicle of articulate sound; but to add to the fervour, and delight of the worshippers; and to the dignity, decorum, and solemnity of their worship; that thus it may present some external symbol of that homage which is due from man to God, some fitness at least in its outward aspect for the first end of all our actions whether in, or out of Church, – the glory of God.[26]

The outward form was not merely utilitarian but symbolic, a physical means to a spiritual end. The editors went on to survey the groundwork on which the whole of the future development of the ecclesiological view of music was based:

> In music, as in the other arts, there are certain fixed principles, certain rules of taste which, though liable to derangement through man's ignorance and imperfection, remain in every age the same. Its forms indeed differ; not so its material, and its sentiment.
>
> Thus the voice and ear of man, however they may have been cultivated at one period, and neglected at another, are in their original powers always the same, and though the melody which accidentally charmed in one age may accidentally disgust in another, that which is in accordance with the genius of our common humanity, consonant with our inward perceptions of the sublime and beautiful, ought to please, and will please in every age alike, unless some unhappy perversion of taste contravene... While it is admitted, that both in melody and in harmony, there has been in later times both developement [*sic*] and improvement, we are still disposed to retain all that is really good of the olden time; not because it is old, but because it is good: and if it shall appear that by the neglect of what is true to nature, and fitting the unworldly delights of Christian worship, in the time before us, we have lost anything which is not to be repaid by the improvements in the secular branch of the art, we do think that good service is being done to the Church of Christ by those who labour to

---

[25] *The Ecclesiologist*, 10/76 (February 1850) 342–9. Authorship of this article is uncertain, but its style and content confirms that it was not by Helmore.
[26] *The Ecclesiologist*, 10/76 (February 1850) 346.

> restore her music to ancient simplicity and gravity, – as we are ready on the other hand to receive whatever offering the genius of modern improvement may bring before the altar of God, in the spirit of true humility, faith, and love, provided it can be proved to be suitable to the condition of the giver, and the Majesty of Him to Whom it is offered. While, therefore some would have us reject harmony altogether in our Canto fermo; and others suppose that vocal harmony is not proper or congenial with it, we would retain it both as ancient and as good in itself.[27]

To those familiar with the traditional view that ecclesiologists were adamant supporters of plainsong and Palestrina to the exclusion of all else, this seems remarkable. The date is only February 1850, and already they were quite prepared to admit the possibility that true church music would issue from more modern, even contemporary, times. Thomas Helmore confirmed this position in several addresses to the ECCS in 1851:

> Let no one for a moment imagine, that because we plead for the restoration of Church Music in opposition to the modern school, which usurps both its place and its name, that we are therefore opposed to the highest developement [sic] of the art. We would, by restricting its extravagance, restoring its dignity, and extending its resources, refine and exalt the art.[28]

> I believe that the Church school of music is really better adapted to Church purposes than modern compositions, and that its study must be revived before we shall have any new writings of any kind, simple or florid, suited to the grandeur and the solemnity of Divine Worship.[29]

The 'Church school of music' was, of course, that of Palestrina's time, prior to the decline of the art of music, as identified by ecclesiologists already in 1846. (: 39) Following the same reasoning that ecclesiologists had used in reference to church architecture, it would be necessary to return to the study of music composed prior to its descent into degeneracy and secularism in order to rescue it (: 27–8).

The role of the clergy

It is important to remember that the overwhelming majority of ECCS members were clergymen, and consequently the Society commanded an exceptionally powerful sphere of influence. After the squire, the clergyman was likely to be the most influential gentleman in any Victorian country parish, and by directing its persuasive efforts toward those who were in positions either to lead or

---

[27] *The Ecclesiologist*, 10/76 (February 1850) 346–7.
[28] 'On hymnody.' A paper read before the ECCS by the Revd Thomas Helmore on May 22, 1851. *The Ecclesiologist*, 12/84 (June 1851) 174.
[29] *The Ecclesiologist*, 12/85 (August 1851) 253. Also quoted in the *Guardian*, 291 (2 July 1851) 473.

to suppress church revival in whole parishes, rather than toward the general populace, *The Ecclesiologist* maximized the potential influence of its polemical ingenuity.

For church music as with architecture, *The Ecclesiologist* used all of its powers of reason to convince the clergy that its views were irrefutable, orthodox and practical. We have seen that, from the beginning, *The Ecclesiologist* was extremely dissatisfied with the state of church music in the universities (: 32, 36–7), and it is important to realize that in saying so it was among the first to join what soon became a general chorus of disapproval. A dozen years earlier the Revd J.A. Latrobe had suggested, 'perhaps the only effectual remedy would be to strike at the root, and make music an indispensable part of clerical education';[30] but the time was not ripe, and Latrobe's is but one of a few lone voices 'crying in the wilderness.' By the early 1840s the climate had changed. In 1843 the Revd John Jebb published his own censures of choral worship in the universities;[31] and later in the same year the *English Churchman* asserted:

> what seems to us our pressing want, we would say, let ecclesiastical music become, at once, a part of the study of every young clergyman, and of every young man preparing for holy orders. Until music is more generally cultivated among the clergy, as the *British Critic* well observes, there is little hope of our choirs being properly regulated.[32]

Not surprisingly this was an urgent theme of the Society for Promoting Church Music throughout its existence (1846–51).[33] In his original call for the formation of the Society (1845), the founder, Robert Druitt, urged the clergy to make the first move toward reform.[34] In its first annual report, he stated that the main difficulty in reforming church music was not lack of funds, bad and tasteless organists, or prejudiced and ignorant congregations, but rather:

> the insuperable impediment is an unmusical clergyman, be he ever so pious, and zealous, and gifted, – he is the great hindrance of the public praises of God's house! And so it will be till the present generation has passed away.[35]

In an early notice and review of the *Parish Choir*, the *Oxford and Cambridge Review* lent its weight in sympathy to the cause:

> the necessity of some knowledge of music is stated to be indispensable to the clergy. We only wish they would think so in right earnest; for on *them* of

---

[30] Latrobe (1831) 438. Latrobe devoted the whole of his third chapter to the clergyman's responsibilities regarding church music; see also Latrobe (1831) 289–90; and Peace (1839) 18–19, 25–6.
[31] Jebb (1843), 136–46, 182.
[32] *The English Churchman*, 1/43 (October 23, 1843) 684.
[33] *Parish Choir*, vol. 1: 1; vol. 2: 6–7; vol. 3: 5, 32, 46–8, 108, 124, 189, 197.
[34] Druitt (1845) 46, 54–5, 61–2.
[35] *Parish Choir*, 2/22 (October 1847) 6, 7.

course it mainly depends whether a reform shall be effected or not. Let every priest be seen to take his part, and there will not be wanting some to support him.36

When signs of a possible revitalization of church music in Oxford became evident, the *Parish Choir* observed:

If there be one place where, more than another, it is important to have the music of the Church properly performed, it is Oxford, where so many, perhaps a majority, of our clergy take the initiative, as it were, and receive impressions which often adhere to them throughout their whole ministerial career.37

Samuel Sebastian Wesley, whose virulent antipathy toward plainsong isolated him from the ecclesiological arm of the choral revival,38 also identified this point and added his voice. He indignantly relates having attended evensong at Christ Church, Oxford, to find only one lay clerk present in the choir stalls, and him an inaudible beginner:

And this was in a University town, where the first impression as to the efficacy of Church Music must be formed in the minds of young men preparing for holy orders, our future Deans of Cathedrals, to whom the character and fortunes of musicians become entrusted.39

Later the same year (1849) the *Parish Choir* proclaimed, 'The clergy have no right, and never had a right to be ignorant of music.'40 This tone of urgency is characteristic of those who promoted the necessity of musical training for the clergy throughout the early 1850s. One staunch High Churchman and Cambridge graduate, the Revd W.B. Flower,41 who wrote repeatedly in defence of choral worship, stated (1851):

Let the clergy be taught plain-song. The professorships of music at our Universities should be converted to really practical purposes, and the future clergy instructed in the noblest science which can claim their attention. 'A clergy (says an able writer in the *English Review*,) well-trained in music, would go forth well prepared to render every part of Divine service, as far as possible, worthy of its end. They would be able, at least, to superintend the instruction of their flocks; and knowledge on their part would provoke knowledge on the part of their congregations. Parishes would cease to have fits of music and fits of

---

36 *Oxford and Cambridge Review*, II (May 1846) 347.
37 *Parish Choir*, 2/39 (March 1849) 156.
38 'Some would reject all Music but the unisonous Chants of a period of absolute barbarism, – which they term "Gregorian." ...These men would look a Michael Angelo [sic] in the face and tell him Stonehenge was the perfection of architecture!' S.S. Wesley (1849) 49.
39 S.S. Wesley, *A Few Words on Cathedral Music*, quoted in the *Parish Choir*, 3/45 (September 1849) 28, and referred to again in 3/47 (November 1849) 46–8.
40 *Parish Choir*, 3/47 (November 1849) 46.
41 Flower took his BA in 1843 (Magdalene College), and was therefore in Cambridge during the earliest years of the Cambridge Camden Society. His name, however, does not appear among those on the lists of members.

unmusicalness; such fits depending on the accidental absence or presence of some musical or unmusical clergyman for the time. There would be a *continued* system at work, varying only in intensity or in degree of excellence, according to the keener or less lively love of music in the clergy for the time.'[42]

When one considers the percentage of the clergy who were educated at Cambridge and Oxford at mid-century, one understands why there was so much concern about the deficiencies in the services of the college chapels, the lack of congregational choral services which could function as models suitable for imitation, and the absence of any instruction for future ordinands in the subject of church music. Oxford trailed Cambridge slightly in the overall number of ordinands it trained throughout the period, but together they supplied the significant majority: 81.9 per cent from 1834–43; 71.9 per cent from 1844–53; 66.2 per cent from 1854–63; and 63.8 per cent from 1864–73.[43]

Given these statistics, it is not surprising that one of the first musical topics which *The Ecclesiologist* took up in depth in 1850 concerned the priest's part in the performance of the liturgy. The *cantus collectarum* was identified as the liturgical music for the monotoning of the daily prayers[44] and, as such, was obviously a most important starting place for the restoration of choral service. For those who objected to 'singing their prayers', Thomas Helmore observed that the ancient Church had done so, that the Catholic Church still did, and in fact, that both the Western and Eastern branches of the Church had done so continuously, as far as could be determined, since the time of the apostles. He wondered how those who were so quick to object to singing 'have mercy upon us, miserable sinners' could logically turn around and sing the metrical version of Psalm 51:

Have mercy, Lord, on me,
As Thou wert ever kind,
Let me, opprest with loads of guilt,
Thy wonted mercy find.

He pointed out that anyone who had ever attended a Nonconformist chapel knew that even dissenting ministers lapsed into a quasi-chant in their effusive extemporaneous prayers, and not only that, but observed that chant was the natural and common mode of prayer for many religions and peoples throughout the world, including the worship of the Jewish temple. Many ethnic groups believed that the mode of ordinary conversation was not a suitable manner of addressing the Almighty. In view of all of this, it was illogical to suppose that

---

[42] Flower (1851), 18–19.
[43] Haig (1984) 32, Table 2.2.
[44] Not to be confused with the *cantus prophetarum, epistolarum,* or *evangelii,* which was identified as the more inflected music for the chanting of Old Testament lessons, epistles, and gospels. (ref. Dyce's preface)

the *cantus collectarum* was suitable only for cathedral worship. No such distinction had existed before the Rebellion, and therefore there was no reason why it should not cease to be limited to the cathedrals 'as soon as the zeal, the piety, and the skill of the people and Clergy generally' were capable of instituting it. The *cantus collectarum* had wrongly come to be considered the privilege of only the best-provided churches; it should not be denied in any church where its due celebration could be undertaken. Caution was urged only to the extent of avoiding giving offence by innovation, and it was suggested that the restored use could be introduced most safely in additional services, which would not interfere with established ones.[45]

The following month (May 1850) Thomas Helmore read another paper on the same general subject before a meeting of the ECCS.[46] He drew a broad picture of the great power of music in worship, either for good or ill. St Augustine had been moved to tears upon first hearing the Milanese chant, an experience to which anyone might well relate who had attended the services of St Mark's College, Chelsea, or had heard the combined choirs assembled for the laying of the foundation stone for the Church of St Mary Magdalene, Munster Square, or had taken part in the octave of services in conjunction with the consecration of St Barnabas', Pimlico. On the other hand, Richard Hooker had felt that some kinds of harmony were 'pestilent', and Pugin's excited anticipation of an opportunity to worship in the magnificent cathedral at Cologne had been completely destroyed in the actual event by a crashing orchestral mass sung by a few operatic soloists. Pugin exclaimed:

> The mighty pillars, arches, vaults – all seemed to disappear; I was no longer in a cathedral, but at a Concert Musard, or a Jardin d'hiver! I never before felt so strongly the superiority of sound over form, and architect as I am, I would infinitely prefer solemn chants in an ugly church, than to assist in the finest cathedral in Christendom, profaned by those diabolical fiddlers.[47]

If such was the power of music, Helmore maintained, then,

> surely it becomes a matter of the utmost importance, that in its present extension, care should be taken in the first place, by the rulers of the Church, (whom it most concerns,) and next to them by all who desire the welfare of true religion, and have any influence in the regulating of such matters, that in the restoration of our Services throughout the length and breadth of the land, the true province of music in relation to the worship of ALMIGHTY GOD, should be properly understood, and that the movement now going on... should, so far as it has to do with the music in churches, be guided and controlled by the spirit at least, if not by the letter, of those ancient (but not antiquated) laws

---

[45] *The Ecclesiologist*, 10/77 (April 1850) 378–86.
[46] Printed in *The Ecclesiologist*, 11/79 (August 1850) 104–110.
[47] Quoted in *The Ecclesiologist*, 11/79 (August 1850) 105.

which the Church Catholic has enacted, and which there is no reason for imagining our own Church has at any time annulled or superseded.[48]

A quotation from Queen Elizabeth's 49th Injunction of 1559, instructing 'that there be a modest and distinct song so used in all parts of the common prayers in the church,' seemed to clinch the argument. Helmore appealed to all who wished 'to remove from our Church all that is out of conformity with true Catholic use' to restore the plainsong of the services immediately, as set out by Merbecke, and to restore the *cantus collectarum*. 'The Cantus Collectarum, or Church monotone, is the warp of our Choral Service; and from this constructive part of the Priest's musical pronunciation, all the rest branches out', he said, but warned that singing a service would not guarantee devoutness any more than saying it, since 'neither the one nor the other can attain the end desired, if the true spirit of prayer and supplication be wanting.'[49] He concluded with a challenge to ecclesiologists throughout the English-speaking world to show by their actions that the mode of service he advocated was 'the *only* right way to restore our public worship to primitive simplicity and primitive fervour', that their worship should be made a model for imitation by all other churches, and that, even if circumstances proved it to be a local necessity, they should not encourage the adoption of a twofold distinction between cathedral and parochial use. The rubrics were everywhere the same, and if those institutions which most should have set the example to parish churches, i.e. cathedrals, collegiate churches, and the Royal Chapels, would not be moved to reform for love of God, then the application of external pressure was justified, and they should be moved by holy rivalry, out of jealousy for hearing their own music 'more fully, more devoutly, and more ecclesiastically performed *without*, than *within* their venerable walls.'[50]

The role of the choir

In the early zeal of ecclesiologists to restore congregational singing, some confusion arose over the place of anthems and what constituted proper choral music for worship. We have seen that, already in 1846, they were prepared to allow that anthems should be chosen from among 'the grandest and most artistic compositions, provided that they be in a solemn and devotional style.'[51] But by 1850 the Society was struggling with the issue of hymnody. As has been alluded to, metrical psalmody was scorned by some as an innovation of the Puritans, and since the Church had never officially authorized its use,

---

[48] *The Ecclesiologist*, 11/79 (August 1850) 106.
[49] *The Ecclesiologist*, 11/79 (August 1850) 107, 108.
[50] *The Ecclesiologist*, 11/79 (August 1850) 109, 110.
[51] *The Ecclesiologist*, 5/– (May 1846) 174.

many High Churchmen and Tractarians rejected hymnody altogether, whether ancient or modern. Some had decided that the 'grandest and most artistic compositions' advocated in 1846 included modern semi-operatic anthems; and the ECCS was bound to step in.

At the eleventh anniversary meeting on 16 May 1850, F.R. Wegg Prosser, M.P., delivered a paper which stated unequivocally that those 'productions' which constituted 'modern Protestant anthems' should be expelled from contemporary worship. He went on to make an etymological connection between the terms 'antiphon' and 'anthem' (which the editor of *The Ecclesiologist* admitted was 'pressed rather too far'), and decided that if the congregation, at least *in theory*, was supposed to have joined in the ancient antiphons of worship, then congregational music, including hymns, might profitably be substituted for the anthem on most occasions. By this time the *Hymnal Noted* had made it apparent that ancient Latin hymnody sung in English translation was to be the next ecclesiological standard, and so one is not surprised to find that its use was suggested as a corrective. Wegg Prosser hastened to add:

> Now we do not say that pieces of music which are not congregational, are to be entirely excluded; but we do say that they are not the highest, nor the best, nor the most edifying, nor the most devotional, kind of church music; and our own feeling is, that the less we hear of them the better.

Such a radical stance is fairly typical of the way in which a perceived abuse was likely, in the first instance, to elicit a drastic reaction from the more extreme ecclesiologists. This would later correct itself, as in this instance, when a more reasoned solution had been worked out. The objection was not only to the semi-operatic nature of contemporary church music, but to the employment of professional singers who, left to themselves, were inclined to vocal exhibitionism. Until the clergy intervened personally, there was little hope that choirs would sing music 'calculated expressly and solely for solemn devotion.' Wegg Prosser thought that the most complicated sacred music might make for more profitable recreation in the home than the morally objectionable secular music which so often served such purposes.[52]

In the discussion which followed Wegg Prosser's paper, someone suggested that the anthem might be considered a sort of 'musical sermon.' *The Ecclesiologist* promptly laid any such notion to rest, asking how any ecclesiologist could raise the place of preaching, as did the Puritans, above that of prayer and praise, and suggested that the only similarity between the two was that 'a long, bad anthem, and a long, bad sermon' were 'equally wearisome.'[53]

Three years later *The Ecclesiologist* identified four classes of anthems:

---

[52] *The Ecclesiologist*, 11/78 (June 1850) 28–31.
[53] *The Ecclesiologist*, 11/78 (June 1850) 31.

1. those which predated the mid-seventeenth century, and a few full anthems of later date,
2. English verse anthems from the previous two hundred years,
3. extracts from oratorios, Handel and Mendelssohn being the largest contributors, and
4. adaptations from the foreign church music of Haydn, Mozart, and others.

The first class constituted a 'valuable stock for daily use', while the second contained some worthy pieces 'amidst a vast quantity of frippery.' Few oratorio extracts were appropriate for liturgical use, and those could not be performed adequately by the number of singers in an ordinary cathedral choir. Those parts of the sacred music of Haydn and Mozart which were sufficiently solemn to be fit for performance in churches should only be played as voluntaries, since their construction was 'thoroughly instrumental.'[54]

An 1853 review of *Remarks on the Protestant Theory of Church Music* by Steuart Adolphus Pears, one of the assistant masters at Harrow, provided an opportunity for *The Ecclesiologist* to affirm and encourage parish church choirs. Pears had written, 'the tendency of all congregations is to formalism and apathy, and we take the surest way to indulge this disease, when we supply so good an excuse for silence as a well-trained choir.'[55] He had concluded, therefore, that in order to restore congregational singing, church choirs ought to be disbanded altogether. *The Ecclesiologist* pointed to St Barnabas', Pimlico, as evidence that a good choir could as easily *promote* excellent congregational singing. It went on to assert that, 'where the music is not too difficult, and the people take any delight in the worship of God, and are encouraged to let their voices be heard', there would be no need to disband the choir to attain the desired end.[56] In 1854 *The Ecclesiologist* agreed with the rector of Liverpool that, of all the modes of sung praise, congregational singing was 'the most devotional, and the most sublime', and that a 'powerfully concentrated choir' was necessary to obtain it since, even with the aid of an organ, congregational singing too often proved to be a 'complicated discord.'[57]

The Motett Society

Any possible doubt about the ECCS's commitment to ecclesiastical choirs was completely eradicated when it revived the Motett Society in 1852. The possibility of reviving the Motett Society, which had been inactive since 1849, was first recorded to have been discussed by representatives of the two socie-

---

[54] *The Ecclesiologist*, 14/97 (October 1853) 340–1.
[55] Pears (1852) 19–20.
[56] *The Ecclesiologist*, 14/95 (April 1853) 129–31.
[57] *The Ecclesiologist*, 15/101 (April 1854) 95.

ties on 23 June 1851, and since no great obstacles were identified, it was decided to pursue their union. In early July, William Dyce, Honorary Secretary and one of the founders of the Motett Society, wrote to Helmore to say that he thought the merger advisable in principle, but it must be up to the ECCS to propose acceptable terms:

> There must be some tangible advantage held out as the ground of uniting the two bodies. As the case now stands the *Ecclesiological Society* proposes to get possession of our collection of Music, and by way of return is to be so obliging as to accord to members of the Motett Society privileges which anyone, whether member of the Motett or not, may obtain: and on the same conditions: *viz:* by paying the annual subscription. No. There must be some guarantee that the objects of the Motett will be carried out – some guarantee that so many musical performances shall take place annually.[58]

At a meeting of the Committee of the ECCS in January 1852, a motion by A.J.B. Hope, seconded by Benjamin Webb, was carried: 'That this Society embracing the whole of the objects intended to be promoted by the Motett Society is anxious to give greater effect to the Society's operations by receiving its members into itself.'[59] Three public performances per year were guaranteed; and at a meeting of the Committee of the Motett Society on 5 June 1852, it was unanimously agreed to accept the terms of the proposed amalgamation. Although ecclesiologists had recruited many of England's most important defenders of church music to its ranks prior to this union, revival of the Motett Choir brought virtually all of the remaining proponents of choral service into the fold of the Ecclesiological late Cambridge Camden Society, who found at their disposal, in *The Ecclesiologist*, an established international forum for the propagation of their views.

In announcing this to the public, *The Ecclesiologist* asserted that church music could not be 'efficiently reformed' without 'great personal exertions' by those who wished for its improvement. Two other societies had laboured successfully for the oratorio (one of which was certainly the Sacred Harmonic Society); John Hullah, aided by the National Society, had taught great masses of people to sing; and the Motett Society had directed the movement toward the Church through its publications of ancient church music and public meetings; still, the work was not done. The choral revival had not yet been fully appropriated by the Church for its own benefit:

> Musical skill is increasing, and therefore needs direction, encouragement, and absorption (if the phrase may be allowed) into the practical and every-day working of the Church. Some one model which we could regard as perfect in design and respectable in execution, (so far at least as human infirmity might

---

[58] Letters from Dyce to Thomas Helmore, 1 and 5 July 1851. Tate Gallery: Dyce Papers, Microfilm TAM 54/23.
[59] *The Ecclesiologist*, 14/97 (August 1853) 275; 12/85 (August 1851) 286; 13/91 (August 1852) 235–6.

allow) would do more good than volumes of elaborate discussion, or thousands of exhortations from the pulpit or the lecturer's platform.

Characteristically ambitious, the point of establishing the Ecclesiological Motett Choir was,

> to form a band of numerical strength and practical skill equal to the development in the church itself of the full grandeur of ritual music, and the sublimity of the liturgy and offices when duly performed, with all the fervour of hearty worship, and all the devotion of skill and talent, which ought to be found at least in the worship of churches in cities and in large towns.[60]

The new Motett Choir was comprised of volunteer men and women, together with members of the St Barnabas Choral Society.[61] During the first year no professional members were employed, and although this was not ruled out as a desirable course for the future, the Committee felt that the goal of education was well met by the arrangement. During 1852-3 the Choir met fourteen times,[62] and so markedly did diligence increase their zeal, that they met twenty-four times during the second year. Improvement was retarded somewhat by a 'constant influx of new members, and the non-attendance of some', a problem which plagued the Choir for some years, but 'great repetition and constant practice' seemed to yield general satisfaction. Twelve additional sets of the Motett Society's publications were added to the Choir library during 1853-4, and an appeal for financial support was made (due to the need to buy music, rather than for engagement of boy trebles).[63] The Choir for a public performance on 13 July 1854 is recorded to have been comprised of eleven first trebles, five second trebles, nine altos (which are enumerated as three women, two boys, and four men), six first tenors, six second tenors, and nine or ten basses. The boys were Thomas Helmore's from the Chapel Royal, who regularly assisted him even when he travelled great distances, (: 127) and possibly some from the London choirs of other member clergy. At the same meeting one of the Choir members, Mr George Grove (then Secretary to the Crystal Palace), was added to the Choir committee and appointed to manage the Choir fund. Donations were solicited on the grounds that the Motett Choir's influence was bound to continue to grow, being 'the only musical society in the country established with the special design of cultivating what has been pronounced by all competent critics, the very highest school of Church Music.' The work must press forward, it was insisted,

> until the songs of Sion ascend, as of old, from the lips as well as from the hearts of the ten thousands of her people, and until every sanctuary throughout

---

[60] *The Ecclesiologist*, 14/94 (February 1853) 28–31.
[61] The Grammar School attached to St Barnabas', Pimlico, was the frequent site of early meetings of the Ecclesiological Motett Choir.
[62] *The Ecclesiologist*, 14/97 (August 1853) 275–6.
[63] *The Ecclesiologist*, 15/103 (August 1854) 269; 14/96 (June 1853) 193–4.

> our land shall have its well-instructed choir to present before the Throne of Christ the highest offerings the musical art can furnish on earth, in lowly imitation of the worship of heaven.[64]

During the ten years in which the two societies were affiliated, the Ecclesiological Motett Choir gave three public performances annually. In addition to five complete masses and nearly thirty motets by Palestrina, these concerts provided the public with an opportunity to hear masses by Anerio, Lassus, and Victoria; anthems and motets by Byrd, Croce, Farrant, Gibbons, Lassus, Lupo, Morales, Nanini, Tallis, Victoria, and the anonymous, now well-known setting of 'Rejoice in the Lord alway'; plus a vast number of plainsong hymns and antiphons, and carols for Christmas and Easter (see appendix). In deference to Protestant traditions of the Church of England, all Latin texts were sung in English translation, or new English texts were adapted to fit the music.

At a public meeting held on 7 April 1853, A.J.B. Hope, who occupied the chair, spoke of the Society's mission to preserve and restore the music of the English Church from the Reformation to the Great Rebellion, and cautioned against the use of the popular style of music employed by the modern Roman Catholic Church.[65] But the Motett Choir's labours were not limited to early music. At the same meeting an anthem by the Society's treasurer, the Revd S.S. Greatheed, was performed, which was hailed by *The Ecclesiologist* as an example of what could be achieved by contemporary composers who studied the ancient masters, but not in servile imitation. 'Original compositions must always have some advantages over adaptations as regards force of expression', it suggested;[66] and throughout the ten years of the Motett Choir's formal association with the Ecclesiological Society, modern compositions were a regular adjunct to the staple diet of ancient church music. In addition to five anthems and a setting of the *Magnificat* and *Nunc dimittis* by Greatheed, compositions were performed by other members, including the Revd H.L. Jenner, the Hon. Frederick Lygon (6th Earl of Beauchamp), and carols for Christmas and Easter which were the result of continued collaboration between J.M. Neale and Thomas Helmore. Contemporary works by non-members which found a place in the repertoire included two by the organist of St Paul's Cathedral, John Goss, who lived literally next door to Thomas Helmore in Cheyne Walk;[67] and five by the Revd Sir Frederick Ouseley, a friend of Helmore's brother, Frederick, from undergraduate days at Oxford. Ouseley's curacy at St Barnabas', Pimlico (1849–51), had put him in close and frequent

---

[64] *The Ecclesiologist*, 15/103 (August 1854) 271–3.
[65] *The Ecclesiologist*, 14/96 (June 1853) 193.
[66] *The Ecclesiologist*, 14/96 (June 1853) 197.
[67] F. Helmore (1891) 73.

contact with Thomas Helmore, and they enjoyed a close friendship for the rest of their lives.[68] (: 128–9)

Developments within the University of Cambridge

The Ecclesiological late Cambridge Camden Society continued to exert an influence in its alma mater after its 1846 disassociation from the University. Two student societies in particular looked to the musical example of ecclesiologists and closely imitated it during the early 1850s. Three of the colleges are known to have made efforts to improve their chapel services during this period: Corpus Christi, Queens', and Peterhouse.

The Cambridge Architectural Society

Originally formed in 1846 to fill the gap created by the Cambridge Camden Society's disassociation from the University and relocation in London, the Cambridge Architectural Society acted as a firm ally of the ECCS and continued its mission among members of the University, especially among junior members. The local Society was formally admitted to union with the ECCS in 1847.[69] Notable members included the Regius Professor of Hebrew, Dr W.H. Mill (Trinity); the Revds P. Freeman (Peterhouse, and Principal of Chichester Diocesan Theological College), T.S. Woollaston (Peterhouse), William Butler (Trinity College, Rector of Wantage), H.R. Luard (Trinity), Benjamin Webb (Trinity), G.F. Reyner (St John's), Professor Willis (Caius), Harvey Goodwin (Caius, then Dean of Ely), G.E. Corrie (Master of Jesus), John Gibson (Dean of Jesus), Gordon Williams (King's), W.M. Campion (Dean of Queens'); Messrs A.J.B. Hope (Trinity), and John Sutton (Jesus), among many others.[70]

Although the Cambridge Architectural Society had to be careful not to offend members of the University over questions of theology and churchmanship as the Cambridge Camden Society had done, its pursuits were not exclusively architectural. Soon after the ECCS actively took up the subject of ecclesiastical music in 1850, J.H. Smith (BA, Trinity College) read a paper before the Cambridge Architectural Society advocating a return to the severe style of early Church music, which is reported to have elicited 'warm discussion.'[71] Early in 1853 H.J. Braithwaite (Clare Hall) read an impressive paper

---

[68] Rainbow (1970) 159–60; F. Helmore (1891) 75–6, 91. This reveals much about the generous characters of the two men, who held such opposite and well-known viewpoints on plainsong.
[69] *The Ecclesiologist*, 8/61 (August 1847) 39.
[70] CUL: Minute Books of the Cambridge Architectural Society 1847–53, 1853–9.
[71] *The Ecclesiologist*, 12/133 (April 1851) 141.

on 'Aesthetics in the Church',[72] which made reference to several of the ecclesiastical arts. He maintained that if any art forms were appropriate for use in worship of the Creator of all, it was illogical not to employ them all with equal zeal. Mankind's greatest and least offerings were equivalent in the eyes of an omnipotent God, Braithwaite stated,

> but our greatest and best is nevertheless the greatest and best manifestation of our desire and intention to honour the Creator, and to approach Him, so far as we can, in a manner according with His majesty. Must it not be an omission to express this desire worse than we can? Why are discord in church-singing, disproportion in a column, want of harmony in colour better than would be bad grammar in a prayer?[73]

He went on to point out that believers were admonished to judge a tree by its fruit, and maintained that those who attacked the employment of the highest arts in worship were guilty of condemning the tree *because of* its fruit. Concerning the present revival, Braithwaite found himself safely within mainstream ecclesiological thought, even when he suggested that true church music was the best model of taste for the other ecclesiastical arts:

> No change is desired but such as is manifestly reasonable or soundly expedient: and these changes are just, because as we have said it is our place to work for this century and to enrich it with new creations, not merely to people it with the ghosts of the past.[74]

This principle of ecclesiology was also proclaimed in the next paper read before the Cambridge Architectural Society. Sabine Baring-Gould, a secretary of the Society, warned against the dangers of merely reproducing Gothic, of straining after details without understanding or achieving its intended total effect: 'there is a spirit in it, not a mere dead formularising.' It was vain and foolish, he thought, to attempt to stem the inevitable tide of change:

> A few zealous antiquaries may strive to pond the stream back from overwhelming their precious field, but it will only do the more harm when it does sweep over it as it eventually will; how much better will it be to direct the flood, and then it will fertilize the field instead of destroying it.[75]

Some years later, in 1860, it was proposed that the Cambridge Architectural Society should form a Motett Choir 'for the study of the ancient choral music of the Church, and more especially that of the school of Tye, Byrd, Tallis, and

---

[72] Braithwaite, Papers of the Cambridge Architectural Society, read on 23 February 1853. CUL: Add. 2760.
[73] Braithwaite, 4, 5, 7.
[74] Braithwaite, 8, 15–16.
[75] S. Baring-Gould, 'On the principles of Gothick architecture, and the manner of carrying them out', 17, 28. Papers of the Cambridge Architectural Society, read on 11 May 1853. CUL: Add. 2760.

Orlando Gibbons.'[76] The Revds H.R. Luard (Trinity) and Gordon Williams (King's) were among those who favoured such a scheme, and the matter was referred to committee for discussion of the way in which it might best be realized. In 1861 the formation of a separate 'Church Music Society' (a different organization from the one discussed below) was announced which, though not connected with the Cambridge Architectural Society, was described as an 'offshoot' of it.[77]

Thus ecclesiology remained a potent force within the University, and not only for its educational role among junior members within the discipline of ecclesiastical architecture. They remained abreast of national thought concerning general principles of the art revival, and reflected their share of the interest in ecclesiastical music which manifested itself so significantly among ecclesiologists by the early 1850s.

The Cambridge University Society for Promoting the Study and Practice of Church Music

This Society was formed during the academic year 1853–4, and was Cambridge's clear response to the example set by the Ecclesiological late Cambridge Camden Society in 1852 when it merged with the Motett Society. The formation in the sister university of the Oxford Society for the Study and Practice of the Plain Song of the Church on St Cecilia's Day 1853 was also a direct fruit of the ECCS's lead. Each society arose not from the efforts of professional musicians, but from the common vision of about one hundred fellows and undergraduates.

The 'Cambridge Church Music Society', as the cumbersome title was sometimes shortened, began by engaging the Revd Thomas Helmore as its musical director, just as the Oxford Plain Song Society had done. He gave a series of introductory lectures and oversaw the establishment of twice-weekly practices (held in the rooms of the Cambridge Architectural Society)[78] during which members, divided into elementary and advanced classes, learned the rudiments of musical notation and singing. Their goal was to become able to participate intelligently in the congregational music of parochial services. Notable members of the Committee of the 'Cambridge Church Music Society' included the President, the Revd John Gibson (Dean of Jesus); Vice Presidents, the Revds W.M. Campion (Dean of Queens'), J.H. Henderson (Precentor of Ely), Harvey Goodwin, W.B. Hopkins (St Catharine's), and G.F. Reyner (St John's); the Treasurer was the Revd R.H. Cooke (Sidney Sussex); the Secretary was Mr J.H. Cooper (Trinity); and the remaining members of the

---

[76] *The Ecclesiologist*, 21/141 (December 1860) 385.
[77] *The Ecclesiologist*, 22/142 (February 1861) 55; 22/147 (December 1861) 403.
[78] CUL: Minutes of the Cambridge Architectural Society, 5 May 1854.

Committee included the Revd F.J.A. Hort (Trinity), Messrs John Sutton (Jesus), F.C. Gleadow (St John's), R.W. Blundrit (Christ's), and J. Pilditch (Queens', who conducted most of the meetings for practice).

The first report admitted that 'Societies for similar purposes had a previous existence in several Colleges,' but asserted that the overwhelming greeting with which the Cambridge University Society for Promoting the Study and Practice of Church Music had been received was justification for its existence as well. Members were immediately offered honorary membership in the Oxford Society for the Study of Plainsong, a gesture which was reciprocated by the Cambridge group. The Society's first report (1854) also stated:

> Your Committee hail with satisfaction the establishment of Choral Services in not a few of our College Chapels, and these too supported not by paid singers, but by the resident members themselves; and they would be glad if the working of our Society should in time produce similar results in all, for they think it impossible to overestimate the importance of improving our College worship as a school for future operations.[79]

The importance of this, considering the number of future priests who took their Divinity degrees at Cambridge or Oxford, has already been noted. (: 70–3)

These developments were welcomed with much pleasure by the Ecclesiological late Cambridge Camden Society. In the annual report of its musical committee for 1854, Thomas Helmore told of this 'unexpected and most important movement, meeting and co-operating with [the ECCS's efforts], if not originally derived from it.' Not only had church music societies been formed in both universities, but,

> In Cambridge, also, with a pliancy and freedom from formality not to be lightly spoken of when rightly directed, many of the colleges and halls are one after another restoring, at least on festivals and their first vespers, choral services, not slovenly performed by hirelings, caring little or nothing for the holy work, but by ardent and voluntary choirs formed among the members themselves.[80]

The fact that both Queens' (: 87) and Corpus Christi (: 86) colleges gave official sanction to the establishment of choral services in January 1854 would seem to be a direct response to the establishment of the Cambridge University Society for Promoting the Study and Practice of Church Music during the 1853–4 academic year. No fewer than nine undergraduates and three Fellows of Queens', including the Dean of Chapel, are included in the list of ninety-nine members published by that Society in Michaelmas 1854. There is not a single member listed from Corpus Christi; but one may surmise that Corpus was one of those colleges mentioned in the Society's first report which already

---

[79] *The First Report of the Cambridge University Society for Promoting the Study and Practice of Church Music, with Laws, List of Members, &c*, Michaelmas 1854.
[80] *The Ecclesiologist*, 15/103 (August 1854) 270.

had an organization that fulfilled similar purposes.[81] Clearly Corpus was responding to the general movement for the revitalization of choral worship.

According to a report of the Oxford Plain Song Society, no fewer than nine Cambridge colleges had some sort of choral service by midsummer of 1854, and plainsong was thought to be in use in at least one of them.[82] This would have included King's, Trinity, St John's, Peterhouse, Jesus, Queens' and Corpus Christi colleges; which two the others may have been remains obscure.[83] *The Ecclesiologist* took this as a positive sign that the clergy were becoming more musical, and aside from the obvious practical benefits this promised for the worship life of the Church of England at large, it hoped that her cathedrals might soon find themselves with a whole generation of precentors who would be capable of enriching the repertoire with first-rate sacred compositions.[84]

Reform in Cambridge college chapels

Peterhouse. John Pratt, organist of King's College 1799–1855, was appointed organist of Peterhouse in 1813.[85] Regarding the Sunday evening services at Peterhouse, a correspondent to the *Parish Choir* reported in 1848:

> The choir consists of boys only. The arrangements here are very slovenly. The boys stand in a row in front of the organ, and do not wear surplices. The chanting, moreover, is not antiphonal. The Psalms and Canticles are chanted to every variety of chant, ancient and modern, single and double. Services and anthems are not used.[86]

John Pratt's infirmities prevented him from executing his duties at Peterhouse no less than at King's. Yet upon his resignation from his post at Peterhouse in February 1852, the Master and Seniors granted him an annual pension of £20, provided that £5 thereof be given to Mr J.H. Robson, who by that time had

---

[81] *The first report of the Cambridge University Society for Promoting the Study and Practice of Church Music* (Michaelmas 1854) 9. CCCA: The Chapter Acts for 27 January 1854 reveal that a College Choral Society was already established, and on that date it was given permission to hold twice weekly practices of an hour and one-half in the College's new lecture room.

[82] *The Ecclesiologist*, 15/103 (August 1854) 279.

[83] One may have been Christ's College, since the *Parish Choir*, 2/29 (May 1848) 62, reported that there was 'some talk of reviving the Choral Service' there. No college records exist to confirm whether or not this came to pass imminently. Certainly there were trebles employed there by the late 1860s, since the St John's Choral Society brought in extra trebles from King's, Trinity, Christ's, and Peterhouse for a major concert in 1868. SJCA: SOC4.1.

[84] *The Ecclesiologist*, 15/104 (October 1854) 309.

[85] West (1921) 125.

[86] *Parish Choir*, 2/29 (May 1848) 62.

acted as deputy organist for 'nearly 20 years'[87] (a capacity in which Robson also served at King's and Great St Mary's).

Within four months of Pratt's resignation a contract was agreed upon to pay the organbuilders, Hill and Co., £150 to add a set of pedals, pedal couplers, and to make various other repairs to the Peterhouse Chapel organ.[88] The new College organist was William Amps who, upon Pratt's death in 1855, also succeeded him as organist of King's College. Beginning in Michaelmas 1852, four additional choristers were added to those already in place, and no further changes were made to the choir or their duties until 1866, when two more choristers and four men were engaged to assist in the choral service. The lay clerks were employed until Michaelmas 1883, when the first choral students of the College (called 'Chapel Clerks') were elected.[89]

Corpus Christi College. Early in the spring of 1856 the minutes of the Cambridge Architectural Society, printed in *The Ecclesiologist*, announced the erection of a new three-manual organ in the west gallery of Corpus Christi Chapel and stated that, although the case was objectionable, pains and expense had not been spared on the instrument. The notice continued, 'But this is of small account when compared with the complete and generous scheme for re-establishment of Choral Service adopted by the College during the past year.'[90]

The Chapter Acts of Corpus Christi College for 27 January 1854 record details of this generous provision for choral worship. On that date it was resolved, 'That during this and the following Term the College pay for the Hire of an Harmonium and six choristers; also for the services of a Singing Master to train the Choristers and such Students as may be approved by the Dean & Singing Master.' An undergraduate, T.J. Jones, was appointed choirmaster, and a precentor was named.[91] Later in the same year it was resolved that the special fund set up in honour of the Quincentenary celebration of the foundation of the College should 'be employed for generally improving the Chapel'[92] and, later, that it would be desirable to place an organ in the Chapel.[93] On 17 October 1855 the new organ was officially opened by the consultant, Dr Buck, organist of Norwich, with assistance from his cathedral

---

[87] Peterhouse Archives, Order Book of Meetings of the Master and Fellows, 16 February 1852. Robson died a few months later.
[88] Peterhouse Archives, Order Book, 3 June 1852.
[89] Peterhouse Archives, Order Book, 22 October 1852; 12 October 1866; 25 August and 13 October 1883 (the last is misdated 1882).
[90] *The Ecclesiologist*, 17/113 (April 1856) 148.
[91] CCCA: Chapter Book, 8 February 1854; 22 October and 13 November 1855.
[92] CCCA: Chapter Book, 23 March 1854.
[93] CCCA: Chapter Book, 20 October 1854.

choir; and early in 1856 it was decided to strengthen the College choir by the addition of six more choristers.[94]

The fact that the Corpus Christi College had a strong Evangelical reputation, which became even more pronounced in the 1860s, made the introduction of choral worship there all the more exciting. One must not make the mistake of thinking that only High Churchmen enjoyed music in church. The introduction of choral service in an Evangelical college is a clear example that, by the mid-1850s, the propriety of choral service was well enough established in theory for Low Churchmen to be able to begin to work out how they would respond to its claims.

Queens' College. Despite the efforts of undergraduates to render chapel services chorally in 1848 (: 58), Queens' College took no official action to support choral service in its chapel until January 1854, when £10 was granted toward the expense of maintaining one.[95] This was evidently for the purpose of paying chorister boys, introduced that year, and such payments are evident annually for many years thereafter.

It was not until the Michaelmas term 1860 that a Cambridge college elected a choral scholar to sing in its chapel, and Queens' led the way.[96] This followed closely on the pioneering example of New College, Oxford, which had elected three choral scholars the previous year to begin singing from Michaelmas 1859. At that time the *Guardian* had warmly welcomed the new scheme in the belief that it had the potential to reconstitute 'on a higher principle' not only the New College Choir, but to 'raise the tone of all the choirs in England.'[97]

Quires and places where they sing

Although parochial church music was the foremost of the ecclesiologists' musical concerns, it is manifestly clear that they admired the daily rigour of cathedral worship as the theoretical ultimate of earthly praise. Handling the subject occasionally during the first half of the 1850s, *The Ecclesiologist* maintained an unequivocally high view of it and, indeed, seemed to take for granted that its readers concurred. The purpose of worship in choral foundations, they stated, was,

---

[94] CCCA: Chapter Book, 5 February 1856.
[95] Queens' College Conclusion Book, 10 January 1854.
[96] Queens' College Conclusion Book, 11 October 1860; see also 9 January 1862, 11 October 1862, and 14 October 1865. Twigg (1987) 275, gives the erroneous impression that the first choral scholar was elected at Queens' on 9 January 1862. The infrequent and scanty number of elections to choral scholarships suggests that other men must have participated in the choir.
[97] *The Guardian*, 698 (20 April 1859) 391; 707 (22 June 1859) 539.

to offer, day by day, the sacrifice of prayer and praise in as perfect a form as the circumstances of the country admit: that this ought to be done, both because we are taught that such acts are acceptable to Almighty God, through the Divine Head of the Church; and because it is a great benefit to every devout Christian to have an opportunity of joining in such specimens of public worship – a kind of worship which, in proportion as the true idea of it is realized, approaches nearer and nearer to that which will be the employment of a blessed eternity.[98]

The Ecclesiologist stated that it was reasonable that choral services should be 'more elaborate' in cathedrals than in parish churches, 'provided it be also such as unprofessional ears can *listen to* with edification.'[99]

Following the example given by the ECCS in 1850, other architectural societies around the country began to consider the subject of church music. In November 1850, Robinson Thornton of St John's College, Oxford, read a paper before the Oxford Architectural Society,[100] which simply restated the principles outlined in articles published earlier that year in *The Ecclesiologist* (: 69–70). Three years later, the Revd E. Miller of New College, Oxford, brought the subject before the Oxford Architectural Society again, during the same month in which the Oxford Society for the Study and Practice of Plain Song was formed, and *The Ecclesiologist* reported, 'Mr Miller concluded by urging the importance of union between the promoters respectively of Church Architecture and Church Music.'[101]

In the spring of 1853, Sir Henry Dryden read a paper before the Architectural Society of the Archdeaconry of Northampton, 'On Church Music, and the fitting of Churches for Music', which 'attracted considerable attention' nationwide.[102] It was reviewed and partially reprinted in two instalments in *The Ecclesiologist*. Dryden proclaimed that cathedral service was 'the noblest form of worship', and was certain that it would lack no public support if the clergy learned music, attended regularly, and saw to the proper maintenance of their choirs. To those who objected to chanted services, Dryden replied that the liturgy was as much an art form as the consecrated architecture in which it was celebrated, and that it would be inconsistent to suggest that the art of music alone was somehow undevotional, while the others were held to be appropriate and good. He neither cared whether everyone liked choral worship, nor demanded that all participate in it, but he did object to the gross presumption of those who personally could not appreciate sung services and who proceeded to disparage them as universally undevotional. To do so was to claim a sort of

---

[98] *The Ecclesiologist*, 14/97 (August 1853) 237. See also chapter five. Among many others, Jebb (1843) 22–3, put forward the same view.
[99] *The Ecclesiologist*, 17/112 (February 1856) 13.
[100] *The Ecclesiologist*, 12/82 (February 1851) 62–3.
[101] *The Ecclesiologist*, 15/100 (February 1854) 46. Quoted also in the *Guardian*, 417 (30 November 1853) 801.
[102] *Guardian*, 422 (4 January 1854) 7.

personal superiority over the collective experience of at least 1400 years of Christian history:

> You cannot... pretend that your piety is greater than that of hundreds of men who have approved of choral service, from the time of S. Augustin [sic] to the present day. You will not, I think, dare denounce as irreligious the practices of the noble army of martyrs.[103]

Dryden drew a distinction between cathedral and parochial service, asserting that in a cathedral the congregation were meant to join in silence, while it was needful that all should join vocally in the worship of a parish. To this *The Ecclesiologist*, of course, took exception, maintaining that the Prayer Book rubrics were the same for cathedrals and parish churches alike, and that those parts of the service which were meant to be congregational should be so wherever a service was held.[104]

Dryden's distinction between cathedral and parochial service found support the following year in *Two Papers on Church Music, read before the Liverpool Ecclesiastical Music Society*, by the Revd Augustus Campbell, rector of Liverpool. *The Ecclesiologist* reasserted that the distinction was 'utterly false and illusory', and added that it arose from a fundamental misunderstanding of the role of a cathedral:

> If the cathedral is not the mother church of all around it, – its services, model services, – its clergy, patterns, – its bishops, a working acting ruler over the diocese: – if it is not this, it is nothing to the parish, – a *caput mortuum* which none would miss, if it were gone.[105]

Models were meant to be imitated.

An 1854 review of S.S. Wesley's *Reply to the Inquiries of the Cathedral Commissioners, Relative to Improvement in the Music of Divine Worship in Cathedrals*, occasioned *The Ecclesiologist*'s most vehement attack on the state of cathedral music. It thought that the real insipidity of English services lay in the fact that they tended to be a continuous string of ideas, unrelated to one another either musically or liturgically. A great improvement would be effected if a hint were taken from the *Hymnal Noted*, and a seasonal scheme of services were adopted, and the bad ones allowed to fall into disuse altogether. Cathedral organists had spent too much time during the past century improving their keyboard skills, *The Ecclesiologist* thought, and this, together with the German style of instrumental composition ('of all styles the one least suited for voices'), had adversely affected English organists' ability to compose for the Church. And S.S. Wesley was no exception: the reviewer suggested that if there were such a thing as a Dis.Doc. (Doctor of Dissonance), Wesley should

---

[103] *The Ecclesiologist*, 14/99 (December 1853) 399–405. Quotation, 404.
[104] *The Ecclesiologist*, 14/99 (December 1853) 402.
[105] *The Ecclesiologist*, 15/101 (April 1854) 94–7. Quotation, 96.

be the first recipient.[106] 'We have observed with regret,' *The Ecclesiologist* continued,

> that the education of English musicians is too generally very defective in matters which do not immediately relate to their art and yet have an important bearing upon it. The faults of many composers are chiefly owing to want of general intellectual cultivation.

It was hoped that the increased study of music among the clergy would eventually yield precentors who would themselves be capable of writing first-rate compositions for the Church, and proposed that it would be well if the possession of a musical degree were required of all precentors.[107]

In 1855, the Revd C.T. Heartley[108] published *Our cathedrals and their mission*, in which he made several ambitious suggestions for the reform of cathedrals and their choirs, which were welcomed wholeheartedly by *The Ecclesiologist*. 'Our Cathedral services,' he wrote, 'are beautiful; sometimes they degenerate into pretty, but they are never grand or sublime. They want vigour, power, mass; and this can only be got by the introduction of more voices.'[109] St Mark's College, Chelsea, was the model he had in mind, and hence he thought that cathedral choirs should be 'not merely doubled, but increased something like ten-fold', which would also have the beneficial effect of encouraging congregational participation.[110] If each cathedral were attached to a theological college, if students were recruited from the National Training Schools and their model schools, and if volunteers were taken from the city, the numbers would soon be at hand. Heartley thought that lay clerks should be put to work teaching music and singing to students in the theological and National Training colleges, and was not in favour of augmenting either their number or their cathedral salaries, since the excess leisure thus created would make them susceptible to greater temptations!

Heartley thought that small cathedral choirs explained the frequency of 'long and often uninterrupted solos' in English sacred compositions of recent times. Composers had written for the insufficient forces at hand; but Heartley insisted, 'It is the opinion of many persons who are well able to judge that solos and duets ought to be excluded from Cathedral music.' At the very least they had become too frequent, and he felt,

---

[106] *The Ecclesiologist*, 15/104 (October 1854) 307–310. An explanation for the reviewer's especially harsh treatment of Wesley may lie in the fact that Wesley had been such a vocal opponent of plainsong.

[107] *The Ecclesiologist*, 15/104 (October 1854) 310.

[108] Heartley was, at that time, assistant curate to the President of the ECCS, Archdeacon Thorp, at Kemerton, Gloucestershire. The daily choral services and the choir which he helped build up were admired nationally as a model for imitation. (: 94–8)

[109] Heartley (1855) 9.

[110] Heartley (1855) 6–7, 30.

> If our Cathedral choirs are strengthened, a more dignified style of music would quickly prevail; we should find that the lighter music would soon be discovered to be unsuitable, and the superiority of such men as Orlando Gibbons, perhaps the prince of English Church composers, would quickly be made apparent.[111]

This was not to suggest that the school of English church music was dead or dying. Those who strove to revive a school which had 'done so much to produce a true spirit of devotion among the members of the English Church' deserved all encouragement.[112]

It is well known that the revival of church music and performance standards did not permeate the cathedrals until later in the nineteenth century. The movement had to start on the outside, in the parish churches, and work its way up, and ecclesiologists realized this. In 1857, the report of the musical committee to the Ecclesiological Society stated:

> On the whole, the Committee are of the opinion that the prospects of ecclesiastical music in the English Church are hopeful; that although the strongholds of choral worship – the Cathedrals and Collegiate churches – are as yet but partially affected by the movement with which the Society is identified, in favour of a purely devotional style of music in the solemn offices of the Church, yet a work is nevertheless going forward, through the media of the Choral Societies of our towns, and the choirs and schools of our villages, which will eventually leaven the whole country, and compel even cathedral authorities to acknowledge, that reverence, earnestness, and heartiness, are worthier characteristics of the worship of a Christian congregation than the mere display of musical ingenuity and artistic talent.[113]

---

[111] Heartley (1855) 28, 29.
[112] Heartley (1855) 30.
[113] *The Ecclesiologist*, 18/120 (June 1857) 189.

CHAPTER FOUR

Contributions of individual ecclesiologists to the revival of church music

Without exception the primary officers of the Ecclesiological (late Cambridge Camden) Society and the members of its Musical Committee cultivated significant personal spheres of influence in the promotion of church music. The Society's senior leading figures, by virtue of both age and public distinction, were the President (1839–59), the Venerable Thomas Thorp; and the Revd William Hodge Mill, Regius Professor of Hebrew at Cambridge (1848–53). The Honorary Secretaries for Music were the Revd Thomas Helmore (1850–56) and the Revd Henry Lascelles Jenner (1856–62). The other most active members of the musical committee included: the Revds Benjamin Webb, John Mason Neale, Samuel Stephenson Greatheed, and John Lake Crompton; and Messrs Alexander James Beresford Hope, Francis Henry Dickinson, John David Chambers, and William Dyce.

The Venerable Thomas Thorp

As we have seen above (: 20), Archdeacon Thorp's[1] willingness to accept the presidency of the Cambridge Camden Society lent it a public credibility which greatly contributed to the speed with which it gained the enthusiastic support of members of the University of Cambridge at all levels. Benjamin Webb's diaries show that Thorp took an active role in the early workings of the Society, and was responsible for introducing Webb to many influential people who would later play key roles in the movement. To Benjamin Webb, Thorp was not only a mentor but a friend.[2]

Archdeacon Thorp's active participation in the daily workings of the Cambridge Camden Society dropped markedly after it reorganized as the Ecclesiological late Cambridge Camden Society in 1845 and made London its new centre. During his twenty years as President (1839–59), however, he

---

[1] Thomas Thorp, BA 1819, MA 1822, BD 1842, Trinity College, Cambridge; elected Fellow of Trinity in 1820, served as Assistant Tutor 1822–34, Junior Dean 1829–32, Tutor 1833–44, and Vice Master 1843–4. He was Archdeacon of Bristol 1836–73, and rector of Kemerton, Gloucs., 1839–d. 24 February 1877. Venn, *Alumni Cantabrigienses*.

[2] Webb diaries. It could be said that to Thorp Webb owed both his money and his wife, i.e. 'maintenance grants' amounting to £50, a debt Thorp forgave him on 17 March 1845; and an introduction to his future wife, Miss Mill, on 18 April 1841.

served an important role as the Society's most senior and respected public spokesman. E.J. Boyce states, 'No one contributed more to the success and wide-spread influence of the CCS than did the President by his annual address and his unflinching defence of its main principles.'[3] High praise of his eloquence as an orator was also paid him in the *Guardian's* review of the first Oxford Architectural Congress (1858), the brainchild of the Hon. Frederick Lygon, M.P. (later the 6th Earl of Beauchamp), which stated that Thorp's speeches were 'by far the most effective of any which were addressed to the congress.' The report continued:

> He [Thorp] maintained that, however much it was a subject of congratulation that ecclesiology had become independent of controversy, yet the vast material movement had during its progress been most beneficially connected with the restoration of Church principles, and would probably never have succeeded without them.[4]

Kemerton

In 1839 Archdeacon Thorp was presented to the rectory of Kemerton in the diocese of Gloucester and Bristol, a village with a population of barely more than five hundred. Village life was evidently to Thorp's liking, since he turned down the more prestigious offer of Great St Mary's, Cambridge, in 1843,[5] and remained rector of Kemerton for the rest of his life. With the help of a succession of gifted and zealous curates he engineered and oversaw a remarkable transformation in his little village.[6]

So eager was Thorp to secure the services of Benjamin Webb that he offered him the curacy of Kemerton more than a year before Webb's ordination. On 17 December 1842 Webb made his subscription to the Thirty-Nine Articles, was charged by the Bishop of Gloucester and Bristol to 'keep to the *via media*' and, on the following day, was ordained deacon.[7] In June 1843 an invitation to preach at Brompton resulted in the unexpected offer of that church's curacy by the incumbent, the Revd W.J. Irons, but Webb's sense of loyalty dictated that he 'could not desert Thorp.'[8]

Benjamin Webb finally arrived at Kemerton to take up his duties on Friday, 4 August 1843. He lost no time in setting to the work of ecclesiological reform. Only two days later, on his first Sunday, he notes, 'Placed stools in chancel as sedilia. I preached *in surplice*. (Flute and bass viol in choir).' The

---

[3] Boyce (1888) 10.
[4] *Guardian,* 654 (16 June 1858) 48.
[5] Webb diaries, 11 December 1843.
[6] Wakeling (1895) 208–9.
[7] Webb diaries. The curacy was originally offered on 20 November 1841, on which date the possibility of a chaplaincy at Trinity College, Cambridge was also discussed.
[8] Webb diaries, 23 June 1843.

next day he 'pulled down the pens [i.e., pews] in church', and on Wednesday he 'gave Charles Smith the Clerk some Gregorians to practise.' On Friday J.M. Neale arrived for a visit, and two days later four clergy vested and took part in the Sunday services. The Gospel and the Epistle were read at the rood screen, and there were sixty-eight communicants.[9] Altar candles were introduced at evensong the next month.[10] There is no indication that any of these innovations caused the slightest disturbance, which suggests that the people had been well prepared for them by Thorp and his curates during Thorp's first four years as rector. Before the end of September 1843, Webb had organized the parish school into three classes; and one of the Cambridge Camden Society's favoured architects, Carpenter, had paid a visit to survey the site designated for a new school, the foundation stone for which was laid the following New Year's Day.[11] Soon thereafter Webb left Kemerton to return to the work of the CCS in Cambridge and London.

The next item on Thorp's agenda for Kemerton was the restoration of the parish church. By November 1846 work was well under way and *The Ecclesiologist* announced admiringly, 'We must mention the gratifying circumstance, that during the whole of the course of the very extensive works, the celebration of daily matins and evensong within the church has not once been omitted.'[12] In 1849 the *Guardian,* which at that time acted as a primary organ for High Church and Tractarian views, carried a report on the anniversary celebration of the consecration of Kemerton parish church, and revealed that Archdeacon Thorp, with partial assistance from the congregation, had spent £5000 on the restoration. One-third of the parish's 560 inhabitants were said to be communicants, a very high proportion for those days, particularly when one considered that the religious loyalties of the village were split between the parish church, one Roman Catholic church, and two Nonconformist chapels, and children were not communicants prior to confirmation. Matins on the occasion had included the Tallis responses sung by the choir and 'followed generally by the congregation'; psalm 24 was chanted by the choir, led by the assistant curate, the Revd C.T. Heartley (: 90–1); the *Te Deum* was chanted to the 5th Gregorian tone; the *Benedictus* was Battishill's in F; and the anthem was *Unto Thee, O Lord,* attributed to Farrant. The litany was chanted, again using the Tallis harmonies, and the *Old 100th Psalm* was sung as an introit to Communion, which was intoned by the rector, Archdeacon Thorp.[13]

Four years later the *Guardian* carried several letters to the editor remonstrating in favour of better choral services at St Paul's Cathedral and Westminster Abbey. On 9 November 1853, 'P.P.' wrote to say that he had

---

[9] Webb diaries, 4,6,7,9,12, and 13 August 1843. Original underlined.
[10] Webb diaries, 18 September 1843.
[11] Webb diaries, 27, 29, and 30 September 1843; 1 January 1844.
[12] *The Ecclesiologist,* 6/53 (November 1846) 194.
[13] *Guardian,* 198 (31 October 1849) 717.

recently attended the dedication festival of a small country parish, and that the special choral service which had been sung by the choir on that occasion had so pleased the parishioners, that they had begged the rector to continue it on a regular basis. This provided a whipping stick for the metropolitan churches: if such a thing could be accomplished in the country, what possible excuse did more populated and wealthier districts have? The correspondent continued,

> I would recommend this subject especially to the consideration of colleges in our Universities, which collect in their chapels daily a greater number of youths of quick intellect and refined pronunciation, than all the rustic pig-driving boys of the village I speak of, whose Dorian dialect had to be broken up and moulded into good English by the indefatiguable Curate who framed them, before they could be qualified to perform their part in a scene which showed what the Church could do with her services if she would only use the materials to her hand.[14]

Later that month another correspondent asked if the person responsible for this remarkable feat could share how he had accomplished it, for the benefit of fellow curates who wished to do the same among their own people.[15] This prompted a long letter from the Revd Charles Tebbott Heartley, who had taken his BA from Queens' College, Cambridge, in 1849, and since that time had been assistant curate at Kemerton. The village choir in question was Kemerton's; and his letter, together with two by Archdeacon Thorp published several years later, provide a detailed history of their remarkable parish choir.

The spiritual foundation for the formation of a choir had been laid in 1845 and 1846 by one of Heartley's predecessors, the Revd Robert Suckling.[16] At first Suckling had been suspicious of choral service, but he had become convinced of its value shortly before his death, when he saw the good it worked in the hearts of his former people.[17] Unable to do more because of ill health, he had taught a few boys to sing a small number of psalm chants and metrical hymn tunes by rote. When Heartley arrived in 1849, he added three boys to the five who were already in place, and persuaded them to attend practices four or five times each week for three months, during which time they learned to read music. Since it was common in the country for boys to go to work at age ten, Heartley managed to get together enough money to pay them each six pence per week, so that their parents would allow them to stay at school longer, and therefore remain also in the choir. (He recommended that no other curate undertake such a work without some guarantee of at least £20 per annum to sustain it.) Two older boys began to learn to play the organ. At the end of the three months, volunteer men were invited to join the practices

---

[14] *Guardian*, 414 (9 November 1853) 748.
[15] *Guardian*, 417 (30 November 1853) 796.
[16] *Clergy List*, 1845, 1846.
[17] Letters by Archdeacon Thomas Thorp, *Guardian*, 518 (7 November 1855) 824; and, 521 (28 November 1855) 875.

two nights a week. So great had been the progress, Heartley wrote, that 'we now have full choral service every night. We are masters of about fifty anthems, and of such a number of chants and psalm tunes as are necessary for the performance of service.' It was true, he said, that they had been requested to continue full choral service on Sundays since the last commemoration. Not only had these services attracted parishioners who had not attended church regularly for years, but people were walking distances of up to five miles to worship with the congregation.[18]

Thorp revealed that, since the introduction of choral services, it had been his policy to have one service on Sunday afternoon 'said plainly', i.e. monotoned, with catechising and only the canticles and a metrical psalm sung. It was this service which, after the commemoration of 1853, the congregation had asked 'almost unanimously' to have changed permanently to full choral service; but Thorp had declined, 'out of deference to the habits and prejudices of those who attend at no other time.' He had, however, introduced an additional Sunday evening service during the six winter months with an elaborate anthem and chanted psalms. Writing in the autumn of 1855, Thorp confirmed that this service was by far the most popular one; the congregation which attended it was 'ten times that in the afternoon.' On the previous Sunday, he reported, 'the church, which is large enough to contain the whole parish, including three denominations of Dissenters, was every place filled; and, I may add, except when engaged in prayer or praise, every voice and limb as still as death.'[19]

The services were intoned morning and evening on Sundays and weekdays. Introduction of the practice of intoning the service at Kemerton had been a 'spontaneous and unforeseen consequence of a choral necessity'; in fact, Thorp argued, it was a logical necessity to maintain the unity of the service, and had come about gradually and naturally. On Sunday and weekday evenings, the psalms were sung antiphonally by the choir to a single chant. 'In this,' Thorp added, 'a great number of the congregation join; and it is the most affecting, stirring, inspiring element of congregational worship.' Thorp gave C.T. Heartley full credit for having perfected the choir. He insisted, 'I know nothing of music' (although he had learned to intone the services when that had become desirable), and continued:

> I could not... train a choir. I have done nothing here but (1) find out the best instruments, (2) afford them full scope for doing that particular thing they were made to do; (3) give everybody and everything a fair trial; (4) fear nothing and nobody; and (5) 'whatever my hand found to do, do it with all my might.'[20]

---

[18] Letter by Heartley dated 12 December 1853, *Guardian,* 420 (21 December 1853) 858–9.
[19] *Guardian,* 518 (7 November 1855) 824.
[20] *Guardian* 521 (28 November 1855) 875.

These words provide a fair summary of Thomas Thorp's whole life and ministry. It was an admirable model for younger ecclesiologists.

The anniversary of the consecration of Kemerton parish church provided an annual occasion for parish festivities. In regard to the special services held in October 1854, the *Guardian* reported, 'The Revd Sir F. Ouseley presided at the organ, and, altogether, the performance was one that would have been creditable to many of our cathedrals, the neighbouring one of Gloucester certainly not excepted.' This fact would hardly surprise anyone, however, since the *Guardian* was sure that, 'Our readers are aware that Kemerton is famed for possessing a parish choir of no mean excellence, formed out of the rugged materials found in a village numbering only [528] in population.'[21]

There are several interesting connections between Ouseley and Kemerton. Having served his first curacy at St Barnabas', Pimlico during its troubled infancy under the Revd W.J.E. Bennett, Ouseley had been in frequent contact with leading Tractarians and ecclesiologists, where he formed an intimate friendship with the Bennett family. In 1851 the Revd F.H. Bennett (brother of the Tractarian vicar of St Paul's, Knightsbridge and St Barnabas', Pimlico) moved to Kemerton. Having experienced persecution for his church views and for restoring plainsong in the services as curate-in-charge of St John's, Worcester during the widespread 'no-popery' riots of 1850 and 1851, F.H. Bennett decided to give up his work as a parish priest, but chose to live in Kemerton, which had already achieved a reputation as 'one of the centres of progress, especially in Church music.'[22]

We are told by W.J.E. Bennett's biographer that on one of Ouseley's visits to F.H. Bennett in Kemerton, a discussion was held concerning the problematic question of how to point psalms for Anglican chants. Bennett is reported to have concluded his comments by quipping that, after all, Gregorian chants were, in fact, better. 'On this,' we are told, 'Sir Frederick exclaimed, waving about his arms in agony, "Then I've lived in vain!"'[23] It is interesting to note that single Anglican chants played such a large role in the music of Kemerton parish church. It is also informative to note that the music chosen for the morning and evening services of the 1854 commemoration of the church's consecration included the 'full responses of Tallis', and selections from the 'elaborate compositions of Nares, Rogers, King, Crotch and Elvey.'[24] This is not the repertoire one might expect to find in the parish church services of the president of a society which is generally supposed to have promoted the use of plainsong and counterpoint from the era of Palestrina, Byrd and Gibbons. Certainly the music performed in Kemerton is indicative of the personal

---

[21] *Guardian*, 464 (25 October 1854) 817; the population figure was corrected in the next issue of the *Guardian*, 465 (1 November 1854) 842.
[22] F. Bennett (1909) 283, 285.
[23] F. Bennett (1909) 151.
[24] *Guardian*, 464 (25 October 1854) 817.

musical taste of the curate, C.T. Heartley. His sympathy with the views of Ouseley is apparent from the fact that Heartley eventually left Kemerton to become Headmaster (1856–1861) of Ouseley's model choir school, St Michael's College, Tenbury. But it is also clear that Archdeacon Thorp's views on church music were no less catholic than on other matters.

Thorp and the 'mutilation' of choral service at St Mark's College, Chelsea

One of the most notorious attacks on the movement to revive choral worship occurred in May 1855, when Sir Henry Thompson induced the National Society to review the manner in which the services were conducted at St Mark's College, Chelsea. It was an attack upon the very heart of the movement, as well as the person most responsible for it, Thomas Helmore. Knowing full well that the Bishop of London opposed the practice of intoning, Thompson persuaded the Governing Committee of the College to confer with the Bishop on the matter and, on the basis of their conversation, the Committee resolved on 24 May 1855 'that the intoning of the prayers should henceforth be discontinued.' Initially the decision was hushed up, since it would not take effect until the following academic year, but when it came out in the pages of the *Guardian* on 1 August 1855, indignation and fury hardly suffices to describe the reaction from ecclesiologists. The *Guardian* served as the forum for the controversy's public battleground until the end of November. That this should have caused a national outcry among the supporters of choral service is not surprising; yet it is a significant fact, which has not previously been emphasized,[25] that their protest was organized under the highly vocal leadership of Archdeacon Thomas Thorp. Thorp wrote four lengthy letters to the *Guardian*, and undertook to solicit and gather signatures for the official petition of protest.

Opponents of intoning the choral service cited the following objections:

1. it was offensive to some of the St Mark's Council members and to many London clergy;
2. too much of the students' time and too much of the National Society's money – an alleged additional £1000 – was spent on it;
3. choral services tended to produce schoolmasters with 'undesirable' theological tendencies, i.e. High Churchmen who, by implication, tended toward 'popery';
4. schoolmasters were being educated for parochial work, and therefore the worship of their chapel should be one which was a realistic reflection of what parochial worship would be, rather than one which might make them dissatisfied with something less;

---

[25] Rainbow (1970) 190–2.

5. schoolmasters should not take on the role of musical missionaries;
6. the general introduction of choral services would be injurious to the Church of England; and
7. identification with intoned choral services linked the National Society to one party of the Church of England, which was therefore injurious to the reputation it wished to preserve for its catholicity.

Claiming to represent the views of 'thousands' of clergy and laity, Thompson summed up:

> My move against the superfluous music at St Mark's is of no significance or power as a High Church or a Low Church proceeding. If it has any meaning as a movement amongst Churchmen, its language is merely this – 'We believe the Church of England to be a very large place, and we will not allow any party to claim to themselves the exclusive merit of orthodoxy. The National Society is intended to occupy a basis as broad as that of the Church of England.[26]

Needless to say, such flawed reasoning did not go unanswered.

Supporters of choral service in its integrity immediately threatened to withhold their subscriptions to the National Society, and were quick to point out:

1. The offence which a few anonymous London clergy and board members felt for intoned services was essentially irrelevant in a situation where the vast majority of those who actually participated in the services on a regular basis wanted it. A former student of the College wrote of the great and general regret which the innovation would cause among his fellow alumni: 'there is no single point connected with the college on which we all set so much store as our much-loved service.'[27] Furthermore, for twelve years St Mark's had been admired nationally by a large section of the clergy as a model for parish worship; and for the country clergyman who eagerly attended services when passing through London, the services had been,

    > a momentary realisation of an ideal which he carries back to his parish, and recollects with satisfaction amidst the grievances of his village choir; which he talks of, to which he takes his friends in order to convert them to the idea of a worship beautiful as well as sincere.[28]

2. Thompson was taken to task for fabricating the accusation that the choral services occasioned any additional outlay of funds. There was no evidence whatsoever to substantiate this, his opponents claimed,[29] and the fact that neither he nor anyone else ever contradicted them suggests that they may have been right. Moreover, it was absurd to imply that students would lose

---

[26] Letters from Sir Henry Thompson, *Guardian*, 510 (12 September 1855) 692; and 514 (17 October 1855) 771–2. Quotation, 772.
[27] *Guardian*, 512 (3 October 1855) 740.
[28] Editorial, *Guardian*, 509 (5 September 1855) 677.
[29] *Guardian*, 511 (26 September 1855) 723.

any less time to choral services if the priest's part were read instead of intoned.
3. Choral service inculcated a love of duty. Of the two hundred and eleven teachers who had been trained at St Mark's, two hundred and two were known still to be actively engaged in teaching, a greater percentage than from any other training institution, and not one had converted to Roman Catholicism.[30]
4. Any intellectual education should aim at 'correctness of apprehension and reasoning', and this should include opening the mind to be susceptible to the perception of beauty. Such an end could not best be obtained by lowering an artistic standard to the level commonly associated with parochial life.[31] If it were injurious to one's future in a parish to experience great art as a student, *The Ecclesiologist* chimed in satirically,

> then on the same principle King's College Chapel ought to be pulled down without delay at least to half its height, and a plain timber roof substituted for the groining, as the sublimity of that building must occasion dissatisfaction with the humbler architecture of village churches.[32]

5. The assertion that schoolmasters should not be musical missionaries begged the question of why the National Society had so actively trained its teachers in the art and practice of music since Hullah started his singing classes in 1841. The real problem was obviously that Thompson and his cronies' personal prejudice was based on ignorance. They were afraid that the well-trained graduates of St Mark's would promote a kind of music which they had neither the requisite knowledge nor the inclination to appreciate and, by extension, a form of worship which demanded more of them than they cared to give.
6. Archdeacon Thorp challenged those who objected to choral services to produce tangible reasons for their objection. Until they could do so, St Mark's ought to be governed by established principles, rather than the fluctuating whims of individuals. These individuals, he said, should,

> listen to those who ought to know something about the matter, having worked at it in every imaginable way of experiment, and against every kind of hindrance and discouragement, for many years, and who, while they are divided as to the suitableness of choral service to general use – many of them believing it to be the most devotional kind of worship for devout worshippers, but nearly all concurring in the conviction that our present congregations are not yet devout enough to appreciate it – are unanimous in deprecating, as at once unnecessary and inexpedient, the abrogation – and still more the mutilation – of it in an Educational institution where it is already established.[33]

---

[30] *Guardian*, 504 (1 August 1855) 593; and 510 (12 September 1855) 694.
[31] *Guardian*, 518 (7 November 1855) 825.
[32] *The Ecclesiologist*, 16/110 (October 1855) 310.
[33] Archdeacon Thorp, *Guardian*, 518 (7 November 1855) 824.

The Ecclesiologist added, 'We are no advocates for the general or indiscriminate adoption of Choral Service in Parish churches.' The kind of worship which Thompson advocated, it continued, was a vast improvement on the 'model' services of thirty years earlier, but if improvement was admitted as a possibility, then one wondered how the proposed change could possibly be designated as such. It was only to be expected that further improvements would yet be discovered which would make the services more edifying and popular; and at the same time, the extravagances of current experiments would surface and be discarded.[34]

7. Choral service should not be identified as a badge of any party in the Church of England, Thorp demanded, and even if people perceived it as such, that perception had nothing to do with reality. He reiterated that even dissenters, notably the Revd Thomas Binney, promoted choral services, a fact which others used to heap scorn on the untenable position taken by enemies of choral services that such worship led to Rome.[35] The *Guardian* insisted that advocates of choral service did not support it because of any supposed connection with the High Church party, but because,

it is good and beautiful in its kind – because it is a successful experiment in a direction in which they believe that experiments ought to be tried boldly – a successful attempt to render available for the service of God that susceptibility to beauty which surely He has not given us in vain.[36]

Archdeacon Thorp stated that no supporter of the choral service had ever made any exclusive claim to orthodoxy; that if, in fact, the National Society wished to make any claim to catholicity, and Thompson and his supporters really believed that the Church of England was a 'very large place', then there should be no objection to retaining choral service in this *one* of the three training colleges. In September 1855 Thorp identified the purpose of the attack on choral worship as a simple attempt by Thompson and his party to undermine the successes of their rivals; by November, Thorp feared that the real design of the opposition was to put down choral service and to drive its supporters out of the Church.[37]

In late August 1855, Thomas Helmore wrote to the *Guardian* to explain that the new prohibition of intoning was intended to apply only to Morning Prayer on ordinary days and on Sundays; yet he encouraged those concerned about the innovation to make their protest known. Ecclesiologists and their High Church allies were fighting for a principle; and compromise was not a concept which came into a matter of principle. *The Ecclesiologist* put it, with its usual directness:

---

[34] *The Ecclesiologist*, 16/110 (October 1855) 309.
[35] *Guardian*, 518 (7 November 1855) 824; and 504 (1 August 1855) 593.
[36] *Guardian*, 518 (7 November 1855) 825.
[37] *Guardian*, 510 (19 September 1855) 708; and 518 (7 November 1855) 824.

> The principle we speak of is one that has been acted on by every devout person, from the time when 'Abel brought of the firstlings of his flock, and of the fat thereof,' to the present day; namely, that what we offer to Almighty God should be the best that we have.[38] (: 43, 61–2, 88, 159–60)

Clearly a service which was only read, when the congregation and clergy were not only perfectly able and willing to sing it, but desired to do so, was not the best offering they could make. Unfortunately for ecclesiologists, this was neither the first nor the last time when no amount of reasoning could change the minds of those in power.

The Revd Professor William Hodge Mill

In 1813 William Hodge Mill took his BA degree from Trinity College, Cambridge, as Sixth Wrangler, and was elected Fellow of the College. In 1820 he became the first Principal of Bishop's College, Calcutta, where he served until his return to Cambridge in 1838. Dr Mill's involvement with the Cambridge Camden Society began during its first year of existence. He joined the Society at its first evening meeting on 28 March 1840, which was reported to have been 'remarkably full.'[39] On 14 May 1840 Benjamin Webb wrote to his (unbeknown to anyone at that time) future father-in-law to ask him to invite the Archbishop of Canterbury, to whom Mill had served as examining and domestic chaplain in the late 1830s,[40] to become a patron of the Society. Two days later Mill wrote back to say that the Archbishop had accepted. In spite of this correspondence, Webb's diaries reveal that he was not actually introduced to Mill until the following November.[41]

Dr Mill's role in the Cambridge Camden Society and the ECCS was one of advisor and counsellor, very much 'behind the scenes', but very substantial in influence. Writing shortly after his death, *The Ecclesiologist* revealed,

> though he was not concerned with the management of our pages, yet from his position in the committee of the Ecclesiological Society, [he] was in habits of the closest intercourse with all who are responsible for our good and evil... his loss is a personal and irreparable blow. How great that loss is none know but those who were privileged to profit by his counsels.[42]

Regarding his character, they who knew him better than anyone else continued:

---

[38] *The Ecclesiologist*, 16/110 (October 1855) 310. Helmore in *Guardian*, 507 (22 August 1855) 644.
[39] *Cambridge Chronicle*, 4 April 1840.
[40] *Guardian*, 421 (28 December 1853) 884 gives the year 1838; Venn *Alumni Cantabrigiense* gives the year 1839.
[41] Webb diaries, 14 and 16 May 1840; 7 November 1840.
[42] *The Ecclesiologist*, 15/100 (February 1854) 4–5.

Without technical knowledge of the details of manipulated construction, he had a keen and intuitive perception of aesthetic beauty: his eminently candid and open character gave him a deep insight into what was truthfulness in art: while in some branches of our associated pursuits, such as music, he possessed a rare and scientific knowledge which, unusual in any age, is almost unknown in our own. Add to which his mild wisdom and loving counsels often prevailed it may be, to curb petulancies, and to check indiscretions, from which, pardonable perhaps in the outset of our career, we trust that we have long since been withheld. We trust that his spirit may be with all our labours.[43]

Three days after his death on Christmas Day 1853, the *Guardian* wrote:

Dr Mill threw the weight of his learning, his character, and his influence, into the ranks of those who have conducted the Catholic revival of the Church of England in our own time, and as circumstances invested him with the responsibility of a leader, there is probably no single person whose loss will be more deeply and generally felt.[44]

Evidence of Dr Mill's musical ability and love of ecclesiastical music abounds. We have seen that the *Hymnal Noted* was the result of a musical evening in his Brasted rectory, where ancient Latin hymns of the Church had been sung. (: 65–6) In 1849 Dr Mill's musical competence as a priest received brief notice in the national newspapers. In October 1848 he had been elected Regius Professor of Hebrew at Cambridge, a position which was attached to a canonry of Ely Cathedral. In late 1848 the Dean of Bristol Cathedral, the Very Revd Charles Lamb (who was also Master of Corpus Christi College, Cambridge), issued an order that henceforth the intoning of services by his cathedral clergy would be discontinued; a move which was the result of the recent appointment of a musically incompetent minor canon. This caused a national outcry which raged in the press during the latter months of 1848 and most of 1849, resulting in the restoration of cathedral service in its full integrity following a visitation by the Bishop of Gloucester and Bristol. Early in the controversy, the Precentor of Ely, the Revd J.H. Henderson, wrote to the *Guardian* to point out that, rather than further mutilating the service, cathedrals should work to restore them to the splendour which was meant to be theirs. Ely had recently restored the practice of intoning the Litany, he wrote, and it was the practice of all of the canons of Ely, including the recently elected Professor Mill, to intone the service.[45]

Brasted, Kent

In 1843 Archbishop Howley presented Dr Mill to the rectory of Brasted, near Sevenoaks in Kent. Benjamin Webb declined Mill's offer of the Brasted

---

[43] *The Ecclesiologist*, 15/100 (February 1854) 5.
[44] *Guardian*, 421 (28 December 1853) 884.
[45] *Guardian*, 159 (31 January 1849) 75.

curacy in January 1846, but by Easter of the same year he seems to have been more or less in permanent residence there. No doubt Maria Mill, to whom Webb became engaged in June 1846 and whom he married on 21 April 1847, was a primary attraction; but it is evident from Webb's diaries that he took an active part in the life of the parish church, whether his presence was in an official capacity or not. The Revd H.L. Jenner (: 19, 129–32, 210–11) was a frequent visitor; and many evenings were spent by all together in the Mills' rectory singing and playing music. On 11 August 1846 Palestrina became the first composer whose works were specifically mentioned in Webb's diaries to have been sung within this context.[46]

During this time ecclesiological reforms were undertaken in Brasted parish church. On Easter 1846, new hangings were introduced into the chancel, and the roodscreen was draped with yew and a garland of flowers. The Tuesday after Easter 1846, four clergy (including Mill, Webb, and Jenner) sang evensong at Brasted, 'sitting in *choir:* for first time.' In March 1847 Webb reports 'a long vestry, which at last determined to let us pull down our west gallery'; and with typical speed, lest anyone have time to change his mind, demolition began only three days later.[47]

Benjamin Webb returned to Brasted (diocese of Canterbury) as curate in December 1848. At first Archbishop Sumner refused to license him 'on account of Durandus'; but a meeting between the two was arranged, and Webb records, 'The Abp kept me 95 minutes: snubbed Durandus: read 2 Sermons: & was satisfied. He was very kind: but awfully Lutheran.'[48] The licence was granted, but the Archbishop had not heard the last of Brasted.

Not only did Dr Mill effect the collaboration of Thomas Helmore and John Mason Neale on the idea of a hymnal during 1849, but the assistance of Frederick Helmore was enlisted to form a choir in Brasted. On 19 December of that year, the younger brother of the more famous Thomas Helmore arrived in Brasted and, accompanied by Benjamin Webb, went to the parish school to choose boys for a choir. Daily rehearsals began on 21 January 1850, after which the adults often concluded the evening by singing Gregorian hymns and early church polyphony at the Mills' home. Within one week Webb pronounced the choir's performance of choral service 'really very successful', with nearly thirty people in the choir. On 3 February Webb composed a set of

---

[46] Webb diaries, 1846: especially 7 January, 6–12 April, 23–25 June, 11 August. According to Webb's diaries, evenings at Brasted divided roughly into three types: musical evenings, 'dull' evenings, and evenings spent with visitors.

[47] Webb diaries, 11 and 14 April 1846; 19 and 22 March 1847. On Wednesday of Holy Week 1847, after only five days as curate of Christ Church, St Pancras, Webb persuaded the incumbent, the Revd William Dodsworth (former incumbent of Margaret Chapel), to introduce a white altar frontal there on Easter. Webb diaries, 31 March 1847.

[48] Webb diaries, 11 December 1848.

rules for the governance of the choir, which he explained to the parents of the choristers on the following day during personal calls to each; on 8 February he notes, 'unison adopted, & Laws accepted.' From the beginning of the new choir, Webb's diaries show that he regularly attended its rehearsals. It would appear that, except when Frederick Helmore was in residence for the purpose of intensive training, Webb and his fellow curate of Brasted 1849–52, Thomas Edmund Heygate, not only oversaw but conducted the rehearsals.

The happy success of the new choir was not long to remain unchallenged. The 'Papal Aggression' of the restoration of the Roman Catholic hierarchy in Britain and the resulting anti-popery riots of 1850 (: 67) disturbed the peace not only in populated centres like London (the riots at St Barnabas', Pimlico, being the most notorious), but also in small villages like Brasted. November 1850 found Dr Mill, Benjamin Webb, and Thomas Heygate embroiled in a local agitation which ecclesiologists came to see as an important battle for their principles. It eventually caught the attention of the national newspapers because of the perplexing positions taken by the diocesan, Archbishop Sumner, due to the possibility that his stance might have widespread ramifications for the Church at large.

A series of letters from Webb to Mill (who spent four months of the year in Ely and Cambridge) reveal that two residents of Brasted, Sir Stephen Hancock and a Mr Faulkner, had begun to stir parishioners up already by 6 November 1850. Faulkner was a trouble-maker who had stopped attending the parish church years earlier when he imagined incorrectly, and was told so by Dr Mill, that a curate had advocated the doctrine of transubstantiation in a sermon. Ever since then Faulkner had slandered Mill as being 'Romish.'[49] Sensing that Hancock and Faulkner saw a golden opportunity to harass Dr Mill and gain public prestige by setting themselves up as valiant defenders of Protestantism, Benjamin Webb urgently requested Dr Mill to write some moderate form of protest against the 'Papal Aggression' which could be circulated before Hancock and Faulkner had time to create radical trouble. This Mill did. Hancock and Faulkner were enraged. They responded by denouncing the Puseyites, accusing Mill and Webb of teaching popish doctrines, attacking the work of the parish choir, and circulated a rival petition. Initially Webb felt secure, since the doctrinal charge was blatantly untrue, and he thought that the 'enemy' underestimated the fact that the choir was 'essentially popular, and would like to be suppressed as little as we should.'[50] If objections were made concerning the ritual of parish services, Webb pointed out, 'There has not been the least alteration in the ritual since we went into the choir – in 1846', and the

---

[49] Lambeth, MS 1491, Papers of William Hodge Mill. f.133–7. Letter from Mill to Archbishop Sumner, 29 November 1850.
[50] Lambeth, MS 1491, f. 88–100. Letters from Benjamin Webb to Dr W.H. Mill; 6,7,13, and 14 November 1850.

use of candlesticks on the altar could hardly be denounced, since they had been there for five years without complaint.[51]

Thomas Heygate suggested that a Sunday evening choral service be added during Advent, so that the afternoon service could be merely read, thinking that this would quell the impending storm.[52] F.H. Dickinson (: 137–9) wrote to urge that moderation was the best tactic with extremists.[53] But when John Mason Neale heard of the attack about to be made on chanting, he wrote to Mill, 'I do trust... that you will allow the Archbishop to take any steps, if he dares, sooner than give way. If it were to be said that you had given it up, your example would of course be triumphantly quoted by our enemies.'[54] Benjamin Webb and Dr Mill agreed that it was not the time to make any change which might look like a concession, since there was no certainty that anything would be gained by it, and the validity of the principles involved might be undermined in the public eye.[55]

At the same time, Faulkner announced that he intended to memorialize the Archbishop and demand the abolition of the choir. Before the end of November he had managed to get up a petition with three hundred and seven signatures, the substance of which read:

> In our own Parish Church we no longer recognise the 'House of Prayer' which was endeared to us by the sweet recollection of former years. A large portion of the Service including the Litany, and several of the prayers and other Solemn devotions are chaunted to music, ill adapted, as we feel it, to the occasion and discordant to our notions. We object to the numerous Choristeur [sic] Men and Boys, dressed in white Surplices, who excite Curiosity and derision in the profane, and distract the attention of the devout, frequent movement from place to place, genuflexion, and other superstitious practices of the Romish Church.[56]

Even considering that the petition included the signatures of a large number of dissenters, and that one hundred and seven of the names included were those of illiterate people, many of whom in all probability did not understand what they were being asked to sign, but made their mark when asked by their social superiors to do so, such a long list of signatures naturally gained the attention of the Archbishop. Trouble continued, and on 1 December 1850 Webb reported to Mill, 'They burnt the Pope, & nine *choristers* (in honour of us) in effigy at Sundridge on Friday.'[57]

---

[51] Lambeth, MS 1491, f.101–2. Letter from Webb to Mill, 16 November 1850.
[52] Lambeth, MS 1491, f.101–2. Letter from Webb to Mill, 17 November 1850.
[53] Lambeth, MS 1491, f.117–118. Letter from F.H. Dickinson to Mill, 20 November 1850.
[54] Lambeth, MS 1750, f.116–117. Letter from Neale to Mill, 20 November 1850.
[55] Lambeth, MS 1491, f.107–9. Letter from Webb to Mill, 20 November 1850.
[56] Lambeth, MS 1491, f.111–115. Memorial to W.H. Mill from parishioners of Brasted.
[57] Lambeth, MS 1491, f.139–40. Original underlined.

A countermemorial was drawn up in support of the choir which expressed the great satisfaction many parishioners felt with the choral service; and in spite of the fact that it gained the signatures of nearly all of the most 'respectable' people in the parish, the Archbishop was not disposed to favour the practice of intoning, and he took action the following March. On 7 March 1851, Benjamin Webb noted in his diary, 'Archiepiscopus scripsit ad Dr Mill, cantum probutens!!' On Sunday 9 March, the afternoon service was conducted without music. The following Sunday an evening choral service was added, in an apparent attempt to save it from total abolition. Attendance figures recorded at the end of the month show that the parish was indeed split: 11 a.m. celebration: 156 persons; 3:30 Evening Prayer with catechism, without music: 103 persons; 7 p.m. choral evensong: 101 persons.[58]

This should have accommodated all parties, but Faulkner, who persisted in inciting trouble, was out for blood. On 27 August 1851 the *Guardian* reported renewed rumours that the Archbishop of Canterbury intended to prosecute clergymen in his diocese for intoning the service. This was confirmed in a leader in the *Times*,[59] and finally led to a monition dated 15 September 1851, which was served not on Mill, as before, but on Benjamin Webb. It forbade Webb:

1. to process with surpliced lay attendants at morning service,
2. to intone morning prayer or litany,
3. to say the Lord's Prayer during administration of the Lord's Supper anywhere else than at the north end of the Communion table,
4. to mix water with the wine, or
5. to withhold wine from the communicants.[60]

Apparently at the suggestion of one of the Archbishop's advisors,[61] Faulkner took it upon himself to observe and report whether the monition was obeyed. In August 1851 the *Guardian* ridiculed the 'gentleman' who had instituted the suit [Faulkner] for attending services not to worship, but to look for ways to continue to persecute the clergy.[62] Webb tells us that one of the churchwardens and Faulkner attended matins the Sunday following the monition, 'making notes and behaving shamefully.'[63] In an article entitled 'The Inquisition at Brasted', the *Guardian* chronicled the Archbishop's appointment of a

---

[58] Webb diaries, 7, 9, 16 and 30 March 1851.
[59] Also cited in the *Guardian* 300 (3 September 1851) 633.
[60] Lambeth, MS 1491, f.152. It is utterly unbelievable that Webb would have withheld wine from communicants. Obviously he had been accused of a blatantly Roman Catholic practice by his enemies.
[61] Lambeth, MS 1491, f.162–3. Letter from Archbishop Sumner to Mill, 18 October 1853.
[62] *Guardian*, 299 (27 August 1851) 613.
[63] Webb diaries, 28 September 1851.

proctor, the proctor's appointment of a spy, the unseemly and reprehensible way in which such spying reflected on the Archbishop, and denounced the whole affair as 'indecent' and 'disgraceful.'[64]

On 29 September 1851 Dr Mill wrote to the Archbishop to report that everything previously sung during the service was now read, 'because the absence of proper vestment in those who should have been the chief singers (which was by implication condemned in the monition) would have impaired the character of a choral service.' This included the prayers, psalms, canticles, litany with prayers and response, the Nicene Creed before the Sermon, the *Sanctus* and the *Gloria in excelsis*.[65] The Archbishop replied that he could well imagine that a portion of the congregation would find this painful, but that he had acted 'on account of those *without* rather than those *within* the pale; and who made it a subject of complaint that they were unable to comprehend the service so conducted.' He continued:

> I had not designed to interdict the chanting of the Canticles: but I trust you will not return to the chanting of more of the Psalms than the Venite, as they must necessarily be a blank to many of those who can read, and to all who cannot. I regret that you persist in *intoning* or *monotoning* the prayers. Nothing, as it seems to me, can be less like S Paul's determination to 'pray with the understanding.' I shall think it my duty to refuse my licence to any curate who follows that practice.[66]

That anyone could advocate the singing of the *Venite*, 'O come, let us sing unto the Lord,' and then insist that the rest of the psalms be read was something which ecclesiologists never could understand. Dr Mill staunchly defended the choral service in its full integrity, and continued to have the evening services intoned as they had been prior to the monition. In the end the introduction of a non-choral morning service on alternate Sundays was the concession made, an arrangement to which the Archbishop acceded.[67]

The Revd Benjamin Webb

We have seen that music played a large part in Benjamin Webb's life before and during his student days at Trinity College, Cambridge (: 11, 14–15), that he was an early ecclesiological link to the Motett Choir and its leaders (: 32–3),

---

[64] *Guardian*, 310 (12 November 1851) 786.
[65] Lambeth, MS 1491, f.158–60. Letter from Mill to Archbishop Sumner, 29 September 1851.
[66] Lambeth, MS 1491, f.162–3. Letter from Archbishop Sumner to Mill, 18 October [1851].
[67] *Morning Chronicle* reprinted in the *Guardian*, 309 (5 November 1851) 777; and Lambeth, MS 1491, f.164–5. Letter from Archbishop Sumner to Mill, 24 October 1851.

that he introduced Gregorian chants at Kemerton (: 94), and was intimately involved in the formation of a choir in the parish church at Brasted (: 104–5).

During his curacy under the Revd William Dodsworth at Christ Church, Regent's Park, St Pancras (March 1847–November 1848)[68], Webb was in frequent contact with all of the major figures in the Tractarian and ecclesiological revival. On All Saints' Day 1847, Margaret Chapel was transferred to a temporary site so that the Church of All Saints', Margaret Street (: 118–21) could be constructed on the original one. At the morning service, the Revd Henry Wilberforce celebrated, Benjamin Webb served as deacon, Upton Richards as subdeacon, and five other clergy took part, including William Dodsworth and William Scott. Pusey preached in the afternoon.[69]

Sheen, Staffordshire

At the height of the troubles in Brasted, on 22 August 1851, Alexander James Beresford Hope offered the perpetual curacy of Sheen in Staffordshire to Benjamin Webb, an advowson which Hope had acquired in or before 1848. Due to the remoteness (even by twentieth-century standards of transportation) and inconveniences of the location, Hope persuaded Webb to accept the living only by planting in his mind the goal of making the village into a model parish, and offering substantial financial backing to make it possible. It was 'a sort of ecclesiastical Australia', Hope observed: undeveloped, but with untold possibilities. On 2 October 1851 Webb wrote to the Archbishop and resigned his Brasted curacy in order to accept the offer. On 5 December of the same year Webb was licensed by the Bishop of Lichfield, and he commenced his duties in the parish.[70]

The first item of business was to put the buildings in order, which included the rebuilding of the church, the existing one having been erected between 1828 and 1832. It had no chancel, which ecclesiologists considered to be absolutely essential to the proper performance of the liturgy, and it had never been consecrated. Already under Webb's predecessor, Hope had undertaken to have the necessary work done, and had met the resulting protest by the parishioners with an ultimatum pointing out that either they could allow him to rebuild the church, which was already in poor repair, at no cost to themselves; or they could foot the costs themselves, persist in worshipping in an unconsecrated and unlicensed building, and continue to ignore the question of the legality of the rites performed therein, including marriages. The parishioners were eventually persuaded to accept the offer, and Hope spent £1700 adding a chancel and substantially renewing the building in works designed by

---

[68] Webb diaries, licensed 26 March 1847; 23 October, 22 November 1848.
[69] Lawson (1910) 162; Webb diaries, 1 November 1847.
[70] Law (1925) 184–6; Webb diaries, 22 August, 2 October, 5 and 7 December 1851.

Butterfield. Butterfield also designed an immense new parsonage, and finished a curate's house and parish school from plans begun by C.W. Burleigh, a Leeds based architect.[71] By the time the works were done and Webb had transformed the parish, Hope had come to refer to Sheen as the 'Athens of the moorlands.'[72]

The original scheme discussed by A.J.B. Hope and Benjamin Webb included the establishment of a choir school, which would have predated Sir Frederick Ouseley's at Tenbury (1856) by a number of years. Although the Sheen choir school was never built, Webb was not thereby prevented from establishing choral services. As had been his practice in other parishes, saints' days were observed without fail even before there is evidence of choral service, and within three months of Webb's arrival at Sheen, on St Matthias (24 February) 1852, he recorded in his diary, 'Canticis Litan[ia] et Hymno *Eterna Christi* cantatis.' On 28 April he noted that he had sung matins, and '*Cantavimus psalmos*'; three days later he went 'ad Sheen ad ix, ad exercit[ationem] chori', an entry which would soon become routine; and on 3 May he wrote, 'Choir began practice.'[73] This marks the official formation of a new choir of boys and men. The boys were given breakfast and tea six days a week, began singing daily services as soon as they could manage them, and from June a new schoolmaster, Mr Colson, was engaged for the parish. In July 1852 fifty copies of the words for the *Hymnal Noted* were purchased for the parish church, which suggests that the choir was already learning the ancient hymns.[74]

On 4 August 1852 the completed parish Church of St Luke, Sheen, was consecrated in 'thronged' ceremonies, underwritten by the patron, A.J.B. Hope. The clergy and choir processed in surplices chanting psalm 43, taking up psalm 24 at the entrance to the church, where they were joined by the Revd S.S. Greatheed, who accompanied on the organ. The Revd Thomas Helmore served as precentor for the day. The consecration service, including matins and Holy Communion, began at 10 a.m; the Bishop of Lichfield (Spencer) celebrated, assisted by Webb, and Dr Mill preached. This was followed at 3 p.m. by Litany and confirmation; 5 p.m. first evensong, at which the Bishop preached; and a second evensong at 7 p.m., at which Helmore preached. All four services were 'wholly choral, the Canticles and psalms being chanted, and the *Kyrie, Sanctus,* and *Gloria in Excelsis*, sung to ancient Gregorian melodies.' The hymns *Veni creator* and *Angulare fundamentum* were also

---

[71] A.C.F. Nicoll, *St Luke's Church and Parish, Sheen*, (1984) 43, 45–7.
[72] Law (1925) 190.
[73] Webb diaries, 24 February, 28 April, 1 and 3 May 1852.
[74] *Sheen Church Expenses Account Book,* 1852; *Sheen School Accounts,* 1852. The Webb diaries, 14 July 1855, give a short account of attending vespers and compline at the Cathedral in Chartres, France, during which was sung 'the *O lux beata Trinitas* which we sing on Saturday evenings at Sheen.'

sung. The *Guardian* announced that morning and evening prayers were to be said [i.e. sung] daily in the new church, and that Holy Communion would be administered on Sundays and holydays.[75]

The establishment of the parish choir in 1852 coincided with the appointment of a curate at Sheen, Webb's old friend and fellow curate at Brasted, the Revd Thomas Edmund Heygate. Together they had trained the choir in Brasted, and together again, with the financial support of their patron, they worked an even more rapid transformation in the parish life of Sheen, from one 'inconceivably behindhand into one of model excellence.'[76] The fact that Webb was no longer solely responsible for the parish also allowed him the freedom to spend substantial periods of time away, whether in London on ecclesiological business, with Dr Mill during his residences as canon of Ely, or visiting the Beresford Hopes at Bedgebury, their country estate. In 1858 he exchanged parishes with Dr W.J. Irons, of Holy Trinity, Brompton, for two months.[77] No doubt these breaks from country life helped to prevent Webb from becoming weary of the seclusion of Sheen.

In addition to the daily services, the choir had a regular practice on Saturday mornings. Music-making multiplied exponentially in January 1854, when the schoolmaster started a Friday evening singing class for the villagers, for which he was paid £5 per annum from school funds.[78] Webb attended regularly, to encourage the residents to improve themselves through leisure activities which were less morally dangerous than drinking themselves into oblivion at the local pub, and also to socialize and thereby build bonds of affection with his parishioners.

Apart from their parochial duties, the Webbs and Heygates were in constant social contact. Nearly as often as not, the Heygates would come to tea and stay for an evening of music-making. The two couples must have comprised a vocal quartet, since singing was their primary pastime. By 1856 Benjamin Webb's diary notes 'musica' or 'madrigals' or 'Palestrina' virtually every night; Palestrina (including his *Lamentations* during Lent) is specified seventeen times in eight months of that year. Other composers specified include Mendelssohn (including his 'Quartetts'), Byrd, Wilbye, Mozart, Victoria, Dowland, and Morley.[79] During the first three months of 1857, despite a week's absence in London and intensive writing for various periodicals, no fewer than thirty-five evenings included social music-making, and most of them were held in the parsonage.

---

[75] *Guardian*, 349 (11 August 1852) 541–2; Webb diaries, 4 August 1852.
[76] Obituary of Benjamin Webb, *Saturday Review* (12 December 1885) in OBL: MSS.Eng.misc.d.475, ff. 51–2.
[77] Webb diaries, 25 June, 13 July–23 September 1858.
[78] *Sheen School Accounts*, 1854.
[79] Webb diaries, 18, 23, 25 March, 16 and 27 July, 19 October 1856; 8 January, 21 April, 6 May, 12 October 1858.

Other frequent participants in these musical evenings included the Revd R.E. Wyatt, who donated altar candles in November 1852[80] and eventually married Heygate's sister. The Revd S.S. Greatheed, who had become an intimate friend of the Webbs during their residence in Brasted (: 132–3) and taught Benjamin Webb to play the 'cello,[81] often came on long visits: twenty days over Easter 1854, ten days over Easter 1855, twenty-four days during Lent 1856, and so on, not to mention other shorter visits. In addition to being an organist, 'cellist and sight singer, Greatheed also played the flute which, when combined with Benjamin Webb on 'cello and Maria Webb at the piano, made for many pleasant evenings of trio playing.[82]

The slow pace of life in a small country parish allowed Webb the freedom to read and write voluminously, above all for *The Ecclesiologist*. The frequency with which that periodical is mentioned in his diaries provides ample testimony that Webb was the 'one to whom *The Ecclesiologist* is more indebted than to any of its contributors, as its responsible conductor from the first.'[83] In 1855, while out of parliament, Beresford Hope founded the *Saturday Review*, intended to be a moderate newspaper not tied to any particular party. By the end of 1860 Webb had written more than one hundred articles for it on all manner of aesthetic, literary, artistic and religious topics.[84]

St Andrew's, Wells Street

In 1862 Benjamin Webb, through the influence of Beresford Hope and others, was appointed vicar of St Andrew's, Wells Street, London. Although his remarkable work there lies almost wholly outside the dates under consideration here, it is worth brief attention because it provides great insight into the quiet and sincere way in which this leading ecclesiologist went about his parish work, and evinces a pastoral maturity which has sometimes been criticized for its apparent divergence from youthful opinions.

As Webb had done so well at Sheen and had attempted in his earlier curacies, he made his urban charge into a nationally respected model parish. Upon his death in 1885, the high praise bestowed by all shades of churchmen upon his work at St Andrew's, Wells Street, is astounding.[85] The parish's reputation had come to be built on its choral services, which during Webb's tenure were sung by a full professional choir of men and boys (supplemented by a few volunteers) twice daily. The *Church Review* reported:

---

[80] *Sheen Church Expenses Account Book*, 15 November 1852.
[81] Webb diaries, 12 October 1858.
[82] Webb diaries, 6,7,8,17 April 1857.
[83] *The Ecclesiologist*, 15/100 (February 1854) 4.
[84] Law (1925) 214; Webb diaries, publication of his 110th paper in the *Saturday Review* is noted on 29 December 1860.
[85] Obituaries compiled in and quoted from OBL: MSS.Eng.misc.d.475.

> When Mr Webb entered on his work [at St Andrew's] his soul was grieved at having to abandon Gregorian music[,] to which he had been so much attached, and which was in use at the neighbouring church of All Saints, but, like everything he did, he threw himself into the system of Anglican music for which St Andrew's is so justly famous, and every Churchman is aware of the magnificence of the services... The completeness of the parochial institutions of St Andrew's, however, is much less known: its large schools, its *creche*, its classes, its guilds, its arrangements for the instruction and amusement of the young.[86]

The *Saturday Review* wrote that 'the services in their magnificence were one of the sights of London.'[87] *The Banner*, like many others, deprecated the lack of preferment bestowed upon Webb, under whom 'the highest form of musical worship attainable within the walls of a parish church has been brought to exquisite perfection.' *The World* claimed unequivocally that 'St Andrew's has long been famous for the most perfect musical service in the kingdom (they were nicknamed the Sunday Pops years ago), and its parochial machinery is beyond praise.'[88]

The fact that Benjamin Webb spent the last twenty-three years of his ministry in what became a fashionable church, where he appointed Joseph Barnby organist and proceeded to appropriate the masses of Gounod, Schubert, and Mozart (sung to English texts) for use in what became the parish's famous choral Communion services, could be seen as a capitulation. Add to this the fact that congregational psalmody made use of Anglican chants instead of plainsong and it is tempting to infer that Webb merely gave in to popular pressure for modern Anglican music, that he somehow betrayed the hardline stance for early church music and let down the 'higher' side. Such reasoning could be sustained if it could be proved that, by this time, Webb thought Gregorian music was the only appropriate, authorized, or sufficiently congregational music for the service of the Church. But that was certainly not the case. Far from being a betrayal of principle, it was the logical extension of the principle that nothing too good, or ornate, could be lavished on the service of God, especially on the celebration of the Sacrament of Holy Communion. The 'best' which an urban parish could offer to God was in this case considerably more artistic and ornate than what would have been realistic or perhaps even appropriate in rural Staffordshire, and by 1862 the singing movement had so permeated British life that it was no longer the case that the people would only be skilled enough to sing or appreciate something as simple as plainsong. In addition, we shall see that several leading ecclesiologists were annoyed by the 'extreme ritualism' promoted by the incumbent of All Saints, Margaret Street, just around the corner. (: 120–1) The fact that Webb promoted con-

---

86 OBL: MSS.Eng.misc.d.475, ff. 61–2.
87 *Saturday Review*, 12 December 1885. OBL: MSS.Eng.misc.d.475, ff. 51–2.
88 OBL: MSS.Eng.misc.d.475, f. 63.

siderably more moderate worship services than this ritualistic neighbouring parish could hardly have been done without some intent to make a point.

The other principle to consider is that ecclesiologists always saw the revival of medieval art as the means to rescue modern art. Not only did Webb appropriate what he considered to be the best continental sacred music to Anglican worship, but by 1864 he had successfully encouraged the eminent musician, Sir George Alexander Macfarren, to compose for the Communion Service. In gratitude Macfarren wrote to wish Webb well in his 'valuable efforts to advance Church music.'[89] In music, then, as in architecture Webb became committed to the encouragement of contemporary Christian artists; and since a predilection for modern Anglican music was what he found among his parishioners when he arrived at St Andrew's, Wells Street, that is what he promoted. This was precisely the musical extension of the ecclesiological approach to architecture, namely that the study of ancient models would eventually lead to the reestablishment of a valid, contemporary artistic style. (: 27–8) It stood to reason that sooner or later contemporary composers would have to be given their opportunity.

This is a prime example of the pastoral technique of moderation (: 96, 122, 131, 190–2) which Webb also employed in regard to the use of eucharistic vestments at St Andrews, Wells Street. Asked before the Royal Commission on Ritual in 1867 why he did not wear them, even though he believed them to be legal, Webb replied, 'I have no excuse except that I do not wish to do it, considering that my congregation have no desire for it, so far as I know. It is a matter of christian charity, expediency, and prudence only with me.' There was no virtue in risking the loss of his congregation's confidence by making 'unnecessary changes.'[90] Upon Webb's death, *The Literary Churchman* wrote, 'Though noted for moderation of opinion and disinclination to advance in matters connected with the accessories of Worship, he was always regarded as a staunch Churchman even by those who are called "Ritualists".'[91]

W.J. Sparrow Simpson, who claims Webb and St Andrew's, Wells Street, as one of Cambridge's great contributions to the Anglo-Catholic revival, wrote:

> His church was not distinguished for ceremonial. What he introduced was marked by simplicity. But he was far in advance of the standard which was usual at that time. Where he excelled was in his keen appreciation of the value of music in the Sanctuary. He lavished on Eucharistic devotion a wealth of musical expression to which the parish churches of English were complete strangers. If the ceremonial was simple the music was not. It was this which made his church a centre of attraction.[92]

---

[89] Letter, Macfarren to Webb, 8 December 1864. OBL: MS.Eng.Lett.e.86, ff.131–2.
[90] Parliamentary Papers, xx (1867) 766, 772.
[91] OBL: MSS.Eng.misc.d.475, f.62.
[92] W.J. Sparrow Simpson (1933) 28.

The frequent choral celebrations of Communion, choral service sung twice daily by a highly-trained choir, and the impressive array of social relief programmes and societies for self-betterment which characterized the ministry of St Andrew's, Wells Street, during Webb's tenure clearly arose from pastoral motives.[93] Throughout his adult life he was devoted to encouraging the highest praises of God, whether on paper, in stone, in music, or in charitable works. Publishing anonymously, he neither invited attention to himself nor asked for any reward. Such learning, devotion, and integrity are remarkable in any age.

Alexander James Beresford (Beresford) Hope, M.P.

Alexander James Beresford Hope was born (25 January 1820) the youngest son of a wealthy family, which was made even more so when in 1832 his widowed mother married her cousin, Lord Beresford. In 1833 Alexander was sent away to Harrow as a home-boarder under the care of a private tutor, where he excelled in Greek and Latin. In due course he was offered a place at Trinity College, Cambridge, which he took up in the Michaelmas term 1837.[94] There he began his lifelong friendship with Benjamin Webb, who introduced him to the Cambridge Camden Society and 'whose influence made him a Churchman in reality as well as in name, and so altered the whole course of his life.'[95] Inspired by Webb and the developing study of ecclesiology, he left Cambridge upon his graduation 'determined to devote his life to the restoration in the Church of England of divine worship as he understood it, conducted in more dignified surroundings than those which prevailed in his youth.'[96] Like the mature Webb, he was a moderate man, inclined to see a broader picture than John Mason Neale. Upon his death (20 October 1887) the *Family Churchman* wrote,

> It has far too generally been taken for granted that Mr Beresford Hope was an 'advanced' Churchman. In point of fact he was a High Churchman of the Hook and Hooker type, which is a very different thing from saying that he was a ritualist. The English Church Union could not secure him for their platforms.[97]

While ecclesiology was clearly his great passion and avocation, Hope also served as a member of Parliament for most of his adult life, representing first Maidstone (1841–52, 1857–9) and then Stoke-on-Trent (1865–8). He finally

---

[93] Griffinhoofe, 'Benjamin Webb and St Andrew's, Wells Street,' *Church Quarterly Review*, 79/157 (October 1914) 36–57.
[94] Law (1925) 111–13.
[95] Law (1925) 128.
[96] Law (1925) 131. Webb diaries, 24 February 1841: 'Hope took his BA degree.'
[97] Quoted in Law (1925) 241.

realized his life's political ambition when he was elected in 1868 to serve as the member for Cambridge, and so popular was he that Beresford Hope, as he surnamed himself following the death of his stepfather in 1854, was 'returned unopposed at each General Election to the end of his life.'[98]

When Archdeacon Thorp was not present at a general or Committee meeting of the Ecclesiological (late Cambridge Camden) Society, A.J.B. Hope almost invariably took the chair. After 1845 Thorp rarely attended Committee meetings and hence, to all intents and purposes, Hope held the practical executive power. At the twentieth anniversary meeting of the Ecclesiological Society in 1859, Archdeacon Thorp resigned as President, and Beresford Hope's informal position at last became official.

Perhaps Beresford Hope's greatest contribution to the church revival was made in his patronage of model institutions. The three primary ones with which he involved himself were St Augustine's Missionary College, Canterbury; the parish of Sheen in Staffordshire; and All Saints, Margaret Street, in London; and these are the ones which will mainly concern us.

It is worth noting, however, that he was also a major benefactor of St Matthias, Stoke Newington, a model church with which ecclesiologists were intimately involved from its beginning. The vision for this church and its realization was due primarily to Robert Brett, a surgeon and resident of the parish. The foundation stone for the new church, designed by Butterfield, was laid in the summer of 1851; the Revd Thomas Helmore intoned morning prayer; and the Revd William Scott, a pillar of the Committee of the ECCS, assisted with Communion and preached at evensong.[99] The consecration of the church took place on 13 June 1853. It was reported that 'the proper psalms and canticles were most effectively sung by a full choir to Gregorian chants, and the character of the choral service throughout was one of earnest simplicity and beauty.' There were more than five hundred communicants.[100] Ecclesiologists remained keenly interested in the parish for many years. On the seventh anniversary of the church's dedication, the Revd Thomas Helmore again intoned the services. Tallis's responses were used, an anthem by the Revd S.S. Greatheed and offertory sentences composed by the church's organist, W.H. Monk, were sung, and 'the entire service, a Gregorian one, was given in hearty and devotional spirit.'[101] In 1867 the participation of the (Rt) Revd Henry Lascelles Jenner, ECCS Secretary for Music 1856–62, in the anniversary services at St Matthias would lead to accusations that he promoted ultra-ritualism, and resulted in the scandalous proceedings which ultimately resulted

---

[98] Law (1925) 134, 150, 157, 203–8.
[99] *Guardian*, 296 (6 August 1851) 567.
[100] *Guardian*, 393 (15 June 1853) 390.
[101] *Guardian*, 759 (20 June 1860) 547.

in his post-consecration rejection by his appointed diocese as Bishop of Dunedin, New Zealand.[102]

St Augustine's Missionary College, Canterbury

The first of Hope's major benefactions to the Church of England was the reconstitution of St Augustine's College, Canterbury. Hope bought the site in June 1844 after reading a letter to the editor of the *English Churchman* (13 September 1843) from Robert Brett of Stoke Newington, in which Brett hoped that God would 'dispose some pious and wealthy Catholic to purchase and restore the sacred edifice', which at the time was being used as a brewery. Hope bought it for the use of the Church, engaged Butterfield as architect, and, encouraged by the Revd Edward Coleridge, master of Eton, decided to make it into a theological college for missionaries. The consecration of the buildings took place on St Peter's Day (29 June) 1848. Afterwards the group of select guests moved from the small chapel of the College to Canterbury Cathedral, where a congregation of 2000 people, including six hundred clergy, had assembled to celebrate the event. The list of notables in attendance reads like a 'Who's Who' of the Victorian High Church; Benjamin Webb noted in his diary, 'Met nearly everybody one knew.'[103] The University of Oxford granted Hope an honorary DCL in gratitude for this generous benefaction to the Church. Among all the honorands at the degree ceremony, his name is reported to have 'elicited decidedly the loudest and the heartiest' cheers and applause, and an allusion to St Augustine's brought forth 'a burst of approbation that told more forcibly than words the deep gratitude felt for his liberality and the good wishes with which his pious work was regarded.'[104]

Already in June 1845 Hope had tried to persuade Benjamin Webb to become a fellow of the College, writing to him:

> It will be the very place for you, and consider the mediaeval influences among which you will live and the opportunities which you will have of following ecclesiological and ritual studies to so much more advantage than if engaged in parochial duties, and daily choral service in choir and weekly Communions which are purposed.[105]

Hope's biographer suggests that Webb declined because of his secret engagement to Maria Mill, but Webb's diaries would seem to indicate that the engagement did not take place until June 1846. More likely Webb declined because of his youth and a humble sense of inadequacy for the task, a sense

---

[102] J. Pearce (1984) 53–4, 57.
[103] Law (1925) 157–8; *Guardian,* 129 (5 July 1848) 436; Webb diaries, 29 June 1848.
[104] *Oxford Herald,* quoted in the *Guardian,* 130 (12 July 1848) 455.
[105] Law (1925) 159; Webb diaries, 7 June 1845.

which cannot but have been strengthened by the fact that J.M. Neale was 'indignant' at the very idea. Hope tried to reassure Webb:

> you have what is of more importance than book-learning, which is the Catholic tone. Just look at yourself and ask if you are not a mediaeval Fellow – I do not mean an antiquarian, but one who will try to develop present times by the help of our inheritance of ancestral holiness and faith. We want such as you to give the tone to our college.[106]

Webb never accepted a fellowship, yet these lines are important for what they reveal about Hope's vision for the College and his mutual identification with Webb in the feeling that the study of history and its principles should naturally inform a continued evolution in contemporary religious practice.

The first warden of St Augustine's was the Revd William Hart Coleridge, former Bishop of Barbados. As one would expect, Hope had less influence on the College's policies and course of development once it was turned over to the Church. In fact, Hope is said to have been disappointed with the early wardens.[107] No doubt the chapel worship was a source of concern, since services were never choral to the extent that Hope had envisioned. When the first warden died in December 1849, the *Guardian* carried a letter in praise for the work of the College. The writer had attended evensong, during which the students had chanted the *Magnificat* and *Nunc dimittis* and sung an anthem 'in good taste enough', which was, he believed, the pattern of services on Eves, Vigils, Saints' Days, and Sundays only. The evenings were left free for private study and music.[108] It would appear that things changed under the second warden, for on 17 August 1851 J.M. Neale wrote of St Augustine's to Webb:

> That is the most wonderful Institution I ever heard of; the business is all but miraculous. The students are so delighted with Helmore's Psalter that, for their own pleasure, they sing it daily; but are not allowed in Chapel to chant, much as they wish it, and have asked for it.[109]

Students were encouraged to learn to sing and to study church music, but by keeping choral services in Chapel to a minimum, the College avoided what might have been an unhelpful party association.

All Saints, Margaret Street

At least by November 1845 discussions were underway among key ecclesiologists to establish a model church in London. Hope thought that 'it should have, like St Saviour's, Leeds, the spiritual advantage of being planted on a site which very much wants one, combined with greater aesthetical perfec-

---

[106] Law (1925) 159; Webb diaries, 18 November 1845.
[107] Law (1925) 160.
[108] *Guardian*, 206 (27 December 1849) 852.
[109] Lawson (1910) 181.

tion.'[110] Discussions continued in December at "Burns' Motett party", and by the 18th of that month Butterfield, James Burns, William Scott, and Webb were already discussing a circular to promote the idea.[111]

Hope's granddaughter chronicles how he assumed leadership in the legal negotiations to acquire the site, that of Margaret Chapel in the parish of All Souls, Langham Place. It was purchased for £9000 in 1847, Hope's mother, Lady Beresford, being among the major contributors. He undertook to rent a temporary room for the chapel in Titchfield Street to which the congregation moved on All Saints' Day 1847. Hope also guaranteed a substantial portion of the incumbent's salary.

The foundation stone for the new church was laid on All Saints' Day 1850. The *Guardian* reported:

> In addition to the spiritual benefits, of which the founders hope it may be the origin and centre, it has been their wish that the structure may be an example of rubrical correctness, carried out through the means of Christian art, of the highest character in design, and of the richest materials, consistent with good taste, principally as an humble offering to Almighty God of His good gifts, and also as a symbol of faith in the Church of England.[112]

Thus ecclesiologists essentially took over what had been seen as an early flagship for Tractarian worship, with the express intent of refining and perfecting it according to ecclesiological standards.

Hope administered the funds in payment for the new works, which by 1854 included an anonymous £30,000 donation, Hope's own contributions which counted 'by thousands' ('I have to make up deficiencies quarterly,' Hope revealed), and £2300 which had been given by various donors before the work began. Freehold and ownership of the church was retained by Hope until it was completed in 1859 after many delays.[113]

In 1853 one of the major Tractarian publishers, Joseph Masters, released *Introits for the Several Seasons of the Christian Year, as used at All Saints' Church, Margaret Street*, adapted and harmonized by the organist and choirmaster of the church, Richard Redhead. Immediate protest caused the title to be withdrawn, since the church was not even near completion, and ecclesiologists expressed great regret that the collection had ever been published. In its disapproval of Redhead's introits, *The Ecclesiologist* stated:

> it was intended from the beginning of the undertaking that the music and ritual of the new church should be as pure and as authentic as the best endeavours of competent authorities could make it. And to this intention is due, in no small degree, the late increased study of ecclesiastical music, as one branch of Christian art and one special province of ecclesiology, among the members of

---

[110] Letter from Hope to Webb, November 1845, cited in Law (1925) 161.
[111] Webb diaries, 9 and 18 December 1845.
[112] *Guardian*, 254 (2 November 1850) 786.
[113] Law (1925) 161–77.

our society and committee. Several distinguished musicians... were added to the committee, and a great impulse was given to the more general study and practice of the authorised music of the Church of England.[114]

The plan for a model church embodied in All Saints', Margaret Street, then, was a catalyst for the study of music by ecclesiologists, since model worship was the only point of building a model church.

Not only were Redhead's introits a cause for concern, but the building of a choir school as part of the new church complex occasioned a reconsideration of how parochial choirs should be constituted. Hope identified as a fundamental difference between ancient and modern practice the fact that mediaeval choir schools, such as King's College, Cambridge, were established for the purpose of training boys to be clerics. The results of that system were completely different from those in which boys were 'petted and coddled and dressed up at Titchfield Street or St Andrew's' [Wells Street] only to become 'tallow chandlers' at age eighteen. He further objected to the fact that unconfirmed choirboys were allowed within the chancel rails while confirmed laymen were denied access. 'The Anglo-Puseyite chorister system is out of joint,' he suggested, and thought that perhaps the solution was to 'institute parochial choirs under some sort of guild regulations, irrespective of the quality of performance.' In spite of these worries, All Saints' ended up with a fairly typical Tractarian choir school with six to eight boys from the parish. Cause for Hope's earlier worries that the congregational singing of the responses in Margaret Chapel was insufficiently hearty was allayed by the time of the church's consecration. The choir for the occasion was augmented by the boys from the Chapel Royal and students from St Mark's College, Chelsea, and it was reported that, 'Never, perhaps, were Gregorians heard to such advantage, for the whole congregation being trained in them, joined heartily in the singing.' The Revd Thomas Helmore's *Manual of Plainsong* was used. He intoned the service; and the congregation, in which the men and women were divided by sides, sang the psalms antiphonally.[115]

The finished work was never a matter of satisfaction to Beresford Hope. He had continual disagreements with the incumbent, the Revd W. Upton Richards, whose ritualistic sympathies incited frequent difficulties with the successive bishops of London, Blomfield and Tait, who looked to Beresford Hope to guarantee the church's fidelity to the Church of England. Beresford Hope felt that Richards had betrayed his responsibility to pursue the vision of the founders. At one point Beresford Hope wrote to Webb, 'It is quite manifest that all along he used or meant to use us simply as tools towards establishing his directionism; ritualism, etc., being traps to catch flies.' Beresford Hope

---

[114] *The Ecclesiologist*, 14/95 (April 1853) 100. T. Helmore, S.S. Greatheed, W. Dyce, and J.L. Crompton were mentioned specially among the distinguished musicians.
[115] Law (1925) 171–2; *Guardian*, 704 (1 June 1859) 485–6.

disapproved of Richards' love of 'sensuous music and showy altars', for the latter of which Richards was publicly embarrassed when the Bishop of London stopped in the middle of the consecration service on 28 May 1859 and refused to proceed until a plain table cloth be fetched to cover the elaborate altar frontal.[116]

Beresford Hope also fell out with the architect, Butterfield, over details of the interior decoration. In the end he called it,

> very sad. Butterfield has so parricidally spoilt his own creation with the clown's dress,[117] so spotty and spidery and flimsy as it looks in a mass now that it is all done, and worst of all the Church looks so much smaller than it used to do with nothing but the solemn columns to give scale. Butterfield on his side is honestly fanatical about colour doctrines, and completely believes that I have marred the world's greatest work... *Pour moi*, it is all much the same, as I very likely may never go there again.

After the consecration in 1859 Beresford Hope reportedly did not visit the church again until after Richards' death in 1874, by which time Butterfield had also long since left the congregation 'because the verger insulted him.'[118]

Having helped to procure Benjamin Webb's appointment to St Andrew's, Wells Street in 1862, Beresford Hope began to worship there and soon became one of the churchwardens.[119] It seemed a shame that such sacrifice and care on the part of Beresford Hope and other ecclesiologists should have ended in disappointment at All Saints', Margaret Street. Yet it is a telling example of the way in which the nineteenth-century revival of church principles could lead to splits over issues of ecclesiology and 'extreme' ritualism. It is also indicative of the moderate views held by Beresford Hope and other leading first-generation ecclesiologists toward church decoration and ritual.

Beresford Hope as author

According to his biographer, A.J.B. Beresford Hope and Benjamin Webb were 'joint editors' of *The Ecclesiologist*. While there seems to be no other evidence to support this claim, there can be no doubt that the two were in constant contact and that Webb highly valued Beresford Hope's counsel. It is also clear that Beresford Hope was a frequent anonymous author for *The Ecclesiologist*,

---

[116] Law (1925) 166–9. Whitworth (1891) 82, posits the explanation that the Bishop had never seen a fair linen cloth which covered only the top and ends of the altar and, seeing the altar frontal exposed, concluded that there was no linen cloth whatever on the altar and sent for one accordingly.
[117] 'A phrase Dyce had applied to the decoration of the spandrels in the nave.' Law (1925) footnote on 177.
[118] Law (1925) 177.
[119] Law (1925) 190–2.

and also contributed articles to the *Morning Chronicle*.[120] His most enduring journalistic contribution was his foundation of the *Saturday Review* in 1855, a weekly publication edited by John Douglas Cook, who was also editor of the *Morning Chronicle*. The *Saturday Review* was launched on 3 November 1855 to be a periodical 'not bound to any party, but written by a combination of Peelite Conservatives and moderate Liberals, and to be the mouthpiece of the... moderate opinions of thoughtful and educated society.' By the end of 1855 weekly circulation had reached 2000 copies, and by March 1858 it had risen to 5000. Fellow ecclesiologists William Scott (former editor of the *Christian Remembrancer*) and Benjamin Webb were recruited to be regular contributors.[121]

The moderate character of the *Saturday Review* was established from the outset of its publication. In a March 1856 article entitled 'Save me from my friends', nineteenth-century apologists of Christianity were upbraided for failing to treat their opponents with 'the gravity that befits discussions upon the most important of all conceivable subjects.'[122] Regardless of who may have written the article, it is clearly indicative of the views of mainstream ecclesiologists by the mid-1850s, and the principle involved would have applied as well to the apologetics of church music (see chapter 5) or the pastoral technique of moderation (: 114) practised by so many ecclesiologists. The author stated:

> In proportion to the depth of our conviction of the vital importance of the Christian faith to the very existence of human society, is our wish that the controversies relating to its foundations should be discussed with judicial dignity and impartiality. It is a great scandal that any of the heat of personal contests should be permitted to enter into the advocacy of so holy a cause. Nothing gives a greater handle to the enemies of Christianity than depreciation of sceptics as such. Taunts, and mockery, and party spirit are not fit weapons for the defenders of Christian truth. Even the follies and weaknesses with which the enemies of Christianity may be justly chargeable should be dealt with with tenderness and generosity.[123]

In 1861 Beresford Hope published *The English Cathedral of the Nineteenth Century*, which was based upon a lecture originally delivered to the Cambridge Architectural Society and dedicated to that organization. Middle Gothic had followed 'a period of cosmopolitanism and eclecticism', he argued, and he asserted that the art revival of his own day had reached a like point where 'our own superior style' could be constructed upon the basis of re-learned Gothic,

---

[120] Beresford Hope would often write to Webb two or three times in a single day prior to Webb's appointment to St Andrew's, Wells Street in 1862, which allowed them to meet regularly in London. Law (1925) 139, 145, 147.
[121] Law (1925) 214–216.
[122] *Saturday Review*, 1/19 (8 March 1856) 375.
[123] *Saturday Review*, 1/19 (8 March 1856) 375.

enriched by the stylistic variants of contemporaneous continental Gothic.[124] This principle had equal relevance to ecclesiastical music.

Beresford Hope's devotion to choral service is clear, and especially his love for what he was by 1861 content to designate 'Cathedral service.' He wrote, 'There can be no question that the solemn Cathedral service, with all its stately accompaniments, is the highest development of the principle which recognises the value of art and of set order in man's collective approach to his Creator.'[125]

The Revd John Mason Neale

As the only ecclesiologist who has received repeated and fairly exhaustive biographical attention, John Mason Neale's efforts within the realm of church music need be only briefly summarized here. His immense contribution to Christian hymnody is his greatest and most enduring contribution to church music. To him credit is primarily due for the popular restoration of ancient Greek and Latin hymnody (in English translation), originally undertaken by the Ecclesiological late Cambridge Camden Society in its publication of the *Hymnal Noted.* (: 64–8) Although his *Hymns for Children* was issued almost a decade earlier (1842)[126] and he had taken a scholarly interest in ancient hymnody by the mid-1840s,[127] Neale did not issue his first set of translations until 1851. In the end his labours yielded nearly a dozen separate publications, enough to fill 450 pages in the *Collected Hymns, Sequences and Carols of John Mason Neale.*[128] Recent editions of *The English Hymnal* (1986) and *Hymns Ancient and Modern* (1983) each include more than thirty of his translations. There are probably few native English-speaking Christians who would not recognize some of Neale's best-known work (see Table 4.1).

For most of his life, J.M. Neale's role as a priest was considerably different from that of any other leading cleric of the Ecclesiological Movement, simply because he did not minister to a parish. As warden of Sackville College, a private institution for the care of the elderly poor, and as the founder and spiritual father of the Society of St Margaret, he was more or less free to introduce what forms of worship he wished, in spite of his inhibition (May 1847–November 1863) by the Bishop of Chichester. The few souls for which he directly cared were, with notable exceptions, for the most part quite willing to do as their friend and pastor told them. Moreover the relatively light demands of his wardenship allowed Neale to devote most of his time to

---

[124] Beresford Hope (1861) 32.
[125] Beresford Hope (1861) 116–117.
[126] Lough (1962) 86.
[127] Lawson (1910) 125.
[128] Edited by his daughter, Mary Sackville Lawson, 1914.

scholarly pursuits, which included not only hymn writing and translation, but several ground-breaking histories of the Eastern Church and volumes of sermons, to mention only a few.

Table 4.1 Well-known hymn translations and carols from the pen of John Mason Neale

First line of Neale's translation	Latin title or Greek author
A great and mighty wonder[129]	Greek, St Anatolius
All glory, laud, and honour	Gloria, laus, et honor
Before the ending of the day	Te lucis ante terminum
Blessèd City, heavenly Salem	Urbs beata Jerusalem
Christ is made the sure foundation	Angulare fundamentum
Come, thou Redeemer of the earth	Veni, Redemptor gentium
Come, ye faithful, raise the strain	Ave Virgo Virginum
Creator of the stars of night	Conditor alme siderum
Gabriel's message does away	Angelus emittitur[130]
Good Christian men, rejoice	In dulci jubilo
Good King Wenceslas	(an original poem by Neale)
Jerusalem the golden	Urbs Sion aurea
Jesu! – the very thought is sweet!	Jesu, dulcis memoria
Light's abode, celestial Salem	Jerusalem luminosa
Now, my tongue, the mystery telling	Tantum ergo sacramentum
O come, O come, Emmanuel[131]	Veni, veni, Emmanuel
O happy band of pilgrims	Greek, St Joseph of Studium
O Trinity, most blessèd light	O Lux beata Trinitas
O what their joy and their glory must be	O quanta qualia
Of the Father's love begotten	Divinum mysterium
Of the glorious body telling	Pange lingua
Sing, my tongue, the glorious battle	Pange lingua
The day of resurrection!	Greek, St John of Damascus
The Lamb's high banquet we await	Ad cenam Agni providi
The royal banners forward go	Vexilla Regis prodeunt
Ye choirs of new Jerusalem	Chorus Novæ Hierusalem
Ye sons and daughters of the King	O filii et filiae

Neale's isolation from society and from the normal practical considerations inherent in parish ministry allowed him to pursue a spiritual life heavily influenced by the traditions of monasticism. By 1856 keeping the daily offices with the Sisters of St Margaret had given him a practical familiarity with the Sarum Hours,[132] and his translations of Latin hymns and sequences were in

---

[129] Sung to the German chorale tune, *Es ist ein Ros' entsprungen*.
[130] From *Piae Cantiones*, 1582.
[131] Neale's translation began, 'Draw nigh, draw nigh, Emmanuel.'
[132] Lawson (1910) 272. Neale founded the Society of St Margaret during the winter of 1854–55. Chandler (1995) 75.

constant use in these services. Mother Kate recorded that the founder of St Margaret's Convent 'was very particular about the singing of both Sisters and children in the Oratory, and always said his ambition was that one day S Margaret's should be the admiration of the whole countryside.'[133] Although Neale wrote in the mid-1850s that he 'said' and 'read' services for the sisterhood,[134] this does not necessarily mean that they were not sung, for services that were monotoned or sung in simple plainsong were often described by ecclesiologists as having been 'said' or 'read.' (: 152–4) Neale's daughter wrote that evensong in the Chapel of Sackville College was 'read', with one unaccompanied hymn led by Mrs Neale. She also wrote of her father that he 'really loved music, but had only one note in his voice, "made a noise," as he called it.'[135] In fact, Neale boasted that all of the College services were performed chorally after he learned to intone in 1849, by which time he described the rota of worship to have included daily Prime (8 a.m.), Morning Prayer (9 a.m.), Nones (2 p.m.), Vespers (6 p.m.), and Compline (10 p.m.).[136]

The Revd Thomas Helmore

Thomas Helmore was born at Kidderminster on 2 May 1811, the son of the Revd Thomas Helmore, a Nonconformist minister, and Olive Holloway Helmore, who had gained some fame as a 'lady-preacher' prior to her marriage. In order to teach his growing family, the elder Thomas took up the study of music at age forty. Thus began at home the musical education of his two sons, Thomas and Frederick, who would later play such a central role in the revival of Anglican choral worship.[137]

It is significant that Thomas Helmore the younger was born and raised the son of an Independent clergyman. Religion was never a matter of indifference in the Helmore home, and the seriousness with which young 'Tom' regarded his faith from his youth undoubtedly helps to account for the zeal and perseverance with which he pursued his later vocation. His was an unusual road to tread, for he spent his adult life training and encouraging choirmasters, choirs and congregations to participate in choral service, and working for the

---

[133] *Memories of a Sister of S. Saviour's Priory*, (1903) 21–2, quoted in Lough (1975) 118.
[134] Lawson (1910) 274, 275. Neale writes that the sisters habitually sang plainsong hymns at these services.
[135] Towle (1906) 220.
[136] Lawson (1910) 128.
[137] Early biographical details are taken from Frederick Helmore's biography of his brother, Thomas. Frederick eventually became known as the 'musical missionary' in the revival of Anglican parish choirs, travelling the length of Britain to start new choirs, even in the smallest country villages. The first choir he trained was at the request of the Revd Henry Wilberforce in the parish of East Farleigh. F. Helmore (1891) 34–7.

restoration of plainsong and early church polyphony at a time when neither was popular or commonplace.

His preparation for the particular avenue of ministry which later brought him fame began as a young man, when he formed a 'school of music' in Stratford-upon-Avon, where his family had moved when Thomas was not yet ten years old. It was run in conjunction with the school attached to his father's congregation at Rother Market. In addition to the orchestra which eventually resulted from his efforts, he began to train an *a cappella* choir in his father's chapel.

According to his brother Frederick, Thomas Helmore's conversion to Anglicanism was a journey he undertook independently and, 'by anxiously seeking information and advice, and by diligent study, chiefly in Hooker's *Ecclesiastical Polity*, he became thoroughly convinced of the catholicity of the English Church.'[138] Shortly following his baptism and confirmation, the parish church of Stratford-upon-Avon underwent major interior renovations. During the construction there was no organ to accompany the services, and Helmore therefore undertook the training of a choir to lead parish worship. Rainbow has demonstrated that Helmore was clearly influenced by William Crotch in his youthful choice of early church polyphony,[139] for despite the fact that Helmore had no personal acquaintance with Anglican cathedral services or repertoire, the music chosen to be sung by his new parish choir included Gibbons' service in F, which would later become standard repertoire for parish choirs throughout the country.[140]

In 1837 Thomas Helmore matriculated at Magdalen Hall (previously and subsequently known as Hertford College), Oxford. As a university student he studied counterpoint with Dr William Marshall, organist of Christ Church, and advanced his knowledge of English church music through the study of music manuscripts in the Bodleian Library and at Christ Church. He was ordained deacon and priest within a year of the completion of his BA, and spent two years in Lichfield as curate of St Michael's parish and priest-vicar in the cathedral choir, where he became intimately acquainted with the cathedral repertoire. Reportedly it was this experience that also 'perfected' his beautiful tenor singing voice, which was much sought-after in later years to intone festival services in parish churches throughout England.[141]

In 1842 he was appointed Vice Principal and Precentor of St Mark's College, Chelsea. (: 31–2) There he directed a choir of young teacher trainees of the college, and a select group of trebles from the model school on its grounds, to sing and read music in preparation for daily choral services in the

---

[138] F. Helmore (1891) 16.
[139] Rainbow (1970) 61–2.
[140] F. Helmore (1891) 17–18.
[141] F. Helmore (1891) 23–8.

College chapel. Thus he helped to equip a young army of teachers, who went out to serve Britain's schools and often the parish churches nearby, to teach their pupils and fellow villagers to sing. The move to London brought Helmore into close contact with the work of the Motett Society, founded in 1841 for the purpose of publishing and performing early church music adapted to English texts. As has already been noted (: 77–81), his ongoing connection with the Motett Society was integral to its revival in 1852 by ecclesiologists, who recruited him to join their cause in 1850. (: 63–4)

In 1846 the Bishop of London, Blomfield, appointed the Revd Thomas Helmore to be Master of the Children of the Chapel Royal, St James. It was the first time since the Reformation that a clergyman had been appointed to the position, and Helmore assumed his responsibilities with alacrity. Under his predecessor, William Hawes, the discipline of the boys had been allowed to fall to shocking levels. The brutal treatment the older boys routinely meted out upon their younger charges, however, was not tolerated by Helmore. Instead of hiring someone to see to the boys' education, they moved into the home of their new choirmaster and his wife. Overseeing their needs and education personally, Helmore reportedly effected a rapid and remarkable improvement in both their behaviour and their skill as choristers.[142]

Whereas his lay predecessors had made of the Chapel Royal boys a lucrative side-business, hiring them out to sing in all manner of London entertainments, Thomas Helmore restricted their activities to those which he felt befitted their ecclesiastical appointment to the Chapel Royal. Since the boys were only required to sing services on Sundays, he often took them with him to assist in the weekday services at St Mark's College. They formed an integral part of the treble section for the rehearsals and performances of the Motett Society and the Madrigal Society, the latter for the purpose of observing how the great masters of sacred music had treated secular subjects. The boys frequently participated in the oratorio productions of the Sacred Harmonic Society, where some of them had the privilege of singing Mendelssohn's *Elijah* under the baton of the composer himself.[143] Helmore's concern that the boys grow up to be well rounded individuals also led him occasionally to take them out to villages around the country where his brother, Frederick, had been engaged in training up a choir. While assisting with festival services in villages and thus showing support for priests who pursued a vision to disciple the children of their parishes within the context of the choral experience, Helmore exposed both the Chapel Royal boys and their country fellows to the lifestyles of their city and village counterparts.[144]

---

[142] F. Helmore (1891) 50–4.
[143] F. Helmore (1891) 54–5.
[144] F. Helmore (1891) 57–8. These children's choirs sometimes included girls.

Helmore's view of music, ancient and modern

There is much reason to believe that Thomas Helmore's taste in music, like that of so many other mainstream ecclesiologists, was far less narrow than critics realized.[145] For instance, he held regular social musical entertainments in his home at 6 Cheyne Walk, which included music of all types and periods. Frederick Helmore states that these concerts were 'one of the many means taken by Mr Helmore to expand the intellect and prevent the musical taste of his [Chapel Royal] pupils being narrowed into one groove.'[146]

As concerned liturgical church music, it should be noted that in 1854 Helmore wrote to J.M. Neale to urge that the ECCS publish a collection of modern English hymns to supplement the *Hymnal Noted*.[147] The public performances of the Ecclesiological Motett Choir also witness to Helmore's encouragement of modern compositions which he considered to perpetuate an ecclesiastical style. A typical programme, for 7 June 1859, included various psalms from the *Psalter Noted*, three hymns from the *Hymnal Noted*, Palestrina's *Missa Eterna Christi munera* (complete), Sir Frederick Ouseley's *How goodly are thy tents*, and two anthems by the Revd S.S. Greatheed, *The Son of Man* and *Let my soul bless God* (which also suggests that Helmore and Greatheed did not fall out over Goddard's stricture of contemporary composers of sacred music in late 1855). The next month the Motett Choir performed an anthem by the wealthy aristocrat, the Hon. Frederick Lygon, M.P. (later 6th Earl of Beauchamp),[148] somewhat ironically entitled, *In my Father's house are many mansions*. He was a member of the Committee of the Ecclesiological Society, and one of the founders of the Oxford Society for the Study and Practice of the Plain Song of the Church in 1853. (: 83)

Thomas Helmore's close friendship with Sir Frederick Ouseley also reveals that Helmore's musical flexibility did not exclude modern church music. Ouseley was a welcome and frequent guest at the Helmore home in Cheyne Walk. On one musical occasion, Ouseley conducted his oratorio *The Martyrdom of St Polycarp* there, with Frederick Helmore singing the lead role and one of Thomas Helmore's Chapel Royal boys, (later Sir) Arthur Sullivan, taking part in the trio.[149] Helmore and his choristers from the Chapel Royal

---

[145] Scholes, *The Mirror of Music*, 2 (1947) 553–5, quotes attacks on plainsong and its supporters by S.S. Wesley, G.A. Macfarren, Henry Smart.

[146] F. Helmore (1891) 75–6. Thomas Helmore moved to Cheyne Walk from Onslow Square in 1854.

[147] Tate Gallery: Dyce Papers, letter from Thomas Helmore to Dyce, 1 September 1854. This project was never undertaken.

[148] *The Ecclesiologist*, 20/133 (August 1859) 276–7.

[149] Frederick Helmore and Ouseley were friends from their undergraduate days at Oxford. F. Helmore (1891) 91.

took part in the consecration of St Michael's, Tenbury,[150] where Helmore later sent one of his sons, Charlie, to be educated.[151] Over the course of years Helmore was honoured with the dedication of no fewer than eight of Ouseley's anthems.[152]

There is no doubt that Thomas Helmore's primary goal in life was to restore plainsong to its rightful place as a musical handmaid of the liturgy. Yet he had no intrinsic objection to the singing of modern anthems, or even to the performance of non-congregational settings of the canticles in places with proficient choirs, as long as they did not partake of a light and secular style. Late in life he was gratified to learn that his *Psalter Noted* was being used in some of the services at St Paul's Cathedral; but he saw little hope of success for a proposed reprint of James Burns' ancient anthems and services. 'Nothing of that kind seems to take the public taste,' he wrote. 'The belief and the taste is set so decidedly to the modern tonality. This has been somewhat the fault of our over-dosing the ancient perhaps.'[153]

The Revd Henry Lascelles Jenner

H.L. Jenner was one of the originators of the idea to form a High Church club, the Ecclesialogical Society, in Cambridge in 1839.[154] This brought him into an intimate circle of friendship with such leaders of the revival of worship as Benjamin Webb, John Mason Neale, and Harvey Goodwin. Jenner's name is not among those published in the membership lists of the Cambridge Camden Society in 1839 or 1843, but his interest in ecclesiology was surely encouraged by the future leaders of the movement, for his early career as a curate leaves no doubt as to where his sympathies lay.[155]

Jenner took his degree in law at Trinity Hall in 1841, two years before his father, Sir Henry Jenner-Fust (Dean of the Court of Arches), came back to his alma mater to be its Master. Deciding against a career in law, he sought ordination, becoming a deacon in 1843 and priest in 1844. Following a three-year curacy at Chevening near Sevenoaks, Kent, he became curate of

---

[150] Joyce (1896) 89.
[151] F. Helmore (1891) 91.
[152] J.S. Bumpus's 1892 catalogue of Ouseley's works (revised 1896), reprinted in Joyce, Appendix D.
[153] Letters to F. Helmore dated 7 May 1889 and 5 March 1990, cited in F. Helmore (1891) 130, 133.
[154] Webb diaries, 3–15 March 1839.
[155] John Pearce's interesting biography of H.L. Jenner, *Seeking a See*, to which I am much indebted, implies that Jenner was a member of the Cambridge Camden Society before its reorganization as the Ecclesiological late Cambridge Camden Society in 1845. J. Pearce (1984) 20. Biographical details of Jenner are also taken from *Crockford's Clerical Dictionary* and Venn's *Alumni Cantabrigienses*.

St Columb Major in Cornwall (1846–9), where he took part in the restoration of the parish church.

From 1849 to 1851 Jenner was curate to the Revd J.F. Kitson at Antony in Cornwall, who, together with the squire, W.H. Pole-Carew, was sympathetic to the church revival and gave Jenner a 'free hand' in the district of Maryfield. Here we catch our first detailed glimpse of Jenner's pastoral ideal of parish ministry. Daily services were initiated, which he monotoned. He began to wear stoles, placed a cross and candles on the altar, and adopted the 'eastward position' during the consecration of the elements at Holy Communion. His biographer tells us,

> Jenner was a born teacher and a faithful pastor, and, although backed by squire and parson in his innovations, he introduced them only after careful public instruction from his pulpit and private tuition in the peoples' houses, every one of which he visited for the purpose. There was universal consent for the revival at Maryfield.[156]

This careful education prior to innovation would mark Jenner's whole career.

In 1851 Jenner took a temporary curacy at Leigh, near Southend in Essex, in order to be closer to his ill father, which also made it practical for him to participate more actively in the activities of the Ecclesiological late Cambridge Camden Society. Accordingly he was added to the Committee on 18 November 1851.[157]

Early in 1852 Jenner accepted an offer to become curate to Dr W.H. Mill at Brasted in Kent.[158] Brasted was a very familiar place to Jenner, especially from his final months as curate of Chevening, when he had often visited Benjamin Webb (who was courting Maria Mill at the time) and had been a frequent and welcome guest of Dr Mill, whether for musical evenings at the rectory or to participate in choral services in the parish church.[159] Jenner came to Brasted in 1852 to fill the vacancy created by Webb's departure to become perpetual curate of Sheen.

However pleasurable this move must have been for everyone concerned, Jenner's stay at Brasted was to be a short one, for a minor canonry of Canterbury Cathedral fell vacant later in the same year and he was the successful candidate for the position. To Canterbury he took his 'fine tenor voice' and sight singing skills in October 1852, and soon set about founding the Canterbury Amateur Musical Society. Meetings in private homes fitted its purpose as social entertainment, and no doubt his multiple talents as an

---

[156] J. Pearce (1984) 21–4; quotation, 24.
[157] *The Ecclesiologist*, 12/87 (December 1851) 399.
[158] J. Pearce (1984) 25–6.
[159] Webb diaries, 16 November 1845; many dates in April and May 1846.

accomplished keyboard, reed, and, to a lesser extent, brass instrument player served these occasions well.[160]

In 1854 the cathedral chapter presented Jenner to the living of Preston-next-Wingham, a village with a population of 500, which he retained until his death in 1898. As at Maryfield, he began the work of reform with patient education. Pearce tells us that Jenner spent two years preparing the people to accept a proper restoration of the church, which, when it was finally undertaken, was carried out in perfect accordance with ecclesiological ideals. Concerning Jenner's pastoral care we are told,

> He started, on arrival, with daily services. These were at nine in the mornings, and on Saints' Days and their Eves there would be evensong at seven. A choir was started of boys and girls largely drawn from the village school. Very soon men joined the choir and the girls were dropped. There were ten men and ten boys. The Vicar was infinitely patient as a choir master and soon their voices, which were rather rough at first, improved under his guidance. They were taught plainsong chants for the psalms and canticles, and some simple anthems for festivals.[161]

The psalms were sung from Thomas Helmore's *Psalter Noted*, and the hymn collection used was the *Hymnal Noted*. The barrel organ which Jenner found in the church soon had its barrel replaced by a keyboard, and later on the Revd S.S. Greatheed donated an organ of his own design to the church. On Sundays there was a morning service consisting of matins, litany and Holy Communion, and a choral evensong.

> The canticles, and at evensong the Psalms, were sung by the choir to plainsong, but at mattins the Psalms were said, alternate verses by the Vicar and congregation, and the glorias sung. The congregation liked it that way and in deference to their wishes it always remained the practice until Jenner's death in 1898.[162]

Like Archdeacon Thorp at Kemerton (: 96), Jenner raised the tone of his parish services without disenfranchising those parishioners who were too set in their own local traditions to be persuaded to adopt anything wholly new. Dr Mill had attempted the same at Brasted by introducing non-choral services on alternate Sunday mornings and every Sunday afternoon; but the root of the problem there was an irrational anti-Roman Catholic mania which worked itself out in blind personal hostility toward Mill, and the dissidents of Brasted would not be placated. After Mill's death on Christmas Day 1853, Archbishop Sumner appointed a Low Church vicar who had 'no use for popish furniture'; and during the restoration of the parish church at Preston-next-Wingham in

---

[160] J. Pearce (1984) 30, 32.
[161] J. Pearce (1984) 33–4.
[162] J. Pearce (1984) 34.

1856, the churchwardens of Brasted presented Jenner with a set of choir surplices and a fine pair of candlesticks designed by the ECCS.[163]

H.L. Jenner's musical influence was not confined to his own parish. In 1856 Thomas Helmore resigned as Honorary Secretary for Music of the (by then) Ecclesiological Society, and Jenner was appointed to assume the duties. This post he retained until 1862, when the Motett Society was disassociated from the Ecclesiological Society. In 1857 he issued the following statement in *The Ecclesiologist*:

> It is very desirable that the progress of true church music among us should be regularly recorded in our pages. The subject is one of such importance and is so generally recognised as a legitimate branch of our studies, that this Journal, if any, may be considered the natural channel through which such intelligence should be transmitted to those interested in it.[164]

He continued by appealing to precentors and others throughout the United Kingdom, America, and the colonies who were concerned with 'the diffusion of sound views on the subject' to make regular reports of their proceedings, so that the progress of ecclesiastical music could be followed throughout the Anglican Communion. (: 192)

H.L. Jenner left an enduring gift to the Church in his hymn tune, *Quam dilecta*, usually sung in Britain with the words 'We love the place, O God.' It was made popular through frequent use in diocesan choral festivals in the early 1860s. Jenner's influence in the formation and subsequent success of the Canterbury Diocesan Choral Union will be discussed in chapter six. (: 210–11)

The Revd Samuel Stephenson Greatheed

S.S. Greatheed (1813–87) took his BA at Trinity College, Cambridge, in 1835, and in 1837 was elected Fellow. In 1838 he was ordained deacon by the Bishop of Ely. Two years later he was ordained priest by the Bishop of London, and for one year, 1840–1, he served as curate of West Drayton in Middlesex. Of his professional activities virtually nothing further is known until he became rector of Corringham, Essex (1862–87). During the interim, however, there is much documentation of his activities as an ecclesiologist and musician.

Greatheed's name is found among the members of the Cambridge Camden Society as early as 1843. His first significant visibility within the Society came with *The Ecclesiologist's* publication of his lengthy letter to the editor, 'On the various styles of church music, and their analogy with those of church architecture' in October 1848. During 1851 the Greatheeds, who at the time lived in

---

[163] J. Pearce (1984) 33.
[164] *The Ecclesiologist*, 18/118 (February 1857) 51.

Sevenoaks, became intimate friends of Benjamin Webb and his wife. A dinner party in Brasted on 26 April 1851 seems to have been the occasion on which the two couples became acquainted, since immediately thereafter visits occurred several times a week. By the end of June contact was almost daily, and S.S. Greatheed was a frequent participant in the choral services at Brasted, whether as priest or choir member.[165] We have seen (: 112) that this relationship continued after the Webbs moved to Sheen in Staffordshire. Given the timing of this friendship's establishment, it is neither surprising nor accidental that on 12 June 1851 Greatheed was added to the Musical Committee of the ECCS.[166] He attended meetings faithfully, and in 1853 succeeded W.C. Luard as treasurer of the ECCS, a position Greatheed held for eleven years.[167]

An analogy between church music and architecture

Greatheed's 1848 letter to *The Ecclesiologist* was the most extensive attempt made within its pages to draw definite parallels between church music and church architecture.[168] As background, he referred to three previous statements on the subject. In 1846 *The Ecclesiologist* had compared Palestrina to 'Middle Pointed' architecture, Haydn and Pergolesi to the 'beautiful debasements' which followed.[169] During March of the same year the *English Review* had asserted:

> It was well observed by one who is both a good Churchman and a good musician, that at Milan, where the Gregorian tones continue to be used with a laudable tenacity, they seemed too stern for the services; they seemed *like a piece of grand and awful Norman amidst the elaborate delicate fretwork of a florid Perpendicular chapel.* [170]

Finally, Greatheed referred to Lord Lindsay's *History of Christian Art* (vol. 2, letter 1), which maintained that music and architecture were in especial agreement with one another, and differed from poetry, painting, and sculpture because both of them expressed emotion rather than definite ideas.

The first analogy he drew concerned architectural and musical types. Grecian architecture was characterized by horizontal lines, Greatheed maintained, which could be seen to correspond with monody, a single succession of notes varying within the limited compass of the human voice, but essentially one horizontal line. Pointed architecture was predominated by vertical lines, which could be related to the simultaneous multiplicity of pitches which created harmony, a vertical sensation, the height and depth of which was

---

[165] Webb diaries, April–July 1851.
[166] *The Ecclesiologist*, 12/85 (August 1851) 285.
[167] *The Ecclesiologist*, 25/163 (August 1864) 210.
[168] *The Ecclesiologist*, 9/68 (October 1848) 107–113.
[169] *The Ecclesiologist*, 5/– (June 1846) 252. (: 39)
[170] Cited in *The Ecclesiologist*, 9/68 (October 1848) 108.

limited only by the ear's ability to perceive sounds as musical. The multiple planes of decoration indigenous to Pointed architecture were seen to be comparable to the individual musical lines, each possessing its own integrity, which were the architecture of counterpoint and thereby of harmony. Since Greatheed saw harmony as the fundamental counterpart to Pointed architecture, he was obliged to assert that, although the birth of both was more or less simultaneous, harmony had remained in an 'infantine state' while architecture had matured and decayed, and that music had followed a similar cycle at a distance of several centuries. The primary difference between the development of the two was that, unlike architecture, which had regressed to classical models after Pointed architecture had run its full course, music had continually progressed. The explanation for this lay therein, that music had not yet reached maturity and thereby satiated the appetite, and that no early pagan musical models were extant to be imitated.

Greatheed's next task, then, was to compare the progress and decay of music with the same cycle in the period of architecture which ecclesiologists considered to be the best: Pointed (or Gothic). The fundamental idea was:

> Words are to music what symbolism is to architecture. Music without words, and architecture without symbolism, may please the senses and move the feelings, but with them, they not only do this, but also convey positive instruction. Now, in First-Pointed, we know that symbolism was paramount, in Middle it appears to have been declining, and in Third to have been quite extinct. So the earliest musical style was altogether vocal, the second is equally adapted to voices and to instruments, and the third is peculiarly an instrumental style.[171]

For the purpose of comparison Greatheed adopted William Crotch's three musical styles (: 40–2), quoting from the *Parish Choir*,[172] and the result may be seen in Table 4.2.

The immediate difficulty with this analogy was that the ECCS's preferred style of architecture, Middle Pointed, was equated with the *beautiful* rather than the *sublime* style, and thereby to composers who were not in favour with ecclesiologists. Greatheed proceeded to explain why the analogy broke down. He asserted that, in addition to 'natural talent and patient study', a sacred artist must possess a '*devotional feeling*, ardent but reverent', and that this was what architects of Middle Pointed had which was lacking in composers of the Italianate style. In addition, he thought that contemporary familiarity with the secular uses of the Italian style made it less suited to church use.

Greatheed stated that the three kinds of Pointed architecture were merely variations of one style, all of which employed the same materials; and therefore none of them could be said to be perfect in all respects. The middle

---

[171] *The Ecclesiologist*, 9/68 (October 1848) 111.
[172] *Parish Choir*, 1/3 (April 1846) 24.

style should be adopted in order not to lose sight of any. The three musical styles, however, employed different materials and were adapted to different purposes. Ignoring the 'faults' of individual composers, Greatheed believed each of the musical styles to be perfect in its kind. Given this premise, there was no need for the music used in worship all to be of one style. Early vocal music deserved peculiar respect simply because, 'as the human voice is confessedly the noblest of instruments, music for voices only is the noblest kind of homogeneous music.'[173]

Table 4.2 S.S. Greatheed's analogy of church music and church architecture

Architectural style	*Crotch's musical style*	*Greatheed's musical examples*
First Pointed	Sublime	Early polyphony, e.g. Palestrina, Victoria, Tallis, Gibbons, Lassus
(transitional period)		Purcell and most Restoration composers
Middle Pointed	Beautiful	Italianate composers, e.g. Pergolesi, Naumann, Kent
(transitional period)		Haydn, Mozart
Third Pointed	Ornamental	Germanic composers, e.g. Beethoven, Mendelssohn, Spohr

It is somewhat astonishing that *The Ecclesiologist* printed these opinions without a disclaimer and, further, that they prompted no letters to the editor in reply. Greatheed's ideas clearly bore no relation to ecclesiological thought or historical reality, and perhaps as little relation to common sense. Nevertheless they are interesting as an early, if fanciful, attempt to understand how the histories of architecture and music might be compared. At the very least they are another suggestion of an early willingness on the part of some ecclesiologists to countenance a variety of musical styles.

---

[173] *The Ecclesiologist*, 9/68 (October 1848) 110, 112–13.

The Revd John Lake Crompton

John Lake Crompton was born on 15 November 1815 in Norwich. After schooling at Brompton, Middlesex, he matriculated in Michaelmas 1833 at Sidney Sussex College, Cambridge, and migrated to Trinity College in July 1836, where he took his BA the following year. He was ordained deacon in December 1838, priest one year later; and from 1838 to 1842 he served as curate of Wick Risington in Gloucestershire.[174] His resignation was apparently necessitated by health problems, which thereafter forced him to leave England during the winter months. By the early 1850s he is known to have wintered regularly at Funchal, Madeira, where he married Harriet Phelps, a talented pianist and harpist, on 25 November 1854.[175] From the early 1840s until at least 1853, he acted as assistant curate of 'All Saints', Marylebone' during the more temperate months of the year, i.e. Margaret Chapel and its interim chapels while All Saints', Margaret Street was under construction. He is also thought to have assisted for some time at St Mary Magdalene, Munster Square. Involvement in two of the metropolis's most advanced churches in the revival of worship would have put him in contact with all of the leading ecclesiologists.[176]

In 1849 Masters published Crompton's edition of *The Prefaces in the Office of Holy Communion,* which were set to the ancient chant. It contained a lengthy and scholarly introduction, which cited an impressive array of ancient sources to prove that the practice of singing the preface to the Communion Office was a common practice of the Church which dated from before the time of St Gregory. The body of the work gave ferial and festal versions of the *Sursum corda,* the preface, and the proper prefaces for Christmas, Easter, Ascension, Whit Sunday, and Trinity. Although modern notation was used, Crompton advised, 'The Chant is merely *rhythmical*, not *metrical*'; and again, 'The notes generally are to be considered as only expressing an *approximation* to the solemn flow of a devout recitation.'[177] The *Parish Choir* welcomed the volume and hoped that it would be adopted wherever the Communion Service was performed chorally.[178]

This contribution to the revival of worship alone was more than sufficient to justify his inclusion among the original members of the musical committee of the Ecclesiological Society in 1850.[179] But liturgical music was a lifelong

---

[174] 'Lake [post Crompton, J.L.], John,' in Venn, *Alumni Cantabrigienses*; 'Crompton, John Lake,' in *Crockford's Clerical Dictionary*, 1889; and *Clergy Lists,* 1841, 1842.
[175] 'Crompton, Canon John Lake,' in Spencer, *British Settlers in Natal. 1824–1857. A Biographical Register,* 24–30.
[176] See Venn; *Crockford's;* and Whitworth (1891) 61.
[177] Crompton (1849) viii.
[178] *Parish Choir,* 3/44 (August 1849) 20.
[179] *The Ecclesiologist,* 11/79 (August 1850) 135.

interest for Crompton. Even when health removed him to Madeira, he 'enriched' the library of the Ecclesiological Motett Choir with an original composition for use in the English Communion Service, written under his direction by a musician named Dos Santos.[180]

In February 1857 Crompton emigrated permanently to Natal, South Africa, due to his health problems, where he settled in a village called Pine Town. He lost little time before he became involved in the work of church revival and embroiled in controversy over his own ritualistic tendencies. In April of the same year he attended a vestry meeting at his local church, St Paul's, 'causing the meeting frequently to degenerate "into a babel and brawl" because of "his constant interruption, speeches and interpolations"' to point out ways in which he felt canon law was being broken. A letter dated 7 May 1857 reveals that he had already teamed up with the Revd Robert Robertson to adapt the Zulu litany to plainsong.[181] Robertson was a fellow Anglican priest who, as early as December 1855, had firmly established the use of chants attributed to Tallis in worship services he conducted for his Zulu parishioners.[182]

Francis Henry Dickinson, Esq.

F.H. Dickinson (1813–90) matriculated at Trinity College, Cambridge, in 1831 and took his BA in 1835, the same year in which he was admitted to the Inner Temple. In 1837 he inherited his family's estate at Kingweston, Somerset, which served as his primary residence for the remainder of his life. He served as member of Parliament for West Somerset 1841–7, but never sought re-election thereafter.[183] His name appears on the membership list of the Cambridge Camden Society for 1843, and after the Society's removal to London in 1846 he became an active member of its Committee. During 1855 and 1857 he managed to be present at half of the Committee meetings in London despite his many other commitments and the substantial travel which his attendance necessitated.[184]

Residence in Somerset did not in any sense remove him from church society. Throughout the period his name is highly prominent among the lists of notable persons published in the press for having attended various consecrations, celebrations, and other meetings of interest to ecclesiologists. Although much of Dickinson's influence on the church revival has little identifiable

---

[180] *The Ecclesiologist*, 15/103 (August 1854) 269.
[181] 'Crompton, Canon John Lake,' in Spencer, *British Settlers in Natal. 1824–1857. A Biographical Register*, 25.
[182] Darby (unpublished MA thesis, The University of Natal, 1977) 138.
[183] Biographical details from Venn, *Alumni Cantabrigienses*; *Guardian*, 2330 (30 July 1890) 1196, and 2331 (6 August 1890) 1246–7.
[184] RIBA: Ecclesiological Society Minutes, ES/1.

connection with music and often cannot adequately be traced, it seems appropriate to chronicle briefly the achievements of one who was so intimately a part of the ECCS's innermost circle. The musical legacy left by Dickinson, nonetheless, was of immense and lasting value.

Dickinson's first great contribution to the church revival was his initiative to found Wells Theological College in 1840. The idea came about during a visit by Archdeacon Manning (of Chichester, where the first diocesan theological college had been founded in 1839) to Dickinson's estate. Together they visited Archdeacon Brymer (of Bath), who stated that he wished to make a charitable donation of £1000. It was Manning who suggested a theological college, but Dickinson took up the idea the next day, and together with the help of Brymer, Chancellor Law, and Lord John Thynne, he set out to raise the necessary funds.[185] Dickinson and Brymer guaranteed £100 per annum toward the principal's salary, and the Revd J.H. Pindar was persuaded to accept the post.[186] The first student was admitted in May 1840. Until his death in 1890, Dickinson was a stalwart member of the Trustees, and the College history records that 'his intellectual alertness and keen perception in business matters were of infinite value to the College during a period of fifty years.'[187]

It is appropriate to note that he was a 'constant attender' of committee meetings for important church organizations throughout his life, including both the ECCS and the Society for the Promotion of the Gospel. Bishop Edmund Hobhouse, writing in high praise of his friend's contributions to the health and welfare of the Church of England, stated that it was Dickinson's evangelical upbringing which moulded much of his character and fostered his lifelong zeal for religious matters. In 1854 Dickinson 'rebuilt' his parish church 'wholly at his own cost.'[188] Dickinson was among the earliest contributors to the *Guardian* and published frequent letters within its pages, often on Church constitutional matters, up until a few weeks before his death.[189]

A final contribution to the church revival was the publication of the *Sarum Missal* 1861–83, which serves as a fundamental source of reference for musicologists to this day. Dickinson was the primary editor of this work, which was begun in 1855. Benjamin Webb received credit for proof-reading and 'many valuable suggestions', and J.M. Neale, Beresford Hope, and J.D. Chambers were among the other individuals specifically thanked for their assistance. Dickinson stated that the purposes of publication were:

---

[185] Elwes (1923) 1–2.
[186] *Guardian*, 2330 (30 July 1990) 1196.
[187] Elwes (1923) 3, 59, 105.
[188] *Guardian*, 2330 (30 July 1990) 1196.
[189] *Guardian*, 2329 (23 July 1890) 1160.

1. to throw light on the history of the Book of Common Prayer,
2. to gain insight into the religious practice of the forefathers of the Church of England, and
3. to be of assistance in determining the nature of the ritual and services of the early Church.

'Without under-rating the first and second objects, it was the third which principally guided this effort,' he revealed. The great delays in publication were attributed to William Scott's calls for the comparison and collation of various source texts, which unfortunately prevented the material from having an earlier and wider influence; yet there can be no doubt that leading ecclesiologists had access to the knowledge as it was accumulated.[190]

John David Chambers, Esq.

J.D. Chambers (BA 1827, Oriel College, Oxford) appears on the list of members published by the Cambridge Camden Society as early as in 1843, by which time he had taken up his professional life's work as Recorder of Salisbury. He was evidently much in London, however, and knew Beresford Hope and other ecclesiologists, as a fellow attender of Margaret Chapel. Chambers is credited with having been prominent among those who saved Margaret Chapel from closure in 1848 when the lease was due to expire, and is thought to have made himself solely liable for the ground rent.[191] After the Cambridge Camden Society's removal to London in 1846, he became more active in its affairs, and eventually was added to the musical committee in the early 1850s.

In 1852 Joseph Masters published Chambers' first important contribution to the revival of choral worship:

> *The Psalter, or Seven Ordinary Hours of Prayer According to the Use of the Illustrious and Excellent Church of Sarum. And the Hymns, Antiphons, and Orisons or Collects, for the Principal Festivals and Seasons; with the Appropriate Musical Intonation and Melodies. Together with Hymns, and other Devotions, from Ancient English Sources, and the More Important Variations of the York and Hereford Uses. Also, the Litany and Vigils of the Dead.*

The length of the book's title is indicative of the amount of material contained therein. For scholars, relevant supplementary information was supplied in lengthy footnotes, but not at the expense of the book's practicality. Chambers fully intended it to be used for private devotions; all the relevant texts for each liturgy of each day were given in English with their corresponding chants,

---

[190] Preface to *Missale ad usum insignis et praeclarae Ecclesiae Sarum*, ed. F.H. Dickinson (1861–83) i, iv.
[191] Whitworth (1891) 52.

while the original Latin hymn texts were given side-by-side with their English translations.

Hymn translation was Chambers' speciality. His participation on the committee to issue the second part of the *Hymnal Noted* [192] caused a certain amount of frustration on the part of J.M. Neale. Chambers was apparently hesitant or unwilling to collaborate, either to correct Neale's translations or to hear suggestions for the improvement of his own, and Neale did not think that Chambers had sufficient knowledge of ancient hymnody to be doing the task on his own. Furthermore, Neale thought that Chambers' Sarum psalter should have used the same hymn translations as those issued in the *Hymnal Noted*.[193]

Chambers' interest in ancient hymnody continued long after the publication of the *Hymnal Noted*. In 1857 Masters and J.A. Novello both issued part one of his *Lauda Syon. Ancient Latin Hymns of the English and other Churches, translated into corresponding metres*. It consisted of 246 pages of hymns in English, and the second part, which appeared with the subtitle *Hymns of the Saints and Angels* in 1866, provided an additional 116 pages. No Latin texts were given, other than the original Latin titles for each hymn, which were used to index the two volumes. One of Chambers' translations, 'All hail, adorèd Trinity' (*Ave colenda Trinitas*) sung to the tune 'Illsley', is still found in the *English Hymnal*.

The postscript to the second volume of *Lauda Syon*, dated May 1866, commended the two volumes to those engaged in compiling vernacular hymn collections with the following words:

> The compositions of the early and middle age of Christianity, are mostly couched in majestic and solemn language – dignified, yet flowing metres, and always embody and express deep and catholic truths, conjoined with earnest and fervid prayer and ascriptions of praise. To this excellence the sentimental effusions of more modern times scarcely ever attain, although often superior in mere poetical and imaginative feeling.

He did not deny the possibility that modern poets might equal or surpass their spiritual forefathers, but merely set the ancient work before the world as an aid to contemporary devotion and a model for imitation.

William Dyce, Esq.

We have seen that *The Ecclesiologist* noted the musical work of William Dyce and voiced its unqualified support and gratitude for his publication of *The Order of Service... with Plain Tune* in 1843. Benjamin Webb's friendship with

---

[192] *The Ecclesiologist*, 14/95 (April 1853) 118.
[193] Letters from Neale to Webb, 19 March 1851 and 6 September 1852, quoted in Lawson (1910) 175–6, 195.

William Dyce began when the two met at a madrigal party on 13 January 1845, and Dyce was made an honorary member of the Ecclesiological late Cambridge Camden Society soon thereafter. (: 32–3) In 1850 he was one of the founding members of the musical committee of the ECCS. (: 63)

In 1841 Dyce wrote one of the most interesting mid-nineteenth century expositions on the history of church music, which was thoroughly in line with what would became the ecclesiological approach to the subject. He opened a series of four articles for the *Christian Remembrancer*[194] with the question, 'Why is it that the Music of the Church has not yet occupied a place among the researches of the numerous band of inquirers who are now engaged in tracing the influence of Christianity on the arts?' Music, he continued, was 'the only art that comes to us with apostolical commendation' and was 'the first of the arts canonized by ecclesiastical authority.' Music, he thought, was the key to the spiritual revitalization of the Church:

> If the sacred architecture and painting of past ages are justly believed to afford us faithful images of Christian poetry, much more may the sacred music be thought capable of giving us communion with the very spirit that animated them. If the former make us acutely sensible how ruined and dilapidated the outward framework of religion has become, much more may the strains in which the ancient Church breathed forth the incense of her praise, awaken us to a perception of the very different spirit that is borne on the sounds of modern worship.[195]

Dyce insisted that the music of the Church could not be judged by the same criteria as other music; the best church music must be that which most faithfully conveyed 'Christian sentiment.' Although music had added to its resources and power during recent centuries, the rise of opera and the secularization of musical style during the 'vicious and frivolous age of Charles II' were blamed for a decline in the quality of church music. Even Purcell did not escape censure for bowing to the pressure of the theatricality of his age.[196]

The obvious remedy for a debased style of church music, Dyce believed, was to return to earlier models. Accordingly he headed each of the four articles with the inscription *'Revertimini vos ad fontem Sancti Gregorii, quia manifeste corruptis cantilenam ecclesiasticam'*,[197] words which had been uttered by Charlemagne to settle a dispute between Frankish and Italian singers over whose plainsong use was less corrupt. The water would be purer nearer to the fountain whence it issued, he advised, and to it they should return. This was the principle, Dyce thought, on which the reformation of contemporary church music should proceed. In recommending that models from the acknowledged high point of church music be studied and practised,

---

[194] Authorship attributed by Pointon (1979) 71–3.
[195] Dyce in the *Christian Remembrancer*, 1 (February 1841) 104, 105.
[196] *Christian Remembrancer*, 1 (February 1841) 105–110.
[197] Dyce footnotes these words to Joan Diac. Lib. II. c. 9.

he wrote, 'we are only advising that mode of cultivating the taste which in all the arts is reckoned to be the most efficient.'[198] Even if this were done for merely antiquarian reasons, he believed, 'its influence will serve, more than any other cause, to correct the false taste of modern composition.' Still greater rewards were possible, however:

> we trust, also, that, in this new disposition, there is the best groundwork for a reformation of the music of the church. It is not, however, by an ephemeral taste for old music alone that this much-needed and, in many quarters, much desired reform will be effected. There must be, at the same time, as in matters of higher import, a return to first principles.

He hoped that in the study of church music might be found 'safe and legitimate grounds on which to build the superstructure of a reformation', as well as a revelation of 'the spirit in which the art was formerly exercised under the sanction of ecclesiastical authority.'[199] The course which had been taken by the Oxford Movement to regain lost theological principles should serve as an example to those who would labour for the revival of church music, not for antiquarian reasons, but as a means to revitalize Christian art and, thereby, contemporary spirituality.

It is hardly surprising that Dyce was recruited to the ranks of the ecclesiologists. Indeed, the primary principles and convictions of ecclesiology can be distilled from his articles as follows:

1. God is worthy to receive the very best offerings which humankind is capable of giving; conversely, it is the Church's duty and man's appropriate response to offer unto God the best they possibly can.
2. The revival of the aesthetic elements of medieval Christian worship would assist in the revitalization of spirituality.
3. The study and revival of the best artistic models of earlier ages would rescue contemporary ecclesiastical art from its state of degradation and set it on course to develop in a valid and vital way.

Thus we see that ecclesiologists spared no personal labours to put into practice the principles which they identified to guide the revival of choral worship. Such great sacrifices of both time and money cannot be attributed to mere antiquarianism. The revival they sought was clearly a spiritual one.

---

[198] *Christian Remembrancer*, 1 (April 1841) 284–5.
[199] *Christian Remembrancer*, 1 (February 1841) 112.

CHAPTER FIVE

The ecclesiological apologetic for church music

Perhaps the most significant way in which ecclesiologists promoted the revival of choral worship was by their unrelenting defence of it. This they did by their own contributions to expound an apologetic of church music, which often reveal great ingenuity in wielding various polemical skills of persuasion, and also through their regular notices of publications on the subject which sympathised with their views or begged words of correction.

Given the tendency of the Church to look to the past for authority and guidance, it is not surprising that ecclesiologists did just that in their consideration of the music of worship. Combining the study of the pre-Reformation musical heritage of the Church of England, efforts to discover the musical intentions of the Reformers, and appeals to historical documents and apologies for church music by respected Anglican divines, ecclesiologists promoted a conviction among the clergy that choral worship was not only desirable but necessary to the spiritual revitalization of the Church in their own times.[1] It was this which, to a large extent, won the battle for choral worship among the clergy.

The only other extended work in print on this aspect of the choral revival is William Gatens' *Victorian Cathedral Music in Theory and Practice* (1986). The purpose here, however, is not to discuss the theory of cathedral music, but rather the overall apologetic of Anglican church music – historically, spiritually, and practically – as it was believed by ecclesiologists to apply to the Victorian Church. Only the ideas that comprise the ecclesiological apologetic of church music will be discussed. Reference will be made exclusively to sources known to have been read by leading ecclesiologists and to have been formative in the development of their apologetic of church music. This will reveal how the combined force of arguments by many authors succeeded in establishing particular ideas for use in the promotion and defence of choral service. Only those apologists who contributed to the ecclesiological apologetic of choral worship during the first two periods of ecclesiologists' involvement in its revival (1839–55) will be considered. It will be apparent that the apology thus formed was complete in itself, and was thoroughly capable of gaining the support of clergymen whose sympathies broadly conformed to mainstream ecclesiological thought.

---

[1] This idea is stated in countless ways and places, among them in the *Parish Choir*, 1/16 (April 1847) 130.

The purpose of this exercise, then, is not to trace the origin of the ideas themselves but

1. to learn what the common ideas were which lay within the range of opinion espoused by those clergymen who belonged within the general mould of an ecclesiologist,
2. to uncover some of the contemporary Victorian sources of inspiration for these ideas, and
3. to reveal the contribution ecclesiologists made toward spreading them.

In fact, few of the thoughts on church music which were promoted by either the Ecclesiological (late Cambridge Camden) Society or the Society for the Promotion of Church Music were original to them. As ecclesiologists had done in their advocacy of Gothic Revival architecture for churches, they borrowed arguments freely from historical and contemporary writings, and rewrote and amplified them for the good of the cause. It is well to remember that their primary interest, in this as in other aspects of the church revival, was to identify and spread principles of truth, and truth was not something which they proposed to invent. Theirs was primarily the work of *justifying* the revival of choral worship in the minds of clergymen, of working to restore a jewel of Anglicanism which they felt had regrettably been lost, and spreading their principles through every available means.

Allies in Holy War

Ecclesiologists were neither the first nor the only churchmen to enter the battle field to champion the cause of church music. Their most important ally was arguably the Society for the Promotion of Church Music (1846–51). As previously mentioned, in April 1849 *The Ecclesiologist* apologized for having neglected to acknowledge 'that those principles for which we have so long contended' were 'ably and consistently supported by our contemporary the *Parish Choir.*'[2] In his very first article for *The Ecclesiologist* later that year, Thomas Helmore encouraged his readers to:

> consult our excellent contemporary, 'The Parish Choir', which, in addition to its primary object of spreading sound information upon Ecclesiastical Music, urges... the propriety of Catholic arrangement in churches, and a due observance of ritual and rubric. We have great pleasure in expressing our gratitude to it for its valuable services; and if sometimes we see ideas and opinions in it, which we could not ourselves admit, we must remember the prejudices of the

---

[2] *The Ecclesiologist*, 9/71 (April 1849) 336.

people, for whom this publication is chiefly intended, and overlook occasional unsatisfactory expressions, in consideration of the great preponderating good.[3]

The previous month the *Parish Choir* had highly recommended Helmore's newly published *Psalter Noted* to its readers, and lauded Helmore for his significant work for the cause of church music through the influence of the services at St Mark's College, Chelsea.[4] Later that year the *Parish Choir* praised John Mason Neale's anonymous article on English hymnody in the *Christian Remembrancer* for November 1849.[5]

In March 1851 the editors of the *Parish Choir* announced that a decision had been reached to cease publication. The periodical had survived 'childhood', which was more than critics had expected, and it went on:

> We trust, ere long, to be enabled to give evidences of a riper growth, and to pass through a second stage of existence, as favourably as we have achieved our first. In plain terms we contemplate the commencement of a new series of a more advanced character, and with certain new features, which are in course of being matured.[6]

The second series was never published, and it is probable that this was due in part to the fact that *The Ecclesiologist* and the ECCS zealously took up the cause of church music in 1850.

The editor of the *Parish Choir*, Robert Druitt, did not officially join the Ecclesiological (late Cambridge Camden) Society until 1853, and then he did so under the auspices of the Motett Choir.[7] By that time most High Church and Tractarian defenders of church music had already allied themselves under the umbrella of the ECCS. Yet a degree of cooperation between the two societies was plainly evident by November 1850 when, in an advisory capacity to Thomas Helmore, William Dyce wrote that the Revd J.W. Twist[8] had assured him that the periodical's proposed publication of hymns would not interfere with the publication of the *Hymnal Noted*.[9] The *Parish Choir* never made the slightest move to compete with ecclesiologists' musical efforts, but saw them as allies, each of whose work complemented the other. By this date

---

[3] *The Ecclesiologist*, 10/75 (November 1849) 212. From the beginning it had been the avowed policy of the *Parish Choir* to move slowly toward a better style of church music. It stated that its primary purpose was 'to teach principles, and to bring the public by degrees to act upon them.' *Parish Choir*, 1/5 (June 1846) 37–8. (: 44–5)
[4] *Parish Choir*, 3/46 (October 1849) 38.
[5] *Parish Choir*, 3/47 (November 1849) 42.
[6] *Parish Choir*, 3/63 (March 1851) 202.
[7] Reported in *The Ecclesiologist*, 14/99 (December 1853) 436–7.
[8] J.W. Twist was very probably the first musical editor of the *Parish Choir*. Dyce wrote to Twist in 1850 to make sure that the *Parish Choir's* proposed publication of hymns would not interfere with the *Hymnal Noted* (Dyce Papers: TAM 54/22); and the posthumous preface (p. 4) to volume 3 of the *Parish Choir* reveals that its first musical editor had been a knowledgeable clergyman.
[9] Letter from Dyce to Helmore, 2 November 1850. Dyce Papers: TAM 54/22.

the imminent cessation of the *Parish Choir's* publication had probably been discussed.

The views propounded by *The Ecclesiologist* and the *Parish Choir* on church music were so well considered and eloquently presented that it cannot be surprising that both appealed to students in the universities. The continued influence of the ECCS upon members of the University of Cambridge in the early 1850s has been noted already. The significance of the *Parish Choir's* influence upon students at Cambridge who were preparing for holy orders is suggested in a letter from a resident member of Trinity College in 1848:

> A more correct taste [in church music] is spreading among the junior members of the University, which is much encouraged by your invaluable publication, which is well read and appreciated by most of us, and in due time we shall hope to see the fruits.[10]

Due to the common vision and principles held by ecclesiologists and the *Parish Choir*, their demonstrated sympathy and cooperation with one another, their combined influence upon the clergy of the Church of England and upon future ordinands while at University, it is highly informative to survey their work in the theoretical propagation and defence of church music. Reference will be limited to views expressed in *The Ecclesiologist* and the *Parish Choir* and to other writings which were specifically mentioned by them.

The apologists

Reference to the writings of respected divines from past ages formed a significant part of the mid-Victorian crusade for the revival of choral service. Writers for the *Parish Choir*, especially, searched the writings of respected theologians and called attention to many powerful and timely passages. Dispute on the subject of church music, after all, was not unique to the times. Among the many divines thus quoted, two stand pre-eminent throughout the Victorian literature. They were Richard Hooker and Thomas Bisse.

Richard Hooker (c.1554–1600) was '*par excellence* the apologist of the Elizabethan Settlement of 1559 and perhaps the most accomplished advocate that Anglicanism has ever had.'[11] His *Treatise on the Laws of Ecclesiastical Polity* was certainly known to every mid-Victorian Anglican clergyman who held a university degree. In 1836 John Keble published a new edition of Hooker's works, which reached a third edition in 1845 and a fourth by 1863. Keble felt that the dangers which had beset the Church in Hooker's time were neither dissimilar from, nor more perilous than, those which faced the Victorian Church in the early 1840s. He stated in the preface that he would

---

[10] Letter from 'Aliquis' dated 14 March 1848, *Parish Choir*, 2/29 (May 1848) 62.
[11] 'Hooker, Richard,' *Oxford Dictionary of the Christian Church* (2nd edn) 665.

consider his efforts amply repaid if the edition awakened any churchmen to a sense of the present danger, and directed their attention to 'the primitive and apostolical Church, as the ark of refuge divinely provided for the faithful.'[12] The learned Hooker had not overlooked the subject of church music, and his views in turn were quoted by Thomas Bisse, the *Parish Choir*, the *English Churchman*, and mentioned casually by many other mid-Victorian authors.[13] As will be detailed below, Hooker observed the power of music to move the affections, discussed its historical use in Jewish and Christian worship, defended its appropriateness in post-Reformation worship, and commented on its ability to refine human nature and spiritually edify base minds. His view of church music was essentially, 'let ancient custom prevail.'[14]

In 1842 the Revd Frederick Pearce Pocock, (BA 1841, Peterhouse, Cambridge), published a new edition of *The Beauty of Holiness in the Common Prayer. To which is added, A Rationale on Cathedral Worship* by the Revd Thomas Bisse (1675–1731). Credited with having imbued the Three Choirs Festival with a 'religious and charitable character' at a time when it had been a merely musical affair,[15] Bisse was a well-known High Churchman in his own time. So popular were his sermons, Pocock tells us, that they went through ten editions between 1716 and 1744. Pocock had undertaken to have these particular works republished due to their devotional character and relevance to the increasing interest in the due performance of the liturgy among earnest churchmen. He hoped that it would encourage them to rectify the deficiencies in contemporary church music, especially in regard to singing the Psalms of David.[16] No doubt the ensuing popularity of this publication exceeded Pocock's fondest dreams, for Bisse came to be the pre-Victorian apologist most widely quoted and referred to in the defence of choral service during the first twenty years of its Victorian revival.[17]

Nineteenth-century essays on church music that were most frequently cited by ecclesiologists and the *Parish Choir*, and which obviously contributed greatly to the formation and effective propagation of their views on choral worship, included:

---

12 Keble's 1841 preface to Hooker, *Works* (ed. Keble, 3rd edn, 1845) cvii–cviii.
13 Bisse, *Rationale* (ed. Pocock, 1842) 237; *The Ecclesiologist*, 10/76 (February 1850) 344; 11/79 (August 1850) 105; *Parish Choir*, 2/32 (August 1848) 88; *English Churchman*, 1/2 (12 January 1843 – its second week of publication) 28; Druitt (1845) 38–9; Latrobe (1831) 80, 123, 312–13, 321; *Practical remarks* (1849) 2.
14 Hooker, *Ecclesiastical Polity*, Book V, ch. 38, 39 (ed. Keble, 3rd edn, 1845) 159–69; quote from 168.
15 Bisse, Pocock's preface (1842) viii–ix.
16 Bisse, *Rationale* (ed. Pocock, 1842), preface, xi, xviii–xx.
17 *Parish Choir*, vol. 1: 25, 71–2, 91–2; vol. 2: 37, 45; vol. 3: 22. *English Churchman*, I/16 (20 April 1843) 249–50. Jebb (1843) 263, 354, 357, 366, 371, 400, 431, 437–8, 483. Latrobe (1831) 258–9, 275, 318. Favourably reviewed in *Christian Remembrancer*, IV [new series] (July 1842) 99–100.

William Crotch (1775–1847), Professor of Music at Oxford 1799–1847, *The Substance of Several Courses of Lectures on Music read in the University of Oxford and in the Metropolis* (1831).[18] (: 40–2)

The Revd John Antes Latrobe, *The Music of the Church Considered in Its Various Branches, Congregational and Choral* (1831).[19] This lengthy apologium obviously stemmed from a love of sacred music inculcated from a childhood. His father, the Revd C.I. Latrobe, had published an important six-volume set of sacred music earlier in the century.

John Peace (1785–1861), *Apology for Cathedral Service* (1839).[20] Peace was admitted as a mature student to Christ's College, Cambridge, in 1822. Amid many digressions, Peace brought forth a large number of salient observations which inspired later church music apologists.

The Revd John Jebb wrote various oft-cited works, including *The Choral Service in the United Church of England and Ireland* (1843), *Three Lectures on Church Music* (1845), and *The Principle of Ritualism Defended* (1856).[21] Much has been made of Jebb's differences of opinion with ecclesiologists over the role of the choir and congregation in worship, but it is important to note that there was an enormous amount of common ground between them. In 1849 the *Parish Choir* acknowledged his writings to be 'the standard authorities on the subject' of church music; and *The Ecclesiologist* later referred to *The Choral Service* as 'a work which we hope is in every Cathedral library.'[22]

Robert Druitt began his public advocacy of choral worship with *A Popular Tract on Church Music, with Remarks on its Moral and Political Importance, and a Practical Scheme for its Reformation* (1845). He subsequently served as editor of the *Parish Choir*.[23]

John Hullah (1812–84) published *The Duty and Advantage of Learning to Sing* (Leeds lecture, 1846).[24] (: 7–8, 38–9) As noted earlier, he worked closely

---

[18] 'It is now nearly twenty years since the attention of the Church was drawn to the true principles of *Church* music, properly so called.' *The Ecclesiologist*, 12/84 (June 1851) 172. Crotch's lectures are known to have been extremely influential upon the musical views of Thomas Helmore. (: 42) See also *Parish Choir*, vol. 1: 8, 24; vol. 2: 37, 158. *English Churchman*, vol. 1: 202, 332–3, 475 etc.

[19] Cited many times in the *Parish Choir*, especially in 3/54 (June 1850) 109–10.

[20] Referred to by Thomas Helmore as 'one of the most interesting works on this subject' in *The Ecclesiologist*, 10/76 (April 1850) 380, 382, 384–5; 14/97 (August 1853) 238.

[21] *Parish Choir*, vol. 2: 106, 197–8; vol. 3: 27, 148–50; etc. *English Churchman* vol. 1: 425–6, 460–1, 474–6, 501–2, 660–4; etc. Flower (1851) 16–17.

[22] *Parish Choir*, 3/45 (September 1849) 27. *The Ecclesiologist*, 14/97 (August 1853) 238.

[23] *The Ecclesiologist*, 4/– (July 1845) 182.

[24] *The Ecclesiologist*, 5/– (May 1846) 250–3. *Parish Choir*, 1/14 (February 1847) 112–13; 1/16 (April 1847) 129–30.

with Thomas Helmore at St Mark's College, Chelsea (: 32) and was an acquaintance of Benjamin Webb (: 15).

The Revd Thomas Binney, *The Service of Song in the House of the Lord* (1848).[25] The high view of music in worship maintained by this remarkable tract was all the more useful to advocates of choral service because Binney was a well-known dissenting minister. (He was also a colleague and good friend of Thomas Helmore's father.)[26] In its lengthy review and notice of Binney, the *Parish Choir* was obviously delighted that after three centuries of opposition to choral services, 'we find earnest and active-minded Dissenters openly giving their support to most of the more important arguments in favour of Church Music, which heretofore have been maintained by *High* Churchmen alone.'[27]

Practical Remarks on the Reformation of Cathedral Music was published anonymously in 1849, and received glowing praise from both the *Parish Choir*[28] and *The Ecclesiologist*.[29]

There can be little doubt that *An Earnest Appeal for the Revival of the Ancient Plain Song* (1850) by A.W.N. Pugin (1812–52) was a telling exhortation which confronted ecclesiologists at a time when they were significantly increasing their efforts to study and propagate 'true' church music. Pugin admitted that, due to the efforts of ecclesiologists, church architecture had improved of late; but he added, 'we might have hoped and expected, that with the shell they would have revived the *soul*.' To do so begged the revival of the ancient plainsong, without which 'the service and the fabric will be at utter variance, a most humiliating spectacle of ancient grandeur and modern degeneracy.' He continued:

> Indeed, with few exceptions, the Churches that have been raised after the old models are become so many evidences of our degradation and our shame. The altar and the arch may belong to the ages of faith, but the singing drags us down to the concert-room of the 19th century, and is a sad and striking proof of the little sympathy which exists between the architecture and the men.[30]

Pugin had been on intimate terms with Cambridge ecclesiologists during the early years of the Cambridge Camden Society. In December 1841 and June 1842 Benjamin Webb, Joseph Haskoll, and J.F. Russell visited Pugin at his home in Chelsea.[31] In May and November of 1841 members of the Cambridge

---

[25] *Parish Choir*, 2/26 (February 1848) 39–40.
[26] F. Helmore (1891) 26.
[27] *Parish Choir*, 2/26 (February 1848) 39.
[28] *Parish Choir*, 3/48 (December 1849) 58.
[29] *The Eccleisologist*, 12/82 (February 1851) 78.
[30] Pugin (1850) 7, 8.
[31] Webb diaries, 28 December 1841; 30 June 1842 'a delightful evening.'

Camden Society lionized Pugin around Cambridge.[32] Webb specifically notes having read Pugin's *Apology*, and there is no question that ecclesiologists took the keenest interest in everything he wrote, including his views on music.[33] Upon Pugin's death in 1852, *The Ecclesiologist* explained that its occasional criticism of his work had been necessary because Pugin had been hampered continually by building committees: 'his genius, had it ever had full scope, would have manifested itself in works infinitely superior to those, which, as a fact, it has left behind.' As far as ecclesiologists were concerned, Pugin was 'the most eminent and original architectural genius of his time.'[34]

The Revd William Balmborough Flower (BA 1843, Magdalene College, Cambridge) was a High Churchman who published several eloquent tracts in staunch defence of choral worship, including *The Prayers to be Sung or Said. A Plea for Musical Services* (1851), *Choral Service, the Sacrifice of Praise...* (1853), and *Choral Services and Ritual Observances: Two Sermons* (1856). Although he was a student in Cambridge during the earliest years of the Cambridge Camden Society, his name does not appear among the early membership lists. His churchmanship, however, was entirely sympathetic to that of mainstream ecclesiologists. He eventually joined the ECCS in 1847,[35] and his writings were welcomed by them.[36]

The apologia

In general, the arguments put forth in mid-Victorian apologia of church music fell into three categories. The first consisted of arguments based on the history of Christian worship and relevant biblical references, with especial regard for the English Reformation. The second group of reasons dwelt on the spiritual and heavenly aspects of music in worship, i.e. its power to transcend the human condition and give believers a foretaste of eternal bliss. The third type consisted of practical, common-sense and, sometimes partisan observations aimed at those who did not appreciate or could not understand the more profound considerations related to music in worship. Such polemics were not

---

[32] Webb diaries, 2 and 3 May 1842; 28 November 1842. Benjamin Webb took primary responsibility for showing Pugin around Cambridge, and on 2 May entertained him, Neale, Haskoll, Paley and Stokes for dinner. On 3 May they took Pugin to Ely, where Webb 'found Pugin passionately weeping in the Lady Chapel' following evensong. Archdeacon Thorp entertained Pugin, Webb, Neale, Suckling, and Freeman for dinner at The Lamb.
[33] Webb diaries, 13 April 1843. *The Ecclesiologist*, 11/79 (August 1850) 105. *Parish Choir*, 3/60 (December 1850) 171–2.
[34] Obituary in *The Ecclesiologist*, 13/92 (October 1852) 352–7.
[35] *The Ecclesiologist*, 8/61 (August 1847) 38.
[36] *The Ecclesiologist*, 12/83 (April 1851) 113–117. *Parish Choir*, 3/63 (March 1851) 201.

infrequently couched in very sharp and direct language, their purpose being to bring the uninformed into submission, and to silence the vocal opposition through intimidation. Although the arguments which accrued in this final category are often the most entertaining to read, one suspects that they may have been the least constructive, since the besieged undoubtedly ended up feeling either misrepresented or humiliated. Ecclesiologists used all three methods to encourage singing in worship.

A biblical and historical basis for nineteenth-century Anglican choral worship

It was only natural that those who laboured for the revival of choral service would, like their predecessors who sought the revival of spirituality in the Oxford Tracts, derive inspiration and guidance from ancient and Reformation history. As in the field of architecture, ecclesiologists looked for models, prior to the degradation that characterized contemporary church music, which suggested themselves to be part of the valid inheritance of the Church of England.

The first task was to establish that music had always been considered a vital part of Judeo-Christian worship; this was easily accomplished. The Psalms of David were a legacy left to Jewish and Christian worship for all time; and the psalmist's admonishments to 'sing to the Lord' were too many and familiar to require enumeration. Bisse headed his *Rationale on Cathedral Worship* with a quotation from I Chronicles 16: 4–6, which relates King David's appointment of certain Levites to 'minister before the ark of the Lord, and to record, and to thank and praise the Lord God of Israel' with psalteries, harps, cymbals and trumpets. Zadok and his brethren priests were instructed to make offerings upon the altar, *morning and evening*, and the choral establishment, of which the instruments formed a part, was appointed to assist in the services (I Chronicles 16: 37–42).[37] Since Jewish worship was considered to have been divinely ordained through God's servant, David (I Chronicles 28:19), no higher authority could possibly have existed for musical worship.[38]

New Testament references which mentioned or positively enjoined singing were enumerated at length by, among others, William Dyce in his 1841 articles on church music for the *Christian Remembrancer*, and by the *Parish Choir* in 1850.[39] The gospels according to St Matthew 26:30 and St Mark 14:26 revealed that Christ himself had sung a hymn (identified by the *Parish*

---

[37] Bisse, *Rationale* (ed. Pocock, 1842) 211–13. The *Parish Choir*, 3/56 (August 1850) 126, points to the continuation of Davidic worship by reference to Ezra 3: 10–11; Nehemiah 12: 24, 45, 46; and Ecclesiasticus 47: 8–10. See also *Practical remarks* (1849) 6; and Jebb (1856) 23–4.
[38] Jebb (1856) 23–4.
[39] Dyce in the *Christian Remembrancer*, new series 1 (June 1841) especially 442–3. *Parish Choir*, 3/56 (August 1850) 125–8.

Choir as Psalms 113–118)⁴⁰ at the conclusion of the Last Supper. The apostle Paul mentioned singing in various biblical letters, including: I Corinthians 14:15, 'I will sing with the spirit and I will sing with the mind also'; Ephesians 5:18–19, 'be filled with the Spirit, addressing one another in psalms and hymns and spiritual songs, singing and making melody to the Lord with all your heart'; and Colossians 3:16, 'Let the word of Christ dwell in you richly, teach and admonish one another in all wisdom, and sing psalms and hymns and spiritual songs with thankfulness in your hearts to God.' St James (5:13) had admonished the suffering faithful to pray, and the cheerful to sing praise. Clearly Christ and the apostles assumed music to be an integral part of worship and Christian life.

The view that music is an efficacious means to move the human spirit into profound levels of spiritual experience has found numerous and learned advocates throughout the history of Christianity. Hooker, Dyce, and the *Parish Choir* cited the testimonies of St Ignatius (c.35–c.107), Justin Martyr (c.100–c.165), Origen (c.185–c.254), St Basil (c.330–379), St Ambrose (339–97) and St Augustine (354–430), among many others, which clearly demonstrated that the early Church continued to view music as an integral part of worship.⁴¹

What was the music which accomplished this? However incomplete the historical knowledge of early Christian music may have been in the 1840s, it was well known that plainsong had been the music of the liturgy from the earliest days of the Church, that it had probably derived from the worship of the Temple, and that it had been the continuous vehicle of Catholic worship down to their own time. The next task which faced early Victorian advocates of choral service, then, was to try to prove that the Reformers had intended plainsong to be retained in the services of the Church of England. This they did by a number of approaches.

In his preface to *The Order of Daily Service* in 1843, William Dyce suggested that a rubrical direction that something should be 'said or sung' was 'not so much *an order to sing* those portions of the service which the direction precedes, as *a license to read* them in the ordinary tone of voice, provided there is no choir.' Other parts of the service, such as the psalms and canticles, were not specifically designated to be sung in some early versions of the Prayer Book, he maintained, because it would have been so self-evident to the Reformers that they *should* be sung, it would never have occurred to them that

---

⁴⁰ The footnote to Matthew 26:30 in *The New Oxford Annotated Bible with the Apocrypha* RSV (2nd edn, 1971) 1208, confirms that the 'hymn' was probably in fact Psalms 113–118.
⁴¹ Hooker, *Ecclesiastical Polity*, v.39.2 (ed. Keble, 3rd edn, 1845) 164–6. Dyce in *Christian Remembrancer*, new series 1 (June 1841) 440–8. See also Jebb (1843) 277–8, 282; and *Practical remarks* (1849) 6–8.

they ought to indicate it.⁴² The *Parish Choir* quoted Archbishop King (1640–1729), who maintained:

> Where persons *can* sing, they are obliged to do so, in obedience to God's command; but where through any defect of nature they *cannot* sing decently, they may be dispensed with saying; only people ought not by this indulgence to be encouraged to neglect singing altogether, or to think that God does not require it of them, when by a little pains and industry, they may attain to the art of decently performing it in His service.⁴³

With the publication of *Hierurgia Anglicana* by members of the ECCS in 1848, ecclesiologists had proclaimed:

> It was never the intention of the compilers of our present services that their work should be considered as a new fabrick, but as a reformation of the existing system. Consequently many things then in actual use, and always intended to be retained, were not expressly commanded, any more than they were distinctly forbidden, in the new rubrick.⁴⁴

This lent weight to a more convincing argument which revealed itself through the comparison of the rubrics of various unreformed service books with those of the *Book of Common Prayer*. The exercise showed that the words *say, read,* and *sing* in the latter were often literal translations of the Latin verbs *dicere, legere,* and *cantare* in the former. A look at the unreformed rites showed that these terms were used more or less interchangeably, and any of them could signify use of a musical tone. The *Parish Choir* quoted a Latin rubric, '*Ante Matutinum dicitur secreto, Pater noster. Deinde clara voce dicitur 'Domine labia mea aperies.*' Here the verb 'is said' was used twice, the first time to designate a kind of private mumble, the second to refer to words which were specifically provided with musical notes, i.e. a monotone with incipit and termination. Another example was cited from a 'Romish Book' of c.1300: '*Post dicitur hymnus Veni Redemptor gentium; et canit dexter chorus primum, et sinister secundum.*' The hymn to be 'said' was in actuality 'sung' antiphonally.⁴⁵

By the late 1840s it was commonly accepted wisdom among ecclesiologists that rubrics in the Book of Common Prayer which instructed words to be 'said' or 'sung' merely offered the choice to 'monotone' them or to chant them to more ornate music. *Hierurgia Anglicana* (1848) maintained that 'plain chant' in the sixteenth century designated anciently prescribed intonations which were peculiar to the several parts of the various Offices, and that,

---

⁴² Dyce, preface (1843), 2. Quoted at length also in the *English Churchman*, 1/13 (30 March 1843) 203; *Practical remarks* (1849) 5; and in Flower, (1851) 8.
⁴³ *Parish Choir* 3/56 (August 1850) 126–7.
⁴⁴ *Hierurgia Anglicana*, i. Maintained also by Flower (1853) 17 and 20, who stated that present reformers, like those of old, merely wished to achieve unity and uniformity.
⁴⁵ *Parish Choir* 2/37 (January 1849) 126; also 1/10 (November 1846) 73–5. Peace (1839) 115–116, hints at this.

> permission is given to 'say,' i.e. to use the plain chant in quires where more elaborate music cannot be obtained; or to 'sing,' i.e. to employ more ornate chants (known as Services) in cathedral and other establishments where there are 'quires' competent to the performance of the same. It is usual on Festival occasions to 'sing,' and on ordinary occasions to 'say' the Offices.[46]

This view was steadfastly adhered to over the years, and gradually gained at least tolerance, if not acceptance, among churchmen educated in Reformation history as a legitimate (i.e. non-papist) interpretation of the reformed rubrics.[47]

The musical practice of the Chapel Royal was cited as proof that the Reformers meant to retain chanting. Surely it was impossible that chanting would have been tolerated in the model Chapel of the realm, where it was under the immediate and watchful eyes of the most influential divines, if it had been considered a Romish abuse. Furthermore the retention of plainsong in the choral services of cathedral and collegiate establishments was as signal a proof as any that the Reformers meant to encourage its use.[48]

Queen Elizabeth's 49th Injunction (1559) was quoted by virtually every nineteenth-century apologist for choral service.[49] *Hierurgia Anglicana* printed it under the heading, *'Plain Song,' Enjoined in All Churches by Queen Elizabeth*:

> Item, because in divers collegiate, and also some parish churches heretofore, there hath been livings appointed for the maintenance of men and children, to use singing in the church, by means whereof the laudable service of musick hath been had in estimation, and preserved in knowledge: The Queen's Majesty, neither meaning in anywise the decay of anything that might conveniently tend to the use and continuance of the said service, neither to have the same in any part so abused in the church, that thereby the Common Prayer should be worse understood of the hearers, willeth and commandeth, that first no alteration be made of such assignments of living, as heretofore hath been appointed to the use of singing or musick in the church, but that the same so remain. *And that there be a modest and distinct song so used in all parts of the Common Prayers in the church, that the same may be as plainly understood as if it were read without singing.*[50]

It is interesting to note that, almost without exception, mid-Victorian quotations of this Injunction ended with a full stop at this point, although the last sentence actually continues:

---

[46] *Hierurgia Anglicana* (1848), 356.
[47] *The Ecclesiologist*, 22/145 (August 1861) 231; 27/174 (June 1866) 146–7. *Practical remarks* (1849) 5; Flower (1853) 18.
[48] *Parish Choir* 2/37 (January 1849) 127.
[49] *Parish Choir*, 1/10 (November 1846) 75; 3/44 (August 1849) 20; 3/49 (January 1850) 60. *The Ecclesiologist*, 10/76 (February 1850) 343; 11/79 (August 1850) 107. Bisse, *Rationale* (1720, ed. Pocock 1842) 244. *Practical remarks* (1849) 11; Flower (1851) 9–10, and (1853) 18. Peace (1839) 86–7.
[50] Italics added by the editor of *Hierurgia Anglicana* (1848) 356.

and yet nevertheless, for the comforting of such that delight in music, it may be permitted that in the beginning, or in the end of common prayers, either at morning or evening, there may be sung an Hymn, or such like song, to the praise of Almighty God, in the best sort of melody and music that may be conveniently devised, having respect that the sentence of the Hymn may be understood and perceived.[51]

Ecclesiologists would have had no desire to provide lovers of metrical psalms and modern hymns with any ammunition to justify their neglect of rendering the service itself chorally.[52]

The *Parish Choir* cited a long line of writers since the Reformation which 'afford distinct proof that the Choral Service was sanctioned by all lawful authorities' from Edward VI to George III. Many of the same writers were also quoted or referred to by *The Ecclesiologist*. Among others these included Archbishop Cranmer, Merbecke, Barnard, Clifford, Lowe, Playford, and Boyce.[53]

Ecclesiologists, as we have seen, insisted that the Reformers had meant the services of the *Book of Common Prayer* to be choral in both cathedrals and parish churches.[54] (: 37, 73–4, 89) There was but one set of rubrics for both; and the music used in pre-Reformation worship, from simple monotone to elaborate polyphony, was intended to be continued or adopted as was most appropriate to the circumstances of each place of worship. In this opinion ecclesiologists were supported by the *Parish Choir*, which stated early in its existence that the 'legitimate and perfect mode of celebrating Divine service' was the choral mode, and that what was commonly known as 'parochial service', denoting a merely read service, was 'a degradation, which has crept in through carelessness, or poverty, or loss of correct principles.'[55] They

---

[51] le Huray (revised 1978) 33. Dr le Huray has modernized the spelling.
[52] The single quotation of this latter portion of the Injunction in *The Ecclesiologist* occurred shortly after the publication of the *Hymnal Noted*, Part I, in 1850. *The Ecclesiologist*, 11/79 (August 1850) 107.
[53] *Parish Choir* 2/37 (January 1849) 127; and 3/49 (January 1850) 59–62, which details contributions by Cranmer, Queen Elizabeth, the Canons of 1604, Edward VI, and Lowe. See also *The Ecclesiologist*, 10/75 (November 1849) 209; 10/76 (February 1850) 342–4; 12/83 (April 1854) 117–19; Jebb (1843) 259; *Practical remarks* (1849) 9–12; and Flower (1853) 18. The scholarship of Drs Peter le Huray and Nicholas Temperley confirms the validity and importance of these sources: le Huray (revised 1978) on Cranmer, 4–7; on Merbecke, 22; on Clifford and Lowe, 159–60; and Temperley (1979) on Playford, 119.
[54] *The Ecclesiologist*, 10/77 (April 1850) 385; 11/79 (August 1850) 109; 14/99 (December 1853) 402; 15/101 (April 1854) 95–6; *Practical remarks* (1849) 17–18.
[55] *Parish Choir*, 1/8 (September 1846) 58. John Jebb agreed on this principle, although, as Gatens points out, Jebb thought the service should ideally be sung by a highly trained choir and less gifted singers should be silent. Jebb (1843) 18–20; Gatens (1986) 30. Jebb's views on this elicited a stern rebuke from the *English Churchman*, 1/27 (6 July 1843) 425–6, and 1/29 (20 July 1843) 461. Flower (1853) 18.

reminded churchmen that plainsong did not fall out of use until the Commonwealth, and that it had become identified with 'cathedral service' only since the Restoration.[56]

A foretaste of heaven

Any in-depth discussion of worship cannot proceed except from a well-formed conception of its essential nature. The Victorians approached the task of definition in two ways, by identifying what worship was, and by specifying what it was not.

The Revd Thomas Bisse, to whom so many Victorians looked for guidance, maintained that the central aspect of worship was praise and thanksgiving. These two acts accounted for most of the service. Parts of the service which did not constitute acts of worship were the lessons, which, 'though a portion of the service, are not part of our worship, being inserted, not as matter of adoration, but of instruction', and the prayers. He concluded:

> by the intention of our Reformers, the daily public worship of our Church doth and ought to consist chiefly of praises and thanksgivings, manifested in doxologies, hallelujahs, in psalms, hymns, and anthems; and that prayers, supplications, and intercessions, as set forth in the Collects and Litany, though necessary duties, should only follow as appendages to that nobler work.[57]

In 1839 John Peace had asserted that preaching was not an essential part of the service. This observation was elaborated upon in 1848 by the Revd Thomas Binney, 'Prayer and praise are the two principal parts of Divine worship; or, perhaps, more properly, the only exercises that *are* worship.'[58] The *Parish Choir* quoted Binney, the Dissenter with higher church views than most Anglicans of the day, almost gleefully:

> Preaching is not worship. The preacher is not worshipping when he speaks, nor the hearers when they hear. More especially, 'preaching the gospel,' in the strict and proper acceptation of the phrase, is not worship; for this may be addressed, with perfect appropriateness, to an assembly of persons, not one of whom may be in a condition qualifying him to unite with the speaker in any Christian act at all.[59]

According to the popular theory of the day the 'end and aim' of public worship was personal edification. This was identified by ecclesiologists to be only one reason for attending divine service, and that a subsidiary one. Its greater aspect was the collective binding together of the members of Christ's mystical Body to intercede for all and to join in the sacrifice of praise. In worship, they

---

[56] *Parish Choir*, 3/49 (January 1850) 61.
[57] Bisse, *Rationale* (ed. Pocock, 1842) 218–23; quotations from 219, 223.
[58] Peace (1839) 39–41; Binney (1848) 1.
[59] *Parish Choir*, 2/26 (February 1848) 39; from Binney (1848) 1.

insisted, believers joined with the saints of all ages, and the service should therefore as nearly as possible imitate that sort of worship which was revealed in the Bible as characteristic of heaven. Bisse proclaimed unequivocally, 'worship *is not for man, but for the Lord God.*'[60]

Binney pointed out that worship services consisted of three kinds of acts – preaching, prayer, and praise – and drew a striking parallel to the well-known scripture, I Corinthians 13:13, 'So faith, hope, love abide, these three; but the greatest of these is love.' (The King James Version of this verse, which would have been the one familiar to Victorians, speaks of faith, hope, and *charity*.) Like faith, preaching would be unnecessary in heaven; and hope, like prayer, would be superseded. But love (charity) and praise would be unending realities. Just as love would be the inward sentiment that would bind together men and angels, so praise would be the outward exercise in which all would unite; and to these *ends* preaching and prayer and faith and hope were but *means*.[61] This analogy bore remarkable resemblance to Bisse's belief that:

> they that are redeemed... have nothing to do in heaven but to sing praises to their Redeemer; which they do before the throne, as we read, resting *not day and night*. Perpetual hallelujahs are represented to be the employment of the heavenly choir... So that we may measure the excellency of praise above prayers and supplications with the same argument as St Paul doth the excellency of charity above faith and hope, not only from its properties, but from its duration – because it *never faileth*. Praise ceaseth not with this state of mortality like the other, but will accompany the saints into heaven even as charity will.[62]

The *Parish Choir* thought that Binney had taken his ideas from Bisse, but later reported that the coincidence was just that, since the former had never read the latter.[63] Because Latrobe found no scriptural authority for the immortality of the sister arts, he felt that the eternal nature of music made it the highest of them all. Certainly, he wrote, music was 'the most enchanting vehicle for the communication of ideas, as well as the most natural and refreshing mode of utterance to an overflowing soul', and 'the most powerful engine to arrest and exalt the feelings on whose wings the breathings of thousands ascend now to the throne of the Holy One.'[64]

The belief that the vision of heavenly worship provided in the Bible should be imitated by the Church Militant was fundamental to the principles which

---

[60] *Parish Choir*, 1/8 (September 1846) 60. Flower (1853) 12–14. Bisse, *Beauty of holiness* (ed. Pocock, 1842) 2.
[61] Binney (1848) 2–3.
[62] Bisse, *Rationale* (ed. Pocock 1848) 219. Quoted also in *Parish Choir*, 1/4 (May 1846) 27; and referred to by Jebb (1856) 12. The Bible verse referred to by Bisse is Revelation 4:8.
[63] *Parish Choir*, 2/26 (February 1848) 39; 2/27 (March 1848) 48.
[64] Latrobe (1831) 80, 146–7.

ecclesiologists espoused for contemporary choral worship.[65] The rich conception of worship in heaven was drawn primarily from the biblical Book of Revelation. Bisse had made numerous references to Revelation (4:8, 14:2–3, 15:2–4), and Jebb based the sermon he preached at St Michael's, Tenbury, on the evening of its consecration on Revelation 5:11,12.[66] In a generally favourable review of *Two Papers on Church Music* (1854) by the Revd Augustus Campbell (Rector of Liverpool), *The Ecclesiologist* complained about the 'total omission of one most important line of argument... the correspondence of services on earth with the worship of heaven.'[67] By this time it had become such an obvious and central apologetic that it seemed irresponsible not to have included it.

The idea that earthly worship takes place in the company of the saints and angels is a biblical one (Hebrews 8:1–5), and the concept had been retained in liturgical practice by the English Reformers during the *Book of Common Prayer* rite for the celebration of Holy Communion. The familiar text follows the proper preface and immediately precedes the *Sanctus*: 'Therefore with Angels and Archangels, and with all the company of heaven, we laud and magnify thy glorious Name; evermore praising thee, and saying, Holy, holy, holy...' In his *Laws of Ecclesiastical Polity, Book V* (Chapter 39), Richard Hooker had provided his own inspiration for this concept by stating that it applied to the whole of Christian worship. He spoke of joining with the angels in 'so many heavenly acclamations, exultations, provocations, petitions, songs of comfort, psalms of praise and thanksgiving.'[68]

A host of witnesses were called upon to demonstrate that this view of worship had been common throughout the history of the English Church. Among them was George Herbert (1593–1633) of whom it was written, 'His chiefest recreation was music, in which heavenly art he was a most excellent master.' So great was his love of music, that he walked to Salisbury twice a week to attend choral services in the cathedral, 'and at his return would say: "that his time spent in prayer, and Cathedral-music, elevated his soul, and was his heaven on earth".'[69] The vision of ideal worship held by ecclesiologists, that of a spiritual experience enhanced by the finest of arts, could want no finer advocate than John Milton (1608–74), who had been sufficiently enraptured by architecture and sacred harmony to write:

---

[65] *Parish Choir*, 1/4 (May 1846) 26. Jebb (1843) 22–3, and (1856) 9–14.
[66] Bisse, *Rationale* (ed. Pocock, 1842) 219, 228. Jebb, *The principle of ritualism defended* (1856).
[67] *The Ecclesiologist*, 15/101 (April 1854) 94.
[68] Hooker (ed. Keble, 3rd edn, 1845) 163.
[69] Quoted from Walton's *Life* in Latrobe (1831) 432; mentioned in Peace (1839) 76.

> Let my due feet never fail
> To walk the shadowy cloisters pale,
> And love the high embowèd roof,
> With antique pillars massy proof,
> And storied windows richly dight,
> Casting a dim religious light;
> Then let the pealing organ blow
> To the full-voicèd quire below,
> In Service high and anthem clear,
> As may with sweetness through mine ear
> Dissolve me into ecstacies,
> And bring all heaven before mine eyes.[70]

Even the respected Evangelical missionary, Henry Martyn (1781–1812), whose greatest spiritual influence as a student at St John's College, Cambridge, was the leader of the Evangelical Revival, Charles Simeon (1759–1836),[71] was moved to note in his journal, 'During the anthem I seemed to have a foretaste of heaven, and could have wished to die, or to live always in that frame in which I found myself.'[72] In 1849 the *Parish Choir* printed an extract from *Angels' work, or the Choristers of St Mark's* (St Mark's College, Chelsea), prefaced with an editorial smile of satisfaction, 'The idea is a *natural* and a *happy* one.'[73]

If earthly worship was to imitate that of heaven, then it followed that the arts employed in its celebration should be 'exceeding magnifical.' This was King David's vision for the temple which his son, Solomon, was to rebuild (1 Chronicles 22:5), and Bisse stated that if such splendour was appropriate for the building, then the worship performed in it should be of equal glory:

> Since the worship of God is the greatest and most honourable among all the acts and employments of the children of men... surely this universal work or duty of man ought to be set off with the greatest order and magnificence, with *the beauty of holiness.* [74]

Bisse pointed to those periods of Christian history during which no pains or expense had been considered too great to be bestowed upon the House of the Lord, and stated that, as David had *'set singers also before the altar, that by*

---

[70] Milton, 'Il penseroso', referred to by Peace (1839) 77; Jebb (1843) 383; and quoted by Beresford Hope (1861) 119. See also Hooker, *Ecclesiastical Polity*, v.38.1 (ed. Keble, 3rd edn, 1845) 160.

[71] Simeon was a Fellow of King's College, Cambridge 1782–1836, vicar of Holy Trinity, Cambridge, 1783–1836, and one of the founders of the Church Missionary Society in 1799. 'Martyn, Henry' and 'Simeon, Charles,' *Oxford Dictionary of the Christian Church* (2nd edn) 881, 1276. (: 13)

[72] Journal entry for 20 May 1804, quoted in Peace (1839) 82; referred to by Thomas Helmore in *The Ecclesiologist*, 10/77 (April 1850) 382.

[73] *Parish Choir*, 2/41 (May 1849) 172–3.

[74] Bisse, *Beauty of holiness* (ed. Pocock 1848) 1–2.

their voices they might make sweet melody, and daily sing praises in their songs', so it was appropriate for Christians to follow David's example, as the English Reformers had intended, since 'the majesty of Him who is higher than the highest, cannot be manifested among men any other visible way, but by the greatness of his temples, and the glory of the daily ministrations therein.'[75] Flower used this line of argument as a rebuke to those of his generation who lived in amazing wealth, yet begrudged all but the most barren plainness to the House of God; and he intimated that this was unworthy by comparison to forebearers who had been content to live in utmost simplicity and yet spared nothing on their churches.

> Will you not ask yourselves... whether it be right that the world should have all its signs of honour, and dignity, and state, and God the Giver of all should have none in His most Holy Temple – that man, the redeemed, should be so had in honour, and that the God-Man the Redeemer should not be held, to say the least, in like regard?

Flower's conclusion was simply, 'There is *nothing too good for God.*'[76]

Naturally this principle applied to all aspects of worship, including church music. The *Parish Choir* stated as unequivocally, 'whatever is offered to Almighty God ought to be the best of its kind.' It pointed to the way in which the children of Israel had provoked the wrath of God by offering as sacrifices animals which were not 'whole and perfect in their kind' (Malachi 1:7–8), and extrapolated a biblical principle that what was cheap or common or unclean was not worthy to be offered to the Almighty.[77] Flower encouraged his readers, 'Nay, rather be it our richest joy, as it is our blessed privilege like the Magi of old, to offer unto Him our choicest store, and not to honour Him with that which costs us nothing.'[78] In truth, the conviction that God demanded the very best and deserved to be offered nothing less was the central and single most important principle in the revitalization of worship at mid-century.

What were the implications for the style of church music to be employed? In 1831 the inferiority of modern liturgical music to ancient church music was brought before the public by William Crotch. (: 40–2) Ten years later William Dyce (: 141–2) and John Jebb expanded on the theory of its gradual decline into secularity.[79] Given the dearth of worthy contemporary music for ecclesiastical purposes in the 1840s and early 1850s, and the growing conviction that God should be offered only the best in His temple, it is hardly surprising that

---

[75] Bisse, *Rationale* (ed. Pocock 1848) 213–14, 264–5; Bisse's italics. Footnotes in Pocock's edition refer to Ecclesiasticus 47:9 and 1 Chronicles 13:8. See also Flower (1856) 45–6.
[76] Flower (1856) 16–17, 45–6.
[77] *Parish Choir*, 1/18 (September 1846) 60; 3/45 (September 1849) 21.
[78] Flower (1856) 17.
[79] Crotch (1831) 71–8. Dyce in *Christian Remembrancer*, new series 1 (February, April, June 1841) 104–112, 284–292, 440–8. Jebb (1843) 382–4.

ecclesiologists and their allies turned to the past. Under such circumstances Druitt (1845) explained that the revival of old church music was the *safest* option for churchmen who sought real quality:

> Not, as some bigoted people think, that nothing is good which is *not* old; for in all ages the proportion between good and bad is nearly alike. But the flimsy and trivial soon vanish from the face of the earth, whilst that only which is really good is handed down to posterity.[80]

Whatever music was used, it should be 'chaste, severe, and simple in its style... all superadded embellishment, any phrase introduced for mere effect, should be rigidly excluded.'[81]

It was often easier to say what characteristics church music ought not to exhibit than to enumerate those which it should. The wise Hooker provided a degree of counsel which was well known to nineteenth-century defenders of choral service:

> In church music curiosity and ostentation of art, wanton or light or unsuitable harmony, such as only pleaseth the ear, and doth not naturally serve to the very kind and degree of those impressions which the matter that goeth with it leaveth or is apt to leave in men's minds, doth rather blemish and disgrace that [which] we do [rather] than add either beauty or furtherance unto it. On the other side, these faults prevented, the force and equity of the thing itself, when it drowneth not utterly[,] but fitly suiteth with matter altogether sounding to the praise of God, is in truth most admirable, and doth much edify[,] if not the understanding[,] because it teacheth not, yet surely the affection, because therein it worketh much.[82]

Bisse warned against the danger of falling into 'theatrical levity', which constituted an 'unnecessary condescension to the world.'[83] If he considered this to be a problem in his own day (c.1720), then how much greater it had become by the early nineteenth century! Pugin asserted that the spiritual revitalization of the Church would certainly never be attained by 'lowering the externals of religion to the worldly spirit of this degenerate age', but only by 'rising to the high standard of ancient excellence and solemnity.'[84]

Already in the early eighteenth century Bisse had pointed to the compositions of the ancient masters as models:

---

[80] Druitt (1845) 36.
[81] Druitt (1845) 38.
[82] Hooker, *Ecclesiastical Polity*, v.38.3 (ed. Keble, 3rd ed., 1845) 161–2. Quoted also by Druitt (1845) 38–9; Latrobe (1831) 123; and *Practical remarks* (1849) 2.
[83] Bisse, *Rationale* (ed. Pocock, 1842) 270. Quoted also in *Parish Choir*, 2/26 (February 1848) 37. This point is also made in *Practical remarks* (1849) 6. *The Ecclesiologist*, 17/97 (December 1856) 463, gives approving notice of the USA Bishops' triennial Pastoral Letter, which condemned 'theatrical music' in churches.
[84] Pugin (1850) 4.

> What stateliness, what a gravity, what a studied majesty walks through their airs! ...being free from the improper mixtures of levity, those principles of decay which have buried many modern works in oblivion, these remain and return in the courses of our worship.[85]

This reference is clearly to pre-Commonwealth composers, and this was the compositional style which ecclesiologists identified as true and inherently sacred music. For them 'Church music' was not a generic term which applied to any composition with a sacred text. When it was not used in reference to plainsong, it denoted liturgical music written in an essentially contrapuntal style, the best models of which were to be found in the church music of the sixteenth and seventeenth centuries. Robert Druitt was hardly without justification, therefore, when he asserted that 'there is as much difference between the style of [ancient] church and of [modern] profane music, as between the language of the Liturgy and the flippant dialogue of a comedy.'[86]

In 1849 S.S. Wesley provided an excellent crystallization of what most defenders of choral service would have agreed constituted an appropriate church musical style:

> [it] courts no external favour or loud applause, – has no strongly marked rhythm, – nothing to quicken pulsation and excite animal spirits. It bends the mind to devotion, removes all impression of mere sublunary things, and brings home to man an overwhelming sense of his own insignificance and the majesty of the eternal.[87]

In itself this is testimony to the fact that unity on the subject of music in worship was much more easily achieved in matters of theory than in practice. We have seen that in practice ecclesiologists were no great admirers of Wesley (: 89–90), yet they were prepared to support him on a matter of theory even if some of them did not believe it was borne out in his music.[88] This unwillingness to settle into rigidly opposing camps was not atypical for ecclesiologists. In *The Ecclesiologist's* extensive review of Sir Henry Dryden's lecture *On Church Music* read before the Northampton Architectural Society in 1854, the editors disagreed with Dryden on a number of practical points, and then stated: 'From details Sir Henry reascends to general principles, in which we quite agree with him.'[89]

The Revd J.W. Twist, whose connection with the *Parish Choir* has been mentioned above (: 145 footnote 8), believed that the inappropriateness of the current church musical style was a problem which would work itself out:

---

[85] Bisse, *Rationale* (ed. Pocock, 1842) 271.
[86] Druitt (1845) 35. Latrobe (1831) 206, 331–3, had also made this point.
[87] Wesley (1849) 45.
[88] The *Parish Choir* approvingly quoted S.S. Wesley on several occasions, 3/45 (September 1849) 27–8 and 3/47 (November 1849) 46–8.
[89] *The Ecclesiologist*, 14/99 (December 1850) 404.

When men *feel* like true Churchmen, and realize in some degree the majesty of Him to whom the praises of the Church are offered, they will no longer be contented with the light operatic style of music, which, until the late partial revival, has superseded the solemn and devotional strains in which our forefathers praised God. It needs only a generation of *true Churchmen* to raise up a race of composers to emulate the great authors who are the glory of the English Church.[90]

Druitt also scolded those of his generation who were willing to spend vast amounts of money on the theatre and opera, but entered church with the attitude that 'neither care, nor skill, nor expense' was necessary for its music.[91] This constituted the reverse side of the central principle. To refuse God one's best, and to offer instead light and inferior music which partook of a debased secular style and was badly performed, was effectually an affront to the Almighty. The theme was taken up eloquently by the Revd Thomas Binney, who did not mince words. He rebuked churchgoers of higher rank and intelligence for abandoning singing to chance:

as if *anything would do for it;* as if it was of no consequence, so long as *they* had their preaching, whether God has praise, – that, while the one was to them as music, it was no matter if to Him the other was a mockery.[92]

The extraordinary power of music over the spirit, mind and affections has been a subject of concern to the Church throughout the ages. Bisse asserted that everyone who attended the theatre recognized this power, and that it was irresponsible not to take the greatest care in the employment of such a tool as well for 'the purposes of devotion as of diversion.'[93] Hooker wrote:

there is nothing more contagious and pestilent than some kinds of harmony; than some nothing more strong and potent unto good. ...there is that [which] draweth [us] to a marvellous grave and sober mediocrity[94], there is also that [which] carrieth [us] as it were into ecstasies, filling the mind with an heavenly joy and for the time[,] in a manner[,] severing it from the body. So that although we lay altogether aside the consideration of ditty or matter, the very harmony of sounds being framed in due sort and carried from the ear to the spiritual faculties of our souls, is by a native puissance and efficacy greatly available to bring to a perfect temper whatsoever is there troubled, apt as well to quicken the spirits as to allay that which is too eager, sovereign against

---

[90] *Parish Choir*, 2/42 (June 1849) 183, editorial paraphrase of a lecture by Twist in Hampstead.
[91] Druitt (1845) 7. Also Sir Henry Dryden in *The Ecclesiologist*, 14/99 (December 1853) 400.
[92] Binney (1848) 44.
[93] Bisse, *Rationale* (ed. Pocock, 1842) 231.
[94] Mediocrity here indicates a calm, composed state of mind, as opposed to being subject to extremes of emotion.

> melancholy and despair, forcible to draw forth tears of devotion if the mind be such as can yield them, able both to move and to moderate all affections.[95]

Hooker thought that this required 'no proof but our own experience.'

Thomas Helmore made this same observation in his first public address to the Ecclesiological late Cambridge Camden Society on 16 May 1850, and insisted that the great power of music either for evil or good ought to make it a matter of 'utmost importance' to 'the rulers of the Church, (whom it most concerns,) and next to them by all who desire the welfare of true religion.' It was up to such as these to guide and encourage the movement according to 'the spirit at least, if not by the letter, of those ancient (but not antiquated) laws which the Church Catholic has enacted, and which there is no reason for imagining our own Church has at any time annulled or superseded.'[96]

Bisse, like many others, went back in history to quote those who contributed to form the Church's ideas on music, including St Basil:

> For whereas the Holy Spirit saw that mankind was to virtue hardly drawn, and that righteousness is the least accounted of by reason of the proneness of our affections to that which delighteth; it pleased the wisdom of the same Spirit to borrow from melody that pleasure, which, mingled with heavenly mysteries, causeth the smoothness and softness of that which toucheth the ear, to convey as it were by stealth the treasure of good things into man's mind.[97]

Flower quoted St Augustine's highly emotional account of the effect which the plainsong of the Church had on him:

> How many tears I shed during the performance of Thy hymns and chants, keenly affected by the notes of Thy melodious Church. My ears drank in those sounds, and they distilled into my heart as sacred truths, and overflowed thence again into pious emotion, and gushed forth into tears, and I was happy in them.[98]

Modern notables were not neglected. Peace quoted Lord Byron, 'I always took great delight in the English cathedral service; it cannot fail to inspire every man, who feels at all, with devotion', as evidence that choral services could move minds otherwise uninclined toward religion; and pointed to Henry Martyn as proof that music could be an important and regular means of inspiring devotion among the faithful. Martyn described the chanting at King's College, Cambridge, as having elicited 'the same emotions of devotion as I generally have' on such occasions.[99] Flower concluded:

---

[95] *Ecclesiastical Polity*, v.38.1 (ed. Keble, 3rd edn, 1845) 160.
[96] *The Ecclesiologist*, 11/79 (August 1850) 106.
[97] Bisse, *Rationale* (ed. Pocock, 1842) 234–5. Quoted also by Hooker, *Ecclesiastical Polity*, v.38 3, and v.40.4 (ed. Keble, 3rd edn, 1845) 162, 168; Latrobe (1831) 321 (quoting from Hooker); and Flower (1853) 22.
[98] Flower (1853) 22.
[99] Peace (1839) 80, 82; quoting from Medwin's *Conversations of Lord Byron*, 106; and Martyn's *Letters and Journals*, 20 May 1804.

> Music and devotional feelings act and react one upon another. Music uplifts the soul to heaven, and gives wings to devotion, whilst devotion springing from Love Divine gifts music with life, and renders it an offering acceptable to God.[100]

A related and important power which music was noted to possess was its ability to aid the recollection of words and associations, an attribute that had obvious value for the edification of the faithful.[101]

Inherent in the Victorian acknowledgement that music possessed a great power to move the affections was the belief that it had the power to refine human nature. The two ideas were, in fact, inseparable. Hooker recalled the way in which God's people of old had always resorted to music 'with hope and thirst that thereby especially their souls might be edified.' Not only was music a spiritual force which 'filleth the mind with comfort and heavenly delight, stirreth up flagrant desires and affections correspondent unto that which the words contain,' but it:

> allayeth all kind of base and earthly cogitations, banisheth and driveth away those evil secret suggestions which our invisible enemy is always apt to minister, watereth the heart to the end it may fructify, maketh the virtuous in trouble full of magnanimity and courage, serveth as a most approved remedy against all doleful and heavy accidents which befall men in this present life.[102]

Bisse added:

> music is allowed to sit among, or rather above human pleasures, as a refiner; it raises the mind and its desires above their low level, drives out carnal thoughts and inclinations as dross, and leaves it like pure gold, which like that too is most ductile and susceptible of good and heavenly impressions; it lifts us up as into heaven, and fits us for the society of heaven.[103]

The *Parish Choir* quoted William Crotch's assertion that music written in the sublime style 'does not strike and surprise, dazzle and amuse, but it *elevates and expands the mind.*'[104]

Practical 'polemicks'

Perhaps the most telling argument of a common-sense nature employed by Victorian advocates of choral music was one which Hooker had already identified in the late sixteenth century; namely, that those who denounced choral services were guilty of exalting their own personal taste above the witness and practice of the whole Church throughout Christian history. Hooker wrote:

---

[100] Flower (1856), 47–8.
[101] Flower (1853), 21–2.
[102] Hooker, *Ecclesiastical Polity*, v.39.4, (ed. Keble, 3rd edn, 1845) 168.
[103] Bisse, *Rationale* (ed. Pocock, 1842) 227.
[104] *Parish Choir*, 2/26 (February 1848) 37.

> we are wont to suspect things only before trial, and afterwards either to approve them as good, or if we find them evil, accordingly to judge of them; their counsel must needs seem very unseasonable, who advise men now to suspect that wherewith the world hath had by their own account twelve hundred years' acquaintance and upwards, enough to take away suspicion and jealousy. Men know by this time if ever they will know whether it be good or evil which hath been so long retained.[105]

Defenders of choral service in Victorian times had reasons to fear for it not unlike those who faced the Puritan threat in Hooker's time. The possibility that the Ecclesiastical Commissioners might reduce the size of cathedral choirs in 1839 caused Peace to exclaim:

> And is this service to be stripped of its majesty, and consigned to the smallest possible number of individuals by whom it can be carried on! Does the sagacity of an enlightened age consist in finding out that, by the prodigality of our ancestors, more servants have been assigned to the Most High than are needful?[106]

The Ecclesiologist carried Thomas Helmore's warning against the danger of falling into 'the snare too often successful in these, as well as S. Jude's times, of speaking evil of dignities.' It also quoted Sir Henry Dryden, who pleaded for the choral service and chanted prayers (i) as the common form of worship ever since the formation of liturgies some 1400 years earlier, in his estimation, and (ii) as the rightful inheritance of the English Church, being in congruity with 'the opinions and practices of many of those great and pious men who preferred death by fire to life in communion with what they thought the idolatrous Church of Rome.' Given this, Dryden bluntly challenged the adversaries of choral service:

> You cannot... pretend that your piety is greater than that of hundreds of men who have approved of choral service, from the time of S. Augustin [sic] to the present day. You will not, I think, dare denounce as irreligious the practices of the noble army of martyrs.[107]

It was grave error to treat the music of worship as a matter of mere taste, as if there were no objective and historical principles to guide its use. Latrobe denounced those clergymen who presumed to know better than the Reformers by taking the liberty to omit the anthem; and in 1849 the *Parish Choir* took the Archbishop of Canterbury (J.B. Sumner) to task for having stated, 'Especially I regret the introduction into our parish churches of a mode of worship which, however proper and suitable in our cathedrals, appears too artificial and elaborate for simple and general devotion.' The *Parish Choir* said it was 'distressed' to be forced to disagree publicly with a spiritual superior, but felt

---

[105] Hooker, *Ecclesiastical Polity*, v.39.2 (ed. Keble, 3rd edn) 166.
[106] Peace (1839) 127–8.
[107] Helmore in *The Ecclesiologist*, 10/77 (April 1850) 385; and Dryden in *The Ecclesiologist*, 14/99 (December 1853) 404.

compelled to 'adhere to that which the Church herself not only sanctions but enjoins, and which not even the Primate, amiable and excellent man though he be, can rightly treat as an affair of personal taste or private judgment.'[108]

A second line of argument taken against detractors of choral worship was that their personal inability to appreciate sung services disqualified them from making any valid judgment of them. So cleverly did various authors express themselves on this opinion that they will be allowed here to speak for themselves.

Not surprisingly, this line of reasoning was not original to mid-Victorians. Having expounded upon the spiritual power of church music, Bisse admitted:

> I grant, there are persons that... are wholly insensible to these impressions of harmony, being unhappily cut off from them by some natural defect or untunableness of the ear, as others are shut up from the delight of prospects by a natural shortness of sight. But how careful are these latter to conceal their defect: should not the former do the same? for though these defects be natural, they are defects, and the objects of pity. But if either of these should pretend to object that there are no such delights in prospects or harmony, because they enjoy them not, then compassion is justly turned into derision.[109]

He referred to Hooker's statement, 'They must have hearts very dry and tough, from whom the melody of psalms doth not sometime draw that wherein a mind religiously affected delighteth,' and went on to decry the sacrilege of the lingering Puritanical portion of the Church, which in its not-so-distant past had plundered the cathedrals and disestablished choral services.[110]

This line of reasoning was taken up by Latrobe, who related it to the Body of Christ imagery used by the apostle Paul in I Corinthians 12: though there be one body, it is comprised of many unique members, each of which has its own purpose. 'No one has a right to despise the services of another', Latrobe wrote, 'prayer may not reject praise, nor praise prophecying.' In relation to music, this principle begged the question:

> Is a man authorized to declare musical accompaniments to scripture truths inadmissable in the house of God; because his perceptions are blunted, his taste uncultivated, and his edification diminished? May it not be, that at the very time that he is yielding to listless impatience, the souls of others are experiencing that 'divinest glow', which anticipates the joys of the blest, and breathes as it were the atmosphere of the New Jerusalem?[111]

Peace asked what right those who were insensible to choral service had to deprive others of it. He asserted that 'they who most invectively do pierce it

---

[108] Latrobe (1831) 334. *Parish Choir*, 2/38 (February 1849) 135–6. See also Flower (1851) 16; George Smith in *The Ecclesiologist*, 21/141 (December 1860) 355–6.
[109] Bisse, *Rationale* (ed. Pocock, 1842) 235–6.
[110] Bisse, *Rationale* (ed. Pocock, 1842) 237–9. Hooker, *Ecclesiastical Polity*, v.38.3 (ed. Keble, 3rd edn, 1845) 162. Quoted also in *Practical remarks* (1849) 2.
[111] Latrobe (1831) 310.

through are themselves 'deaf as the dead to harmony', and should therefore abstain from offering judgment on the matter.' He admitted that if the spiritual wants of such people were not amply provided for elsewhere, they might have some grounds for complaint; but such was hardly the case.112 The fundamental point at issue was that it was arrogant and small-minded in the extreme for detractors of choral service to suggest that God's majesty was so small that He should only be praised in ways which they themselves could appreciate. The basic premise behind the reasoning of such zealots was essentially, 'worship which I myself cannot comprehend, or which I find in any way unfamiliar, uncomfortable, or offensive, is not a valid form of worship for *anyone*, and does not deserve to exist *anywhere*.' Perhaps the greatest wonder is that defenders of choral service did not attack their most bigoted opponents even more vociferously.

However firmly advocates of choral service felt the need to defend this point, a degree of moderation of their parts was not lacking. Hullah thought it prudent of music lovers to attempt to understand the feelings of those 'to whom melody is frivolity, and harmony chaos.' Yet, he continued in his own inimitable way,

> we regret deeply that a fountain of such sweet waters should be untasted by, or distasteful to any sincere Christian. But if, as is too common, these people with four senses shift their ground, and seek to account for these feelings by anything other than their own imperfect organization, we claim at their hands the same charity they ask at ours, and that when they feel inclined to say that intonation is *unnatural*, and the Choral Service *undevotional*, and the like, – things which we hear said every day, – they will ask themselves whether they have seriously considered the rationale of the whole question, and whether, when they have done so, their self-confessed physical infirmities do not prevent their opinion being of the smallest weight? We may grieve over the privations of the blind, and the dumb, and the lame; we may do all that lies in our power to relieve them; but we do not take them into council on questions relating to colour, elocution, or gymnastics.113

Whose opinion on church music, then, was worthy of consideration? Thomas Helmore stated near the outset of his official connection with the Ecclesiological late Cambridge Camden Society:

> the fitness or unfitness of any musical mode of expression, as applied to the Offices of the Church, can only be judged of by the *Church* musician; not by the ritualist who is no musician, nor by the musician who is no ritualist; far less by the *common-sense* view of those who are notoriously neither.114

---

112 Peace (1839) 72–4.
113 J. Hullah (1846) 5.
114 *The Ecclesiologist*, 11/79 (August 1850) 109.

This is indicative of a principle which the Society adhered to throughout its existence, in all of its various pursuits. In the one hundredth issue of *The Ecclesiologist,* the editors wrote:

> Some people think that in knowledge of Church architecture as in knowledge of pictures or poems, we all stand on an equality. In other words, they cannot understand that æsthetics in music, art, and architecture, have laws, and grammar, and syntax: that is, that they have exact elements. We say however distinctly that it is not every person who sees a pretty church who has a right to form an opinion about it, still less to object to the honest judgment of those who are possessed with canons of taste and the learning of the subject. We are quite aware that everybody who hears a song or a sonata will say, How pretty! or, How ugly! But we take the liberty of saying that just as they only who know the laws of composition have a right to an opinion, so it is with churches.[115]

Given such a conviction, it was fairly easy for ecclesiologists to predict their own future: 'What we are we shall most likely continue to be. We are neither bigots nor waverers. It has happened to us to reconsider details: our principles, as we have not foregone, we are not likely to alter.'[116]

It was a favourite tactic of advocates of choral service to use the zeal of dissenters for congregational singing as a polemical stick with which to beat Low Churchmen for their neglect. The *Parish Choir* was especially fond of this method of persuasion,[117] the object apparently being to shame those churchmen into action who could not be budged by principles or reason.

As early in the revival as 1841 William Dyce had attributed the 'cold and heartless' aspect of Anglican worship, of which dissenters complained, to its non-choral performance. He insisted, 'if we are to attract dissenters by the music of the Church, it must be by its real and legitimate use, and not by exhibiting to them, in an inferior form, the very counterfeit invented by themselves.'[118] Ten years later *The Ecclesiologist* was surprised and pleased to observe the popularity of the *Hymnal Noted* among dissenters.[119]

In 1849 the *Parish Choir* favourably reviewed the publication of *Psalms and Hymns from Holy Scripture*, a collection of prose rather than metrical texts provided with chants (including two Gregorian ones), published for the use of the Revd Thomas Binney's congregation at Weigh-House Chapel, Fish Street Hill, in London.[120] Two months later the *Parish Choir* took up this opportunity to jibe churchmen again, stating its satisfaction at the fact that prejudice against chanting was 'at length beginning to be dispelled – at any rate among certain influential sections of the Dissenting community.' It was a

---

[115] *The Ecclesiologist*, 15/100 (February 1854) 7.
[116] *The Ecclesiologist*, 15/100 (February 1854) 6.
[117] *Parish Choir*, vol 1, pages 146, 175–6; vol 2, pages 39–40, 128; vol 3, pages 20, 27–8, 31, 77.
[118] Dyce in *Christian Remembrancer*, new series II (September 1841) 200, 201.
[119] *The Ecclesiologist*, 12/87 (December 1851) 395; 13/88 (February 1852) 22–3.
[120] *Parish Choir*, 3/44 (September 1849) 20.

welcome development that 'the Puritanical pretence that chanting in public worship is one of those Romish corruptions which were overlooked at the Reformation,' was being refuted by the practice of Dissenters themselves.[121] In 1855 the *Guardian* held up Binney and the example of Weigh-House Chapel as a scornful reproof to those churchmen who had achieved the mutilation of the choral services of St Mark's College, Chelsea.[122] (: 98–102)

A final reason for daily choral worship arose from Bisse's insistence that national strength derived directly from national worship. This concept, he pointed out, was at least as old as the Edwardine Injunctions, which stated that the establishment of the liturgy would be 'most profitable to the estate of this realm, upon the which the mercy, favour, and blessing of Almighty God is in no wise so readily and plenteously poured, as by common prayers.' Neither strong armies and alliances nor great wealth, Bisse wrote, would induce God to look favourably upon the realm, and he instanced the 'vials of God's wrath' which had been poured upon the state during the Rebellion, when the daily sacrifice of praise had been abrogated throughout the land.[123] In 1848 the *Parish Choir* quoted Bisse approvingly on this subject. Some years earlier Robert Druitt had stated his conviction that church music was not a mere matter of form, taste, or usage, but that 'it might be an instrument of the greatest moral and political benefit.'[124]

Whatever political benefits there may have been in the promotion of singing and choral services, this was not the aspect of church music which ecclesiologists were interested in promoting. Their primary aim was to convince churchmen, and especially the clergy, that choral worship was a powerful means to true and spiritual communion with God, and that its adoption would lead to the spiritual revitalization of the Church. Robert Druitt wrote in 1845:

> Looking then to Church Music, whether as a mere political means of producing uniformity of sentiment, or as one vehicle of divine truth to the soul, and a means of infixing it there, we would urge its claims on the attention of our spiritual superiors. We would earnestly hope that the clergy might be induced to study it, as a most necessary preparation for their sacred calling.[125]

The appropriateness of singing in worship

Using historical, spiritual, and practical means of persuasion, ecclesiologists and other advocates of choral service developed a strong apologetic for the appropriateness of singing in worship:

---

[121] *Parish Choir*, 3/46 (October 1849) 31.
[122] *Guardian*, 504 (1 August 1855) 593.
[123] Bisse, *Rationale* (ed. Pocock, 1842) 267–8; p. 268 quotes the Acts of Uniformity, 5 and 6, Edward VI, cap. 1.
[124] *Parish Choir*, 2/27 (March 1848) 45. Druitt (1845) 57.
[125] Druitt (1845) 61–2.

1. The faithful were meant to join together *in one voice* to praise their Maker. This was impossible if no musical tone was used, since no two individual speaking voices would ever naturally speak at the same pitch and with like inflection. Singing also moderated the discordant effect of various accents.[126] In addition to union one with another, Pugin believed,

> The distinct and graduated Chaunt offers no impediment to the perfect union of the heart and mind with the words, as they are sung; and in lieu of a mere empty and vain display of vocal eccentricities [from operatic singers in a gallery], we have a solemn, heartfelt, and, we may trust, an acceptable service to the honour of Almighty God.[127]

2. Bisse wrote that singing the service,

> gives still a higher dignity, solemnity, and a kind or degree of sanctity to divine worship, by separating it more, and setting it at a farther distance from all actions and interlocutions that are common and familiar; chanting being a degree and advance in dignity above the distinct reading or saying used in the Church, as that is and ought ever to be above that manner of reading or speaking which passes in common conversation and intercourse among men.[128]

This concept found wide support among Victorian advocates of choral service. Early in the history of the *Parish Choir* Druitt stated,

> whatever is offered to Almighty God ought to be the best of its kind; that the tone of voice used in God's house ought not to be of that dull, prosaic sort, with imperfect and irregular inflections, which we use in common speech; but that, whether addressing the people in God's name, or in reading His word, or in offering prayer to Him, it ought to be of that clear elevated character which bespeaks earnestness of purpose, and to have all its cadences and inflexions regulated in the manner most conducive to solemnity and devotion.[129]

3. Singing was a *natural* and appropriate means of prayer and praise. Not only had this been the case throughout Judeo-Christian history, but it was the witness of all religions. John Peace wrote the most thorough nineteenth-century vindication of this theory, which was referred to on several occasions by Thomas Helmore in *The Ecclesiologist*. Peace's reasoning was nothing if not creative, but to many churchmen it must have seemed a little far-fetched. Of those who denounced chanting as artificial and unnatural, Peace asked, 'if chanting be artificial what are we to think of the "Art of Reading"?'

---

126 Hooker *Ecclesiastical Polity* v.39.1 (ed. Pocock, 1842) 163. Bisse, *Rationale* (ed. Pocock, 1842) 248–50, quoted also by Latrobe (1831) 258–9. *The Ecclesiologist*, 5/– (May 1846) 173. Druitt (1845) 18, 20. Peace (1839) 84–5.
127 Pugin (1850) 6–7.
128 Bisse, *Rationale* (ed. Pocock, 1842) 241–2.
129 *Parish Choir*, 1/8 (September 1846) 60. See also Druitt (1845) 18; Latrobe (1831) 207; Dryden in *The Ecclesiologist*, 14/99 (December 1853) 404.

> The objectors appear to have forgotten that we sing before we talk, and...
> though we must be taught to read with great pains, we all chant without any
> teaching whatever. If a child that has just learnt to talk, receive unkind
> treatment from a playfellow, it chants out its little griefs in the mother's ear,
> with eyes filled with tears that give sufficient evidence of sincerity and
> naturalness.[130]

Why, then, should it be unnatural to intone prayers to God? Flower pointed out that everyone would concede that the psalms should be sung, yet the psalms, together with large portions of the canticles (e.g. the *Te Deum*) were written in the language of prayer. To deny music to the prayers of the liturgy, then, was an illogical double standard.[131]

As further evidence for the naturalness of chanting Peace cited (i) the example of the West Devonshire ploughboy, who chanted directions to his horse all the day long, because it was less wearing on the voice; (ii) Bishop Heber's encounter with the Bheels in India, a whole race who chanted their ordinary conversation; (iii) the use of chant in Islamic religious rites; (iv) the 'low buzzing, musical sound' in which Quakers delivered their exhortations; and (v) the way in which Dissenting ministers so often chanted their sermons.[132] The *Parish Choir* drew attention to the experience of Anglican missionaries that the *neglect* of chanting in worship was often an obstacle to converting the heathen, 'since they cannot conceive, and will not be induced to believe, that any act of prayer or public devotion can be effectively offered unless robed in the decorous garb of chant.'[133] Druitt asserted:

> Whatever... the cultivated intellect of the civilised man does universally like,
> that we may assert it is natural for him to like; and hence we can argue, from
> the universal consent of all nations, that when (as in addressing the Deity)
> grand and awful sentiments are clothed in sublime language, the tone in which
> they are recited should be in a corresponding degree, elevated, sonorous, and
> modulated by art.[134]

Hence proof of the fitness and naturalness of chanting in Christian worship was – it was claimed – to be found in the use of a quasi-musical tone in the involuntary expression of deep human emotion, and in its almost universal use in the rites of the various religions of the world. Jebb unequivocally stated that chant was 'the VOICE OF THE CHURCH.'[135]

4. Singing was a means of stirring up devotion. Bisse wrote, 'Chanting the service is found more efficacious to awaken the attention, to stir up the

---

[130] Peace (1839) 90–1. *The Ecclesiologist,* 10/77 (April 1850) 384.
[131] Flower (1853) 19–20.
[132] Peace (1839) 90–1, 99–107. *The Ecclesiologist,* 10/77 (April 1850) 384–5; 11/79 (August 1850) 109.
[133] *Parish Choir,* 3/45 (September 1849) 21.
[134] Druitt (1845) 22.
[135] Jebb (1843) 171.

affections, and to edify the understanding, than plain reading of it',[136] a view which was supported by Hooker. *The Ecclesiologist* quoted Peace's references to the personal testimonies of (i) an American divine, Orville Dewey, who wrote that he found the music and singing of English 'cathedral services' to be "admirable, well fitted to touch the imagination and move the heart," and that he could "very well conceive of it as natural to sing out thoughts in a state of high devotional excitement"; and (ii) Henry Martyn, who recorded in his journal for 29 May 1804, "In my walk I was greatly cast down, except for a short time on my return, when I was *singing*, or rather *chanting some petitions*, in a low plaintive voice, I insensibly felt myself engaged in prayer."[137]

5. Singing increased the intelligibility of words by carrying them on uniform sound waves throughout a vast room. This was common knowledge to anyone who had ever attended services in a large church or cathedral. The history of this justification for the retention of chanting in the Church of England went all the way back to Queen Elizabeth's Injunctions (1559) and King Edward VI's Prayer Book, which instructed that the lessons should be sung 'to the end the people may better hear.'[138] (: 154)

6. Singing attracted people to want to join in worship actively. Referring to the very earliest days of the Church in England, Bisse wrote:

> It is known to have brought many of all conditions and complexions to the holy place of worship, which otherwise would have gone nowhere; and it is as known, that many who at first came out of the unhallowed motive of mere pleasure, have in a course of time come out of principle; 'weaker minds being,' as St Austin there speaks, 'by the delight of the ear, raised up to the real affection of piety.'[139]

Latrobe called church music 'a bait to allure persons into the house of God', and in particular pointed out its appeal to the young. 'If the affections are indeed the most susceptible in youth', he wrote (with good intentions, if somewhat unfortunate imagery), 'how important is it to place them under the spell of so powerful a magician as Religious Harmony!'[140] The *Parish Choir* suggested that people were sometimes driven to leave the Church in favour of dissenting chapels because the singing was so dire in the former and so hearty and attractive in the latter.[141]

---

[136] Bisse, *Rationale* (ed. Pocock, 1842) 242. Hooker, *Ecclesiastical Polity*, v.39.4 (ed. Keble, 3rd edn) 168.
[137] *The Ecclesiologist*, 10/77 (April 1850) 382; from Peace (1839) 80–3, who cites Dewey, *Old World and the New*, i.165, and Martyn, *Letters and Journals*.
[138] Bisse, *Rationale* (ed. Pocock, 1842) 246–7; quoted by Latrobe (1831) 258–9. Also Dryden in *The Ecclesiologist*, 14/99 (December 1853) 404; Peace (1839) 86–7, 110.
[139] Bisse, *Rationale* (ed. Pocock, 1842) 233.
[140] Latrobe, 99, 103.
[141] *Parish Choir*, 3/56 (August 1850) 128.

7. Choral services were part of the rightful inheritance of the Church of England, and were not, as some detractors charged, 'popish.' In the wake of the 'Papal Aggression' and the riots at St Barnabas', Pimlico, in late 1850, the *Parish Choir* used Pugin's *An Earnest Appeal for the Revival of the Ancient Plain Song* as proof that contemporary services of the Roman Catholic Church were neither such as ought to be imitated, nor were they likely to be attractive to earnest Anglicans.[142] Advocates of choral service were frequently called upon to defend it against accusations that it led to 'popery.' All of the reasons cited in this chapter were used to refute them.

The ecclesiological apologetic of church music thus formed and propounded was relentlessly brought to the attention of those who comprised the ecclesiologists' sphere of influence, primarily the clergy. It is clear that ecclesiologists felt that it was at least as importance for clergy to understand *why* the best music should be employed in the service of God as it was for them to learn *how* to do it. Once the clergy began to be convinced that music was an appropriate and integral part of worship, and that it could lead to the spiritual revitalization of the Victorian Church, the major obstacle to the revival of choral worship had been overcome.

---

[142] *Parish Choir*, 3/60 (December 1850) 171–2.

CHAPTER SIX

The Ecclesiological Society 1856–62 and the diffusion of the Anglican choral revival

The year 1856 marks a turning point in the revival of church music, both for ecclesiologists and for the wider movement. Early in that year the Revd S.S. Greatheed wrote a pointed letter to *The Ecclesiologist* repudiating a recent statement in its pages to the effect that modern composers were incapable of writing true church music, which was symptomatic of a growing rift between hard-line ritual antiquarians and mainstream ecclesiologists.[1] At midsummer 1856 Thomas Helmore resigned as the Ecclesiological Society's Honorary Secretary for Music, and H.L. Jenner was appointed to replace him.[2] On the feast of St Michael and All Angels (29 September) Sir Frederick Ouseley's model choir school at Tenbury was consecrated.[3] At Lichfield the first diocesan festival of parish choirs was held on 14 October,[4] beginning a movement that gave official diocesan encouragement to the revival of choral service in parishes. It also created a powerful platform for church music enthusiasts to prosecute their own musical ideals, and instead of uniting people in one voice as ecclesiologists hoped, the use of plainsong sometimes ended up dividing them. In Cambridge, Thomas Attwood Walmisley died; and the consequent re-establishment of an entirely separate choral foundation at St John's College[5] (: 200) was indicative of the gradual change of attitude toward choral worship in the University. The fact that 1856 was also the year during which the Ecclesiological late Cambridge Camden Society officially shortened its name to simply the 'Ecclesiological Society' seems almost symbolic.

---

[1] *The Ecclesiologist*, 16/111 (December 1855) 327–30; 17/112 (February 1856) 19–20.
[2] RIBA: Ecclesiological Society Minutes, 5 June 1856; *The Ecclesiologist*, 17/115 (August 1856) 297).
[3] Joyce (1896) 88–90.
[4] Lichfield Joint Record Office: MS D30/7/6/5, f.78.
[5] SJC Dean's Order Book, October 1856; G.M. Garrett, 'The Choral Services in Chapel,' *Eagle*, XVI (1891) 229.

The claims of modern church music composers

The insult to contemporary composers of church music occurred in *The Ecclesiologist* within a notice regarding a proposed edition of sacred choral works by Palestrina. The Revd Edward Goddard stated:[6]

> In the present total degeneracy of church music, and the absence of any modern compositions emanating from a true religious spirit, the attention of all who still desire that the music performed in our churches and cathedrals should correspond with its real object, *viz.*, that of elevating the mind and inspiring genuine feelings of devotion, is directed to the compositions of former ages.[7]

Interest in old music was gaining ground throughout Europe, especially in France and Germany, he maintained, where the 'higher clergy are exerting themselves to the utmost to reform the state of church music.' The implication, of course, was that English clergy should do likewise, but that Palestrina and his contemporaries were the *only* composers who had ever succeeded in realizing music's true potential and purpose in worship. The implication was that modern composers lacked some spiritual quality which made them inherently unfit to write for the Church.

This the Revd S.S. Greatheed could not bear. As a composer and cleric who certainly would have considered that he possessed a 'true religious spirit', he could not sit back and allow *The Ecclesiologist* to be seen to condone such sentiments by its editorial silence. The matter was discussed at the next committee meeting of the Society, which evidently gave Greatheed its blessing to write a letter in reply,[8] since Greatheed did so in the next issue of *The Ecclesiologist*. He cited specific publications of W.H. Havergal, Dr George Elvey, W.H. Monk, and Sir Frederick Ouseley, all of which he thought proceeded from the requisite religious spirit, and stated that his lack of acquaintance with the first two gentlemen relieved him of any possible accusation of personal bias. As to his own compositions, Greatheed wondered why the Ecclesiological Motett Choir performed them with approbation if they were actually unworthy specimens of church music? It was as though the author of the insult had been asleep for twelve years, then written the article without informing himself about what had happened during the interval, and Greatheed called upon him either to justify his statement or to retract it.[9] Greatheed concluded:

---

[6] Authorship attributed in RIBA: Ecclesiological Society Minutes, 12 December 1855. See also *The Ecclesiologist*, 17/115 (August 1856) 269–70.
[7] *The Ecclesiologist*, 16/111 (December 1855) 327.
[8] RIBA: Ecclesiological Society Minutes, 12 December 1855: 'Mr Greatheed begged leave to write to *The Ecclesiologist*, in defence of modern church-musicians from Mr Goddard's strictures in the last *Ecclesiologist*.'
[9] *The Ecclesiologist*, 17/112 (February 1856) 19–20.

It should be borne in mind that the question is not as to the amount of genius, talent, or acquired skill displayed in the works of modern Church composers; nor even whether they exhibit an equal *degree* of religious spirit with Palestrina. If the derogatory sentence had related only to these points, I should not have thought it worth while to write anything against it.[10]

It cannot be assumed that, as Musical Secretary, Thomas Helmore would necessarily have screened musical articles before they were published in *The Ecclesiologist*. The traditional and misleading belief that he was averse to any church music but old church music cannot, therefore, be relied upon to explain the statement's appearance. One wonders why Benjamin Webb, as chief editor, allowed such a strong deprecation of modern composers to be published in *The Ecclesiologist*. The Committee's subsequent agreement that a more moderate rejoinder should be made clearly signalled that the Society did not condone an exclusively antiquarian tendency in church music. Surely Webb should have been able to predict this.

It is tempting to jump to the conclusion that Thomas Helmore's resignation from the post of Musical Secretary so soon after this exchange was the result of a falling out caused by the Ecclesiological Society's unwillingness to champion the old church music exclusively. One might also think this from the matter-of-fact way in which *The Ecclesiologist* reported the change:

> The Revd T. Helmore having expressed his wish to resign the secretaryship for music, it was agreed to accept his resignation, and the Revd H.L. Jenner was elected to the office. Mr Helmore kindly undertook to retain his office of precentor of the Motett Choir.[11]

It seems suspicious that the resignation was accepted with no apparent protest, and that the notice included no expression of thanks for services rendered or regret that they were being terminated.

But Webb's handwritten Minute Book provides another angle: 'The Revd T. Helmore having expressed a wish to resign the secretaryship for music, and to confine himself to the office of precentor of the Motett-Choir, it was agreed to nominate the Revd H.L. Jenner.'[12] This gives the impression that Helmore was simply over-extended and wished to concentrate his efforts on that which he loved best of all. Certainly this was a valid reason. His constant duties as Precentor of St Mark's College, Chelsea; his responsibilities to the boys of the Chapel Royal, St James, who boarded in his home;[13] ever increasing demands upon his time as a lecturer on church music and as a participant in church anniversary celebrations and parish choir festivals around the country; his involvement with church music societies in Cambridge and Oxford (: 83, 127);

---

[10] *The Ecclesiologist*, 17/112 (February 1856) 20.
[11] *The Ecclesiologist*, 17/115 (August 1856) 297.
[12] RIBA: Ecclesiological Society Minutes, 5 June 1856.
[13] F. Helmore (1891) 50–4.

all these combined to yield a schedule which would have wearied the most energetic person. In February 1857 *The Ecclesiologist* reported that the activities of the Motett Choir had been curtailed of late 'owing to very severe illness in the family of the Precentor.'[14] This may also have contributed to his decision to cut back on his Ecclesiological Society duties the previous summer.

In any case Helmore's resignation as Secretary for Music did not mean that the Society was losing his services. He retained his most important duty as precentor of the Motett Choir and continued as an active member of the Committee, attending four of the seven meetings in 1857.[15] The fact that he remained on friendly terms with all of his friends from the Committee of the Ecclesiological Society also suggests that there was in fact no 'falling out.' Furthermore the Society was blessed with an abundance of gifted musicians from which to choose a successor, and they could afford to respect Helmore's wishes.

By the mid-1850s responsibility for writing specific reviews and notices for *The Ecclesiologist* was routinely delegated to various musical members of the Society during meetings of the Committee.[16] With so many capable musical writers, it is possible that, once assigned, articles were sent directly to the publisher with little, if any, editorial interference; and it is plausible that, even if he had the opportunity, Webb may not have bothered to read what appeared merely to be a notice regarding the publication of sacred choral works by Palestrina, an undertaking which any leading ecclesiologist would have condoned wholeheartedly. In addition, it was not unknown for *The Ecclesiologist* to reprint articles or extracts with which they did not wholeheartedly agree, merely to provoke thought or discussion. This was the case with Helmore's first article in *The Ecclesiologist*, in which he had advocated singing Gregorian chant exclusively in unison[17] (an opinion he changed not long after, evidenced by the fact that vocal harmonies were issued for the *Hymnal Noted*); and in 1854 a large portion of Sir Henry Dryden's paper *On Church Music, and the Fitting of Churches for Music* was reprinted, 'as there

---

[14] *The Ecclesiologist*, 18/118 (February 1857) 51. Rehearsals were resumed that month according to *The Ecclesiologist*, 18/119 (April 1857) 119.
[15] This marks no tell-tale difference from 1855, when he attended five out of seven Committee meetings. Attendance statistics derived from RIBA: Ecclesiological Society Minutes, 1855, 1857.
[16] For example, on 12 December 1855 the Committee requested Greatheed to review Thijm's *Oude en Niewere Kerst-Liederen*; on 29 January 1856 F.H. Dickinson was assigned Daniel's *Thesaurus Hymnologicus*; on 17 April 1858 H.L. Jenner was asked to attend the Southwell Festival of Parochial Choirs in order to review the proceedings. RIBA: Ecclesiological Society Minutes.
[17] *The Ecclesiologist*, 10/75 (November 1849) 211.

is nothing in it that will not be entertaining, if not instructive to our musical readers, and the latter predicate is applicable to the greater part of it.'[18]

Eclecticism and Christian Art

Without reference to the Ecclesiological Society's views concerning the revival of the other ecclesiastical arts, it is impossible to understand why its leaders not only countenanced but positively encouraged the use of contemporary music in worship during the late 1850s and 1860s. Architecture was the first and most consuming of their concerns, and therefore it was primarily in regard to architecture that their principles were first developed. It will become obvious below, however, that the principles which they developed to guide their architectural pursuits consistently transferred to the other branches of ecclesiology.

In 1856 and 1857 S.S. Greatheed was one of two identified parties in a three-way discussion of the principle of eclecticism in regard to the creation of a valid contemporary style of architecture and music. This presented rather different issues from the eclectic principle of church restoration debated ten years earlier.

The subject of eclecticism and modern art was raised by the French architect, M. Lassus, in a letter addressed to A.J.B. Beresford Hope following the Lille Exhibition in 1856, which Benjamin Webb had attended in order to write a full report for *The Ecclesiologist*.[19] Prefaced by *The Ecclesiologist's* 'entire conviction of the value' of what Lassus had written, Lassus defined eclectism:

> In philosophy, as in art, it characterises a whole school – that of those persons who admit the possibility of creating a new art, or an entirely new philosophical doctrine, by borrowing the elements of their creation from all styles, or from all philosophical systems.[20]

In this way, he warned, artists deluded themselves into thinking they were creating a new art, when in fact all they were doing was propagating the 'indifferent intermixture' of various artistic styles which were fundamentally incompatible with one another, throwing aside all rules and principles and destroying any sense of unity. 'Eclectism,' Lassus wrote, 'admits no other law than the will and the taste of the artist, no other guide than his reason. It is the doctrine of absolute liberty.' This was thought to be peculiarly dangerous because by it 'the taste of the public is perverted; and art is descending by great steps to a complete decadence.' Unity of style, he insisted, was the true

---

[18] *The Ecclesiologist*, 10/75 (November 1849) 208; and 15/101 (April 1854) 97.
[19] Webb diaries, 12–14 and 20 March 1856. William Scott accompanied Webb to Lille.
[20] Letter from M. Lassus to A.J.B. Beresford Hope, *The Ecclesiologist*, 17/115 (August 1856) 285.

foundation of art, and unity of style was the goal that should be pursued. How was this to be done? In common with the longstanding belief of ecclesiologists, he suggested:

> as we have no art belonging to our own time – everybody is convinced of it and deplores it – there is only one thing for us to do: that is, to choose one from among the anterior epochs, not in order to copy it, but in order to compose, while conforming to the spirit of that art.[21]

With a profound knowledge not only of the technique but also of the sentiment of such a style, an artist would be enabled to create or invent new 'dispositions' and even to conquer any new problems which might arise without deviating from a unity of style.[22]

In the next issue of *The Ecclesiologist*, S.S. Greatheed replied that he had always considered himself an eclectic, and that Lassus's opinions required some qualification. No artist, Greatheed thought, would randomly combine elements of different styles; but an artist's style might be derived from a multiplicity of sources, which was perfectly acceptable insofar as the artist was able to discern which elements of various styles were compatible with one another, and understood the principles which would allow their combination. Greatheed felt that unity of style was a principle that had been followed too closely between music for the Church and music for the theatre.[23]

The debate over eclecticism continued in the December issue of *The Ecclesiologist* with a lengthy letter signed 'Phœnix.'[24] This gifted polemicist stated that there were three conflicting elements in art – eclecticism, development, and originality or invention – which stood in tension with one another:

> In the revival of art, there must of necessity be, for a little while, a preponderance of Eclecticism. It is, and must be, used till art has regained some footing, and is to be looked upon, not in the light of a benefit, but of a *necessary evil*, to be for a short time tolerated from lack of a higher principle to take its place. Its place, in due time, *is* taken by Developement [sic]. Developement brings forth unity of style and harmony of design. But Developement *alone* cannot move forward. It requires to be set in motion. It is like an engine without motive power. Something else *besides* Development [sic] is needed for high art. This need is Originality or Invention, – the fire of genius, the very spirit and life of art.[25]

---

[21] *The Ecclesiologist*, 17/115 (August 1856) 286.
[22] *The Ecclesiologist*, 17/115 (August 1856) 284–7.
[23] S.S. Greatheed, *The Ecclesiologist*, 17/116 (October 1856) 362–4.
[24] Authorship is anonymous, but given J.M. Neale's admiration for Benjamin Webb's superior knowledge in the field of aesthetics (: 17), the general style of the article itself, and the fact that Webb was the Ecclesiological Society's delegate to review the Lille Exhibition (which elicited the letter that began the series of correspondences), the author was almost certainly Webb.
[25] *The Ecclesiologist*, 17/117 (December 1856) 414–15.

In defining a style, an artist needed to enter personally into the ideas and principles which formed that style, a much deeper and more difficult undertaking than merely understanding its physical expression. Whether a modern utterance of an ancient style would be inferior or superior to the original model depended, Phœnix thought, entirely on the ability of the artist. Unity of style would result when a set of principles became generally understood, and this could only happen if many sympathetic artists agreed to struggle together to discover and refine what was 'good and true' in art. Once the principles and rules had been agreed upon, then invention and originality would naturally come into play: but it was the *idea*, the writer cautioned, which needed to be original, not the language. It was neither necessary nor desirable to despise one's inheritance:

> let us not cast it aside in order to compile an entirely new code, but only let us labour to remodel and to reform the old, – infusing into it such new life and new energy as shall make it worthy of the spirit of our own highly-cultivated, enlightened, and scientific age.[26]

An imperfect art might continue to 'satisfy the cravings of an indifferent multitude', but it would never elevate or refine them; and to be of any real and lasting benefit, it needed to be 'something like universal.' If only artists would agree to combine into a sort of fraternity to pursue unflinchingly the same high standards of artistic integrity, the writer asserted, 'what weight would they not have in forming the standard of taste!'[27]

In advocating a general, undeviating pursuit of excellence, 'Phœnix' was merely appealing for the same unified and concerted course of action which ecclesiologists had attempted to follow from the beginning. Isolated individuals who could agree together to propagate their common views would soon constitute a movement: there was strength in numbers, and an initial degree of dogmatism was an effective tool to draw attention to abuses, potential error, and principles of reform.

A rejoinder from Lassus commended Greatheed's dispassionate and reasoned reading of his initial letter to Beresford Hope, which Lassus held to be proof that ecclesiologists, unlike emotive French advocates of eclecticism, 'seek above all things the *truth*.'[28] Lassus stated that Greatheed had confused the concept of 'unity' with that of 'uniformity', or 'identity.' Indeed, music for the Church and theatre had recently shared an unfortunate uniformity of style;

---

[26] *The Ecclesiologist*, 17/117 (December 1856) 419–20.
[27] *The Ecclesiologist*, 17/117 (December 1856) 420–1.
[28] M. Lassus, *The Ecclesiologist*, 18/118 (February 1857) 47. Truth was indeed the ultimate goal. Having questioned whether Ruskin's *Seven Lamps of Architecture* was wholly conclusive or logical, Benjamin Webb's review of it eight years earlier stated, 'he has forced upon our minds the conviction that there is no success to be gained in Christian art without those guiding principles, self-sacrifice, truth, obedience.' *The Ecclesiologist*, 10/74 (October 1849) 120.

but real unity of style would produce variety in expression, whereas uniformity would not. Examination of Gothic architecture revealed an infinite variety of detail; but there was no doubt as to the general harmony of the *ensemble*. The unhappy state of contemporary art demanded 'heroic remedies'; and only by faithfully adhering to the principles of an anterior and flourishing period of art could one hope to be inspired to equal or greater creations. 'It is, in a word, to seek to complete it; to appropriate it to our wants and to our materials.'[29]

The fundamental difference of opinion between Lassus and Greatheed lay in the fact that they proceeded from different definitions of 'eclecticism.' The Frenchman's definition of eclecticism proceeded from his viewpoint as an architect, in which it would produce an unprincipled amalgamation of individual aspects of incompatible styles, purely according to the whim of the artist and without regard to tradition or form. As a musician, Greatheed viewed eclecticism as the principled fusion of various compositional techniques. Any elaborate composition, he stated, consisted of principal subjects, their development, harmony, accompaniment, and instrumentation; and since 'few, if any, of the great masters have been equally skilful with respect to all these elements', why should a musical student not study them all, with the purpose of 'bringing together out of each whatever is most valuable'? And if a musician could be so improved, why not a painter or an architect? Greatheed conceded Lassus's distinction between unity and uniformity; but refused to agree that eclecticism, in its purest form, was contrary to unity.[30]

This discussion of eclecticism and modern art hailed the beginning of a significant shift of emphasis for ecclesiology, a move into maturity. From the beginning ecclesiologists viewed the revival and study of ancient models as the only means to set a correct course for modern art. Up to the mid-1850s, the primary need had been to look to the past. But now that a style was gradually becoming engrained into the very nature of artists and of society, it was time to look forward, to consider how to turn a revived artistic language into the vital contemporary style for which everyone hoped.

The discussion of eclecticism also serves as an example of one of mainstream ecclesiologists' most laudable mature traits: their ability to disagree among themselves on matters of theory or practice, and to discuss their differences dispassionately in a public format without adversely affecting personal friendships or drawing battle lines within their own ranks. It was perspicacious of Lassus to observe that ecclesiologists sought 'above all things the *truth*.'[31] When freed from a petty or personal investment in 'winning' an argument among themselves, the polemical interaction of great minds could

---

[29] *The Ecclesiologist*, 18/118 (February 1857) 47–9.
[30] S.S. Greatheed, *The Ecclesiologist*, 18/119 (April 1857) 89–91.
[31] M. Lassus, *The Ecclesiologist*, 18/118 (February 1857) 47.

serve only to further the real end which they all desired: the more perfect praise of God, and a more efficacious ministry to God's people.

On the future of art in England

This was the topic that the architect, George Edmund Street, brought before the nineteenth anniversary meeting of the Ecclesiological Society in 1858, although his view of the recent past comprised his most interesting comments. The Society had been an 'undeniably powerful helper' in the general revival of religious art, he agreed, but it was unwise to ignore the other forces which had lent themselves to the cause. Its origins, he thought, were to be seen throughout northern Europe, beginning with the end of the eighteenth century and arising from various national reasons. In England it had been aided by the Society of Antiquaries. A greater external aid was necessary, however, and Street attributed this mainly to Sir Walter Scott,

> who, himself possessed with an enthusiasm of the most genuine kind for old story, legend and song, created the same enthusiasm in the minds of all who read his works. Unconsciously the world came to regard the past with a new feeling and a warmer love; his skill had invested it with a glory which was not undeserved: and it was no unnatural consequence that men should have longed to attempt some revival of the art of an age which they had begun to regard thus enthusiastically.[32]

Street thought that this new tone had probably indirectly influenced the great religious revival which had begun in Oxford nearly thirty years earlier, which had in turn combined to give the impetus to the subsequent revival of ecclesiastical architecture. 'To the religious revival we owe the existence of this society, and to this society I think most of us may, without shame, admit that much of our success as ecclesiastical architects is attributable.'[33]

The subject was taken up by Benjamin Webb in the first issue of *Bentley's Quarterly Review* in March 1859.[34] In writing for periodicals even on the most complicated subjects, Webb normally accomplished his task within the space of a couple of days; but his diaries indicate that he took the greatest pains over 'The Prospects of Art in England', spending eight complete days on the first draft and an additional seven revising it.[35] It is a deeply considered statement and is worthy of close attention.

---

[32] G.E. Street, 'On the future of art in England,' *The Ecclesiologist*, 19/127 (August 1858) 233.
[33] Ibid.
[34] Benjamin Webb, 'The Prospects of Art in England,' *Bentley's Quarterly Review*, 1/1 (March 1859) 143–82.
[35] Webb diaries, 19 January to 4 February 1859.

Webb began with a broad background of revivals of art throughout history. 'The periods of greatest intellectual activity have not uniformly recurred under similar conditions of political, religious, or social life', he observed.

> Nor, again, have the most important historical developments of science, art, and literature been strictly parallel or contemporaneous. At first sight it would seem probable that all the chief branches of human study would flourish simultaneously in an age of great intellectual progress. But the theory is not borne out by facts. Music, for example, did not reach the culminating point of its mediaeval stage under Palestrina till its sister arts had long passed their maturity and entered upon their decline. But then, again, it was music that, under Mozart and Beethoven, anticipated that modern revival which, in its special relation to architecture, painting, and sculpture, it is our present purpose to examine.[36]

This reveals an important development in attitude toward classical and early Romantic music. From Webb's private music making and the kinds of concerts he attended in London, it is clear that he had always enjoyed the music of Mozart and Beethoven. To designate this music as a forerunner to the revival of other branches of ecclesiastical art suggests that he approved of the stylistic developments in which it partook, and was beginning to consider that it might be used validly within the context of worship. The principles which later allowed him to spare nothing to make the choral services of St Andrew's, Wells Street, as magnificent and elaborate an offering to the Almighty as possible, and to employ modern continental music to that end, had essentially been formed. Rainbow sees this development as an aberration: 'Benjamin Webb's *volte face* in musical policy some quarter of a century after the Choral Revival began, represents one of the least predictable features of the movement's history.'[37] In the light of mainstream ecclesiology's view of artistic revival, however, Webb's evolution in this regard is considerably less unpredictable than one might think.[38]

Webb continued by summarizing the background of the movement, since this was the most logical source of clues to its future. He qualified the attempt of some to trace the origin of 'romantic mediaevalism' to the novels of Sir Walter Scott, insisting that Scott 'was not so much the originator and prophet of a new faith as an exponent of a general movement which was beginning in his time to stir the whole European mind.' Webb alluded to Fouqué in Germany and Victor Hugo in France as Scott's continental counterparts. It is

---

[36] *Bentley's Quarterly Review*, 1/1 (March 1859) 143, 144.
[37] See Rainbow (1970) 278.
[38] Rainbow (1970) 276–8, uses St Andrew's, Wells Street, as an example of how far choral services had declined from the pristine Tractarian ideal of total congregational participation. It should be noted, however, that according to Webb's own testimony the congregation at St Andrew's participated in singing the psalms and hymns. Webb had not, therefore, totally abandoned the ideal. Parliamentary Papers, *Royal Commission on Ritual.* xx (1867) 770.

nearly always futile, Webb thought, to attempt to trace the origin of any movement to one person or place; since many events and ideas must inevitably combine to create the conditions in which an individual can become a conspicuous agent of revival:

> All great changes of opinion are the growth of years and the result of numberless co-operative and converging forces. When the time has come, and men's minds are ripe for it, the new sentiment shows its universality by manifesting itself in a thousand forms and places at once. And such a movement, unless we are mistaken, is that recurrence to sounder principles of taste which in so many different departments of art and literature distinguishes our own times.[39]

If it was difficult to trace the origins of the movement, at least its progress could be observed; and although its present provided no ground for a 'confident prediction' regarding the future, one could speculate, and possibly 'even affect the future very materially by directing the course of the stream as it flows on.'[40]

Webb summarized his own view of the revival of church art as:

> a reaction from corrupt conventional standards, and a recovery of first principles with a view to an improved practice. The last qualification, severs it wholly in essence from archaeology pure and simple; but inasmuch as it was necessary to go back before a fresh step could be taken forward, the revival, for a certain way, was scarcely distinguishable from antiquarianism. And even now the divorce between the two is not complete. The more progressive artists of the day are denounced by mere antiquaries as rash innovators, and by their opponents as mere archaeological copiests. The truth is, that their advance is made from a new starting-point which they could only reach by a preliminary retrogression.[41]

Clearly this is an encapsulation of the mainstream ecclesiological view of the revival of ecclesiastical art.

Webb maintained that the revival of ecclesiastical architecture had led to the current revival of art in general. Although there had been isolated defenders of Gothic in the first quarter of the nineteenth century, Webb thought that they had not constituted what could be termed a 'movement.' It was at Cambridge, he asserted, that,

> the first principles of Pointed architecture were practically recovered, and dogmatically enunciated, not without the polemical language and hasty generalization which are the characteristics and defects of youth and sincerity, yet with a substantial accuracy which no further investigation has materially impugned.[42]

---

39 *Bentley's Quarterly Review*, 1/1 (March 1859) 145.
40 *Bentley's Quarterly Review*, 1/1 (March 1859) 144.
41 *Bentley's Quarterly Review*, 1/1 (March 1859) 145.
42 *Bentley's Quarterly Review*, 1/1 (March 1859) 151.

He proceeded to identify three stages in the Gothic revival, using language which left no doubt that he felt them to be the logical progression in the revival of any art. The first stage was characterized by much mere 'copyism.' No originality was apparent, and artists did not fully understand the adopted style or its adaptability to various purposes. This was not a phase, the shortcomings of which were undetected by ecclesiologists as the church art revival moved through it. John Mason Neale had written to Benjamin Webb on Candlemas 1844, 'have not all our creative attempts, S Albans, the New Zealand Cathedral, etc., been failures?'[43] The second stage Webb called the 'eclectic' period. Those who wished to inaugurate the architecture of the future had demanded the freedom to borrow from continental Gothic; and debate over the starting point of such a movement had yielded an agreement to begin with Second Pointed or Middle Gothic. In borrowing from the best features of French and Italian Romanesque, Webb thought that actual practice had guided architects more than theory, and eventually a new, less specifically English style had begun to reveal itself. 'Their works were no longer elaborate combinations and tesselations of the fragments of a dead style, but a living language clothing original thought.' Webb believed:

> Our own architectural style was thus enlarged and improved by contributions from the cognate varieties of continental Gothic; and a judicious eclecticism borrowed from France or Italy, in due subordination to the prevailing spirit of the style, was calculated to give it additional strength, grace, or beauty, in its arduous task of supplying the manifold requirements of a refined and highly civilised age.[44]

Webb believed that the ecclesiologists' model church, All Saints', Margaret Street, was the earliest example of eclecticism, as well as the 'most fruitful in its consequences', and agreed with John Ruskin that it was '*the* original work of modern English art.'[45] Already in 1853, six years before its completion and consecration, Ruskin had proclaimed All Saints' to be the first piece of modern architecture which was 'free from all signs of timidity or incapacity', and had asserted:

> it challenges fearless comparison with the noblest work of any time. Having done this, we may do anything; there need be no limits to our hope or our

---

[43] This admission occurs within a criticism of Pusey's suggestion that nineteenth-century churchmen did not posses the 'purity of heart and life' to make them 'great Church builders in a Catholick sense.' Neale asserted, 'it is absurd to say that it does not often please God to raise up, as defenders of His truth, men even of immoral lives: witness many of the Popes. If of His truth, why not of His beauty? Thus it is necessary that a S Athanasius or S Cyril should be men of eminent personal holiness; they were, for the first time, developing truth. But it is not necessary for its mere defenders should be so.' Lawson (1910) 70–71; Towle (1906) 51–2.
[44] *Bentley's Quarterly Review*, 1/1 (March 1859) 153, 154.
[45] *Bentley's Quarterly Review*, 1/1 (March 1859) 154, 155.

confidence; and I believe it to be possible for us, not only to equal, but far to surpass, in some respects, any Gothic yet seen in northern countries.[46]

Webb attributed much influence to Ruskin in the spread of interest in the art revival:

> We believe that the startling paradoxes and splendid inconsistencies of this brilliant author have been exceedingly useful in provoking criticism, in arresting people's attention, and interesting them in art-questions... doubtless we owe to him in great measure the wide acceptance, or at least recognition, of many wholesome principles, which perhaps have gained their popularity less through their inherent truth than through his persuasive declamation.[47]

Webb was not prepared to suggest that every detail of All Saints', Margaret Street, was beyond reproach, citing especially the polychroming of the interior. It was important because it was truly Gothic, yet unlike any ancient Gothic cathedral; it was perfectly suited to its purpose and situation, but 'indebted to no architectural *Gradus ad Parnassum* for its several details', neither was it a mere imitation of a foreign building. It was original, and Webb considered its contribution toward the advancement of the eclectic principle to have been catalytic.[48]

It was the third and mature stage of the revival of English architecture on which Webb thought the nation was embarking:

> It is full of promise and overflowing with vigour. We stand on the threshold, it would seem, of a great future. The capabilities of the improved and enriched Gothic of our day, in its secular as well as its ecclesiastical adaptations, will be explored and developed by an able and enthusiastic band of votaries. And there is more hope than there has yet been at any period of the revival of the general adoption of an architectural style which will fairly represent the wants and characteristics of the age.[49]

In treating the other branches of art, Webb attributed the awful state of sculpture in Britain to the 'absurd iconoclasm' which had 'denuded nearly every niche in our churches of its occupant.' In the absence of a general public familiarity or even sympathy with sculpture, its prospects seemed dim. Painting and fresco were in a far more encouraging position. Public interest in them was high, and the increasing prosperity of society was producing patrons. It was, Webb thought, a good sign that 'the artistic improvement of modern London is the result of private taste and spirit, and not of imperial magnificence imposing its will on a submissive municipality.' The latter had been the case under King Ludwig in Bavaria, whose supposed revival of art had not been 'genuine'; indeed, it had begun to languish even before his abdication.[50]

---

[46] Ruskin, *Stones of Venice*, III/196; quoted in Whitworth (1891) 9–10.
[47] *Bentley's Quarterly Review*, 1/1 (March 1859) 170–1.
[48] *Bentley's Quarterly Review*, 1/1 (March 1859) 154, 155.
[49] *Bentley's Quarterly Review*, 1/1 (March 1859) 157.
[50] *Bentley's Quarterly Review*, 1/1 (March 1859) 159–66.

A movement from below would be far more thorough and long-lasting in its effects, and Webb dismissed as 'absurd' the old superstition that the English mind bore an inherent inaptitude for the fine arts: 'So it used to be said that the English would never be a musical people: – a prophecy completely stultified by the extraordinary cultivation of this art of late in every part of the country.'[51]

Webb warned that in any revival of art there would be many failures and much mediocre work produced. 'But,' he wrote, 'if we must make up our minds to the patient endurance of a vast amount of mediocrity, we need not on that account fix at a low mark that higher excellence which is to be attained by the few.' The new lesson which was being learned was that 'art, in its highest function, does not so much represent to us what is as what ought to be.' Education, he thought, would continue to advance the art revival. Its strength lay in the fact that the movement was no mere literary, aristocratic, or accidental phenomenon, but rather:

> a true practical work of recovery and progress – a necessary correlative, as some have thought, of the higher spiritual tendencies that are strongly operating upon modern society, a deep and wide movement of the whole national mind. It is, we say again, no mere dilettantism, no fashionable pursuit of some evanescent development of artistic fancy, but a thorough and honest inquiry into the principles of art with the practical resolution to carry those principles into practice.[52]

A parting of the ritual ways

In 1858 the Revd John Purchas published the *Directorium Anglicanum; being a Manual of Directions for the Right Celebration of the Holy Communion, for the Saying of Matins and Evensong, and for the Performance of Other Rites and Ceremonies of the Church, according to Ancient Uses of the Church of England.* It has been represented as a key point in the development of extreme ritualism, and a divergence from mainline Tractarianism.[53] It cited a multitude of ancient sources in order to give practical guidance to priests on everything from when, how, and in which direction they should bow, to the proper measurements, material, and embroidery for their vestments. Purchas acknowledged that the manuscript had been proof read by many notable Tractarians and ecclesiologists in an effort to achieve utmost correctness, including the Revds John Mason Neale, Thomas Chamberlain, F.G. Lee, and Philip Freeman.[54] Several paragraphs on music were taken from John Jebb's *The*

---

[51] *Bentley's Quarterly Review*, 1/1 (March 1859) 180.
[52] *Bentley's Quarterly Review*, 1/1 (March 1859) 168, 171, 182.
[53] Herring (unpublished Oxford D.Phil dissertation, 1984) 283.
[54] Purchas (1858) xxiii.

Choral Service (1843), and Thomas Helmore contributed appendix VIII, 'On the Music of the English Church.'

Not surprisingly the ideal advocated by the *Directorium Anglicanum* was thoroughly choral services with Gregorian tones for the psalms.[55] Helmore reiterated his view that there was never meant to be any essential difference between cathedral and parochial service, and thought that 'what is required whenever it may be attained is a full Choral Service of the Plain Song order.'

> The rule to be followed is, that 'all things should be done to edification;' and this involves the proper use of all available means, and lawful appliances – the only bar to the use of the highest style of Choral Service properly regulated in every Church is the inability to perform it. In proportion as zeal for the honour and glory of God's worship inspires the ministers and people of any particular Church, so will their worship rise in the scale of musical grandeur and choral dignity.[56]

Purchas urged that either anthems or hymns could be sung in the place of the anthem, as long as they were appropriate to the day or the liturgical season, and thought that 'it would be well to have a fixed rule as to the Anthems from which a selection should *invariably* be made' during the special seasons of Advent, Lent, the octaves of great Festivals, and the period between Easter and Trinity Sunday.[57] Concerning the use of instruments, Helmore added simply:

> All the instrumental aid which can be made subservient to general devotion and that of the performers themselves, ought by inference to be considered *lawful*, though perhaps a good organ and a competent organist are all that will be found in general *desirable*.[58]

In a review for *The Ecclesiologist*, Benjamin Webb[59] acknowledged the usefulness of a practical survey of the historical precedents of the *Book of Common Prayer*, in the belief that it would make people grateful for the great extent to which the Church of England had preserved the ancient modes of worship in the reformed rite; and he admitted that the *Directorium Anglicanum* contained much interesting and instructive material, 'a singular mixture of mere antiquarianism and of practical common sense.'[60] He observed that Purchas had based his book on the dispassionate instructions prefixed to the *Churchman's Diary*, 'the best compendium hitherto published', but Webb regretted that Purchas had not left it at that. 'There is such a thing as proving too much; and we can foresee possible results from this publication, which its

---

[55] Purchas (1858) 96–8, 100, among other places, (including Thomas Helmore in Appendix VIII, 178–80).
[56] Helmore in Purchas (1858) 180.
[57] Purchas (1858) 112–113.
[58] Helmore in Purchas (1858) 180.
[59] *The Ecclesiologist*, 20/130 (February 1859) 31–4. Authorship revealed in Webb diaries, 13 January 1859.
[60] *The Ecclesiologist*, 20/130 (February 1859) 33.

excellent compilers would be the first to regret.' He was afraid that the book might provide more ammunition for the foes of ritual propriety than help to its friends: 'We are bidden to be "wise as serpents," and are warned against throwing pearls before swine.'[61]

Specifically, Webb regretted Purchas's apparent inability to attribute to the Holy Communion its deserved centrality without depreciating the importance of the daily cycle of morning and evening prayers.[62] Most of all, however,

> we must put on record our regret, that the old English use of Sarum has not been more religiously followed in the matter of precedent. It is, doubtless, a great temptation in liturgical matters to choose eclectically from differing rituals, and especially to borrow explanations or practices from modern Roman usage, where the ancient practice is obscure or doubtful. But we are satisfied that this is a wrong principle, and entirely evacuates our legal standing ground in matters of ritual. We inherit the old English traditions, and none other. We know that this rule has its perplexities, and that the unreformed use of Sarum is sometimes less convenient, as a precedent, than the reformed Roman. But if we are to choose our models, it becomes a mere question of individual taste. *The practical lesson to be drawn from the difficulties of the subject is one of cautious moderation which, in matters of ritual, most of us would do well to learn.*[63]

From this, from the individual biographies of Archdeacon Thorp, Dr Mill, A.J.B. Beresford Hope, Benjamin Webb, and H.L. Jenner in chapter four, and from the discussion of Thomas Helmore's broader views on modern music (: 128–9), it is readily apparent that, once ecclesiological principles had begun to win their way, the primary leaders of the Ecclesiological Society were essentially men of moderation. Recent insight into the ministry of mainstream Tractarians can be applied with equal validity to leaders of the Ecclesiological Movement:

> instead of confronting hostility head-on, they seem to have deliberately done all in their power to avoid unnecessary antagonism. The themes of caution, patience and diplomacy are found throughout their manuals, sermons, diaries and letters in the generation after 1845, and it was so typical of them that it deserves to be treated as a distinctive pastoral technique in its own right, something which seems to have been peculiar to them in so marked and developed a degree; and which sets them apart from the headstrong attitudes of the new Ritualists of the 1860's.[64]

As early on as the publication of *Hierurgia Anglicana* (1848), ecclesiologists had felt it needful to urge one another:

> Let us endeavour to restore everywhere amongst us the Daily Prayers, and (at the least) weekly Communion; the proper Eucharistick vestments, lighted and

---

[61] *The Ecclesiologist*, 20/130 (February 1859) 32.
[62] See Purchas (1858) viii, ix.
[63] *The Ecclesiologist*, 20/130 (February 1859) 33. Italics added.
[64] Herring (unpublished Oxford D.Phil dissertion, 1984) 240.

vested altars, the ancient tones of Prayer and Praise, frequent Offertories, the meet celebration of Fasts and Festivals... *but let us be careful not to retard the general return of the Clergy to Rubrical regularity, by attempting as individuals, and by adoption of isolated practices, to do more than our Church sanctions in the ceremonial departments of Divine Service.*[65]

An article in the January 1865 issue of the *Christian Remembrancer* provoked J.M. Neale to publish *Extreme Men; a letter to A.J.B. Hope, Esq.*, its author, soon afterwards. Among other things, Beresford Hope had advocated moderation in the current battle for clerical vestments, fearing a counter-productive tumult if 'extreme men' pressed the issue too far. Neale replied that he had never read anything which gave him so much pain. He reminded Beresford Hope how, twenty-five years earlier, the Ecclesiological Movement's 'extreme men' had contended for churches with chancels and without pews; both of these issues had been highly controversial, but both battles had been won resoundingly. Later they had fought for chancel screens, altar vestments, colour in churches – crusades over which All Saints', Margaret Street, had been 'the first seal of our complete victory.'[66] Neale thought it ludicrous to draw an 'arbitrary line' at the issue of clerical vestments, especially since one country tradesman had sold sixty sets of them during the previous year. As far as Neale could see, this battle, too, was about to be won, and he wondered if Beresford Hope had ever known of 'anything worth fighting for that was gained without one?'[67]

In response to the publication of this letter, Benjamin Webb wrote to Neale:

> neither B Hope nor I have ever argued against *vestments*. Their revival is a question of expediency not of legality... Not so, *nobis judicibus*, the lighted candles (since the Privy Council decision)...

> This is the point at issue. Vestments are carried, we at least, shall not grumble. But to us, men in the world, the *Church Times* and its supporters seem to be living in a fool's paradise. What we fear is that their imprudence may, sooner or later, pull down the whole fabric about our ears. You would do well to consider the significant 'short and easy method' which the State now applies to Convocation to alter canon or rubric. In any one new session we may find we have lost *all* we value, by proper ecclesiastical legislation. It is this want of discrimination which we charge against your 'extreme man' of 1865.[68]

Certainly this fear was not unfounded. In 1867 a Royal Commission on 'Ritualistic Practices in the Church of England' was appointed to review the issue, and by 1874 opponents of ritual had seen to the passage of the Public

---

[65] *Hierurgia Anglicana* (1848) v. Italics added.
[66] Neale (1865) 5.
[67] Neale (1865) 7.
[68] Lambeth, MS 1491, f.183–4, Letter from Webb to Neale, 9 June 1865.

Worship Regulation Act in an effort, in Disraeli's words, "to put down Ritualism."[69]

Too often ecclesiologists have been painted as 'extreme men', but the facts simply do not support such a generalization. There is no doubt that John Mason Neale was an extreme man, and it is primarily due to the fact that he has traditionally been considered to be representative of the viewpoints of ecclesiologists that this misunderstanding exists. It has been demonstrated above that he took an ever-diminishing role in guiding the affairs and policies of the Ecclesiological (late Cambridge Camden) Society. (: 16–18) And it is quite evident that he was cast of a very different temperament from the men who actually managed the Society throughout its mature years.

The Musical Committee of the Ecclesiological Society 1856–62

The Revd H.L. Jenner's desire to expand the scope of *The Ecclesiologist's* coverage of the church music revival to include the entire Anglican Communion (: 132), as the *Parish Choir* had more or less done up until 1851, was never quite fulfilled. As he assumed his role as the Ecclesiological Society's Honorary Secretary for Music in 1856, the revival of choral service was picking up sufficient momentum to guarantee an almost self-propelled increase. (: 210–12)

By the mid-1850s church music was a subject that concerned all shades of churchmen. As had been the case in the revival of church architecture, the books and tracts and articles issued by early proponents of choral worship had deprived conscientious clergymen of any possibility to harbour either complacency or active disregard for the music of the sanctuary. In 1854 *The Ecclesiologist* confidently proclaimed: 'Among the Clergy, as would seem natural, even among those most opposed to our church sympathies, the ignorance of the past is impossible.'[70] And as the number of voices increased, the opinions expressed concerning church music became ever more kaleidoscopic. Considering how splintered into parties the mid-nineteenth century Church of England was, it is not surprising that no single faction or society would preside over the course of the revival indefinitely.

Reviews of music and books on church music continued to be a regular feature of *The Ecclesiologist*, but their content changed significantly. The vast quantity of apologies and polemical writings on church music during the 1840s and early 1850s had more or less won the theoretical battle. By the late 1850s no informed churchman would have advocated the liturgical or musical status quo of former times, but everyone seemed to have an opinion about

---

[69] Law (1925) 208–9.
[70] *The Ecclesiologist*, 15/100 (February 1854) 4.

what should be done instead. Consequently the work of church music revival shifted from proclaiming artistic principles and historical precedents to a discussion of practical details and technicalities. Between 1861 and 1868, when *The Ecclesiologist* ceased publication, more than a dozen articles and lengthy correspondences appeared in its pages concerning the division of the psalms for chanting and the manner of their actual performance. Yet however important such issues were, they could hardly generate the same general interest as did fundamental questions concerning the heritage and catholicity of the English Church and its modes of worship.

The tone of musical reviews during this period varied from the moderate to the dogmatic. If anything, incompetence was even more severely denounced; as the revival progressed, there were ever fewer excuses for inferior publications. An 1859 review stated dryly, 'The professed object of this pamphlet is certainly good: as to the means employed for the attainment of that object, we will assist our readers to form their own opinion.'[71] And it did. Chant collections were an obvious target for criticism. In the same year *The Ecclesiologist* stated that of the *Twenty-five Chants, Single and Double* issued by the Revd E.T. Codd, just six were worthy. The rest should be burned, and it was suggested that the reverend gentleman should study counterpoint before sending any more music to press.[72] Three years later the preface to a collection of chants by the Manchester musician, Benjamin St John Baptist Joule, was dismissed with the following words: 'Whatever Mr Joule's attainments in music may be, his attainments in the science of logic are most miserable.'[73]

In 1859 Jenner's report to the anniversary meeting of the Ecclesiological Society stated that there was, in fact, little for the musical committee to report. Since the completion of the *Hymnal Noted* (Part II appeared in 1854), their operations had been 'chiefly confined to the practical exemplification of their principles by the public performances of their Motett Choir.'[74] He stated that these performances continued to be held regularly, and that the press continued to bestow praise on them.[75] It could not be expected that such meetings would ever become popular in the sense that oratorio and secular concerts were popular; but he was sure that in its quiet way the Motett Choir was doing significant work in spreading a taste for early church music:

---

[71] *The Ecclesiologist*, 20/135 (December 1859) 370; regarding H.J. Gauntlett's *Notes, Queries, and Exercises in the Science and Practice of Music; Intended as Aids to Clergy, Churchwardens, and Others, in the Examination of Candidates for the Appointment of Organist in Parish and Other Churches*.
[72] *The Ecclesiologist*, 20/130 (February 1859) 44–5.
[73] *The Ecclesiologist*, 23/148 (February 1862) 41.
[74] *The Ecclesiologist*, 20/133 (August 1859) 269.
[75] For example, *The Ecclesiologist*, 19/124 (February 1858) 63, quotes the *Daily News*, 'the performance was not a little impressive, and highly interesting.'

> The compositions of Palestrina are not more strange to English ears at the present time, than were the works of Sebastian Bach, a few years ago. The latter have, by the force of their own intrinsic value, obtained a considerable and increasing share of public favour; and there seems to be no reason why the great Italian master and his successors should not, in due time, take the position to which their unrivalled merits so justly entitle them.[76]

He thought that the 'most practically important branch of the Committee's musical operations' consisted of its demonstrations of the plain song of the Church at each performance of the Motett Choir. The chanting of the psalms at the recent consecration of All Saints', Margaret Street, had, he thought, been 'triumphant proof of the value of the ancient tones of the Church, in securing a full and sonorous flood of song in this portion of the service. We have scarcely ever heard anything that so nearly approached our idea of what Psalmody ought to be.'[77]

The Ecclesiological Motett Choir to 1862

Musically the meetings of the Motett Choir maintained the pattern set in its early years. Since the primary goal had always been to introduce the public to the music of the ancient Church, it is not surprising that plainsong hymns, sequences, antiphons, and sixteenth and seventeenth-century polyphony predominated. It is interesting to note that at its meeting in April 1858, two translations from the *Hymnal Noted, Part II* which have since gained universal adoption were sung 'for the first time', namely *O Filii et Filiae* for Easter, and *Veni, veni Emmanuel* for Advent.[78] One or more modern anthems were always included in the programmes, and carols for Christmas and Eastertide were also featured regularly.

Between the costs of music, rental of rooms for practice and performance, and hiring boy trebles, running the Motett Choir was always an expensive venture, and at various points throughout its existence appeals for funds were made.[79] In 1860 H.L. Jenner reported to the Ecclesiological Society that the Motett Choir had 'undergone considerable modification, amounting almost to a re-formation', which he was sure would improve its efficiency.[80] As a result, a circular was issued to remind interested parties that the purpose of the Choir was 'to effect for Church Music a revival of sound principles and correct details, similar to that which within the last twenty years has happily arisen in Church Architecture', due primarily to the Ecclesiological Society's efforts.

---

[76] *The Ecclesiologist*, 20/133 (August 1859) 269–70.
[77] *The Ecclesiologist*, 20/133 (August 1859) 270.
[78] *The Ecclesiologist*, 19/127 (August 1858) 264.
[79] *The Ecclesiologist*, 19/127 (August 1858) 264–5.
[80] *The Ecclesiologist*, 21/139 (August 1860) 245.

Much work remained to be done for the cause of church music, Helmore wrote, and 'zealous and efficient' singers were required. From 1 November 1860 an initial entrance fee of a half-sovereign would be added to an annual subscription of the same amount (although members of the Ecclesiological Society could subscribe one guinea per annum, and would be elected by the Choir committee upon recommendation by a member of the Choir); and it was stated that irregular attendance at meetings for practice would result in exclusion from the Choir. Meetings were announced for every Monday evening, not being a 'red letter day' (a major saint's day or festival of the Church), except during the months of January, and August–October inclusive.

In December 1860 the public performance of the Motett Choir was held in the Architectural Exhibition rooms in Conduit Street for the first time. The promise which this location held for greater publicity and influence caused negotiations to be undertaken to transfer all subsequent meetings for practice and performance there. The *Ecclesiologist* stated:

> We trust that the increased outlay recently made by the choir themselves, and now to be incurred by the hire of these rooms, will induce the friends of Church music to increase in every way in their power the support and encouragement which are so essential to give permanent efficiency to the efforts of the society, and more especially of their choir.[81]

By the summer of 1861 Jenner was able to report to the Ecclesiological Society that 'competent judges have observed a decided improvement in the general efficiency of the choir, to the members of which our accustomed tribute of thanks was never more justly due.'

At the same time Jenner noted that a new Plain Song Choral Union had been formed in London under the direction of the Honorary Precentor of the Motett Society, Thomas Helmore, and the presidency of another member of the Ecclesiological Society.[82] The other gentleman was the Hon. Frederick Lygon, who as an undergraduate had been a founder of the Oxford Society for the Study and Practice of the Plain Song of the Church in 1853.[83] (: 83, 128) No doubt the formation of a Plain Song Choral Union in London arose from a desire to reach more people than the Motett Society could, in a setting which would allow an exclusive focus on that mode of congregational song, and without the strict attendance policy which the Motett Society necessarily had to enforce in order to ensure the effective performance of elaborate polyphonic church music.

It would seem that a breach of protocol by Thomas Helmore eventually brought to light underlying questions about the practicality of the continued

---

[81] *The Ecclesiologist*, 22/142 (February 1861) 45.
[82] *The Ecclesiologist*, 22/145 (August 1861) 249.
[83] *Guardian*, 797 (13 March 1861) 251. The Plain Song Choral Union's first meeting for practice was announced for 11 April 1861.

partnership between the Ecclesiological Society and the Motett Choir. By 1862 the Society's commitment to practical music-making had grown so large that the Motett Choir had become a financial burden. Webb reports on a Committee meeting of the Ecclesiological Society on 24 June 1862:

> The President [Beresford Hope] called attention to the fact that, without the consent, or even the cognizance, of any other officer of the Society, the Precentor of the Motett Choir [Thomas Helmore] had advertised a repetition of the second Motett Performance of the season as 'under the patronage of the President, Vice President, and Council of the English Church Union.'[84] He read a correspondence between Mr Helmore and himself on the subject. After an explanation from the Precentor, the Treasurer [Greatheed] stated that the costs of the Motett meetings made it necessary to reconsider the Society's obligations with respect to them. The Secretary [Webb] stated that the Honorary Secretary for Musical Matters [Jenner] had expressed to him his conviction that the time had come for dissociating the Motett Choir from the Ecclesiological Society, and accordingly he proposed that steps should now be taken for dissolving the union that had existed between the two bodies for the last ten years.

Accordingly, the following resolution was passed:

> That in the opinion of this Committee it is desirable for the Ecclesiological Society to terminate those functions which they have for some years undertaken in connection with the prosecution of Church Music: and that it be referred to the Officers of the Society to take steps for dissolving such union as at present exists between the Ecclesiological Society and the representatives of the late Motett Society.[85]

At a meeting on the morning of the twenty-third anniversary of the Ecclesiological Society, 1 July 1862, it was decided to defer the question of the future of the Motett Choir to the new Committee, to be elected that evening. Consequently the annual report stated only:

> The Motett choir have continued their labours with increased diligence, and the public music meetings have been more than usually successful. There has been, however, an increase of expenditure in the musical department which has pressed heavily on the very small funds of the society, and it will therefore be necessary to reconsider the whole matter of their musical operations in the ensuing year.[86]

On 15 July 1862, the new Committee, attended by Beresford Hope, Greatheed, Webb, J.F. France, William Scott, Thomas Helmore and Frederick Lygon 'agreed that the connection at present existing between the two bodies should

---

[84] It is probable that Beresford Hope was concerned that the Motett Choir's public association with the English Church Union would attach to the Motett Choir an undesirable church party association. Due to its ritualistic tendencies, Beresford Hope could never be induced to speak on the platforms of the English Church Union. (: 115)
[85] RIBA: Ecclesiological Society Minutes, 24 June 1862.
[86] *The Ecclesiologist*, 23/141 (August 1862) 219, 226.

terminate at the close of the present season.'[87] With this move the musical committee of the Ecclesiological Society was also disbanded, and the Honorary Secretary for Music, H.L. Jenner, became an ordinary member of the Committee.[88]

This must be construed neither as disapproval of the undertakings of the Motett Choir nor as loss of interest in its mission. Neither was the separation a death blow to the Motett Choir's work. On 4 August 1862 former members of the committee of the Motett Choir and interested parties from the late musical committee of the Ecclesiological Society met to form a new committee of the Motett Choir, consisting of the Precentor (Helmore) and nine other men, who pledged themselves to see that its work continued. In a circular printed by the reformed Motett Society and reprinted in *The Ecclesiologist*, the disunion of the two societies was referred to as a 'friendly dissolution.' The public was apprised of the fact that the Motett Choir continued to enjoy the 'good wishes, sympathy, and support' of the Ecclesiological Society, and that it had been thought that 'by a division of labour, and a simplification of its machinery' the Motett Choir would be 'more free to plan and stronger to execute such operations as in future may seem best calculated to fulfil the high and important aim which it hitherto *has* kept, and by God's help *will keep*, in view.' In an appeal for financial support at this 'crisis' in its history, the public was reminded that no other Society promoted ecclesiastical music with 'equal attention to Church authority and ritual, Church history, Church propriety, and Church wants and requirements.' To those who felt that the Motett Society's mission had already been accomplished, since ancient models were now readily available for modern composers to 'imitate, and perhaps surpass',[89] Helmore submitted:

> the restoration and improvement of the Music in our churches are not to be obtained merely by placing good books within the reach of composers. An actual singing and hearing of the best models – the practice of the Music of the old Italian and other Continental Masters, as well as those of the English school still heard in our Cathedrals; a trial, by persons somewhat qualified by such a course of study, of new compositions for the Church; above all, the keeping together [of] a body of Singers and Musicians who can from time to time be listened to while they perform either the ancient compositions accepted as the models of greatest excellence, or modern Music formed upon these as their patterns, or at least by authors enjoying the advantage of a thorough acquaintance with them – are objects claiming the continuance of the work which, though well begun, cannot, in any practical view, be deemed to have been completed by the original founders of the Motett Society.[90]

---

[87] RIBA: Ecclesiological Society Minutes, 15 July 1862; *The Ecclesiologist*, 23/142 (October 1862) 298.
[88] *The Ecclesiologist*, 24/157 (August 1863) 228.
[89] *The Ecclesiologist*, 23/142 (October 1862) 298–9.
[90] *The Ecclesiologist*, 23/142 (October 1862) 300.

Subscribers were forthcoming, and *The Ecclesiologist* soon carried the Motett Choir's intelligence that its first season under new management had been a success.[91]

During 1860 and 1861 there had also been various calls for the Ecclesiological Society to provide a new Gregorian psalter. Profound gratitude was expressed for Helmore's *Psalter Noted,* but everyone was aware that there were inconsistencies in the pointing; and greater variety was felt to be desirable in the chants for the canticles, which, it was suggested, should be included in the same publication. The more ambitious scheme was put forth by Edmund Sedding, who thought that those members of the Society who were so highly qualified to do so should unite to produce a complete English *Gradual.*[92] Both schemes would have constituted valuable contributions to the furtherance of the movement, and with the precedent of the *Hymnal Noted*, the Society should have felt no compunction in undertaking them. Yet neither came to fruition.

Why did the Ecclesiological Society seemingly abandon its efforts on behalf of church music? It would seem that the primary reason was the increasingly heavy personal responsibilities of those who would have taken part in such a work. At the twenty-third anniversary meeting of the Society in July 1862, the Secretary, Benjamin Webb, stated in his general report:

> It is to be regretted that the press of other business has prevented your committee from dealing with those many musical subjects which might otherwise most properly have claimed their attention; and this must excuse the absence of any musical report this year.[93]

A number of years later, at the conclusion of 1868, *The Ecclesiologist* ceased publication due simply to the 'growing pre-occupations of those whose pens have for so long chiefly kept it alive.' At the same time the editors proclaimed, 'We have the satisfaction of retiring from the field victors.'[94] The feeling that the battle had been won was anything but new in 1868. In the 25th annual report to the Society in 1864, the President (since 1859), A.J.B. Beresford Hope had stated proudly:

> In the way of church-worship it is very little indeed to say that the exertions of a great many people, of whom we claim, and dare to assert the claim, that we were among the most prominent and the earliest, have effected a revolution in the idea of worship throughout the Church of England.[95]

At the same meeting Benjamin Webb declared that most of the objects for which the Society had been founded twenty-five years earlier had been

---

[91] *The Ecclesiologist*, 25/160 (February 1864) 47–8.
[92] *The Ecclesiologist*, 21/139 (August 1860) 246; 22/145 (October 1861) 346–8.
[93] *The Ecclesiologist*, 23/141 (August 1862) 226.
[94] *The Ecclesiologist*, 29/189 (December 1868) 314.
[95] *The Ecclesiologist*, 25/163 (August 1864) 209.

accomplished. 'Its present and its future work,' he continued, 'seems to be the watching, aiding, and (it may be) guiding the growth and diffusion of true principles of taste in every branch of Christian art.'[96]

Transition in the old Cambridge choral foundations after 1856

King's College. Upon the death of John Pratt in 1855, William Amps (Peterhouse) was appointed to succeed him. Amps seems to have been a rather colourless character, for virtually nothing is known of him or his ability as a choir trainer.

By early 1858, however, signs that improvements unrelated to Amps were being made appeared in the national press. It was reported that a 'Conduct' was about to be appointed to the Chapel staff. The *Guardian* wrote:

> We are glad to hear that the musical qualifications of the Clergymen who are candidates will be carefully tested, as it is intended to restore the *choral service* in its integrity. Of late years there has been a discord between the choir and the reader, although many can remember the time when the service was intoned in the regular way. In such a chapel certainly the service should be as perfect as human skill can make it.[97]

Six weeks later it was announced that the successful applicant had been the Revd Arthur Beard, BA of St John's College, Cambridge. His title was reported to be chaplain.[98]

In August 1859 *The Ecclesiologist* announced the forthcoming rebuild of the King's College Chapel organ by Messrs Hill and Co:

> This... will be the second great improvement which the Provost and Fellows of King's have made in the choral service of their chapel; the first being the substitution of a musical for an undefinable polytonic recitation by the priest of the versicles and prayers in the daily service. We hope that a third improvement will be affected [sic] before long, namely, a thorough reformation with respect to the music in use.[99]

This most likely refers to the Sunday 'parades' (: 48), oratorio excerpts, the extrovert settings of the canticles which were commonly sung during prior decades. There was certainly was an abundance of fine works by ancient masters in the anthem library (: 52–6, 202–3), but whether any of them were actually performed in the 1850s and 60s is unknown.

---

[96] *The Ecclesiologist*, 25/163 (August 1864) 210.
[97] *Guardian*, 634 (27 January 1858) 63.
[98] *Guardian*, 640 (10 March 1858) 203.
[99] *The Ecclesiologist*, 20/133 (August 1859) 296.

Trinity College. Since Trinity had determined to raise the standard of its Choir and their manner of conducting choral service during the 1840s, there was little for John Larkin Hopkins (1820–73) to do upon his arrival at Trinity (Michaelmas term, 1856) but to maintain an already high status quo. The next major reorganization of the Trinity Choir began in the early 1870s.

St John's College. By the time Thomas Attwood Walmisley died, four days short of his forty-second birthday in 1856, St John's was of the mind, and took the opportunity, to re-establish a completely independent choral foundation. On 7 May 1856 the College Council 'agreed to appoint Alfred Bennett Organist and Choirmaster during our pleasure at a Salary of £100 per annum payable quarterly.'[100] It is clear that there was a strong desire at St John's to strengthen and expand the role of music in the worship of the College Chapel, since the number of choral services increased significantly. With a completely independent choir (Trinity and King's continued to share a set of lay clerks until midsummer 1871),[101] St John's was no longer compelled to plan its choral services around those of its neighbours, and from Michaelmas 1856 the Choir sang on Saturday evening, twice on Sunday, on the Eves and evenings of Saints' Days, and twice on Christmas and Ascension. If the additional services are an indication of a growing appreciation of music in general and choral service in particular, they were certainly not the last.

As it happened, Alfred Bennett's tenure as Organist of St John's was short-lived, due to his desire to pursue a career in India, and he was succeeded later in the year of his appointment by a man who would be a dominant figure in the musical life of Cambridge for thirty years. George Mursell Garrett (8 June 1834–8 April 1897) was born in Winchester, son of William Garrett, a Cathedral lay clerk and Master of its Choir School. In 1844 the younger Garrett entered the Choir of New College, Oxford, where he boarded with the other choristers in the home of the Choirmaster, Stephen Elvey. Glandular fever forced his return to Winchester after three years, where he was soon articled to a Mr B. Long, Samuel Chard's permanent deputy as cathedral organist. When Samuel Sebastian Wesley assumed the position of Organist at Winchester Cathedral in 1849, Garrett's articles were transferred, and he eventually became Wesley's first deputy. Garrett ended his studies in Winchester in 1854. On 16 October of that year Thomas Attwood Walmisley wrote to inform him that the Chaplain to the Bishop of Madras, India (who was also the Bishop's son), had applied to him for a recommendation to fill the post of Cathedral organist, and that Walmisley had recommended Garrett, whose ability he would have known from visits to S.S. Wesley in Winchester.

---

[100] SJCA: Conclusion Book, 7 May 1856.
[101] TCWL: Muniments Room, shelf 1, #35, Minutes of the Trinity College Choir Committee, 6 February 1871.

A friendly letter of congratulation followed from T.A. Walmisley on 26 November, after the position had been formally offered and accepted.[102] Garrett presumably sailed in December 1854 or early in 1855; he was destined to stay abroad for only about a year, however, for:

> the climate proved too much for him, and he had to return home. He was not long idle. His successor as senior pupil of Dr Wesley was Alfred Bennett, who, in 1856, was made Organist of St John's. Bennett, however, was preparing to start for an appointment at Calcutta, and he invited his fellow pupil to come up to Cambridge and try for the appointment he was leaving. There was no competition; Dr Garrett played a few services and was elected forthwith. He then settled down to his life's work.[103]

Thus it was that George Garrett became Organist of St John's College. He was officially appointed by the College Council on 17 December at a salary of £100 per annum, and entered upon his duties on 31 December 1856.

At St John's singing was encouraged by the formation, at least by 1861, of the St John's Choral Society. It is possible that this was the 'Church Music Society' which the Cambridge Architectural Society stated to be an offshoot of itself in 1861. (: 82–3) Elementary and advanced classes met weekly under Dr Garrett's direction, the latter group being assisted by boy trebles, in order that a wide variety of sacred and secular part-music could be practised. At the general meeting of its members on 4 December 1861,

> it was decided that it would be desirable to strengthen the chapel choir by two altos, two tenors, and two basses selected from this society, who should practise with the choir and sit in seats reserved for them in the chapel.[104]

However good the idea was, at the next meeting the secretary reported that he had discussed the proposal with Dr Garrett, and that 'it had been found impracticable... for the present.' Students played no official part in the music of the Chapel until 1869, when a 'Voluntary Choir', its membership drawn from the students of the College, was formed to assist in certain services.[105]

It is interesting to note that the increase of interest in sacred choral music corresponded to a gradual move toward High Church practices in the St John's College Chapel, especially in terms of more frequent celebrations of the Eucharist. From 1840 (possibly much earlier), the Sacrament had been observed only six times a year: on Christmas, Easter, Whit Sunday, the first Sunday after the division of Michaelmas and Lent term, and on the fourth Sunday of Easter term. In 1858 it was ordered that from Michaelmas Holy Communion should be celebrated twice each term, double the previous custom. During Michaelmas 1864 bi-weekly communions at 8 a.m. were

---

[102] Letters in the possession of Mrs Olwen Way, granddaughter of George Garrett.
[103] Garrett (1897) 591.
[104] SJCA: SOC4.2, Minutes of the St John's Choral Society.
[105] SJCA: D103.84, Letter from George Garrett to the Senior Dean, 20 April 1887.

instituted. These were delayed by one week whenever they would have coincided otherwise with a 10 a.m. celebration. The practical result of this was that Holy Communion was held nearly every Sunday as one of the morning services. The Revd S. Hiley, who had been Senior Dean for one year from June 1862, wrote to the Senior Bursar, the Revd G.F. Reyner on the 28th November 1864:

> During the time I was Dean, as you are aware, 80 undergraduates, or thereabouts – almost a third of our number – presented me with a petition for this change, to be laid before the Master and Seniors. This was done, and you see the result. I am much pleased with your early Communions, as all parties may now possibly be accommodated... If...changes are to be made, our Colleges should be amongst the first to shew the example.[106]

The old College Chapel having been outgrown, by 1862 discussions and plans were well under way for the erection of a new one, which would be built according to the architectural ideals of the Cambridge Camden Society. With its completion in 1869 the general move toward more frequent Sunday Communions continued. On 3 November 1869 the Revd P.H. Mason, Senior Dean, recorded that it had been 'Agreed that the Holy Communion be celebrated in the College Chapel every Sunday during Term time and during the months of July and August.'[107]

Anthem repertoire at King's, Trinity, and St John's Colleges, circa 1858

The best clues concerning the anthem repertoire in the old Cambridge choral foundations after the arrival of their new organists in 1855 and 1856 survives in the form of the appendices which they added to Thomas Attwood Walmisley's 1844 *Collection of Anthems* for use in their chapels. It should be observed, however, that the purpose of these appendices was not to remould the repertoire, but primarily to fill in the gaps in Walmisley's collection (1844) which were the natural product of time. Obviously the new organists each introduced anthems which suited his own taste, music which his predecessor either did not know, preferred not to perform, or which had been composed since 1844. Hence the appendices do not provide an overall view of the anthem repertoires of the three choirs, but they constitute the body of works with which each organist was most eager to supplement the established repertoire upon his arrival.

William Amps added an appendix for *King's College* in 1856. It consists of forty-seven texts for forty-nine compositions by twenty-six composers. Four of the composers (15.4 per cent) are foreign, and their twelve compositions account for 24.5 per cent of the appendix. The composers represented are:

---

[106] SJCA: D92.1.49.
[107] SJCA: DS1.1, Dean's Order Book.

S.S. Wesley	7	Spohr	3	G.J. Elvey	2
Mendelssohn	5	W. Amps	2	Ouseley	2
Palestrina	3	Blow	2	Rogers	2
Purcell	3	Crotch	2		

One each: J.E. Beckwith, Boyce, Chard, J. Clark, Forster, Calcott, Attwood, P. Hayes, Longhurst, Nares, Novello, Tye, Webbe, Wise, Zingarelli

The inclusion of three adaptations of Palestrina is noteworthy.

The precise date of J.L. Hopkins' appendix for *Trinity College* is not known, but it is probably from the late-1850s. It consists of fifty-one texts for fifty-two compositions by seventeen composers. Only two of the composers (11.8 per cent) are foreign, but their seventeen compositions account for 32.7 per cent of the appendix. The composers represented are:

Mendelssohn	14	Spohr	3	G.J. Elvey	2
S.S. Wesley	8	Attwood	2	E.J. Hopkins	2
J.L. Hopkins	5	Croft	2	Purcell	2
Sterndale Bennett	4	Crotch	2		

One each: Allen, Goss, Handel, Nares, Malan, Sturges

This list anticipates the devotion to the works of Mendelssohn which was so common in the cathedral repertoire throughout England later in the nineteenth century. The addition of works by J.L. and E.J. Hopkins is unsurprising, as is the inclusion of four works by Walmisley's successor as Professor of Music at Cambridge, William Sterndale Bennett.

George Garrett added an appendix for *St John's College* in 1858. It consists of forty-seven texts for forty-eight compositions by twenty different composers. Seven of the composers (35 per cent) are foreign, and their eighteen compositions account for a similarly large proportion (37.5 per cent) of the appendix. The composers represented are:

S.S. Wesley	7	Attwood	3	G.J. Elvey	2
Mendelssohn	6	Sterndale Bennett	3	Mozart	2
Spohr	6	Crotch	2	Purcell	2
Garrett	5				

One each: Beethoven, Goss, Handel, Haydn, Hayes, Kent, Malan, Luther, Nares, Righini

The fact that two Germans are found at the top of the list is an indication of Garrett's sympathies in terms of compositional style. A decided predilection on the part of Henry B. Walmisley (Thomas Attwood Walmisley's brother) for German music is revealed in a series of letters to George Garrett during 1854–

5,[108] and their tone reveals that the writer's sentiments were shared by Garrett. By the time service lists began to be printed for the College Chapel in 1877, the works of Mendelssohn had eclipsed those of all other composers in popularity.

A trend established in Walmisley's Collection which is continued in two of the three appendices is the gradual introduction of a greater percentage of works for full choir. In Matthews' 1827 collection 86 per cent of the selections included work for solo voices. This was reduced to somewhat less than 80 per cent of the whole in Walmisley's 1844 Collection. Only the appendix for Trinity by J.L. Hopkins did not advance the trend toward more full anthems, with 81 per cent of his selections including work for solo voices. Solo voices were required in just 71 per cent of Garrett's selections and only 57 per cent of William Amps' appendix.

Thus we see that the old Cambridge choral foundations responded to ecclesiologists' calls for reform and to the choral revival at large by strengthening their professional choirs, and that the college organists continued the performance of an essentially traditional 'Anglican' repertoire which relied heavily upon the use of solo voices. King's and St John's introduced a larger proportion of less 'showy' music into the repertoire, and all three colleges restored choral service 'in its integrity' (i.e. the priests learned to intone their parts of the service). But none of them succeeded in becoming the models that ecclesiologists hoped for during the first two decades of the revival of choral worship. Ironically, it was the demands of Evangelicals later in the century which succeeded in altering the choral services at Trinity to include more active congregational participation.

Ecclesiologists and the Diocesan Parish Choir Festival Movement

The rise of diocesan choral associations signalled a sort of coming-of-age for the Anglican choral revival, ushering in a new era and giving ecclesiologists great hope for the future of choral service in parishes throughout the realm. Until such societies were formed, rural church choirs functioned more or less within the isolation of their own parishes, and owing their existence to the good fortune of having an enthusiastic curate, vicar, schoolmaster, or musician who could train them. Diocesan parish choir gatherings radically changed the face of the revival. Brought together with dozens of other choirs for a festival service, these isolated parish choirs suddenly knew themselves to be part of a much larger movement. They became conscious of the kinds of music their neighbours were aspiring to sing, strong opinions on church music vied to gain

---

[108] Letters in the possession of Mrs Olwen Way.

the validation of popularity, and one suspects that there was an occasional sense that it might be important to, as it were, keep up with the neighbours.

The diocesan choral associations were not the first associations to unite parish choirs; several towns and rural districts led the way with smaller local organizations in the early 1850s. Perhaps the most influential of these early societies was the Cheadle Association for Promoting Church Music, formed in late 1848 or 1849 under the patronage of the Bishop of Lichfield for the purpose of encouraging good congregational singing.[109] Its first massed gathering was held in Cheadle (Staffordshire) on 4 October 1849. A correspondent to the *Parish Choir* recommended that other clergy follow the Cheadle association's example, and reported that its great success was due to the appointment of a 'most efficient choir-master to give a systematic course of musical instruction to each of the choirs within the limits of the Association.'[110] The fifth annual meeting of the association in Cheadle on 30 August 1853 included two full 'cathedral services', with the responses by Tallis, the *Venite* and psalms sung to 'appropriate' chants, Boyce's *Te Deum* and *Jubilate* in C, Hayes' *Great is the Lord,* Gibbons' *Magnificat* and *Nunc dimittis* in F, and Creyghton's *Praise the Lord.* The *Guardian* marvelled:

> When we consider that upwards of a hundred choristers, chiefly from rough country parishes and parochial schools, should be able, after a training of so short a time, to execute, without instrumental aid, vocal music of so high a character, we cannot but be struck with the great amount of good which the Cheadle society has been the means of accomplishing, in purifying and reforming so important a part of our Church service, and wish that similar societies were generally established throughout the country.[111]

The wish was not long in being fulfilled.

The Lichfield Diocesan Choral Association

The *Guardian* eventually credited Cheadle's example as the origin of the whole diocesan choral festival movement. The general success of the early meetings of that association led to a desire for a larger gathering in a grander building, and consequently the first diocesan choral festival was held in Lichfield Cathedral on 14 October 1856. About twenty-six choirs participated the first year, and so great was its success that the second Lichfield festival in 1857 attracted forty-seven choirs.

---

[109] The *Parish Choir*, 3/58 (October 1850) 152, reported that it was formed 'about a year' ago; the *Guardian,* 405 (7 September 1853) 601, reported that it was formed 'about five years ago.'
[110] *Parish Choir*, 3/58 (October 1850) 152.
[111] *Guardian,* 405 (7 September 1853) 601.

The moving force behind the Lichfield gatherings was the Precentor, Canon John Hutchinson;[112] but he promoted the choral association in consultation with many advisors. Benjamin Webb first discussed the music for the 1857 festival ten weeks before the event, but was too late to influence its choice that year.[113] The music was entirely 'Anglican' (Rogers in D; *Sanctus* and *Gloria in excelsis* by Tallis; and Anglican chants). Thomas Helmore was invited to lead the services for the day.

Benjamin Webb reviewed the gathering for *The Ecclesiologist* saying that 'the idea was worthy of the highest praise.'[114] The event silenced those who attacked cathedrals as useless to the diocese by showing it 'in its true light, as a model and pattern. What was aimed at in each parish occasionally and imperfectly', he wrote, 'was there seen to be ordinary and habitual.' In addition, the service united the trained singers of the diocese and its clergy around their bishop in magnificent worship, imbued by the surroundings with 'a dignity and beauty such as could not fail to elevate and impress those whose highest ideal of worship had hitherto been that of a town parochial church.' There were no dominant personalities seeking attention for themselves, as in the popular preaching assemblies of the day, and the sheer number of singers made it impossible for any individual singer to 'show off.' Webb deprecated a proposition to hold district festivals (although this was necessary in 1858 and 1859 due to restoration work on the cathedral), since it would destroy the positive effects to be gained by directing the affections of the diocese to its true spiritual centre, and there was danger that smaller gatherings could become the forum for 'party manifestos.'[115] To encourage future improvement he pointed to various organizational shortcomings of the Lichfield festival, including the lack of a procession, the type of service music chosen, and its standard of performance, and asserted:

> As... the object is to give the choirs music which they can all sing, and by joining in bring out and feel their united strength and beauty, it seems a mistake to neglect those wealthy stores of the great church composers – music, be it remembered, of the highest class – who wrote as if they always had in view those very dangers which were fatal to much of the Lichfield music.[116]

In 1858 district meetings of the Lichfield Diocesan Choral Association were held. As Secretary for the Ashbourne District, Webb was carefully consulted about the choice of music to be sung there.[117] His influence is obvious in the

---

[112] LJRO: D30/7/6/5 (78) and D30/7/6/8 (198); *Guardian*, 880 (15 October 1862) 983.
[113] Webb diaries, 19 August 1857.
[114] Authorship is attributed in the Webb diaries, 12 and 13 October 1857. *The Ecclesiologist*, 18/123 (December 1857) 360–3.
[115] *The Ecclesiologist*, 18/123 (December 1857) 360–2.
[116] *The Ecclesiologist*, 18/123 (December 1857) 363. The choirs had difficulty singing in time together.
[117] Webb diaries, 30 March, 14 and 20 April 1858. LJRO: D30/7/6/5 (2).

choice of Gibbons 'in F' for both the morning and evening services, the Merbecke Nicene Creed, and Tallis *Sanctus* and *Gloria in excelsis*. The anthems were Purcell's *O God, Thou art my God* and Crotch's *We will rejoice*.[118] One suspects that Gregorian chant must have been employed (although no mention of it is made in the *Guardian*), since the following week's report on the district festival held at St Mary's, Lichfield, reveals that Gregorian chant was used for the morning canticles, a psalm before Communion, and the *Magnificat*.[119] Merbecke was still used in 1862 for the Communion service, but in that year the Revd Sir Frederick Ouseley 'offered' to serve as advisor to the Lichfield Diocesan Choral Association.[120] The previous year Ouseley had served as 'Rector Chori' for the Lichfield festival, and in thanking him for an anthem (based on II Chronicles 5:13,14) composed for that occasion, *The Ecclesiologist* had hoped that the anthem's employment of unison passages would be allowed in future to extend to the admission of plainsong hymns and psalms:

> We are... grateful to the most accomplished clerical musician of our Church for this splendid composition, and trust that, if called upon to prepare the programme and preside (as we trust he may) at many other similar solemnities, he will allow his own excellent taste to pervade the whole arrangements, unfettered by that kind of homage to inferior genius which we fear has too long kept both himself and other admirers of Anglican Church music from throwing themselves heart and soul into the cause of Church Musical Reform.[121]

One wonders if these generous wishes did not occasion regret in their fulfilment. In Ouseley's subsequent capacity as 'Honorary General Visitor' to the Lichfield Diocesan Choral Association, Gregorian chant and early service settings became decidedly less conspicuous, while Ouseley's own specially composed festival anthems, chant services, and other 'Anglican' music became the norm.[122]

Lichfield never became the model diocesan choral festival which ecclesiologists hoped for; the diocesan association was, notwithstanding, a remarkable success. By 1864 membership in the diocese of Lichfield alone was estimated at 1500 persons, and the association was happy to boast of its 1856 example which, in just eight years, had come to be imitated by seventeen other English and Welsh cathedrals. The combined membership of all of the diocesan choral associations was estimated to be about 13,000 persons.[123]

---

[118] *Guardian*, 671 (13 October 1858) 802.
[119] *Guardian*, 672 (20 October 1858) 818.
[120] LJRO: D30/7/6/5 (27).
[121] *The Ecclesiologist*, 22/147 (December 1861) 395–6.
[122] LJRO: D30/7/6/5 (28, 70) and D30/7/6/8 (142, 198).
[123] LJRO: D30/7/6/8 (141).

Southwell Minster: the Nottinghamshire Choral Union

Lincoln was the second diocese in which a parish choir festival on the model of Lichfield was inaugurated. It was founded primarily due to the zeal of the Revd John Murray Wilkins (BA 1841, Trinity College, Cambridge), Rector of Southwell, where the festivals were held. The Revd H.L. Jenner was dispatched by the Committee of the Ecclesiological Society to observe and review the proceedings.[124]

Jenner opened by admitting that there were as many opinions as people on how best to improve church music:

> Now we do not think this diversity of opinion an unmixed evil. The question is obviously one on which considerable latitude may be allowed, without serious prejudice to the cause, which, we may presume, all have at heart. The whole subject requires deep investigation; and this, if fairly and impartially conducted, will, we may hope, in process of time, reduce the number of conflicting theories, and furnish some intelligible and consistent principles, to guide the course of present and future reformers of Church music.[125]

For this very reason, choral festivals were held to be important as a means of testing the various theories. Jenner hoped that the example set at Southwell would be the most beneficial one yet made for the cause of English church music.

Three hundred and fifty singers participated in the first meeting at Southwell Minster on 28 April 1858. Two hundred persons in surplices processed singing Psalm 122 to the fifth tone; single Anglican chants were used for the morning psalms and canticles, and Tallis' *If ye love me*, which would become a great favourite at parish choir festivals, was sung as the anthem. The litany was sung from Helmore's *Brief Directory of Plain Song*. But it was the evening service which Jenner proclaimed 'undoubtedly the great success of the day.' With the sole exception of the Tallis responses, the music at evensong was taken from Helmore's *Psalter* and *Canticles Noted* and the ECCS's *Hymnal Noted*, and was sung in unison with organ accompaniment.[126] 'The psalms and canticles thus poured forth by 350 voices,' Jenner wrote, 'were grand beyond description.' It was conclusive proof, as far as Jenner was concerned, that

> this style of music, and this mode of performance, are the best that have yet been devised for congregational worship; the best suited, therefore, to our present services, which are so essentially congregational.[127]

For its continued commitment to plainsong as an integral part of the annual gatherings, Southwell came to be the ecclesiologists' model festival of parish

---

[124] RIBA: Ecclesiological Society Minutes, 27 April 1858.
[125] *The Ecclesiologist*, 19/126 (June 1858) 175.
[126] *The Ecclesiologist*, 19/126 (June 1858) 175–6.
[127] *The Ecclesiologist*, 19/126 (June 1858) 177.

choirs. Of the Southwell festival for 1859 *The Ecclesiologist* reported that much improvement had been realized due to the appointment of a peripatetic choirmaster.[128] The festival was still marred, however, by two major shortcomings: first, the festival had not used ancient music exclusively, although *The Ecclesiologist* admitted that 'a certain concession to tastes formed in the modern corrupt schools of Church music is, on such occasions as these, not only tolerable, but necessary', and second, that the bishop had not sung his part of the service. 'Until our clergy, whether bishops, priests, or deacons, are *'mediocriter docti in plano cantu,'* however well trained the choirs may be, the work of our choral associations will be only half done.' The reviewer, almost certainly Jenner, continued:

> It is intolerable that, where such evident care has been taken, as at Southwell, that all the services should be worthily rendered, the chiefest of all, the Holy Sacrifice itself, should be marred by the unwillingness or incompetence of the celebrant – usually, of course, the principal dignitary present – to recite the very easy Plain Song of the English Liturgy.[129]

No matter how closely Southwell came to the ecclesiologists' ideal, there was always room for improvement; and the seriousness with which the whole movement was taken by them is revealed in the statement, 'It is not easy to exaggerate the value and importance of these choir festivals, or of the associations under whose auspices they are organised, and of whose activity and success they are the result, as well as the test.'[130] In 1861 *The Ecclesiologist* stated flatly, 'There is no reason whatever... why this sort of gathering should not be held annually in every cathedral and collegiate church in England.'

The Ely Society for the Promotion of Church Music

The Ely diocesan parish choral union was formed in 1858 under the auspices of Dean Peacock, who died a few months later. His successor, Harvey Goodwin, had been an original member of the Ecclesialogical Society, the High Church club formed in 1839 with J.M. Neale and Benjamin Webb (: 19), and he extended his enthusiastic support to the cause of church music. At the Ely Society's first festival in May 1859, more than 600 singers joined the cathedral choir in the presence of a congregation estimated at 3000 people, and Dean Goodwin preached a 'vigorous defence of musical services.' In an early attempt to accommodate all musical parties, the psalms were sung to Anglican chants and the canticles to Gregorian chants at both the morning and evening

---

[128] *The Ecclesiologist*, 20/132 (June 1859) 189–91.
[129] *The Ecclesiologist*, 20/132 (June 1859) 190.
[130] *The Ecclesiologist*, 20/132 (June 1859) 189.

services.[131] This compromise soon became common at parish choir gatherings.

By 1861, however, Ely had abandoned the use of Gregorian chant in their district and diocesan festivals. With the contact between choirs that resulted from the Ely parish choir festivals, the use of Gregorian chant had become a divisive issue, and Dean Goodwin prided himself on being unattached to any party.[132] By this time Gregorian chant had been roundly denounced by many influential musicians, and even the *Guardian* had turned its back on the music it had once promoted. In 1861 the *Guardian* lauded the improvement of the Ely Cathedral Choir under the new Precentor, W.E. Dickson, and praised Dean Goodwin for the constant support he showed the choral revival through his impressive and reverent manner of intoning the daily services. Then it went on to congratulate the Ely Society for choosing music which was 'free from the antiquated barbarisms of a period when the art was in its infancy, as well as from the florid vulgarities of modern times.'[133] In 1862 the Ely Society for the Promotion of Church Music found itself unable to agree upon the recommendation of any style or collection of music for general diocesan use in the singing of the psalms and canticles.[134] It is a clear example of the way in which parish choir festivals sometimes reached a practical impasse because individual parties within the Church, whose local parish choirs may happily have sung whatever the choirmaster introduced to their autonomous little parishes in the past, now found themselves thrown in with neighbours who thought that *their* preferred style was best. Those who felt compelled to advocate a uniform, 'proper', or 'correct' style of church music drew battle lines which did not go unchallenged.

Canterbury Diocesan Choral Union

It was due to the initiative of the Revd H.L. Jenner that the Canterbury Diocesan Choral Union was founded early in 1862. For the next five years Jenner acted as its precentor, the post which carried the greatest share of practical responsibility. The Dean of Canterbury, Alford, who had also been a regular participant in the Canterbury Amateur Musical Society (: 130) since arriving there in 1857, consented to be the first President. The object of the Union, like others which had been formed since Lichfield set the example in 1856, was 'to promote the glory of God by improving the singing in the parish churches'; and the public was assured, 'It is not intended to interfere with, in any way, the selection of music in parish churches, but only to assist its more

---

[131] *Guardian*, 704 (1 June 1859) 470.
[132] *Guardian*, 681 (22 December 1858) 1030.
[133] *Guardian*, 808 (29 May 1861) 501.
[134] *Guardian*, 808 (29 May 1861) 501; 889 (17 December 1862) 1181.

reverent and efficient performance.'[135] The goal of the Union was pursued by 'affording instruction and superintendence to choirs, in parishes desiring assistance', and by holding general and district choral festivals.[136]

The Union's first annual festival of parish choirs was held the following July in Canterbury Cathedral. Adhering to the plan of musical inclusivity which by then had been adopted for many other choral festivals of the kind, the psalms and canticles for the morning service were sung to Anglican chants, and in the evening Gregorian tones were used. The Tallis responses and anthem *If ye love me*, both of which commonly appeared on such occasions, were sung in the morning; the anthem for the evening service was *I know that the Lord is great* by the Revd Sir Frederick Ouseley.[137] The pastoral consideration of catering to various musical preferences was enhanced by the fact that Anglican chants were matched with Tallis, Gregorian tones with Ouseley. Such diplomacy was exhibited again at a district festival in Folkstone the following November,[138] and at the Union's festivals thereafter.

The second annual festival was held in June 1863, when more than 800 singers from forty-five choirs took part. By this time the *Guardian* had firmly turned its back on plainsong and criticized the Revd S.S. Greatheed's harmonies to the evening psalms: 'If these foreign tones must be used, more expert harmonisers should be found.' It is likely that any harmonization would have failed to please this reviewer, unless the result had made the Gregorian tones sound like diatonic Anglican chants. Whatever the difference of opinion over ancient chant, the *Guardian* stated that to H.L. Jenner 'the highest praise is most justly due, and to him the success of the choral services of the day, and of the now firmly established Union, is mainly to be attributed.'[139]

Ecclesiologists, then, were involved and keenly interested in the parish choir festival movement. Given the size to which the movement so rapidly grew, the choral revival quickly moved far beyond the power of any party or school of thought to control or even effectively guide it. The large, public nature of diocesan choral festivals invited the expression of opinions on church music by anyone who cared to offer them. Whereas individual clergymen previously would have been able to impose their own wills on isolated parish choirs, now the powerful influence of public taste and popularity came into play. In particular, this likely hindered the widespread adoption of the plainsong tones for the psalms and canticles, which ecclesiologists had strongly promoted well into the 1850s.

---

[135] *Guardian*, 848 (5 March 1862) 218.
[136] *Guardian*, 914 (10 June 1863) 551.
[137] *Guardian*, 867 (16 July 1862) 679.
[138] *Guardian*, 884 (12 November 1862) 1067.
[139] *Guardian*, 914 (10 June 1863) 551.

The brief consideration of the Ecclesiological Movement's role in the revivals of church architecture and music

That the influence of ecclesiologists on church architecture in England was virtually all encompassing is a well established fact. Ecclesiological influence on the revival of church music, however, would appear to have been much less complete, and has been considerably less obvious historically. Let us consider some of the reasons for this discrepancy.

Ecclesiologists maintained that, in general, ecclesiastical art had degenerated following the 'Middle Pointed' period in Gothic architecture and the early seventeenth-century in music. The many fine examples of Gothic architecture to be found throughout England stood as living and familiar memorials to religious devotion and artistic genius, and their existence assisted in the task of convincing a public which was increasingly fascinated by the Middle Ages that subsequent architectural developments were debasements, or at least that the revival of Gothic church building might be desirable. In contrast, plainsong, except for the simple intonations used for the daily services in cathedrals, was virtually unknown to Anglicans, the vast majority of whom would have had little or no familiarity with the music of Palestrina, Byrd, or Gibbons either. Whereas the average person's eye could behold the grandeur of Gothic in nearly every cathedral city, the average ear was ill-equipped to appreciate the beauty of plainsong or sixteenth-century polyphony. There was no pure musical tradition preserved in stone. 'Performance practice' was an unknown concept and, practically speaking, it was also an irrelevant one, because the norm in the Anglican choral tradition had been to sing music of the current and immediately preceding generation. Prior to the reprinting of large quantities of early music beginning in the 1840s, if musicians were familiar with pre-Commonwealth repertoire, it was only with a very small, representative sample. Consequently, if early church music was performed at all, whether or not it was performed well enough for valid judgements of its merits to be made, even by the open-minded, is open to question. It could be argued that, musically, ecclesiologists were a hundred years ahead of their time.

Beginning in the early 1840s, the singing movement quickly created a nation that liked to sing and which sang increasingly well. As ecclesiologists and eventually churchmen of all parties insisted that it was everyone's duty to sing whatever part of the liturgy was so designated at the local parish church, music demanded the personal attention and participation of every member of the congregation. Although it would be difficult to prove, it would extremely interesting to know whether Victorian churchgoers were more passionate about their musical tastes or about the architecture of the buildings in which they worshipped. The likelihood that music may have elicited stronger opinions would go far to explain the fact that the ultimate musical goals of ecclesiologists took the better part of a century to be realized, while their revolution for Gothic Revival churches was essentially secured within the space of a decade. Whether the tracery of the lancet windows dated from the best period of architecture or the corbels and capitals were carved with utmost symbolism probably did not occupy the thoughts of the average Victorian parishioner on any given Sunday. What style of music he or she was expected to appreciate and sing, however, certainly must have.

Whereas ecclesiastical architects retained very little professional independence from ecclesiological opinion, professional church musicians as a body never bought into the mid-Victorian, clergy-generated pressure to reintroduce 'plainsong and Palestrina.' It was the composers of the Continent, Handel and later Mendelssohn, who commanded the most adulation among the Victorian populace. Contrary to the ecclesiological view, the public, supported by many influential musicians, was convinced that the art of music had *progressed* rather than *regressed* and, indeed, that plainsong was as 'barbarous' as the epoch from which is issued.[140] Hence the fact that plainsong and early polyphony were adopted to the extent they were is probably more remarkable than the reality that they did not win general support during Victorian times.

Considering that the use of plainsong and the sacred polyphony of the sixteenth and seventeenth centuries did not become the norm in later-Victorian choral worship, it might be tempting to conclude that the musical contribution of ecclesiologists was neither great nor lasting. This view overlooks the reality that for music to flourish within the context of liturgy, the support of the clergy is essential, and it is clear that ecclesiologists worked diligently and effectively to secure that support. It also overlooks the ecclesiological goal to encourage the creation of a truly Victorian style of Christian art, one which derived its inspiration from tradition, but surpassed it in refinement. On the whole Ecclesiologists were neither extremists nor mere antiquarians. According to their own principles, it was both a logical and necessary development that their attention eventually widened to include the promotion of contemporary composers and the performance of modern music.

It hardly seems unreasonable, then, that the creation of a living musical expression of spirituality should have taken priority, in the end, over the resurrection of one which, for the average member of the Anglican Communion anyway, was virtually dead. That this was the goal for ecclesiastical architecture has been demonstrated. Ecclesiologists' resurrection of Gothic church architecture did not result in exact copies of medieval buildings, but buildings which interpreted that style in a manner which is readily identifiable as Victorian. It was not until the early years of the twentieth century that musicians such as Sir Richard Terry (Westminster Cathedral)[141] and Cyril

---

[140] S.S. Wesley (1849) 49; Smither, *Early Music*, 13/3 (August 1985) 339–47.
[141] Elizabeth Roche, *Early Music,* XVI/2 (May 1988) 231–6.

Rootham (St John's College, Cambridge)[142] made early music a major part of the daily choral repertoire. By that time contemporary Anglican church music had regained a higher state of integrity, and early music had become more accessible to the public in inexpensive editions. It could be argued that increased familiarity with early music brought the same sense of sympathy for its revival that had been attained for architecture merely by extolling the virtues of familiar medieval churches. With that same sense of familiarity came the popular estimation that it, too, could constitute a valid expression of contemporary spirituality.

For ecclesiologists to have persisted in advocating the exclusive use of 'plainsong and Palestrina' would have necessitated an underlying belief that all subsequent developments in the art of music were unworthy to be appropriated to the service of God, and that there was no hope for the creation of true church music in the future. Such reasoning could never have been sustained, intellectually or theologically. How inconsistent it would have been if ecclesiologists had promoted the development of a historically based but contemporary style of church architecture, and then insisted on a merely antiquarian approach to church music. Although ecclesiologists continued to believe in the intrinsic value of reintroducing plainsong and polyphony to the worship of the Anglican Church, it is clear that their own views of choral service evolved and matured over time, and that they adapted their early model to adjust to the radical changes in Victorian musical culture which took place at mid-century.

Ecclesiologists believed that, once the principles of a valid antecedent style had been learned, an infinite variety would be the natural result of its contemporary artistic development and evolution.[143] It is clear that, by the mid-1850s, mainstream ecclesiologists no longer felt it necessary or desirable that every parish should adhere to a single model for choral worship, any more than they would have thought it desirable that every church should be architecturally identical. Ecclesiologists themselves admitted that they were divided even on the appropriateness of universal adoption of choral service, although it is clear that most thought it advisable.[144] By their own practice, they showed that some musical flexibility was a pastoral necessity. In a country parish, fully plainsong services might indeed be most appropriate. Even there, however, ecclesiologists built up amazingly well trained choirs, producing not only model worship, but using the choral experience as a means to educate the

---

[142] During George Garrett's tenure as organist 1857–97, more than three-quarters of the anthem repertoire sung by the Choir of St John's College, Cambridge, had been composed within his own lifetime. Within five years of Cyril Rootham's appointment in 1902, three-quarters of the Choir's anthem repertoire had been composed prior to 1750. Source: unpublished repertoire studies by the author.
[143] *The Ecclesiologist*, 17/115 (August 1856) 284–7; 18/118 (February 1857) 47–9.
[144] Archdeacon Thorp, *Guardian*, 518 (7 November 1855) 824.

children of the parish and inculcate in them a love of the Church. Where there was a highly trained choir, however, as there was even in the most famous centre for the choral revival, St Mark's College, Chelsea, it was perfectly acceptable for portions of the liturgy to be sung by the choir while the congregation participated by listening. The psalms and hymns were the two parts of the liturgy which mainstream ecclesiologists always thought should be rendered congregationally. In the end, whatever else a congregation sang was determined largely by the kind of music it preferred and whether a highly trained choir was part of the parish's ministry.

The fundamental points at issue were:

1. Anglican liturgy had historically been sung. For a variety of theological and practical reasons, ecclesiologists believed that in most cases it still ought to be sung.
2. Ecclesiologists believed that it was the congregation's duty to participate in the singing.
3. Only the very best liturgical music should be appropriated for use in contemporary worship.

Summary

It is clear that the Ecclesiological Movement was both formative and integral to the post-Tractarian revival of Anglican choral worship. The principles and convictions which ecclesiologists identified to guide the revival of ecclesiastical architecture were extended by them to include the field of church music, and this informed not only the early stages of the movement to revive choral worship in parish churches, but also the manner in which the movement would develop. It has been shown that the primary leaders of the Ecclesiological Movement took considerable pains to promote the revitalization of English church music, and that they did so for pastoral reasons rather than out of merely antiquarian or musical concerns.

By the early 1850s virtually all of the leading proponents of choral service had been recruited to the ranks of the Ecclesiological late Cambridge Camden Society, and ecclesiologists became the foremost voice within the Church of England in the advocacy of choral service. Included among the efforts of ecclesiologists that led to this widespread visibility were:

1. the Society's formation of a distinguished musical committee in 1850, comprised primarily of clergymen.
2. ecclesiologists' advocacy of the revival of plainsong and early church polyphony.
3. their revival of and amalgamation with the Motett Society in 1852, for the express purpose of cultivating a taste for plainsong and early church music

by providing opportunities to hear it performed.
4. ecclesiologists' permanent gift to the Church of medieval hymns in English translation, published together with the original plainsong tunes in the *Hymnal Noted* (Part I in 1851, Part II in 1854).
5. the Society's energetic, highly visible, and unbending defence of choral worship in *The Ecclesiologist* and other publications.
6. the extraordinary examples of model choral worship which became typical of leading ecclesiologists' parishes.

It has been demonstrated that John Mason Neale's role both in the leadership of the Society and in the development of its policies during the 1850s and 1860s has been overestimated. Unlike Neale, whose opinions have too easily been equated with 'ecclesiological' opinion, most of the members of the Committee, who actually guided the evolution of ecclesiological policy, cannot accurately be described as extremists, ritualists, or ultraconservatives, and none of them, Neale included, were mere antiquarians. In general the leaders of the Ecclesiological (late Cambridge Camden) Society were moderate men, like Benjamin Webb and A.J.B. Beresford Hope, who were deeply concerned that the study of the best ancient models should lead to the development of a valid and vital contemporary style in each of the ecclesiastical arts.

Despite their exceptional resources to do so (wealth, daily chapel services, and colleges full of the nation's brightest young men, many of whom intended to take holy orders), the colleges in the University of Cambridge never responded satisfactorily to the remonstrances of ecclesiologists regarding either the poor state of music of most of the college chapels or the dearth of opportunities for prospective ordinands to study and participate in church music. The frustration thus engendered among the future clergy was probably the University's major contribution to the revival, instilling in the musically inclined a determination to set things in better order in their future parishes. Several significant and positive reforms did take place by the mid-1850s, but these were largely initiated by enthusiastic individuals, often students. The three old choral foundations, King's, Trinity, and St John's, strengthened the efficiency of their professional choirs, but introduced little early church music and no congregational singing into the services until later in the century.

In the late 1840s and 1850s it became a significant part of the Ecclesiological (late Cambridge Camden) Society's work to help establish and propagate an apologium for Anglican choral worship that was both historically and theologically based. This ecclesiologists did through their own publications and by reference to those of respected Anglican divines and contemporary allies. It was arguably their greatest contribution to the revival of choral service, for it was undoubtedly a key factor in gaining the widespread support of the clergy. It was the clergy who comprised the primary sphere of ecclesiological influence, and the apologium for choral worship thus established helped to convince them that they bore much of the responsibility for reviving the music of Anglican worship.

The campaign to revive choral service was essentially won when a broad cross section of Victorian clergy became convinced that music was integral to Anglican liturgy, and that choral worship could be an efficacious means to revive earnest spirituality in their own time. And that, as far as ecclesiologists were concerned, was the crux of the matter.

APPENDIX

Music performed by the Ecclesiological Motett Choir 1853–62

The following repertoire list is taken from the public programmes of the Ecclesiological Motett Choir as published in The Ecclesiologist, *retaining original composer attributions and titles.*

Anthems

Anerio, Felice	Missa	1858
Bach, J.S.	Be present, Holy Spirit	1856
Byrd, William	Bow Thine ear, O Lord	1856
	Save me, O God, for Thy Name's sake	1856, 1857
Certon, Peter	I will always give thanks	1853, 1857
Clari	Gloria in excelsis (excerpts)	1856, 1861
Croce, Giovanni	Behold now, praise the Lord	1858, 1859, 1861
	Behold, I bring you glad tidings	1856, 1858, 1859
	Now unto him that is able to keep you	1857, 1860
	O give thanks unto the Lord	1858
Dos Santos	Communion Service	1854
Farrant	Lord, for thy tender mercies' sake	1853, 1861
Gibbons, Orlando	Communion Service in F	1858
	Hosanna to the Son of David	1856, 1858
	Why art thou so heavy, O my soul?	1853
Goss, John	Almighty and merciful God	1860
	If we believe that Jesus died	1856
Greatheed, S.S.	Let my soul bless God	1859
	Magnificat	1854
	Nunc dimittis	1855
	O God, Thou art worthy to be praised	1853, 1858
	O Lord Almighty, God of Israel	1854
	O Saviour of the world	1853, 1856, 1857
	The Son of Man	1859
Jenner, H.L.	Haste Thee, O God	1856
	We have risen very early (carol for May Day)	1857, 1860
Lasso, Orlando di	For he was a good man	1854
	Missa	1858, 1860
	(for five voices, from Proeske's *Selectus novus Missarum*)	
	Not unto us, O Lord	annually 1853–61
	O praise the Lord, all ye heathen	1853, 1859
Lupi, Eduardi	Now it is high time	1858, 1860
Lygon, Frederick	In my Father's house are many mansions	1859
Mel, Rinaldo del	O praise the Lord our God	1856

Mendelssohn, Felix	Judge me, O Lord (Psalm 43, eight voices)	1861
Monk, W.	Offertory Anthem	1856
Morales	Me have ye bereaved	1853, 1855, twice 1857
Nanini	All Thy works praise Thee, O Lord	1854
Ouseley, Frederick	Blessed is the man that feareth the Lord	1856, 1858
	How goodly are Thy tents, O Jacob	1856, 1859
	O Lord, we beseech Thee	1856, 1857
	Save me, O God, for Thy Name's sake	1857
	Thy mercy, O Lord, reacheth unto the heavens	1856
Palestrina	Behold the Lamb of God	1855
	Break forth into joy	1854, 1857, 1860
	Canita tuba in Sion	1856
	Caro mea vera est cibus	1856
	Coenantibus illis, accepit Jesus panem	1853
	Conditor alme siderum (hymn)	1859
	Derelinquat impius viam suam	1856
	Holy, holy, holy	1855
	I will give thanks	1860
	I will magnify thee	1854, 1856, 1857, 1861
	If thou shalt confess with thy mouth	1853, 1857
	In Festo Pentecostes	1860
	Magnificat and Nunc dimittis	1856
	Miserere mei Deus (hymn)	1860
	Missa ad fugam	1854
	Missa Æterna Christi munera	1853, 1854, 1859, 1861
	Missa Assumpta est	1858
	Missa veni sponsa Christi	1857, 1860, 1861, 1862
	O be joyful in the Lord	1860
	O beata et gloriosa Trinitas	1853, 1859
	O Domine Jesu Christe	1856, 1860
	O God, Thou art my God	1853, 1857, 1861
	O Lord God of our salvation	1859
	O Lord my God	1857, 1859
	O vera summa sempiterna Trinitas	1855
	Peccantem me quotidie	1853
	Quam pulchri sunt	1860, 1861
	These are they that follow the Lamb	1857
	These things have I written unto you	1860
	Why do the heathen rage	1860
Redford, John	Rejoice in the Lord always	1853, 1857, 1858, 1860, 1862
Tallis, Thomas	All people that on earth do dwell	1853
	Hear the voice and prayer	1859
	If ye love me	1854, 1855, 1860
Vittoria	Behold, I bring you glad tidings	1857, 1860
	Communion Service	1858
	It is a good thing to give thanks	1858
	Missa O quam gloriosum	1854, 1855, 1860

220 APPENDIX

Plainsong

Ambrosian melody	Te Deum (Lansdowne MS, British Museum)	1859
Antiphons	O Adonai	1858, 1862
	O Clavis David	1858, 1862
	O Emmanuel	1858, 1862
	O Oriens	1862
	O Radix Jesse	1858, 1860, 1862
	O Rex gentium	1858, 1862
	O Sapientia	1858, 1862
	O Virgo virginum	1858, 1862
	Veni Sponsa Christi (from the Mechlin Vesperale)	1857, 1860, 1861, 1862
Canticles	Benedictus	1858, 1860
	Jubilate Deo	twice in 1860
	Magnificat	1854
	Magnificat and Nunc dimittis	1857
	Nunc dimittis	1853, 1858
'Hymn'	Te Deum laudamus (from Baini's MS)	twice in 1860
Hymns	A song, a song, our Chief to greet	1856
	Ad coenam Agni	1853, 1858
	Adesto Sancta Trinitas	1856
	Æterna Christi munera	1853, 1854
	Angulare fundamentum	1853
	Aurora lucis rutilat	1856, 1861
	Before the ending of the day	1861
	Blessed City, Heav'nly Salem	1859
	Cantemus cuncti melodum	1861
	Chorus novae Hierusalem	1853, 1854, 1861
	Come, Holy Ghost	1859
	Conditor alme siderum	1857, 1858, 1862
	Corde natus ex Parentis	1858, 1860, 1862
	Creator of the stars of night	1859
	Deus tuorum militum	1856
	Eterna Christi munera	1860, 1861
	Jam lucis orto sidere	1853, 1860
	Jesu dulcis memoria	1853, 1854, 1857
	Jesu Salvator saeculi	1853, 1855
	Let us tell the story	1856
	O beata Beatorum	1856, 1861
	O filii et filiae	1858
	O Lux beata Trinitas	1853, 1855, 1857
	O quanta qualia sunt illa Sabbata	1856, 1858
	Omnes una celebramus	1856
	Panga lingua	1853, 1854
	Primo dierum omnium	1857
	Rector Potens	1854
	Rerum Deus tenax vigor	1853
	Sermone blando	1853
	Sing Alleluia, all ye lands	1856
	Te lucis ante terminum	1857, 1860, 1861

	The Royal banners forward go	1855, 1857
	Veni Creator Spiritus	1853, 1854, 1856, 1860
	Veni redemptor gentium	1857
	Veni, veni Emmanuel	1858, 1862
	Vexilla regis prodeunt	1853, 1860
Marbeck	Creed	1856, 1857
	Kyrie, Creed, Sanctus, Gloria	1860
	Magnificat and Nunc dimittis	twice in 1860
Psalms	various	
Carols	A song, a song, our Chief to greet	1855
	Christ was born on Christmas Day	1860, 1862
	Days grow longer	1857
	Earth today rejoices	1862
	Earthly friends may change and falter	1854, 1858, 1860
	Give ear, give ear, good Christian men	1855, 1856, 1861
	Good Christian men, rejoice and sing	1860
	Good King Wenceslas	1860
	Let the merry Church bells ring	1854, 1856, 1857, 1861
	Let the song be begun	1857
	Merry bells are ringing	1860
	O earthly fruits	1862
	Our Master hath a garden (Sedding's Collection)	1862
	Royal Day that chasest gloom	1854, 1858, 1860
	Sing Alleluia, all ye lands	1855, 1861
	The first Nowell (Sedding's Collection)	1862
	The foe behind, the deep before	1854, 1860
	The morning of salvation	1857
	The world itself keeps Easter Day	1856, 1861
	'Twas about the dead of night	1860, 1861

Bibliography

Manuscripts

Cambridge, City Library, Cambridgeshire Collection
    First report of the Cambridge University Society for promoting the study and practice of Church music, with laws, list of members, &c. Michaelmas, 1854, Cambridge, 1854. (pam: c.69.08)
Cambridge, Corpus Christi College, archives
    Chapter Acts Book, 1854–84.
Cambridge, Jesus College, archives
    Chapel Boxes
        2: 1800–49.
        3: 1844–58. First Restoration.
        4: 1850–68. Second Restoration.
        5: 1866–89.
    Conclusion Books
        1825–47. (Col. 4.3)
        1848–84. (Col. 4.4)
    Private papers of Dr G.E. Corrie, Master
        Letters received, 1817–85.
        Correspondence with E.H. Morgan (Dean), 1867–75.
Cambridge, King's College, Rowe Music Library
    Choir partbooks, eighteenth and nineteenth century.
    Mann, Arthur Henry, notes on Cambridgeshire musicians, 2 vols.
    Musical events in Cambridge, 3 vols.
    Notes on music in Cambridge colleges.
    Notebook of music at King's College.
    Annotated copy of the index to E.C. Perry and A.H. Mann, *A collection of anthems for use in King's College Chapel,* Cambridge, 1882. (MS 445)
    Service lists, 1918–22. (Held in the director of music's offices.)
    'Some East Anglian musicians,' a lecture read at the Guildhall School of Music for the East Anglian Society of London, 21 February 1905.
    'Suggestions for improvements of various parts of our sacred services,' a lecture read at Manchester (1910), Ipswich and Norwich (1915), and Peterborough (1917). (box Mn.24)
    'The necessity of a strong central society for the musical profession', a lecture read at Dunfermline, Yarmouth, Glasgow, Cardiff, 1912, 1915.
Cambridge, Queens' College
    Conclusion Book, 1832–88. (archives)
    Dean's Book, 1854–1944. (in the possession of the Dean)

Cambridge, Peterhouse, archives
    College account books
        Yearly College Account Book
            Dean's Book 1822 (1822–3)
            Bursar's Account 1831, (1831–7).
        Computis Collegium 1810–33.
        Yearly College Account Book (1836–42)
        Computis Collegii 1834–57
        (Unnamed) 1843–51.
        (Unnamed) 1853–64.
    Order Book of meetings of the Master and Senior Fellows, 1823–72.
Cambridge, St John's College
    Archives
        Conclusion Books, 1799–1908.
        Council Minutes, 1883–1926.
        Dean's Order Book, 1837–1904. (DS1.1)
        Letterbooks of R.F. Scott, 1890–1929.
        Miscellaneous sources. (D103.138, 140, 216)
        New Chapel. (D33.3.1.g.1, 3–6, 22; D33.10(24))
        Rentals Books, 1794–1925.
        St John's Choral Society
            Minutes, beginning 1861. (SOC4.2)
            Treasurer's Book 1868. (SOC4.1)
        Senior Bursar's Book, 1831–45.
        Volunteer Choir, misc. sources. (D103.84, 189, 190)
    Song School
        Choir partbooks
            Eighteenth century, two sets of eight books each, TrTrAATTBB.
            Nineteenth century, TrTrAATTBBB.
Cambridge, Trinity College, Wren Library
    Bursar's Annual Accounts, 1817–39, 1857.
    Bursar's Minute Books, 1817–28, 1829–56.
    Choir Committee Minutes
        1870–72. (Muniments shelf 1, no. 35)
        1885–1919. (Rec.44A.1)
    College notices, 1892–1912.
    Service lists, 1876–97, 1907–9, 1913–14.
    Walmisley, Thomas Attwood, Letters. Add.ms.c.80(42–3)
    Whewell, William. Journal 1841–6. (MS: O.15.45)
Cambridge, University Library
    Cambridge University Architectural Society
        Minute Book, Michaelmas 1847–25 May 1853. (Add. 2758)

Minutes of Committee meetings, 1 February 1853–26 May 1859. (Add. 2759)

Papers read before the Society, *see titles under authors:* S. Baring Gould, and H. Braithwaite. (Add. 2760)

'*On the study of* Church *architecture.*' A paper read before the Cambridge University Architectural Society.

Misc. receipts, treasurer's reports, papers, and papers read before the Society. (Add. 2761)

Ledger book: receipts and payments, lists of life members. (Add. 2762)

Gray, Alan. Scrapbook compiled by C.B. Hurry. (Add. 8496)

Lichfield Joint Record Office

Lichfield Diocesan Choral Association: records, minutes, leaflets, orders of service. MSS: D30/7/6/5 and D30/7/6/8.

London, British Library

Chapel Royal, St James, services throughout the year [1852?]. MS 39,864, part 3.

Dyce, William, autobiographical notice. MS 28,509 ff.477–9.

Motett Society, prospectus, 1841. (1879.cc.13(7))

The Sacred Harmonic Society, a thirty-five years' retrospect, from its commencement in 1832, to the five hundredth concert, in Exeter Hall, 13th December, 1867. London, 1867.

London, Lambeth Palace Library

Mill, The Revd William Hodge. Letters and papers. MS 1491.

Miscellaneous papers. (regarding J.M. Neale) MS 3120, ff. 31–97.

Neale, The Revd John Mason. Papers. MSS 2677, 2678, 2681, 2683, 2684.

Webb, The Revd Benjamin. Letters, 1850–85. MS 1750.

London, Royal Institute of British Architects Library

Ecclesiological Society (ES/1), Minute Book, 1855–66. (In the hand of Benjamin Webb, Secretary.)

London, St Paul's Cathedral Library

Canon Gregory's Diary.

Service lists, 1873–1914.

Succentor's reports, 1877, 1879, 1880, 1887.

London, Tate Gallery, archives

William Dyce Papers, transcribed by his son, James Stirling Dyce. Microfiche: TAM 54 (7–10, 12–14, 15–26, 28–31)

Oxford, Bodleian Library

Cope, Revd W.H., *Lectures by the Rev. W.H. Cope, M.A., of Magdalen Hall, Precentor of Westminster Abbey, on the Church Choral Service, on Wednesday, the 23rd, and Thursday, the 24th of May, 1849.* (Oxford, 1849?). (G.A. Oxon 8° 52)

Fellowes, E.H. and Buck, P.C., *A catalogue of cathedral music*, compiled 1898. (Tenbury MS. 1482)

Helmore, Revd T., *A practical lecture on plain song. Delivered to the members of the 'Society for the Study and Practice of the Plain Song of the Church,'* Oxford, 1854. (1375.e.6(2))

Merton College Musical Society, programmes 1863–4. (G.A. Oxon 8° 1107)

Oxford University Motett and Madrigal Society (G.A. Oxon 8° 52)
Announcement of formation, with rules, Oxford, 1846.
Annual reports (First–Eighth), 1847–54, Oxford, 1847–54.
Catalogue of books in the library of the Oxford University Motett and Madrigal Society, Oxford, 1853.

Pembroke College Musical Society, programmes 1865–1922. (G.A. Oxon 8° 1112)

Society for the Improvement of Church Music in the Archdeaconry of Monmouth, *Report of the Society... for 1848.* Usk, 1848. (1375.e.6[1])

Society for the Study and Practice of the Plain Song of the Church (G.A. Oxon 8° 1033 (21, 22))
Terminal Report for the Society... with a list a members. Easter, 1854, Oxford, 1854.
Report of the Society... June, 1855, Oxford, (1855).
Rules of the Society..., together with an account of the Second Anniversary Festival, held on Saint Cecilia's Day, 1855. With a complete list of members, Oxford, 1855.
Rules of the Society... with a list of members. June, 1855.

Webb, Benjamin, *Diaries*
1837–44. (MS.Eng.misc.e.406)
1844, foreign tour. (MS.Eng.misc.e.407)
1845–9. (MS.Eng.misc.e.408)
1850–1. (In Latin beginning 10.02.1850) (MS.Eng.misc.e.409)
1852–5. (Latin) (MS.Eng.misc.e.410)
1856. (Latin) (MS.Eng.misc.f.98)
1857–62. (MS.Eng.misc.e.411–16)

Webb, Benjamin, *Letters*
from J. Keble, 1856. (MS.Eng.lett.e.94, folios 93–5)
from Sir G.A. Macfarren, 1864, 1865. (MS.Eng.lett.e.86, ff131–3)
Letters, newspaper cuttings, programmes. (MS.Eng.misc.d.475)

Sheen, Staffordshire, parish church
Church Expenses Account Book, 1852–64.
Offertory Account Book, 1852–3.
School Accounts, 1852–95.

Way, Mrs Olwen (granddaughter of George Garrett; private collection)
Letters to G.M. Garrett from Alfred Bennett, William Sterndale Bennett, H.B. Walmisley, T.A. Walmisley, and S.S. Wesley.

Bibliography

General

Anthems for Three, Four, and Five Voices, Selected Chiefly from the Works of Standard Composers, London, 1845.

Archdeaconry of Ely, *The Music Appointed for Festivals of Parish Choirs, to be held in 1869, in the Chapel of King's College, Cambridge*, Cambridge.

Attwater, Aubrey, *Pembroke College, Cambridge: a Short History*, Cambridge, 1936.

Banfield, Stephen, 'The artist and society', *The Romantic Age 1800–1914*, volume 5: 11–28, Athlone History of Music in Britain, ed, Nicholas Temperley, London, 1981.

Banister, H.C., *George Alexander Macfarren*, London, 1894.

Baring-Gould, Sabine, *The Church Revival: Thoughts Thereon and Reminiscences*, London, 1914.

Baring-Gould, Sabine, *Early Reminiscences, 1834–1864*, London, 1923.

Baring-Gould, Sabine, 'On the Principles of Gothick Architecture, and the Manner of Carrying Them Out', a paper read before the Cambridge University Architectural Society, May 11, 1853. (CUL)

Barrett, Philip, *Barchester: English Cathedral Life in the Nineteenth Century*, London, 1993.

Barrett, Philip, 'English Cathedral Choirs in the Nineteenth Century', *Journal of Ecclesiastical History*, XXV/1 (January 1974) 15–37.

Barrett, Philip, 'The Tractarians and Church Music', *Musical Times*, CXIII/1549,1550 (March, April 1972) 301–2, 398–9.

Bennett, F., *The Story of W.J.E. Bennett, founder of St Barnabas, Pimlico, and Vicar of Froome-Selwood, and of his part in the Oxford Church Movement of the Nineteenth Century*, London, 1909.

Binney, Thomas, *The Service of Song in the House of the Lord, an Oration and an Argument*, London, 1848.

Beresford Hope, Alexander James Beresford, *The English Cathedral of the Nineteenth Century*, London, 1861

Beresford Hope, Alexander James Beresford, *Worship in the Church of England*, London, 1874.

Bisse, Thomas, *The Beauty of Holiness in the Common Prayer, to which is added, A Rationale on Cathedral Worship*, New edition, revised with additional notes by F.P. Pocock, Cambridge, 1842.

Bonney, T.G., *Memories of a Long Life*, Cambridge, 1921.

Boyce, Edward Jacob, *A Memorial of the Cambridge Camden Society*, London and Cambridge, 1888.

Braithwaite, Henry, 'Aesthetics in the Church,' a paper read before the Cambridge University Architectural Society, 23 February 1853. (CUL)
Bright, Michael, *Cities Built to Music: Aesthetic Theories of the Victorian Gothic Revival*, Columbus, 1984.
Brown, James D., and Stratton, Stephen S., *British Musical Biography: a Dictionary of Musical Artists and Composers, Born in Britain and its Colonies*, Birmingham, 1897.
Bumpus, John S., *A History of English Cathedral Music*, 2 volumes, London, 1908.
Burge, William, *On the Choral Service of the Anglo-Catholic Church*, London, 1844.
Burton, Nigel, 'Oratorios and Cantatas', *The Romantic Age 1800–1914*, volume 5: 214–41, Athlone History of Music in Britain, ed. Nicholas Temperley, London, 1981.
Bury, Patrick, *The College of Corpus Christi and the Blessed Virgin Mary, A History from 1822 to 1952*, Cambridge, 1952.
Cambridge Camden Society, *A Few Words to Churchwardens on Churches and Church Ornaments*. [The 1st edition was entitled *A Few Suggestions...*]
    No. 1. *Suited to Country Parishes*, Cambridge, 1st edition, 1841; 14th edition, 1846.
    No. 2. *Suited to Town and Manufacturing Parishes*, Cambridge, 3rd edition, 1841; 6th edition, 1843.
Cambridge Camden Society, *A Few Words to Church Builders*, Cambridge, 2nd edition, 1842; 3rd edition, 1844.
Cambridge Camden Society, *A Few Words to Parish Clerks and Sextons of Country Parishes*, Cambridge, 1843.
Cambridge Camden Society, *Laws &c.* 1839 [and 1841].
Cambridge Camden Society, *Draft of Proposed Laws*, 1846.
Cambridge Camden Society, *Revised Laws*, 1846.
Cambridge Camden Society, *Transactions*, a selection from the papers read at the ordinary meetings in 1839 [–1845], Cambridge, 1841–5.
Cambridge Chronicle, Cambridge, 1762–1934.
Case, Thomas H., *Memoirs of a King's College Chorister*, Cambridge, 1889.
Castle, John, *Cambridge Churchmen: an Account of the Anglo-Catholic Tradition at Cambridge*, Cambridge, [1951].
Chadwick, W. Owen, *The Victorian Church*, 2nd edition in 2 volumes, London, 1970; 3rd edition in 2 volumes, London, 1971; SCM Press reprint, 1987.
Chambers, John David, *The Psalter, or Seven Ordinary Hours of Prayer According to the Use of the Illustrious and Excellent Church of Sarum. And the Hymns, Antiphons, and Orisons or Collects for the Principle Festivals and Seasons*, London, 1852.

Chambers, John David, *Lauda Syon, Ancient Latin hymns of the English and other Churches, Translated into Corresponding metres*, London, 1857 (Part I) and 1866 (Part II).
Chandler, Michael, *The Life and Works of John Mason Neale*, Leominster, 1995.
Charleton, Peter, *John Stainer and the Musical Life of Victorian Britain*, London, 1984.
Christian Remembrancer. new series, volumes 1–56, London, 1841–68.
'Church Music', *Edinburgh Review*, 95/193 (January 1852) 123–45.
Church Music: a Sermon, London, 1843.
Church Music Society Occasional Papers
  1. Fuller-Maitland, J.A., *The Need for Reform in Church Music*, London, 1910.
  2. Bridges, Robert, *About Hymns*, a letter dated 2 October 1911.
  3. *Elizabethan Church Music: a Short Enquiry into the Reasons for its Present Unpopularity and Neglect*. [no date – attributed to Froude, 1912, by Rainbow]
  4. Davies, H. Walford, *Music and Christian Worship*, a lecture delivered 19 February 1913.
  5. Hadow, W.H., *Hymn Tunes*. [no date]
  6. Nicholson, Sydney H., *The Organ Voluntary*. [no date]
  7. Rootham, Cyril Bradley, *Anthems*. [no date]
  8. *The Choral Foundations in the Church of England*, London, 1924.
Church, R.W., *The Oxford Movement 1833–1845*, London, 1891.
Clark, John Willis, *Memories & Customs (1820–1860)*, reprinted from the *Cambridge Review*, Lent Term, Cambridge, 1909.
Clark, John Willis, *Remarks on Trinity College Chapel*, Cambridge, 1867.
Clark, Kenneth, *The Gothic Revival: an Essay in the History of Taste*, London, 1928; 2nd edition, 1950.
Clergy List, The, London, annually 1841–89.
Colles, H.C., 'Music of the Catholic Revival', *Theology*, 157 (July 1933) 11–22.
Crockford's Clerical Dictionary, London, annually since 1860.
Crompton, John Lake, *The Prefaces in the Office of Holy Communion*, London, 1849.
Crotch, William, *Substance of Several Courses of Lectures on Music Read in the University of Oxford, and in the Metropolis*, London, 1831.
Darby, Ian Douglas, *Anglican Worship in Victorian Natal*, Pietermaritzburg: University of Natal, MA thesis, 1977.
Davidson, C.H., *Sir John Sutton – a Study in True Principles*, Oxford, 1992.
Davies, Horton, *Worship and Theology in England*, volume 3: *From Watts and Wesley to Maurice, 1690–1850*, and volume 4: *From Newman to Martineau, 1850–1900*, Princeton, NJ, 1962.

Day, Thomas Charles, 'Old Music in England, 1790–1820', *Belgisch Tijdschrift voor Muziek-wetenschap/Revue belge de musicologie*, XXVI–XXVII (1972–3) 25–37.
Dearnley, Christopher, *English Church Music 1650–1750 in Royal Chapel, Cathedral, and Parish Church*, London, 1970.
Dickinson, Francis Henry, *List of Printed Service Books According to the Ancient Uses of the Anglican Church from 1490*, London, 1850.
Dickinson, Francis Henry, ed., *Missale ad usum insignis et praeclarae ecclesiae Sarum*, 4 parts in 2 volumes, Oxford and London, 1861–83.
Dickson, William Edward, *Cathedral Choirs*, reprinted from *Contemporary review*, December 1867; Ely, 1877.
Dickson, William Edward, *Fifty Years of Church Music*, Ely, 1894.
Dix, Gregory, *The Shape of the Liturgy*, Westminster, 1945.
Druitt, Robert, *A Popular Tract on Church Music, with Remarks on its Moral and Political Importance, and a Practical Scheme for its Reformation*, London, 1845.
Dryden, Sir Henry Edward Leigh, *On Church Music, and the Fitting of Churches for Music: a Paper Read at the Public Spring Meeting of the Architectural Society of the Archdeaconry of Northampton, 1853, with additions read at other places*, London, 1854.
Dryden, Sir Henry Edward Leigh, *On Repairing and Refitting Old Churches*, a paper read May 1854.
Durandus, William (Bishop of Mende), *The Symbolism of Churches and Church Ornaments, a translation of the First Book of the Rationale divinorum officiorum by William Durandus, with an introductory essay, notes, and illustrations by the Rev. John Mason Neale, B.A., and the Rev. Benjamin Webb, B.A. of Trinity College*, Leeds, 1843.
Dyce, William, 'Church Music', in four parts, *The Christian Remembrancer*, 1 (February, April, and June 1841) 104–12, 284–92, 440–8, and 2 (September 1841) 192–201.
Dyce, William, *The Order of Daily Service, the Litany, and Order of the Administration of Holy Communion, with Plain-Tune, according to the Use of the United Church of England and Ireland*, London 1843–4.
Eagle, (The journal of St John's College, Cambridge) volumes 1–26, Cambridge, 1859–1915.
Ecclesiologist, volumes 1–29, London, 1841–68.
Elwes, Edward Leighton, *The History of Wells Theological College*, London, 1923.
Ely, Archdeaconry of, *The Music Appointed for Festivals of Parish Choirs to be held in 1869, in the Chapel of King's College, Cambridge*, Cambridge, [1869].
Engel, Carl, *Reflections on Church Music for the Consideration of Church-goers in General*, London, 1856.

English Churchman, volumes 1–7, London, 1843–49.
Faber, Geoffrey, *Oxford Apostles: a Character Study of the Oxford Movement*, London, 1933.
Flower, William Balmbrough, *The Prayers to be Said or Sung: a Plea for Musical Services*, London, 1851.
Flower, William Balmbrough, *Choral Service, the Sacrifice of Praise: a Sermon Preached at St John's, Bovey Tracey*, London, 1853.
Flower, William Balmbrough, *Choral Services and Ritual Observances. Two Sermons*, London, 1856.
Foster, Joseph, *Alumni Oxoniensis: the Members of the University of Oxford, 1715–1886: their Parentage, Birthplace, and Year of Birth, with a Record of their Degrees*, 4 volumes, Oxford and London, 1888.
Gatens, William J., 'John Ruskin and Music', *Victorian Studies*. 30/1 (August 1986) 77–97.
Gatens, William J., *Victorian Cathedral Music in Theory and Practice*, Cambridge, 1986.
Glover, William, *Memoirs of a Cambridge Chorister*, 2 vols., London, 1885.
Glover, William, *Reminiscences of Half a Century*, London, 1889.
Goodwin, Harvey, *Authorized Report of the Proceedings of the Church Congress held at Norwich, [3–5] October 1865,* 79–80, Norwich and London, 1866.
Gray, Arthur, and Brittain, Frederick, *A History of Jesus College, Cambridge*, London, 1979.
Green, V.H.H., *Religion at Oxford and Cambridge*, London, 1964.
Griffinhoofe, Rev C.E., 'Benjamin Webb and St Andrew's, Wells Street', *Church Quarterly Review*, LXXIX/CLVII (October 1914) 36–57.
Grove's Dictionary of Music and Musicians
   1st edition in 4 volumes, London, 1879–89.
   3rd edition in 5 volumes, London, 1929.
   6th edition in 20 volumes, London, 1980.
Guardian, nos. 21–992 (16 September 1846–7 December 1864), London, since 1846.
Guide to the Church Services in London and its Suburbs, London, 1858.
Hackett, Maria, *A Brief Account of Cathedral and Collegiate Schools; with an Abstract of their Statutes and Endowments*, [London], 1827.
Haig, Alan, *The Victorian Clergy*, London, 1984.
Hammond, Peter, *Liturgy and Architecture*, London, 1960.
Hardwick, Peter, *The Revival of Interest in Old English Music in Victorian England, and the Impact of this Revival on Music Composed into the Twentieth Century*, University of Washington, Ph.D. dissertation, 1973.
Hardwick, Peter, 'The revival of interest in plainsong in English, 1833–1850', *Canadian Association of Univ Schools of Music/Assoc. Canadienne de Ecoles Universitaires de Musique Journal*, IX/2 (Fall 1979) 53–69.

Haweis, Hugh Reginald, *My Musical Life*, London, 1884.
Heartley, Charles Tebbott, *Our Cathedrals and Their Mission*, London, 1855.
Helmore, Frederick, *Church Choirs; Containing a Brief History of the Changes in Church Music During the Last Forty-or-so Years*, London, 4th edition, 1879.
Helmore, Frederick, *Memoir of the Rev. Thomas Helmore, M.A.*. London, 1891.
Helmore, Thomas, *A Catechism of Music*, London, 1878.
Helmore, Thomas, *Accompanying Harmonies to the Psalter Noted*, London, 4th edition, 1857.
Helmore, Thomas, *Manual of Plainsong; containing A Brief Directory of the Plain Song Used in Morning and Evening Prayer, Litany, and Holy Communion; together with the Canticles and Psalter Noted*, London, 1850.
Helmore, Thomas, 'On Church Music', *Authorized report... of the Church Congress held at Wolverhampton, [1–4] October 1867*, pages 334–51, London, 1867.
Herring, George W., *Tractarian to Ritualism: a Study of Some Aspects of Tractarianism Outside Oxford, from the time of Newman's Conversion in 1845, until the First Ritual Commission in 1867*, Oxford University, DPhil dissertation, 1984.
Hierurgia Anglicana; or Documents and Extracts Illustrative of the Ritual of the Church of England after the Reformation, edited by members of the Ecclesiological late Cambridge Camden Society, London and Cambridge, 1848.
Hildyard, James, *The Obligation of the University to Provide for the Professional Education of its Members Designed for Holy Orders, a Sermon Preached before the University of Cambridge (Commemoration of Benefactors), October 31, 1841*, Cambridge, 1841.
Hillsman, Walter Lee, *Trends and Aims in Anglican Church Music 1870–1906 in Relation to Developments in Churchmanship*, Oxford University, DPhil dissertation, 1985.
Hooker, Richard, *The Works of that Learned and Judicious Divine, Mr Richard Hooker: with an Account of his Life and Death by I. Walton*, edited by John Keble, 3 volumes, Oxford, 1st edition, 1836; 3rd edition, 1845; 4th edition, 1863; 7th edition by R.W. Church and F. Paget, 1888. [Hooker's *Ecclesiastical Polity* was originally published in 1672.]
Hope, Alexander James Beresford, *see* Beresford Hope, A.J.B.
Howes, Frank, *The English Musical Renaissance*, London, 1966.
Howson, J.S., ed., *Essays on Cathedrals*, London, 1872.
Hullah, Frances, *Life of John Hullah, Ll.D., by his wife*, London, 1886.
Hullah, John, 'Church Music', *Report of the proceedings of the Church Congress held at Bristol, [11–13] October 1864*, 296–303, Bristol and London, 1865.

Hullah, John, *The Duty and Advantage of Learning to Sing: a Lecture*, London, 1846.
Hutchings, Arthur, *Church Music in the Nineteenth Century*, London, 1967.
Ingle, John, *What is the Use of Our Cathedrals? A letter to Lord Stanley, M.P., on the True Principle of Cathedral Reform*, London and Ely, 1855.
Ingram, ed., *Gregorian and other Ecclesiastical Chants, Adapted to the Psalter and Canticles as They are Pointed to be Sung in Churches*, London, 2nd edition, 1843.
Jackson, T.G., *Modern Gothic Architecture*, London, 1873.
Jebb, John, *The Choral Service of the United Church of England and Ireland: Being an Enquiry into the Liturgical System of the Cathedral and Collegiate Foundations of the Anglican Communion*, London, 1843.
Jebb, John, *Dialogue on the Choral Service*, Leeds, London, and Oxford, 1842.
Jebb, John, *The Divine Origin of Music. A Sermon Preached at the Third Annual Festival of Church Choirs held in the Cathedral Church of Norwich on Tuesday, 30 Sept., 1862*, published by the Committee of the Norfolk and Suffolk Church Choral Association, London, 1862.
Jebb, John, 'The Principle of Ritualism Defended', a sermon preached at St Michael & All Angels, Tenbury, 26 September 1856.
Jebb, John, *Three Lectures on the Cathedral Service of the Church of England*, Leeds, 2nd edition, 1845.
Jenner, Henry Lascelles, *The See of Dunedin, New Zealand: the title of H.L. Jenner to be Accounted the first Bishop briefly Vindicated. With a Few Remarks on a Recent Charge of the Lord Bishop of Wellington, New Zealand*, London, [1872].
Joyce, Frederick W., *The Life of the Rev. Sir F.A.G. Ouseley, Bart.*, London, 1896.
Keble, John, ed., *see* Hooker, Richard.
Latrobe, J.A., *The Music of the Church Considered in its Various Branches, Congregational and Choral*, London, 1831.
Law, Irene, *The Book of the Beresford Hopes*, London, 1925.
Lawrence, A.H., *Reminiscences of Cambridge Life*, privately printed, 1889.
Lawson, Mary Sackville, ed., *Collected Hymns, Sequences, and Carols of John Mason Neale*, London, 1914.
Lawson, Mary Sackville, *Letters of John Mason Neale, D.D.*, London, 1910.
Lee, Frederick George, *The Directorium Anglicanum*, revised, 2nd edition. 1865.
Leek, W.P., *Congregational Singing. An Address to the Religious World, on Singing the Praises of God in Public Worship*, London, 1843.
le Huray, Peter, *Music and the Reformation in England 1549–1660*, London, 1967; revised edition, Cambridge, 1978.
Lough, Arthur Geoffrey, *The Influence of John Mason Neale*, London, 1962.

Lough, Arthur Geoffrey, *John Mason Neale – Priest Extraordinary*, Newton Abbot, 1975.
Lyttelton, Edward, *Memories and Hopes*, London, 1925.
Mainzer, Joseph, *Music and Education*, London, 1848.
Mainzer, Joseph, *Singing for a Million: a Practical Course of Musical Instruction*, London, 1841.
Matthews, Samuel *A Collection of Anthems Used in Trinity and St John's College Chapels, Cambridge*, Bury St Edmund's, 1827.
Milner-White, E., 'Architecture and Art of the Oxford Movement', *Theology*, XXVII/157 (July 1933) 23–34.
Monk, E.G., 'Church Music.' *Report of the proceedings of the Church Congress, held in Manchester, [13–15] October 1863*, 172–5, Manchester, 1864.
Morgan, Iris and Gerda, *The Stones and Story of Jesus Chapel, Cambridge*, Cambridge, 1914.
Musical Antiquarian Society, London
   A collection of anthems for voices and instruments, by composers of the Madrigalian era, ed. E.F. Rimbault, [1845].
   A Mass for five voices... by William Byrd. ed. E.F. Rimbault, [1841].
   Book I of Cantiones Sacrae, for five voices... by William Byrd, ed. W. Horsley, [1842].
   Report of the Third General Meeting of the Musical Antiquarian Society... with list of members, 1842–3.
Neale, John Mason, *Church enlargement and Church arrangement*, Cambridge, 1843.
Neale, John Mason, *see also* Durandus.
Neale, John Mason, *Extreme Men. A Letter to A.J.B. Beresford Hope*, London, 1865.
Neale, John Mason, *'He said, Come' – a Sermon Preached at the Dedication Festival of St Matthias, Stoke, Newington, 1859.*
Neale, John Mason, *Hierologus, or the Church tourists*, London, 1843.
Neale, John Mason, *Lectures Principally on the Church Difficulties of the Present Time*, London, 1852; reissued as *Lectures on Church Difficulties*, with an introduction by W.J.E. Bennett, London, 1871.
Nicoll, A.C.F., *St Luke's Church and Parish, Sheen*, printed privately, 1984.
Nockles, Peter, *The Oxford Movement in Context: Anglican High Churchmanship, 1760–1857*, Cambridge, 1994.
Oakeley, Frederick, and Redhead, Richard, *Laudes Diurnæ: the Psalter and Canticles in the Morning and Evening Service of the Church of England set and pointed to the Gregorian tones*, London, 1843.
Ollard, Sidney Leslie, *The Anglo-Catholic Revival, Some Persons and Principles*, London, 1925.
Ollard, Sidney Leslie, *A Short History of the Oxford Movement*, London, 1915.

234 GENERAL BIBLIOGRAPHY

Ouseley, Frederick Arthur Gore, 'Church Music', *Report of the Proceedings of the Church Congress, held in Manchester, [13–15] October 1863*, 160–76, Manchester, 1864.

Ouseley, Frederick Arthur Gore, 'Musical training of the clergy', *Authorized report... of the Church Congress held at Wolverhampton, [1–4] October 1867*, 324–33, London, 1867.

Oxford and Cambridge Review, volumes 1–5, London, 1845–7.

Oxford Dictionary of the Christian Church, ed. F.L. Cross and E.A. Livingstone, Oxford, 2nd edition, 1974.

Parish Choir, (journal of the Society for Promoting Church Music) volumes 1–3, London, 1846–51.

Parliamentary Papers, *First Report of the Commissioners appointed to inquire into the Rubrics, Orders, and Directions for Regulating the Course and Conduct of Public Worship, &c., according to the Use of the United Church of England and Ireland, with minutes of evidence and appendices*, London, 1867.

Parsons, Gerald, 'Reform, revival, and realignment: the experience of Victorian Anglicanism', *Religion in Victorian Britain*, ed. Gerald Parsons, volume I. Traditions, 14–66, Manchester, 1988.

Peace, John, *Apology for Cathedral Service*, London, 1839.

Pearce, John, *Seeking a See. A Journal of the Right Reverend Henry Lascelles Jenner, D.D. of His Visit to Dunedin, New Zealand in 1868–1869*, Dunedin, 1984.

Pears, Steuart Adolphus, *Remarks on the Protestant Theory of Church Music*, London, 1852.

Perry, E.C., and Mann, A.H., *A Collection of Anthems for Use in King's College Chapel*, Cambridge, 1882.

Pocock, Frederick Pearce, *see* Bisse, Thomas.

Pointon, Marcia, *William Dyce 1806–1864. A Critical Biography*, Oxford, 1979.

Practical Remarks on the Reformation of Cathedral Music, London, 1849.

Prestige, G.L., *St Paul's in its Glory, 1831–1911*, London, 1955.

Pritchard, Brian W., *The Musical Festival and the Choral Society in England in the Eighteenth and Nineteenth Centuries: a Social History*, 3 volumes University of Birmingham, Ph.D. dissertation, 1968.

Pugin, Augustus Welby Northmore, *An Apology for the Revival of Christian Architecture in England*, London, 1843.

Pugin, Augustus Welby Northmore, *An Earnest Appeal for the Revival of the Ancient Plain Chant*, London, 1850.

Pugin, Augustus Welby Northmore, *Contrasts; or, a Parallel Between the Noble Edifices of the Fourteenth and Fifteenth Centuries, and Similar Buildings of the Present Day; Shewing the Present Decay of Taste*, London, 1836.

Purchas, John, *Directorium Anglicanum; being a Manual of Directions for the Right Celebration of the Holy Communion, for the Saying of Matins and Evensong, and for the Performance of other Rites and Ceremonies of the Church, according to Ancient Uses of the Church of England*, London, 1858.

Rainbow, Bernarr, *The Choral Revival in the Anglican Church 1839–1872*, London, 1970.

Rainbow, Bernarr, *The Land without Music; Musical Education in England 1800–1860 and its Continental Antecedents*, London, 1967.

Rainbow, Bernarr, 'Music in Education' and 'Parochial and Nonconformist Church Music', *The Romantic Age 1800–1914*, volume 5, 29–45, 144–167, Athlone History of Music in Britain, ed. Nicholas Temperley, London, 1981.

Rainbow, Bernarr, 'William Dyce', *Musical Times*, 105 (1964) 900–1.

Reardon, Bernard M.G., *Religious Thought in the Victorian Age: a Survey from Coleridge to Gore*, New York, 1980.

Rimbault, E.F. ed., *The Book of Common Prayer with musical notes. Compiled by Marbeck*, London, 1845.

Rimbault, E.F. ed., *Cathedral Music. Selected by S Arnold*, 3 volumes, London, [1843].

Rimbault, E.F. ed., *The Full Cathedral Service as Used on Festivals and Saints' Days,* [by Thomas Tallis], London, 1845.

Rimbault, E.F. ed., *The Order of Chanting the Cathedral Service: with Notation of the Preces, Versicles, Responses, as published by Edward Lowe*, London, 1843.

Roche, Elizabeth '"Great learning, fine scholarship, impeccable taste," a fiftieth anniversary tribute to Sir Richard Terry (1865–1938)', *Early Music*, XVI/ 2 (May 1988), 231–6.

Romilly, J., *Romilly's Cambridge Diary 1832–42,* ed. J.P.T. Bury, Cambridge, 1967.

Routley, Erik, *The Musical Wesleys*, London, 1968.

Rowell, Geoffrey, *The Vision Glorious: Themes and Personalities of the Catholic Revival in Anglicanism*, Oxford, 1983.

Saturday Review of Politics, Literature, Science, and Art, volumes 1–2, London, 1855–6.

Scholes, Percy, *The Mirror of Music 1844–1944: a Century of Musical Life in Britain as Reflected in the Pages of the Musical Times*, 2 volumes, London, 1947.

Selwyn, William, 'Trinity College Chapel', in *The Cambridge Portfolio*, ed. J.J. Smith, London and Cambridge, 1840.

Simpson, William John Sparrow, *The Contribution of Cambridge to the Anglo-Catholic Revival*, London, 1933.

Simpson, William John Sparrow, *The History of the Anglo-Catholic Revival from 1845*, London, 1932.
Smith, W.J., *Five Centuries of Cambridge Musicians: 1464–1964*, Cambridge, 1964.
Smither, Howard E., 'Messiah and Progress in Victorian England', *Early Music*, 13/3 (August, 1985) 339–47.
Spencer, Shelagh O'Byrne, *British Settlers in Natal. 1824–1857: a Biographical Register*, volume 5, Pietermaritzburg, 1990.
Sutton, John, *A Collection of the Anthems Used in Divine Service Upon Sundays, Holy-days and their Eves, in Jesus College Chapel, Cambridge. To which is added the form for the Commemoration of Benefactors*, Chiswick, 1850.
Sutton, John, *A Short Account of Organs Built in England from the Reign of King Charles II to the Present Time*, 1847. Reprinted with introduction by C.H. Davidson, Oxford, 1979.
Temperley, Nicholas, 'The Anglican Choral Revival', *Musical Times*, CXII/1535 (January 1971) 73–5.
Temperley, Nicholas, *The Music of the English Parish Church*, 2 volumes, Cambridge, 1979.
Temperley, Nicholas, Introduction and 'Cathedral Music', *The Romantic Age 1800–1914*, volume 5: 1–10, 171–213, Athlone History of Music in Britain, ed. Nicholas Temperley, London, 1981.
Torry, A.F., *Founders and Benefactors of St John's College, Cambridge*, Cambridge, 1888.
Towle, Eleanor A., *John Mason Neale, D.D., a Memoir*, London, 1906.
Twigg, John D., *A History of Queens' College, Cambridge 1448–1986*, Woodbridge, Suffolk, 1987.
Venn, John, *Alumni Cantabrigienses: a Biographical List of all known Students, Graduates and Holders of Office at the University of Cambridge, from the earliest times to 1900*, Part II, 6 volumes, Cambridge, 1922–7.
Wakeling, G., *The Oxford Movement: Sketches and Recollections*, London, 1895.
Walmisley, Thomas Attwood, *A Collection of Anthems Used in the Chapels of King's, Trinity, and St John's Colleges*, Cambridge, 1844.
Walmisley, Thomas Attwood, 'Organs', *The Cambridge Portfolio*, ed. J.J. Smith, London and Cambridge, 1840.
Webb, Benjamin, Diaries, *see* Manuscripts Bibliography.
Webb, Benjamin, *see also* Durandus.
Webb, Benjamin, *In Memoriam*, London, 1881.
Webb, Benjamin, *Sketches of Continental Ecclesiology, or Church Notes in Belgium, Germany, and Italy*, London, 1849.
Webb, Benjamin, 'The prospects of art in England', *Bentley's Quarterly Review*, 1/1 (March 1859) 143–82.

Webb, Clement C.J., 'Benjamin Webb', *Church Quarterly Review*, LXXV/CL (January 1913) 329–348.
Wedgwood, Alexandra, *A.W.N. Pugin and the Pugin Family,* London, 1985.
Wesley, Samuel Sebastian, *A Few Words on Cathedral Music and the Musical System of the Church, with a Plan of Reform*, London and Leeds, 1849.
Wesley, Samuel Sebastian, *Reply to the Cathedral Commissioners Relative to Improvement in the Music of Divine Worship in Cathedrals,* London, 1853.
West, J.E., *Cathedral Organists*, London, 1921.
White, James F., *The Cambridge Movement – the Ecclesiologists and the Gothic Revival*, Cambridge, 1962.
Whitworth, William Allen, *Quam Dilecta: a Description of All Saints' Church, Margaret Street,* London, 1891.
Winstanely, D.A., *Early Victorian Cambridge*, Cambridge, 1940.
Winstanely, D.A., *Later Victorian Cambridge*, Cambridge, 1947.
Wilkins, J. Murray, *Church Music,* London, 1856.
Wordsworth, John, *The Church and the Universities*, Oxford and London, 1880.
Yates, Nigel, *Buildings, Faith, and Worship: the Liturgical Arrangement of Anglican Churches 1600–1900,* Oxford, 1991.
Yates, Nigel, *The Oxford Movement and Anglican Ritualism,* London Historical Association (General series 105), 1984.

Index

aesthetics xii, 3, 8–9, 30, 82
A Few Words to Church Builders 26
A Few Words to Churchwardens 26, 34
Aldrich, Henry 48
Allegri, Gregorio 42
All Saints, Margaret Street 109, 113–14, 118–21, 136, 186–7, 191, 194
  see also Margaret Chapel
altars 7, 121, 191
Amps, William 86, 199, 202–4
Anglican chant 37, 38, 44–5, 96, 97, 113, 137, 169–70, 206, 208, 209–10, 211
Anglican choral revival ix
  antecedent movements 5–10
  see also choral service; church music
Anglicanism
  Catholic heritage, spiritual and artistic 2, 5–6, 10, 13, 16, 23, 27, 28, 39, 66–7, 73, 74–5, 139, 143, 144–5, 146–7, 151, 174, 189
  spirituality, revival of 2, 103, 143
antiquarianism 5, 10, 18, 40, 118, 185, 216
apologium for church music, *see* church music; *see also* polemical techniques
apostolic succession 5–6
architecture, *see under the name of the architectural style*
artistic style
  development of 27–8, 39, 40–2, 185–8
  interchangeability of principles between art forms 3, 40–2, 133–5, 144, 169, 179
  revival of, by study of ancient models 10–11, 22, 27–8, 42, 70, 114, 122–3, 141–2, 151, 180–1,
  promotion of Victorian art 43, 61, 114–15, 122–3, 179–88, 212–15
  see also eclecticism; Gothic Revival

Bach, Johann Sebastian 49, 53, 54, 194, 218
Balfe, Michael William 39
barbarism 27, 62, 72, 210
Baring-Gould, Sabine 82
Barnby, Joseph 113
'beautiful', Victorian concept in art 39, 40–1, 90, 134–5

Beethoven, Ludwig van 41, 53, 135, 184, 203
Bennett, Alfred 200–1
Bennett, F.H. 97
Bennett, W.J.E. 44, 97
Beresford Hope, Alexander James Beresford 16, 17, 43, 64, 65, 68, 78, 80, 81, 109–12, 115–23, 138, 139, 179, 190, 191, 196, 198, 216
  and *The Ecclesiologist* 25, 30, 121–2
  name change xi, 116
  patronage 116–21
  see also the *Saturday Review*
'best', Christian duty of offering God the 22, 26, 38–9, 43, 61–2, 102, 113, 159–60, 215
Binney, Thomas 101, 149, 156–7, 163, 169–70, *see also footnote citations in chapter 5*
bishops ix, 6, 20
Bisse, Thomas 147, 156, 157, 159–60, 161–2, 163, 164, 165, 167, 170, 171, 172–3, *see also footnote citations in chapter 5*
Blow, John 31, 53, 203
Book of Common Prayer 6, 139, 158
  Reformers' intentions 153, 154, 160, 189
  'sung or said' rubrics 153–4
Boyce, Edward Jacob 19, 20, 21, 93, 203
Boyce, William 48, 52, 53, 155, 203, 205
Braithwaite, H.J. 81–2
Brasted, Kent 42, 65, 103–8, 130, 131–2
Brett, Robert 33, 116, 117
Bristol Cathedral 103
Buck, Zechariah 86–7
Burleigh, C.W. 110
Burns, James 15, 31, 33, 34, 119
Burton, Thomas Jones 14
Butler, William 81
Butterfield, William 33, 109–10, 116, 117, 119, 121
Byrd, William 31, 42, 53, 54, 80, 111, 218
Byron, Lord 164

Caius College, Cambridge 19
Calvinism 7

INDEX 239

Cambridge Architectural Society 81–3, 122, 201
Cambridge Camden Society ix, 13, 19–29, 38, 46, 57, 58, 102, 137
  foundation, 3, 20, 92
  name changes x–xi
  publications 22–9
Cambridge, University of 4, 23, 29–30, 34, 36–7, 46–59, 73, 81–7, 146, 216
  see also 'frustration factor'
  see also under individual college names
Cambridge University Society for Promoting the Study and Practice of Church Music 83–5
Camden, William 20
Campbell, Augustus 89, 158
Campion, W.M. 81, 83
Canterbury Amateur Musical Society 130, 210
Canterbury Cathedral 7, 130
Canterbury Diocesan Choral Union 210–11
canticles 7, 38, 57, 58, 59, 96, 108, 110, 131, 152, 209
carols 80, 194, 221
Carpenter, Richard Cromwell 33, 94
Carter, John 9
cathedrals and cathedral choirs ix, 6, 7, 35, 85, 87–91, 97, 103, 123, 154, 158–9, 164, 166–7, 173, 206, 209
  see also church music, common use for cathedrals and parishes
Catholic heritage of Anglicanism, *see* Anglicanism, Catholic heritage of
Chamberlain, Thomas 188
Chambers, John David 17, 30, 64, 68, 138, 139
chant, *see* plainsong; Anglican chant
Chapel Royal, St James, *see* Helmore, Thomas
Chappell, William 31
Cheadle Association for Promoting Church Music 205
Child, William 48, 53
choirs, *see* church music
choral scholars 87
choral service 1, 6, 8, 87–9, 94–102, 110–11, 112–14, 123, 124–5, 131, 143–74, 199
  common use for cathedrals and parishes 37, 73–4, 75, 88–9, 155–6, 166–7, 189
  see also church music

Christ Church, St Pancras 104, 109
Christian Remembrancer 16, 122, 141, 145, 191
Church Building Act (1818) 10
churchmanship xi–xiii, 99, 101, 192
church music
  ancient 31, 39, 44, 59, 69–70, 80, 104, 125–6, 128–9, 141–2, 160–2, 176, 193–4, 197, 209, 212–15
  apologium for 3–4, 43, 69–70, 73–5, 88–9, 99–102, 141–2, 143–74, 216–17
  choirs, role of 1, 37–9, 45, 75–7, 112–15, 120, 214–15
  choral repertoire 48, 52–6, 57, 76–7, 80, 113, 128–9, 202–4, *see also* Appendix 218–21
  congregational role 1, 39, 56, 69, 77, 208, 215
  diocesan choral festivals 204–11
  early ecclesiological views 33–43, 64–5
  inherently vocal 35, 152–6, 215
  modern 67, 70, 80, 91, 114, 128–9, 176–7, 192–4, 209, 212–15
  poor state of 35, 89, 160, 180
  revival in conjunction with architecture 42, 57, 58, 88, 194–5
  symbolism 28–9
  see also canticles; choral service; hymns; plainsong; psalms and psalm singing; Sarum rite and hymns
Clarke-Whitfeld, John 52, 53
Classical architecture 9, 27
clergy 4, 7, 34, 47, 59, 70–1, 146, 170, 192, 216
  musical responsibilities 36–7, 71–3, 74, 76, 90, 174, 209
Close, Francis 29
Codd, E.T. 193
Coleridge, Edward 117
Coleridge, William Hart 118
Commonwealth, The (1649–60), *usually referred to by ecclesiologists as* 'The Rebellion' 7, 36, 38, 39, 74, 156, 170
congregational singing, *see* church music
Corpus Christi College, Cambridge 47, 84–5, 86–7, 103
Corrie, G.E. 20, 81
Cranmer, Thomas 69, 155
Crompton, John Lake 63, 120, 136–7
Cromwell, Oliver 1, 7

Crotch, William 28, 40–2, 97, 126, 134, 148, 160, 165, 203, 207

Dickinson, Francis Henry 17, 43, 64, 106, 137–9, 178
Dickson, W.E. 47–9, 52–3, 58–9, 210
Diocesan Parish Choir Festival Movement 204–11
dissenters (or nonconformists) 7, 73, 101, 125, 149, 169–70, 172
Dodsworth, William 104, 109
Dowland, John 111
Downing College, Cambridge 13, 14, 46
Druitt, Robert 35, 43, 46, 65, 71, 145, 148, 161, 162, 163, 170, 171, *see also footnote citations in chapter 5*
Dryden, Sir Henry 88–9, 162, 166, 178–9
Dunedin, New Zealand 117
Durandus, William (*Rationale divinorum officiorum*) 28–9, 104
Durham Cathedral 7
Dyce, William 31–3, 34, 40, 42, 43, 46, 63, 66–8, 78, 120, 140–2, 145, 160, 169

East Grinstead, *see* Sackville College
Ecclesialogical Society (1839) 13, 19–21, 22, 129
Ecclesiological late Cambridge Camden Society (ECCS) 81, 144, 146
  musical committee 3, 42, 63–4, 66, 84, 91, 119–20, 132, 133, 137, 139, *see also under* Ecclesiological Society
  name change and formation of x–xi, 29–30, 92–3, 175
  publications 64–8
Ecclesiological Motett Choir 77–81, 128, 137, 145, 176–8, 193–9, 218–21
Ecclesiological Movement ix–xi, 1–3, 22, 46, 212–17
  antecedent movements 5–10, 24, 183, 184–5
  see also Cambridge Camden Society; Ecclesiological late Cambridge Camden Society; Ecclesiological Society
Ecclesiological Society 116
  musical committee 192–4
  name change x–xi, 175
Ecclesiologist, The 4, 16, 22–5, 29–30, 33–9, 40, 78, 112, 178
  editorial control 17–18, 24–5

ecclesiologists
  churchmanship xi–xii
  see also pastoral techniques
ecclesiology, defined 3, 30
eclecticism 59–61, 179–83
Edwardine Injunctions 170
English Churchman 34–5, 68, 71, 117, *see also footnote citations in chapter 5*
English Church Union 115, 196
Elvey, G.J. 176, 203
Ely Cathedral 103, 150
Ely Society for the Promotion of Church Music 209–10
Erastianism 5, 27
Eucharist, *see* Holy Communion
Evangelical Movement 6
Evangelical beliefs xii, 7, 11, 12, 24, 87, 138, 204
Exeter Hall 7, 15

Fallow, T.M. 32–3, 44
Farrant, Richard 31, 42, 48, 80, 94, 218
Fisher, Osmund 57
Flower, W.B. 72–3, 150, 160, 164–5, 172, *see also footnote citations in chapter 5*
Forbes, James Stewart 16
France, J.F. 17, 196
Freeman, E.A. 60
Freeman, Phillip 25, 81, 150, 188
French, William 56
'frustration factor' 58–9

Garrett, George Mursell 200–4, 214
Gauntlett, H.J. 11, 42, 43, 193
Gibbons, Orlando 31, 42, 48, 53, 54, 80, 91, 126, 135, 205, 207, 218
Gibson, John 57, 81, 83
girl choristers 131
Gloucester Cathedral 97
Goodwin, Harvey 11, 13, 14, 19–21, 81, 83, 209–10
Goss, John 80, 203, 218
Gothic Revival architecture 1, 3, 9, 10–11, 25, 28, 32, 122–3, 144, 182, 185–8, 212–13
  analogies to music 39–42, 133–5, 182, 212–13
  preferred style ('Middle Pointed' or 'Decorated') 2, 26–8
  see also eclecticism
Gounod, Charles 113

Greatheed, Samuel Stephenson 17, 45, 64, 68, 80, 110, 112, 116, 120, 128, 131, 132–5, 175–7, 178, 179–82, 196, 211, 218
Great St Mary's (University Church, Cambridge) 11, 23, 47, 56, 86, 93
Gregorian chant, *see* plainsong
Grove, George 79
Guardian 59, 94, 98–102
'guerilla warfare' 23

Handel, G.F. 48, 53–5, 56, 77, 203
Harington, Sir John 44, 63
Haskoll, Joseph 33, 149, 150
Havergal, W.H. 176
Hawes, William 127
Haydn, Franz Joseph 28, 39, 41, 48, 53, 77, 135, 203
Heartley, Charles Tebbott 90–1, 95–8
Helmore, Frederick 65, 80, 104–5, 125, 127, 128
Helmore, Thomas 17, 32, 42, 44, 46, 63–70, 78–81, 83–4, 101, 110, 116, 120, 125–9, 144–5, 149, 164, 166, 168, 171, 177–8, 189, 190, 195–8, 206, 208
  see also the *Manual of Plainsong;* the *Psalter Noted;* St Mark's College, Chelsea
Henderson, J.H. 83, 103
Herbert, George 158
Heygate, Thomas Edmund 105–6, 111–12
High Churchmanship xii, 7, 11, 12, 19, 21, 29, 65, 75, 87, 101, 147, 149, 150, 201
Hill (William) & Co. 49, 86, 199
Holy Communion 6, 107, 110–11, 113–15, 190, 201–2
Hook, Walter Farquhar 12, 14, 33, 38
Hooker, Richard 74, 126, 146–7, 158, 161, 162–3, 165–6, 167, 173, *see also footnote citations in chapter 5*
Hope, A.J.B., *see* Beresford Hope, Alexander James Beresford
Hopkins, E.J. 203
Hopkins, J.L. 200, 202–4
Hullah, John 7, 14, 33, 38–9, 50, 78, 100, 148–9, 168, *see also footnote citations in chapter 5*
Hutchinson, John 206
Hymnal Noted 64–8, 76, 89, 103, 110, 123–4, 128, 131, 140, 145, 169, 178, 193, 194, 198

hymns and hymn singing 7, 37, 76, 123–4, 189, 215
  Latin hymns 14, 65–8, 103, 110, 140

iconoclasm 187
Irish Church Temporalities Bill (1833) 5
Irons, W.J. 33, 93, 111

Janes, Robert 51
Jebb, John 35, 36, 65, 71, 148, 158, 160, 172, 188–9, *see also footnote citations in chapter 5*
Jenner, Henry Lascelles 17, 19, 64, 80, 104, 116–17, 129–32, 177, 178, 190, 192–4, 196–7, 208–9, 210–11, 218
Jesus College, Cambridge 56–8, 85
Jewish precedents for Christian worship 73, 151, 171
Joule, Benjamin St John 193

Keble, John 20, 24, 29, 146–7
  assize sermon 5
Kemerton, Glos. 59, 90, 93–8
King's College, Cambridge 47–9, 50, 52–6, 85, 86, 100, 120, 199, 200, 202–4
  choristers 14, 56

Lamb, Charles 103
Lassus, M. 179–82
Lassus, Orlandus 31, 42, 53, 80, 135, 218
Latin, singing in 55
Latin hymnody, *see* hymns, Latin
Latrobe, J.A. 71, 148, 166, 167, 173, *see also footnote citations in chapter 5*
lay clerks 90
Lee, F.G. 188
Lichfield Cathedral 126, 205
Lichfield Diocesan Choral Association 175, 205–7
Luard, H.R. 81, 83
Luard, W.C. 64, 133
Ludwig, King of Bavaria 187
Lygon, Frederick (6th Earl of Beauchamp) 80, 93, 128, 195, 196, 218

Macfarren, Sir George Alexander 114, 128
Manual of Plainsong 120
Marenzio, Luca 31
Margaret Chapel 14, 24, 104, 109, 120, 139
  see also All Saints, Margaret Street

Marshall, William 126
Martyn, Henry 159, 164, 173
Matthews, Samuel 49, 52–5
Mendelssohn, Felix 53, 77, 111, 127, 135, 203–4, 219
Medieval Revival 8–10
Merbecke 69, 155, 207, 221
metrical psalms 7, 65, 75, 96, 155
Mill, William Hodge 15, 17, 22, 43, 44, 64–5, 81, 102–8, 111, 130, 131, 190
Milner, Bishop John 9
Milton, John 158–9
model parishes 24, 59, 90, 93–8, 103–5, 109–15, 118–21, 131–2
moderation, *see* pastoral techniques
Monk, W.H. 116, 176, 219
Morley, Thomas 111
Morning Chronicle 16
Morris, William 10
Motett Society 15, 31–2, 34, 46, 77–8, 79, 127
  see also Ecclesiological Motett Choir
Mozart, Wolfgang Amadeus 41, 48, 53, 77, 111, 113, 135, 184, 203
Musical Antiquarian Society 15, 31
music, power to move the spirit 152, 163–5

Nares, James 48, 53, 97
National Society for Promoting the Education of the Poor 7, 98–102
National Training College, Chelsea, *see* St Mark's College, Chelsea
Neale, John Mason xii, 12–15, 16, 19–21, 29–30, 33, 94, 106, 115, 118, 123–5, 138, 145, 150, 180, 186, 188
  as author and translator 10, 26, 28, 44, 45, 62, 64–6, 68, 80, 123–5, 140, 191
  ecclesiological influence 2, 5, 16–18, 192, 216
  and *The Ecclesiologist* 16, 25
  unmusicality 14, 34
New College, Oxford 87, 200
Newman, John Henry 5, 24
nonconformist, defined 7
  see also dissenters
Nottinghamshire Choral Union, *see* Southwell Minster

Oakeley, Frederick 3
opera's influence on church music 39–40, 76

oratorio 55, 77
organs x, 33–6, 189
'ornamental', Victorian concept in art 27, 40–1
Ouseley, Sir Frederick Arthur Gore 80–1, 97–8, 110, 128–9, 175, 176, 203, 207–8, 211, 219
Oxford Architectural Society 26, 88
Oxford Society for the Study and Practice of the Plain Song of the Church 83, 84, 85, 88, 128
Oxford Movement ix, xi–xiii, 5–6, 24, 183
  see also Tractarians
Oxford, University of 6, 29, 40, 47, 73, 117

Page, C.W. 32–3
Palestrina 31, 39, 42–3, 53, 54, 70, 80, 104, 111, 128, 135, 176–7, 184, 194, 203, 219
Paley, F.A. 22, 30, 150
'papal aggression', *see* Roman Catholicism
Parish Choir 35, 40, 43–6, 57, 72, 134, 144–6, 166–7, *see also footnote citations in chapter 5*, *see also* Society for the Promotion of Church Music
parish choirs 7, 94–8
parish churches 4, 26
  see also model parishes
pastoral techniques
  appropriation of popular art 10–11
  education prior to innovation 130, 131
  moderation 25, 96, 113–15, 121, 122, 131, 190–1, 211
Peace, John 148, 156, 164, 16–7, 171–3, *see also footnote citations in chapter 5*
Pergolesi 39, 135
Perpendicular architecture 27
Perth, Scotland 34
Peterhouse, Cambridge 85–6
Pine Town, Natal, South Africa 137
Phillpotts, Bishop (Exeter) 12
Plain Song Choral Union (London) 195
plainsong (or Gregorian chant) 34, 36, 38, 43, 44–5, 57, 58, 64–70, 72, 74–5, 83, 84, 93, 94, 104, 110–11, 113, 116, 120, 136, 137, 139–40, 141, 152–6, 169–70, 172–3, 178, 189, 194, 195, 198, 207, 208, 209–10, 211, 219–20
  see also Sarum rites and hymns; *Sarum Missal*

pluralism 6
Pluralities Act (1838) 6
Pocock, Frederick Pearce 146
polemical techniques of ecclesiologists 22–3, 25, 150–70
polyphony, *see* church music, ancient
popery, *see* Roman Catholicism
Pratt, John 48–9, 54, 85, 199
Pre-Raphaelites 9, 10
Preston-next-Wingham, Kent 131–2
Protestantism 6, 7, 76, 105
psalm singing 4, 7, 37–9, 51–2, 57, 58, 59, 108, 110, 118, 131, 147, 151–3, 167, 193, 215
Psalter Noted 64, 118, 128, 129, 131, 145, 198, 208
  see also its successor, the *Manual of Plainsong*
Pugin, A.W.N. 9, 10, 21, 74, 149–50, 161, 171, 174
Purcell, Henry 31, 53, 135, 141, 203, 207
Puritanism 7, 45, 65, 75, 76, 166, 167, 170
Purchas, John 188–90
Pusey, E.B., and Puseyites 109, 120, 186

Queen Elizabeth's 49th Injunction (1559) 69, 75, 154–5, 173
Queens' College, Cambridge 58, 84–5, 87, 95

Randall, John 54
'real, let everything be' 61–2
Rebellion, *see* Commonwealth, The
Redhead, Richard 119–20
Renaissance 8, 28
repertoire, *see* church music
restoration, architectural methods of 60–1
Restoration of the Monarchy (1660) 7, 39, 141, 156
Reyner, G.F. 81, 83, 202
Reynolds, Sir Joshua 3, 40
Robson, John H. 14, 47, 49, 85–6
Richards, Upton 109, 120–1
Rimbault, E.F. 31
Ritualism xii, 30, 113–14, 120–1, 188–92, 196, 216
Rogers, Benjamin 53, 97, 203, 206
Roman Catholicism 5–6, 10, 24, 29, 67–8, 80, 105, 174
Romanesque architecture 27
Romanticism 8–10, 184

Romantic medievalism, *see* Romanticism
Rootham, Cyril 213–14
Rossini, Gioacchino 39
Round Church, Cambridge, *see* St Sepulchre's, Cambridge
Royal Commission on Ritual 114
Ruskin, John 9, 61, 186–7
Russell, John Fuller 14, 32–3, 149
Russell, Lord John 67

Sackville College, East Grinstead 16, 65, 123, 125
Sacred Harmonic Society 78, 127
St Andrew's, Wells Street 44, 112–15, 120, 121, 184
St Augustine 74, 164, 166, 173
St Augustine's Missionary College, Canterbury 117–18
St Barnabas Choral Society 79
St Barnabas, Pimlico 44, 74, 77, 79, 80, 97, 105, 174
St Basil 164
St John's College, Cambridge 47, 49–50, 52–6, 85, 175, 200–4, 214
St John's, Worcester 97
St Margaret's Convent 123–5
St Mark's College, Chelsea 31, 34, 64, 74, 90, 98–102, 120, 126–7, 145, 159, 170, 177, 215
St Mary Magdalene, Munster Square 74, 136
St Mary's, Penzance 35
St Matthias, Stoke Newington 33, 116–17
St Michael's, Tenbury 98
St Paul's Cathedral, London 7, 15, 94, 129
St Paul's, Knightsbridge 44, 97
St Saviour's, Leeds 118
St Sepulchre's, Cambridge 29
Salisbury Cathedral 158
Sarum Missal 138–9
Sarum rite and hymns 66–7, 124–5, 139–40, 190
Saturday Review 17, 112, 122
Schubert, Franz 113
Scott, Sir Walter 9, 11, 183, 184
Scott, William 17, 32, 109, 116, 119, 122, 139, 179, 196
Sedding, Edmund 198
sermons 76, 156
Sheen, Staffordshire 59, 109–12
sight singing, *see* singing movement

Simeon, Charles 13, 159
singing movement 7–8, 111, 113
  appropriation to the benefit of the
    Church 8, 64, 78–9, 141
Smart, Henry 128
Society of St Margaret 123–5
Society for the Promotion of Church Music
  35, 36, 43–6, 71, 144–6, see also *Parish Choir*
Society for the Promotion of the Gospel 138
soloists, choral repertoire including 55–6, 204
Southwell Minster (and the Nottinghamshire Choral Union) 178, 208–9
Spohr, Ludwig 135, 203
Sterndale Bennett, William 203
Strawberry Hill 10
Street, George Edmund 183
'sublime', Victorian concept 39–42, 90, 134–5
Suckling, Robert 95, 150
Sullivan, Arthur 128
Sumner, J.B. (Archbishop of Canterbury) 29, 104, 105–8, 166–7
Sumner, Bishop (Winchester) 13
Sutton, Sir John 56–8, 81, 84
symbolism 9, 28–9, 69, 134

Tallis, Thomas 31, 42, 53, 54, 80, 94, 116, 135, 206, 207, 208, 211, 219
Terry, Sir Richard 213–14
Thompson, Sir Henry 98–102
Thorp, Archdeacon Thomas 20, 43, 90, 92–102, 116, 150, 190
Three Choirs Festival 147
Tractarians ix, xi–xii, 5–6, 8–9, 12, 24, 29, 33, 42, 58, 65, 67, 75, 97, 109, 119, 120, 145, 151, 190
  see also Oxford Movement
Tracts for the Times xii, 5, 11, 12, 13, 24, 29
Trinity College, Cambridge 11, 12, 20, 37, 47, 49–56, 85, 102, 115, 132, 136, 137, 146, 200, 202–4
Trinity Hall, Cambridge 19, 129
truth, spiritual and artistic 10, 27, 144, 181, 182–3

Twist, J.W. 145, 162–3
Tye, Christopher 31, 42, 53, 54

universities, the English 6, 36–7, 71–3, 95, 146
University of Cambridge, *see* Cambridge, University of
University of Oxford, *see* Oxford, University of

Venables, Edmund 19, 25
Verdi, Guiseppe 39
vestments 114, 188, 190–1
Victoria, Tomás Luis de 31, 67, 80, 111, 135, 219
via media 5, 93

Walmisley, Thomas Attwood 37, 38, 49–50, 52–6, 57, 175, 200–4
Walpole, Horace 10
Warburton, Thomas 9
Webb, Benjamin 11–15, 19–21, 32–3, 44, 52, 64–5, 78, 81, 92–4, 102, 103–15, 117–18, 130, 133, 138, 149–50, 179–81, 190, 196, 198–9, 206–7
  as author 26, 28, 34–6, 42, 61, 68, 122, 180, 183–8, 189–90
  ecclesiological influence 5, 16–18, 216
  and *The Ecclesiologist* 22, 24–5, 29–30, 112, 177
Wegg Prosser, F.R. 63, 76
Wells Theological College 138
Wesley, Samuel 40
Wesley, Samuel Sebastian 72, 89–90, 128, 162, 200–1, 203
Westminster Abbey 7, 94
Whewell, William 15, 20, 24, 49, 50–2
Wilberforce, Henry 109, 125
Wilbye, John 111
Wilhem, Louis Bocquillon 7
Wilkins, John Murray 208
Williams, Gordon 30, 81, 83
Willis, Professor 24, 81
Winchester 9, 20, 200
Woollaston, T.S. 81
worship 2, 3, 24, 30, 87
  see also choral service; church music
Wyatt, R.E. 112

Young Englanders 8
Young, James Gavin 19

Zulu litany 137

For Product Safety Concerns and Information please contact our EU representative GPSR@taylorandfrancis.com
Taylor & Francis Verlag GmbH, Kaufingerstraße 24, 80331 München, Germany

www.ingramcontent.com/pod-product-compliance
Lightning Source LLC
Chambersburg PA
CBHW071823300426
44116CB00009B/1409